A Consumer's Guide to Aging

David H. Solomon, M.D.
Elyse Salend, M.S.W.
Anna Nolen Rahman, M.S.W.
Marie Bolduc Liston, M.S.W.
David B. Reuben, M.D.

A Consumer's Guide to Aging

The Johns Hopkins University Press • Baltimore and London

The Johns Hopkins University Press
701 West 40th Street
Baltimore, Maryland 21211-2190
The Johns Hopkins Press Ltd., London

Photographs by Marianne Gontarz, M.S.W.

The paper used in this book meets the minimum requirements of
American National Standard for Information Sciences—Permanence
of Paper for Printed Library Materials, ANSI Z39.48-1984.

Library of Congress Cataloging-in-Publication Data

A Consumer's guide to aging / David H. Solomon . . . [et al.].
p. cm.
Includes bibliographical references (p.) and index.
ISBN 0-8018-4301-4 (alk. paper).—ISBN 0-8018-4302-2 (pbk. : alk. paper)
1. Retirement—United States—Planning. 2. Aged—Health and hygiene—United States. 3. Aging—United States—Psychological aspects. I. Solomon, David H.
HQ1063.2.U6C66 1992
305.26′0973–dc20 91-41587

Note to the reader: Diet, exercise programs, and the use of medications are all matters that by their very nature vary from individual to individual. You should speak with your own doctor about your individual needs before beginning any diet or exercise program. It is especially important to discuss the use of any medications with your doctor. These precautionary notes are most important if you are already under medical care for an illness.

To my wife, Ronnie, whose love and dedication have made our golden years possible. David H. Solomon

To my parents, Anne and Harry Salend, and my husband, Jon, for always being there when I need them. Elyse Salend

To Mom and Dad, whose example has been my inspiration.
Anna Nolen Rahman

To my husband, Bob, for his understanding and support, and to my parents, Bert and Doris Bolduc, and parents-in-law, Morris and the late Ingemie Liston, who have met the challenges and opportunities of their later years with strength and optimism. Marie Bolduc Liston

To Cosmo, who taught me about watchmaking and much more about healthy aging. David B. Reuben

Contents

Acknowledgments

We are indebted to Nancy Watts Stockwell, a social worker and writer, for her editorial and writing assistance and for her upbeat spirit. Without Nancy's help, the process of writing this book would have been both longer and more difficult. The illustrations are the work of Art Dorame and the photographs are by Marianne Gontarz, both talented artists who deftly used their skills to produce the graphics.

We wish to thank our spouses, who lived with us throughout the book's conception, outline, drafts, and rewrites, and who changed their lives to accommodate the birth of this publication. To our children, Jessica, Rebecca, Joshua, Daniel, Gregory, Asif, and Deena, who learned to share priority status with a book—thanks for your humor, patience, and encouragement.

We also want to thank the many "On Aging" readers whose questions and concerns continue to motivate us to find answers, and the many people who welcomed us into their homes and shared with us their heartfelt and often uplifting stories about aging. Thanks are also extended to Al Leeds, President of the Los Angeles Times/Washington Post News Service, whose gentle and persistent prodding to write this book could not be ignored.

Special thanks to Libbie Agran, Marc Hankin, Bob Liston, Jon Pynoos, Muhit Rahman, and Harry Salend, who took time to review some of our chapters and offered constructive criticism.

We wish to thank Jon Alan Webber, our administrative assistant, who devoted nights and weekends to typing drafts of the manuscript and was able to maintain a sense of humor and perspective when others were losing theirs; and Sandy Gordon and Lisa Femrite for their administrative support.

Many thanks are also due to our editor, Jacqueline Wehmueller, for her warmth, wisdom, and professionalism. She shared with us our vision for the book, and helped make our dream a reality.

Introduction

Today's older Americans have been called innovators, pioneers, trailblazers, trendsetters, and even trendbusters. Mature men and women now have more options available to them than any older generation in history. The daughter who thinks her widowed mother is too old to fall in love again is wrong. So is the friend who tells his retired buddy it's too late to start a new career. The fact is, stereotypes are breaking down as mature adults are taking advantage of their options and making diverse choices about how to live their lives.

What can we say about the average 65-year-old? Is he considering retirement or a return to work? Is she worried about her health or training for a marathon? Is he bored with life or so busy there aren't enough hours in the day? All we can say, it seems, is that there is no "average" 65-year-old. In the last few decades, mature Americans have shattered so many stereotypes that many experts now consider chronological age, especially in the later years, the weakest measure of the man or woman. Better, they say, to ask what people are doing with their lives. How have they defined themselves in terms of work, leisure, family, and health? As one expert remarked: "The process of aging is neither inexorable nor immutable. . . . To a considerable degree we ourselves are in control."

But being at the helm is often a mixed blessing. While it allows us the freedom to grow in the directions we choose, it also creates the opportunity to make mistakes. To avoid mistakes, or to limit their frequency and severity, many of us seek advice from others when a new opportunity presents itself or a difficult decision must be made. Small wonder, then, that as our friends encountered the promises and pitfalls of middle and later life, we gerontologists became increasingly popular.

For many years, new acquaintances, upon learning that we

worked in geriatrics, would do one of two things: stare blankly and say, "That's nice, what is it?" or stare blankly, say "That's nice," and then switch the topic to something more familiar. But with time, as the older population grew in numbers (and the press confirmed it with reports that America was graying), the responses of new acquaintances began to change. "Is that right?" they'd say now, drawing it out, lingering a bit as they collected their thoughts for the next question. "You know, I was wondering . . . ," they'd continue, and then quiz us about what we thought of the early retirement program their company was offering, or their decision to invite Mom to move in with them, or the diet they had heard would prevent all sorts of diseases.

These intelligent, successful, mature men and women were becoming increasingly aware of the new challenges confronting them and their families. And yes, they were in life's driver's seat. The problem was that they didn't always know where they were going or, if they did, how to get there. What they wanted was information and guidance to help them add "not just years to their lives, but life to their years."

Once we realized we were hearing many of the same questions over and over again, it occurred to us that a newspaper column would be an ideal way to address the common concerns of many people. That's why, in 1984, we began writing a weekly question-and-answer column called "On Aging." Syndicated nationally by the Washington Post Writers Group, "On Aging" reaches more than six million households. Our readers write to us and ask for advice, just as our new acquaintances do. Janie R., age 59, wants tips on finding a dating partner. Robert K., in his 70s, would like help with estate planning. And Jim T., 64, is wondering about housing opportunities in warmer climates. In response to these and other requests and questions, we research topics of interest to older adults and their families, drawing on our professional experience, findings from state-of-the-art studies, and feedback from men and women who are struggling with or have sailed through transitions common in later life. Then we consolidate what we've learned and present it in a way that's practical and directly applicable to the lives of our readers.

We believe that if we tell Janie R. that she needs to get out and get involved, then our job is only half done. Where is she most likely to meet someone interesting? In what activities should she consider participating? And Robert K.? His friends probably have already suggested he consult a financial planner. But did they tell him what to look for in a planner and where to go for referrals? Jim T. describes friends of his who retired to Florida and are now having the time of their lives. But what does he need to do to determine whether a similar move will work comparable wonders for him and his wife?

Over the years, "On Aging" readers have told us that what they and others like them want is useful advice to help them achieve their new goals. So throughout this book, on topics ranging from fitness and finances to leisure and relationships, that's what you'll find.

This book is directed toward making life better, through knowledge and advice, for aging men and women. We have addressed the needs of the oldest as well as the middle-aged. But who is old? Picasso was not old at 90. A homeless woman, buffeted by unrelenting poverty, may look, feel, and *be* old at 50. "Old" has no single definition. That's why this book deals not with old age, but with the aspects of life that affect apparent rates of aging: physical and mental abilities, attention to healthful lifestyles, social contacts, verve, humor, love, self-esteem, emotional balance, understanding, acceptance without resignation.

The only gold standard we have for "old" is false gold: what we pictured as old when we were very young. This is a distortion partly because young eyes see everyone from Mommy's age on as old and partly because the norm has been a moving target for the past forty years: "Old" has constantly been getting older.

So, discard your stereotypes of aging. In reading this book and in your everyday lives, it is a good idea to think in terms of the first years, the middle years, and the later years. At all phases, the present calls for action if the future is to be better—and it can be.

In recent years, the scientific fields of geriatrics (health care of older people) and gerontology (the study of normal and productive aging) have expanded rapidly, as more and more researchers have become interested in the challenges and problems of our oldest age group. As a result, many of the guidelines in this book are far more explicit today than they could have been just a few years ago.

Life spans in the United States have increased by 60 percent, or twenty-eight years, during the twentieth century, and by about 25 percent in just the last twenty-five years. Our book focuses more on how to improve the quality of life than on how to increase the length of life, but we have by no means censored information that might lead to longer lives. Most preventive measures, which we discuss in chapters 1, 2, and 3, that can add years to life also improve health and hence ensure a state of greater well-being and usually greater happiness.

The other seven chapters, chapters 4–10, are especially designed to enhance the reader's understanding, encourage peace of mind, relieve anxiety, and generally guide the reader through the later years. We hope these down-to-earth, fact-filled chapters will be helpful not only to the oldest generation but to their children and grandchildren as well.

A Consumer's Guide to Aging

CHAPTER ONE

Keeping Fit

I just don't think I'm old. I got a lot of zip yet. You got to keep moving to keep young. Keep the old joints greased up.

—Bill Cota, 86, repairman, as quoted in *Newsweek*

Aging doesn't necessarily mean a life that is sick, senile, sexless, spent or sessile.

—Richard Besdine, director of aging center,
University of Connecticut, as quoted in *Time*

Ah, the ills of old age. The wrinkles and memory loss. Slowing down. Abandoning your sex life. High blood pressure and low energy. Loneliness and depression. Getting fat. Heartburn and indigestion. Stiff joints, flabby muscles, and aching backs. All inevitable, right? Wrong.

We now know that most of the losses traditionally considered a natural part of aging are actually results of illness, stress, and poor health habits, such as smoking, a diet high in fat, inactivity, and abuse of alcohol. Furthermore, we know that many of these losses can be reversed, to some extent, at any age. Our body processes slow down with age, but our functioning is affected by our lifestyle far more than by the number of candles on our birthday cake. Today is the best day to begin changing that lifestyle.

It's Never Too Late to Start

Dean Ornish, a physician at the University of California, San Francisco, has demonstrated that a program of exercise, improved diet, and stress reduction can reverse the effects of heart disease. Middle-aged cardiac patients in his study walked briskly three times per week, performed stress-management exercises (stretching, focused breathing, relaxation, visualization, and meditation) for an hour and a quarter each day, and switched to a diet low in fat and sodium and high in fiber. After a year, ten out of twelve patients had less plaque in their coronary arteries, lower cholesterol levels, lower blood pressure, and a weight that was closer to the ideal for that person. By comparison, a control group treated with standard cardiac drugs had discouraging results. The majority got sicker, and while a few women improved, the only men who improved had taken the initiative to change their lifestyles on their own.

You can make the same changes in your own lifestyle that produced such spectacular results for Dr. Ornish's patients. "Sure," you say, "but I'm crippled up with arthritis and my ticker's no good. I've hardly been out of the house in years, except to go to the doctor and get my prescriptions filled. I'm overweight, and if I started jogging, I'd drop dead of a heart attack. The only fun I have left is drinking beer and eating potato chips in front of the TV, and now you want to take that away from me." Why should you start changing your lifelong habits? Clearly, people need a reason to change their habits; they need to be *motivated.* There are many reasons for people to develop healthier lifestyles. All other things being equal, well-conditioned people with healthy diets

- live longer
- feel happier and less anxious
- have lower blood pressure and cholesterol levels
- are more alert
- look younger
- have more satisfying sexual function
- have better flexibility and range of motion

- sleep better
- digest their food more easily
- have less heartburn and constipation
- control their weight more easily
- suffer less low-back pain
- have denser bones (less osteoporosis)
- have lower rates of cardiovascular disease, diabetes, and cancer
- have better immune function (natural killer cells)

In other words, the rate at which the body declines is greatly influenced by habits we can control. As the *New York Times* states, "The number of years we have lived is not nearly as important a measure of aging as how much our body has deteriorated while the clock ticked away."

For example, osteoporosis, a common condition in older women and men that is characterized by weakened bones that fracture easily, is primarily due to hormone deficiency but is aggravated by inadequate calcium in the diet and lack of exercise. An individual's level of hypertension—the "silent killer"—can be lowered through stress reduction, sufficient exercise, and healthy diet. Diabetes can often be controlled with improved diet and regular exercise. Smoking increases enormously the risk of lung cancer, emphysema, and cardiovascular diseases. According to the American Cancer Society and the American Heart Association, the typical fatty American diet increases our risk of developing colon and breast cancer as well as heart disease. Impotence in older men is often caused by diabetes or chronic alcohol abuse. In some cases, as Dr. Ornish has shown, we can reverse the effects of old habits. In other cases, we can reduce the risk of further disease and disability.

Making choices to improve our health may sound simple, but as we all know, following through may be more difficult. In this chapter, we offer tips for successfully changing your lifestyle, with a focus on improving exercise and diet patterns. In chapter 2, we suggest resources to help you stop smoking. In chapter 3, we offer guidelines for managing stress and coping with alcohol abuse in your family.

Of course, *before you begin any exercise or diet regimen, be sure to share your plans with your doctor. You should have a complete physical exam and be sure that your doctor approves the changes in your exercise and diet. If you are presently taking medications, you may need to take them into account when you choose activities and menus.*

Tips for Changing Habits

For most of us, changing lifelong patterns of eating and physical activity challenges our willpower. We may start off with a bang, enthusiastically joining a health club or signing up for daily exercise classes at the "Y," plunking down a large deposit for a weight-loss program, and promising ourselves that from this day forward we will never fall off the path to the perfect body. By the next week, we are worn out and fed up. Too many sit-ups, too much time in the locker room feeling flabby, too much cottage cheese, and too many raw-vegetable salads. We find ourselves stopping by the doughnut store for comfort after the exercise class or substituting cheesecake for the fresh fruit dessert in the diet plan. Pretty soon, we feel like failures and give up on the whole thing.

Successful changes take time. It has taken you fifty or sixty years to develop your present eating and activity patterns, so you need to give yourself a few months or a couple of years to change them. Here are some tips for success in regaining fitness.

1. Plan small changes that are comfortable for you. If you want to cut down on the amount of fat in your diet, reduce the level gradually. For example, if you love blue-cheese salad dressing, mix it half-and-half with low-fat Italian dressing. Later, when you're used to that combination, perhaps you will be happy with less blue cheese, just enough for flavor. And while you're at it, you can gradually increase the size of the salad to fill up with high-fiber vegetables. But emphasize the vegetables you like and add new ones a little at a time.

2. Plan changes you can enjoy. Choose an activity you've always wanted to try, or one you used to love but somehow stopped pursuing. Have you been dancing lately? Dance classes provide excellent exercise for flexibility and balance as well as a chance to meet new friends. Choose from ballroom dancing, tap, aerobics, jazz, and belly-dancing. Something is available for all interests, so select what piques your fancy. If you're a long-distance runner whose joints are beginning to hurt, you might enjoy lap swimming, another aerobic exercise that you can do for long periods and that puts little pressure on your back, hips, and knees.

3. Enlist the support of family and friends. Let them know you'd like reinforcement and praise for your efforts, not teasing and criticism. Better yet, get them involved in the changes, too. Maryanne and Vern T. walk their dog together every morning and evening; all three of them travel 2 to 4 miles a day, depending on the weather. Three mornings a week, Maryanne picks up her daughter-in-law and granddaughter, and they all go to the gym. The baby plays in daycare while Mom and Grandma swim laps. Then they all have lunch together. Having company makes the exercise time go faster and makes it more enjoyable.

4. Find small rewards for your changes, rewards that mean something to you. Try taping that great TV program for a reward after you take your walk. Or go out for breakfast after you exercise, as people in jogging and cycling groups often do. If you've kept to your eating plan for the day, make yourself a coupon toward something new you've wanted to buy. Save up your coupons, and then be sure to buy that special reward. Don't cheat yourself!

5. Give yourself pats on the back for your efforts. Even if you don't get reinforcement from other people, you can give it to yourself very effectively. Be as kind to yourself as you would be to a good friend. Mentally tell yourself: "Good job"; "I'm getting more flexible all the time"; "I had a hard time getting myself to the exercise class, but I did it after all. I must be tougher than I thought"; "I never thought I could pass up cream pie, but I did it. Good for me." What you tell yourself is powerful, so tell yourself you're a winner.

6. If you slip up, don't dwell on failure. Instead, figure out what you learned from the experience: "Next time I'll eat before I go shopping. I stick to my grocery list better when I'm not hungry." "I didn't feel like exercising today. I'll call a friend and make a date to go walking tomorrow. If I commit myself to go with someone else, I'll get back on track."

7. Keep records of your changes; they will help you see how much you've really accomplished and will reinforce your motivation. You can draw charts or graphs, make notes on your calendar, keep a notebook, or invent your own system. Some people buy pretty stickers and reward themselves with a butterfly or gold star on the calendar when they've done their exercise for the day or eaten according to their plan.

8. Consider joining or forming a group of people who want to make similar changes. Many people like to exercise at a gym or in

a class because they have more fun with company. Throughout the country, YMCAs, YWCAs, Jewish Community Centers, and other recreation centers offer exercise classes and clubs. Some people start new eating or exercise plans with a companion for support and encouragement. For example, next-door neighbors Catherine V. and Leslie S. made a standing arrangement to bicycle a 3-mile route together every morning. If one of them is a little slow or reluctant to get out of the house, the other one gets her going. They enjoy each other's company, and they feel better, more flexible, and stronger for the exercise.

9. Give yourself time to make changes in small increments. Older bodies respond more slowly to changes in eating and exercise, but they do respond. Even though it takes a little longer to build muscle and reduce fat, people often find they have become more fit in midlife than ever before. All it takes is persistence and patience.

Blooming out of Season

Feeling overwhelmed by the job ahead of you? Among the many mature adults who point to fitness programs as the source of their later-life bounce is Virginia Moore, mother of five and grandmother of eight, who has been developing and teaching exercise to people of all ages for the past thirty years. A former Mrs. Maryland, the slim and trim Mrs. Moore has helped more than seven thousand people to feel and look better through regular exercise classes. "Raise your arms, twinkle your toes. Put some music in your life," she encourages her audience on her cable television show, "Fifty and Moore," which features slim and fit guests in their seventies and eighties. The grouchy and surly among us might object, "She's one of those people who has always been thin and athletic. She probably can eat anything and never notice the calories. I'm not like that." Take heart, oh grouchy ones. Mrs. Moore has traveled the same path as the rest of us. Thirty years ago, she recalls, "I was having babies right and left, and I had a size 42 everything—anything you wanted to measure was 42 inches. I considered myself a fat lady."

These days, she boasts the cholesterol count, heart rate, and body weight of a young woman, having rid herself of her "stored potential energy"—excess fat. Fit as she is, she refuses to divulge her chronological age. "People tend to evaluate everything you say and do by a number. Let's just say I've been blooming out of season—for season after season." It's never too late to start blooming!

Exercise after 50

Many older people are models of fitness. Mary T., 72, has climbed Mt. Whitney (14,495 feet, the highest peak in the continental United States) every year since she was 42. She hikes and walks daily, and she has no plans to quit. George J., 78, cycles 5 to 10 miles per day during the week, and he often joins a Florida cycling club on longer outings over holidays. Harold G., 66, climbs mountains in Utah. Edna and Burns W., 65 and 67, respectively, are caretakers for a large farm in the Napa Valley foothills, on which they do the gardening, orchard work, and general repairs. They preserve all their own fruits and vegetables, as well as care for chickens, cows, and other livestock. For relaxation, they often hike for miles, enjoying the scenic woods and countryside nearby. Ross S., 92, has been blind for forty years, but he still chops all the wood for the stove to heat his rural Florida home, and he raises the vegetables for himself and his wife in their family garden. He attributes his long life to his activity and good health habits.

But what about the rest of us? What about the couch potatoes

whose idea of exercise is walking to the refrigerator and back? What about folks with arthritis or limited range of motion from other disabilities? If we want to start increasing our physical activity, how do we do it safely and effectively?

Developing Your Own Exercise Program

First, begin to incorporate more activity into your daily life. Walk around the neighborhood instead of driving or taking a bus. When you ride, allow time to get out and walk the last couple of blocks to your destination. Instead of using the elevator, walk up a flight or two of stairs, and always walk down the stairs. Take part in social activities such as dancing, walking, hiking, bowling (lawn or alley), racquet games, swimming, camping, golfing, cycling, and so on. Work in the garden whenever you can. Even sitting at work or at home, you can stretch your fingers and toes, rotate the joints in your shoulders, arms, and legs, and breathe deeply. These activities will increase your flexibility and overall fitness.

If you've been inactive, start gently with 5 to 10 minutes of exercise twice a week. Add a few minutes each week, going slowly. If you feel well (and you probably will find that you feel better all the time), increase your exercise sessions to 15 to 30 minutes, three to four times a week. It is important to begin and end with stretching and slow movements (warm-up and cool-down) to avoid stiff muscles or injuries. If you are bed-bound or in a wheelchair, try chair exercises and Kegel exercises.

For a program of more vigorous exercise, choose an activity you like; you'll stick with it longer. It's wise to begin with a well-supervised program so that you can obtain instruction and guidance when you need them. As mentioned previously, community centers, senior centers, and gyms in many areas offer exercise classes suitable for older adults. Local high schools and colleges

CHAIR EXERCISES

Being confined to a wheelchair does not disqualify you from the benefits of regular exercise, even if you have been sedentary for quite a while. You may not start off with the routine of Joe S., 67, who works out in the weight room at his gym and then wheels himself to the pool, levers himself out of his chair onto the pool edge, and swims laps for an hour four times a week. Joe's legs no longer function well, but his upper body is strongly developed. His blood pressure, cholesterol, body weight, and other fitness measures, to say nothing of his muscle definition, are the envy of his younger friends.

To start a chair-exercise routine, try these movements. They will keep your joints lubricated, strengthen your muscles, and make you more flexible. They will also improve your outlook and lower your stress level. Not everyone will be able to do every one of these exercises; do what you can, and be certain to consult your physician before you begin the exercise program. Begin slowly, just a few times a week, and work toward a daily routine.*

Deep Breathing

Sit up straight with your lower back pressed firmly against the chair. Hold your head up. Put your hands on your hips. Inhale deeply through your nose, and hold your breath while you count to 3. Exhale by blowing slowly and gently through your lips as though you were whistling. Repeat 3 times.

Yawn and Stretch

Take a huge yawn, and slowly stretch your arms to the ceiling. Then stretch your arms out to the sides and down. Repeat 3 times.

Relax Your Neck

Turn your head slowly to the right, and pause for a count of 2. Now turn it slowly to the left, and pause. Look slowly up to the ceiling, and pause again. Repeat 2 times.

*Adapted from exercises developed by the Medicine Education Program of Los Angeles County.

Apple Picker

One at a time, raise each arm overhead, and then lower it to your side. Inhale as you raise your arm, and exhale as you lower it. Repeat with each arm 3 times.

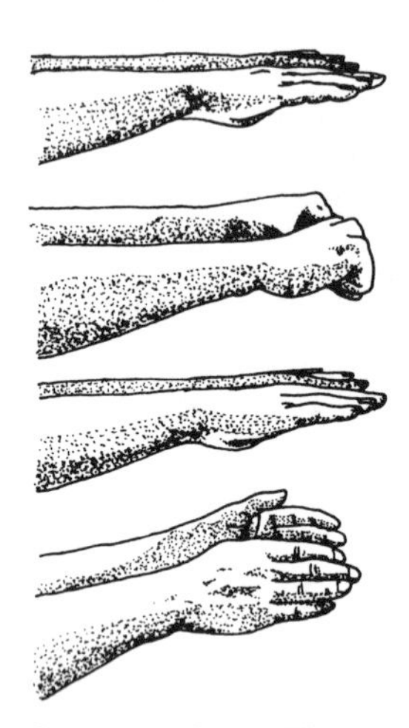

Squeeze Those Fingers

Stretch your arms straight out in front of you with the palms down. Squeeze your fingers slowly, then release them. Repeat 5 times.

Now turn your palms up and squeeze your fingers 5 more times. Now turn your palms down again and shake your hands 5 times.

Roll Your Shoulders

With your arms loosely at your sides (or with hands placed on shoulders), slowly roll your shoul-

ders forward in circles and repeat 5 times. Now reverse the motion: Roll your shoulders backward in full circles and repeat 5 times. Move slowly. Now shrug your shoulders and relax them 5 times.

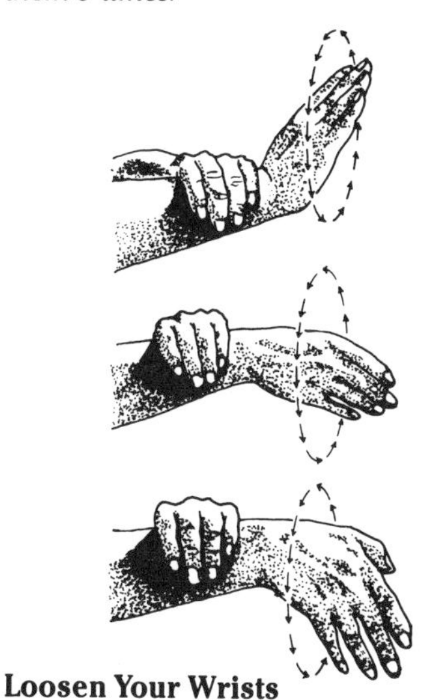

Loosen Your Wrists

Grasp your right hand with your left hand. Keeping your right palm facing down, rotate your right hand slowly, 5 times one way, and 5 times back the other way. Now switch hands, and rotate your left hand slowly, 5 times each way. Feel those joints loosening up?

Side Stretch

Place your left hand on your left hip. Stretch your right arm over your head, and then bend toward your left side while you count to 2. Move gently and smoothly; do not bounce. Return to straight up.

Now place your right hand on your right hip, extend your other arm over your head, and bend smoothly toward the right side while you count to 2. Return to straight up. Repeat the movement on each side 3 times.

Relax Your Lower Back

Sit up straight. Bend straight forward slowly, and then straighten up. Clasp your hands on your left knee, and slowly bend toward your hands. Straighten up.

Now clasp your hands on your right knee, and slowly bend toward your hands. Straighten up. Repeat each movement 3 times.

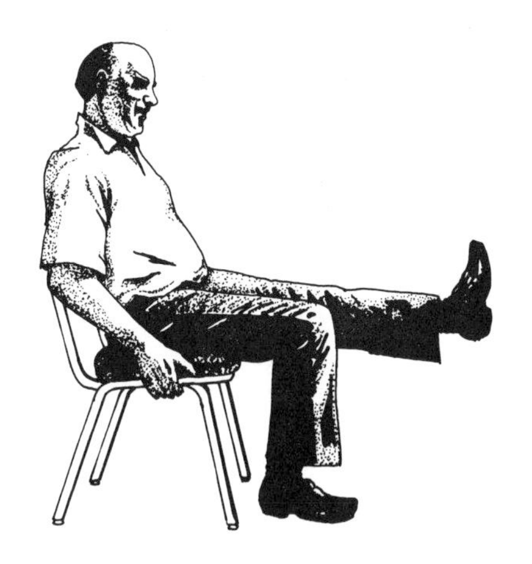

Leg Extensions

Lift one leg off the floor, and stretch it out straight ahead, up to chair height if you can. Lower it slowly. Now lift the other leg off the floor, and stretch it straight out. Lower it slowly. Repeat the movement with each leg 5 times.

Loosen Your Feet and Ankles

Cross one leg over your other knee, and rotate the foot slowly. Do 10 rotations. Now cross the other leg, and rotate the other foot. Repeat 10 times. Eventually, try to rotate each foot both clockwise and counterclockwise 10 times.

With your legs crossed, flex each foot backward and forward. Clench your toes and release. Repeat 5 times for each foot.

KEGEL EXERCISES

Named for the physician who originated them, these exercises improve bladder control for women with stress urinary incontinence (leaking small amounts of urine, particularly when coughing or laughing), as well as for men who have dribbling of urine after prostate surgery. Kegel exercises strengthen the pelvic floor by toning up the ring of muscles around the urine outlet, vagina, and rectum without tensing the leg or buttock muscles. You can feel this pelvic-floor muscle in contact with the chair seat when you are sitting down.

Another way to identify the pelvic-floor muscle is to practice stopping and starting the flow of urine by tightening this muscle while urinating. Stop and start the urine flow for 3 to 4 seconds, several times while voiding. Do not increase abdominal pressure, which will cause pressure on the bladder and work against stopping the urine flow. Once you have identified your pelvic-floor muscle, you can practice the following exercises at any time:

- *Contract and draw up the muscles of your pelvic floor, hold for 3 seconds, and relax. Repeat 5 times. For best results, repeat this exercise several times during the day, building up gradually to 10 groups of 5 muscle contractions. If your muscle begins to be a little sore, relax for a while until the soreness disappears. Then gradually start exercising again.*
- *Contract and relax the muscles as quickly as possible. Start doing 2 contractions and relaxations, and work up to 10 contractions and relaxations, 3 times a day.*
- *To strengthen the lower abdominal muscles and improve urine retention even further, add the "elevator" exercise. Think of your bladder as an elevator you are trying to raise to the top floor. Imagine pulling it up into your abdominal cavity toward your stomach. Raise it floor by floor, and then lower it slowly, gradually relaxing the abdominal muscles. Relax. Then raise your bladder back to the top floor so that the slight tension in your pelvis holds your organs firmly in place.*

may have swimming pools or tracks available to the public as well as classes designed for people with specific problems; for example, water-exercise classes for people with arthritis. Look for qualified instructors, classes with some participants of your own age, and instruction that adapts to individual differences in pace and flexibility.

Whether you are well or disabled, living on your own or in a group facility, an exercise program will help you to function better. Even frail older people who may be considering moving to a nursing home can benefit from an exercise program of stretching, range-of-motion, and deep-breathing exercises. Researchers report that exercise adjusted to individual abilities may allow peo-

SENIOR OLYMPIANS

Burt D., 82, of California, competes in shot put and discus throw. John W., 78, drives 50 miles roundtrip in North Carolina almost every day for his swimming workout, preparing for events at the Senior Olympics. Doris P., 66, of Missouri, also trains for Senior Olympics swimming events.

These master athletes, along with thousands of others across the nation, plan to participate in the national Senior Olympics, a competition held on odd-numbered years. In the intervening years, local competitions give older Americans the fun and opportunity of qualifying for national competition. Participants qualify for nationals by placing first, second, or third at local Senior Olympics. If you happen to be a former Olympian or national record holder, however, you can participate without qualifying at a local site.

Senior Olympians compete in archery, badminton, bowling, cycling, field, golf, horseshoes, softball, swimming, table tennis, track (including walking), and volleyball. What are the benefits of all this training, aside from the pleasure of playing games in groups? Why do three to four thousand people show up at national Senior Olympics? These older adults find that staying fit keeps them feeling younger and healthier, enjoying their lives more. "I feel like I'm a 66-year-old in the body of an 18-year-old," says Doris P. Or, to put it more scientifically, "the average individual loses functional capacity at the rate of (about) 1 percent a year after the age of 30," according to Everett L. Smith, director of the biogerontology lab at the University of Wisconsin. "In my opinion, about 50 percent of the average aging decline is self-induced by lifestyle, and the other 50 percent is due to the genes or the makeup of the individual biological system."

Whatever your level of fitness, you might enjoy getting involved in Senior Olympics. Local events are often sponsored by banks, hospitals, and other businesses. Your local senior center or Jewish Community Center may be able to give you information about upcoming activities. For information about national events and regional organizations, write to the Director, National Senior Olympic Games, 14323 S. Outer Forty Road, Suite N-300, Chesterfield, MO 63017, or call (314) 878-4900.

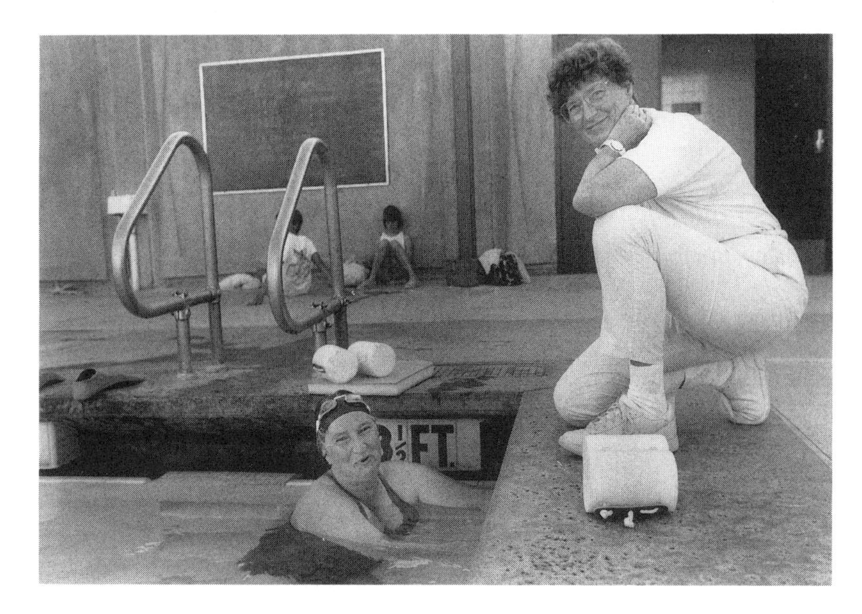

STRETCHES FOR WARM-UP AND COOL-DOWN

If you're designing your own exercise program, you may need a few ideas for safe and effective ways to stretch your muscles and ligaments before vigorous activity. Here are some recommendations from the President's Council on Physical Fitness and Sports.

Wall Stretch

Stand facing a wall about an arm's length away. Lean forward and place the palms of your hands flat against the wall, slightly below shoulder height. Keep your back straight and your heels firmly on the floor. Slowly bend your elbows until your forehead touches the wall. Tuck your hips toward the wall, and hold this position for 20 seconds. Repeat the exercise with your knees slightly flexed to stress an alternate muscle group. Use this exercise to prevent or treat soreness along your shins ("shin splints").

Reach and Bend

Stand erect with your feet shoulder-width apart and your arms stretched over your head. Reach as high as possible while keeping your heels on the floor. Hold for 10 counts.

Now bend your knees slightly *and bend slowly at your waist, touching your fingers to the floor between your feet. Don't strain; if you can't touch the floor, try to touch the tops of your shoes. Repeat the entire sequence 2 to 5 times.*

If you are overweight, or if you have any problems with your back or joints, *do this stretch sitting on the floor instead of standing. Sit with your back straight and your legs comfortably stretched in front of you. Reach straight ahead with your arms, toward the opposite wall. Stop if you feel any pain in your back. Hold your stretch for a count of 5, and relax. Repeat 2 to 5 times.*

Knee Pull

This exercise relaxes and stretches the lower back. Use it before and after exercising. Lie flat on the floor—pad it with a towel or mat—and extend your arms and legs. Clasp your hands around your knees and pull them up toward your chest, raising your buttocks slightly off the floor. Hold your knees gently in this position for 10 to 15 counts. If you have knee problems, you may find it more comfortable to clasp your hands behind your knees. Repeat the exercise 3 to 5 times.

Sit-up

Here are several versions of the sit-up, with the easiest one listed first, the most challenging last. Start with the sit-up that you can do three times without undue strain. When you are able to do 10 repetitions of the exercise without great difficulty, move on to a more challenging version.

1. Lie flat on your back, with your arms at your sides, palms down, and your knees slightly bent. Curl your head forward until you can see past your feet. Hold for 3 counts, then lower your head to the floor. Repeat 3 to 10 times.

2. Lie flat on your back, with your arms at your sides, palms down, and your knees slightly bent. Roll forward until your upper body is at a 45-degree angle to the floor, then return to your starting position. Repeat 3 to 10 times.

3. Lie flat on your back, with your arms at your sides, palms down, and your knees slightly bent. Roll forward to a sitting position, and then return to your starting position. Repeat 3 to 10 times.

4. Lie flat on your back with your arms crossed on your chest and your knees slightly bent. Roll forward to a sitting position, and then return to your starting position. Repeat 3 to 10 times.

5. Lie flat on your back with your hands laced in back of your head, and your knees slightly bent. Roll forward to a sitting position, and then return to your starting position. Repeat 3 to 10 times.

Arm Stretches

Before swimming, stretch your upper arms with these exercises.

1. Extend your right arm out in front at shoulder height. Place your left palm behind your right elbow and pull your right arm over in front of your neck. Stretch the right arm for about 20 seconds. Relax and repeat with the left arm.

2. Raise your right arm above your head, and bend at the elbow until your right hand touches the back of your neck. With your left hand, pull your right elbow toward your head. Keep your head up and your neck straight. Stretch the right arm for about 20 seconds. Relax and repeat with the left arm.

3. Loosen and lubricate your shoulder joints by rotating your shoulders, 20 seconds forward and 20 seconds backward.

ple more years of independent living, helping to keep them out of nursing homes longer than if they remained inactive.

Before starting your new exercise regimen, at whatever level, *always begin with a complete medical exam, including a treadmill test (or some other test of physical tolerance, such as a step-test), to identify your baseline cardiovascular capacity and ensure that your heart rhythms can tolerate exercise.* With your doctor's approval for the pace and type of exercise, begin at a level of activity you can do easily. Then, gradually increase the number of repetitions, the rate of movement, or the distance you travel. A safe and effective exercise session for older adults would include a warm-up period, aerobic activity, and cool-down.

Warm-up (10–30 minutes). Prepare your body to exercise by doing slow, rhythmic activities such as stretching, walking leisurely, or exercising for flexibility. This phase may also include breathing exercises and calisthenics. Gradually increase the intensity of exercise so that your heart rate rises slowly. Your blood will flow more easily to your coronary arteries and your joints and muscles will move more easily—without pain or injury—if you warm up thoroughly before vigorous exercise. You're warmed up when your body temperature rises enough for you to start perspiring.

Aerobic exercise (15–30 minutes). Aerobic exercise makes demands on your body for extra energy and oxygen. Done three to five times per week, aerobic exercise results in a conditioning effect on the heart and lungs, making them stronger and more efficient. Aerobic exercise can reduce hypertension and your cholesterol level as well as improve your ability to control diabetes and obesity. Activities that make you breathe hard and sweat a lot, like brisk walking, jogging, swimming, cycling, rowing, and dancing, make aerobic demands on your body; they condition the

CALCULATING YOUR TARGET HEART RATE FOR EXERCISE

Physical exercise that uses large muscles rhythmically and continuously (walking, swimming, cycling, and so on) forces the body to use oxygen, burning excess calories. This aerobic activity tones the heart, lungs, and arteries by stressing the cardiovascular system. As it adapts to regular exercise, the cardiovascular system works more efficiently, lowering blood pressure and improving the efficiency of oxygen use. A strong heart doesn't have to work as hard to circulate the blood because the heart can pump more efficiently with each beat. So your resting heart rate—that is, your pulse taken before exercise—will become lower as you progress with your exercise program.

It's important not to overstress the system, nor to work at such a low level that the exercise has no effect. You can regulate the stress on your cardiovascular system by taking your pulse during vigorous exercise and making sure that your activity level keeps your heart rate within a safe, effective range. How do you know what is safe and effective for you?

You can find out how hard to exercise by keeping track of your heart rate. Your maximum heart rate is the fastest your heart can beat. According to the National Heart, Lung, and Blood Institute of the National Institutes of Health, the best activity level for building cardiovascular fitness in older adults is 60 to 75 percent of your maximum level. This 60 to 75 percent range is called your target heart-rate zone.

When you begin your exercise program, aim for the lower end of the target heart-rate zone (60 percent). As you get stronger, gradually work at getting your heart rate up to 75 percent of maximum. You will stay in good condition as long as you exercise with your heart rate in this range.

To approximate your maximum heart rate, subtract your age from 220. Your target zone is 60 to 75 percent of this number. Here is a guide to typical heart rates for older people:

To monitor your heart rate, take your pulse (at the wrist or neck) after you have been exercising about 10 minutes. Count for 10 seconds, and multiply your count by 6. If your pulse is below your target zone, exercise a little harder. If you're above your target zone, slow down a bit. Once you're exercising consistently within your target zone, check your exercise pulse at least once a week.

Age (years)	Target Heart-Rate Zone (60–75% of maximum)	Average Maximum Heart Rate (100%)
50	102–127 beats per min.	170
55	99–123 beats per min.	165
60	96–120 beats per min.	160
65	93–116 beats per min.	155
70	90–113 beats per min.	150

heart and burn body fat. The advantages of individual sports as well as adaptations of sports for physical limitations are discussed later in this chapter. With any aerobic activity, an older person should exercise at a pace that keeps his or her heart rate within 60 to 75 percent of its maximum capacity. Take your pulse for 10 seconds several times during the aerobic phase of exercise. If your heart rate is too high for your range, slow down (don't stop), or else make smaller and more contained movements. If your heart rate is too low, make more vigorous movements, raise your arms higher, or move a little faster.

Cool-down (10–30 minutes). The third phase of your exercise session, cool-down, is important to prevent cardiovascular complications after exercise. Walking, stretching, and other slow movements keep your large muscles contracting, allowing the blood to return normally to the heart instead of pooling in the legs and hands. Stopping exercise suddenly, without cooling down, can result in dizziness, fainting, abnormal heart rhythms, or even heart attack. Don't stop—cool down!

At this point you might be thinking, "I couldn't do all that. I've never exercised in my life, and I'm too fat, anyway. I don't want to be seen with all those skinny people in turquoise spandex at the gym." Violet G., 58, finally decided to do something about her weight. At 324 pounds, she was on crutches from arthritis and obesity. She had difficulty with even simple activities, such as walking around her apartment. With her doctor's advice, she enrolled in a nutrition program that emphasized high fiber and low fat. She reduced her calorie intake and changed her eating patterns. She also joined a local gym, after noticing that several overweight, gray-haired women participated in the water-exercise class. The instructor, also an older woman, taught Violet how to adapt the exercises to her own pace. For example, Violet started out by moving on every other beat of the music instead of on every beat. She also limited the range of her movements to her own comfort level, gradually extending them as she lost weight and gained flexibility.

Six months later, Violet has lost 50 pounds, and she moves more comfortably. She attends water exercises four mornings per week and swims an extra 30 to 40 minutes after class. She finds that the water cushions her movements so that her arthritis is not irritated, as it might be in walking or jogging. Like most people, Violet found that regular exercise reduced her arthritis pain. Now she is an exercise convert, giving advice to all her friends and acquaintances about the benefits of fitness!

What to Wear

Exercise can be an excuse for indulging yourself in bright colors and outrageous garments you might never have imagined yourself wearing: skintight black spandex bike shorts, fluorescent windbreakers or vests for road-walking or biking, brilliant leotards and bathing suits, turquoise running shoes, even day-glow shoelaces. But it's not necessary to go to extremes unless you want to—almost any comfortable, loose-fitting clothing will do.

Flora G., 63, complains, "I love my daily walk, but I hate to exercise in cold weather. I get so much colder than I used to. Is something wrong with me?" Of course, Flora's physician can tell her whether she has a medical problem that makes her feel chilled, but most likely Flora feels colder than she used to because she is older. According to the American Physical Therapy Association, older people feel colder because they are colder. Later in life, your thinning skin releases more body heat. Unlike the average 98.6-degree body temperature earlier in life, the older person's body temperature ranges from 98.2 down to 98 degrees. So take care to dress for the weather when you exercise outdoors, understanding that your body will be less tolerant of extreme temperatures at either end of the gauge.

Clothing. For most cool-weather activities, slacks and sweatshirts or jogging suits work well; add extra layers, mittens, scarf, and wool cap when it gets really cold. Shorts and light shirts are suitable for warm weather; add a visor and sunglasses for outdoor activities. It's best not to exercise in extreme heat or cold. The heat your body generates during activity will warm you, so you may prefer to dress lightly rather than become overheated. Natural fibers such as cotton and wool and porous fabrics will help stabilize your temperature by allowing perspiration to evaporate. Wearing several layers of loose-fitting garments allows you to subtract or add as your body temperature rises or falls. Leave tight garments, belts, and girdles at home. Wear cotton socks, not those made of nylon or other synthetic fabrics. Loose-fitting socks may give you blisters.

Shoes. The most important part of your exercise clothing is shoes. Well-fitting shoes can enable you to "walk on air," while poorly fitting shoes can cause pain and even injury to the feet, knees, and back. Many activities put repeated stress on the foot and ankle. To avoid sore feet, purchase comfortable, well-built shoes with an arch support, half- to three-quarter-inch heel, and a firmly cushioned sole made of rubber or crepe. Uppers should be made of mesh cloth or leather, so that your feet can "breathe." For walking or jogging, sneakers and tennis shoes allow too much side-to-side movement. Your balance will be better in good shoes made especially for walking or running.

Aerobic Activities

Although many people think of vigorous exercise in terms of running, long-distance cycling, or working out, recent research has found what Violet discovered—that the benefits from moder-

TROUBLE SIGNS

No matter how much you love your new aerobics class or walking group, it's important to listen to your body's messages. While it is normal to breathe deeply, feel your heart beat harder than usual, perspire, and maybe ache a little when you begin a new exercise program, if you feel uncomfortable, you are doing too much. Slow down, or take a break and start again later. Although most people who start slowly have no problems with exercise programs, you should be alert to unusual signs, including the following:

- *chest pain or pressure*
- *severe breathlessness*
- *joint pain or muscle cramps*
- *dizziness or confusion*
- *nausea*
- *exhaustion or trembling*
- *coughing or difficulty in breathing*
- *pallor*

If you have any of these symptoms, stop exercising and see your doctor. Never exercise when you are sick or in pain. Avoid vigorous exercise when the weather is hot or the air polluted.

During any vigorous exercise, give yourself the talk test occasionally. If you cannot keep up a normal conversation because of breathlessness, you are exercising too fast. SLOW DOWN. When you stop enjoying yourself, switch to another activity. If you're not having fun, you're playing the wrong game!

ate exercise are just as valuable for your health as more strenuous sports. A British study of 18,000 civil servants found that two groups—the vigorous sports enthusiasts and the people who worked energetically in their gardens and walked briskly every other day—had less than half the incidence of heart disease of people who did not exercise. A study of 17,000 Harvard alumni found that people who exercised heavily gained no more health benefits than those who exercised moderately; both groups lived up to two years longer than alumni who avoided exercise.

Weight training and aerobic workouts may seem more macho, but they are no more effective for health than brisk walking, stair-climbing, or dancing. For benefits to your circulatory system, it's important to exercise at least three times per week, preferably on alternate days to give your body recovery time. And select an activity (or alternate among several) that you enjoy enough to continue. You will lose your fitness gains quickly if you get bored and quit for a while. Harvey B. Simon, assistant professor of medicine at Harvard Medical School, uses a rule of thumb for exercisers who "lay out" now and then: "I tell people to figure on two days' buildup for each day out. If you miss a week, it takes two weeks to get back to your baseline. But that's based on my own experiences and practice of medicine."

So choose an activity to please yourself, and if you do get tired of it, switch to something else. Enjoy!

Walking. "I'm 66 years old," says Al R., "and although I'm in good health, jogging has gotten to be too much for me. I'm thinking of developing a walking routine. But I wonder if the physical benefits are worth the effort."

Absolutely. When done on a regular basis, walking can improve your body's ability to use oxygen during exertion, lower your resting heart rate, reduce blood pressure, and increase the efficiency of your heart and lungs. It also helps burn excess calories. Like jogging, walking often makes people feel better and sleep better, while improving their mental alertness by sending more oxygen to the brain.

A national survey found that the highest percentage of regular walkers (39 percent) was among men aged 65 and older. Walking takes longer than running to achieve the same results, but because it's less strenuous, it lets you enjoy the scenery and opportunities for social life more. And the fitness differences are not as great as many people think: One study reported that jogging a mile in 8½ minutes burns only 26 calories more than walking a mile in 12 minutes. Assuming that you maintain the same diet, walking 2 miles in 30 minutes daily (this is brisk walking, about a mile in 15 minutes) can burn off enough excess calories so that you'll lose 15 pounds of fat in a year. Walking an hour a day can burn enough calories so that you'll lose 30 pounds in a year.

Before beginning a walking program, get an okay from your doctor. Always start with exercises to warm up (such as walking at a leisurely pace) and to increase your overall flexibility and body strength (such as stretches or light calisthenics). Then, walk as briskly as your condition permits. The President's Council on Physical Fitness and Sports recommends that you begin by walking for 20 minutes four or five times a week at a pace that feels comfortable for you. Thereafter, you can increase the speed, length of time, or both. If you develop dizziness, pain, nausea, or any other unusual symptom, slow down or stop. If the problem persists, see your physician before walking again.

Here are some tips for walking at any pace:

- Wait an hour after eating heavily before you walk.
- Any movement is exercise, so if you are housebound, walk at home. Walk to the kitchen, walk around the table, get up and walk over to change the TV channel. Walk up and down the halls, outside to the mailbox, over to visit a neighbor.

- Always warm up. Take time for slow stretching and easy movements before beginning your walk. Then, start out with a slow pace and increase it gradually.
- Hold your head erect, back straight, abdomen flat, and arms loose. If your hands feel a little swollen, stop swinging your arms, bend your elbows, and walk for a while with your hands raised to chest level.
- Breathe deeply, fill your abdomen, and then exhale gradually and fully.
- Step out with your heel first, roll forward, bend your knees, and step off the ball of your foot. Point your toes straight ahead. Walk with a relaxed, loose-jointed stride, not stiffly.
- Walk when the weather is pleasant, not too hot or too cold. For example, walk during the early morning and early evening in summer, and during mid-day in winter.
- Use a sunblock and wear protective clothing—a hat, long sleeves, long pants—to prevent skin cancer.
- Cool down. Slow your pace gradually until you stop sweating. Relax your muscles with slow stretches.
- Find a companion and vary the itinerary if you get bored. People in cities often join clubs that walk in shopping malls, in parks, or on nature trails. Walk to a museum or historical site together. Include a challenging hill or two. Find an interested co-worker at your office and take walk breaks together instead of coffee breaks or sedentary lunches.

Jogging. Walking gives you the same benefits as jogging, but without the extra stress on the joints and spine. However, if you are feeling fit enough to jog, the guidelines are similar to those for walking. Start slowly and work up gradually to a faster pace and longer distance; monitor your heart rate frequently; be alert for unusual symptoms or pain, and see your doctor if these occur. One way to begin a jogging program is with walk-jogging: Walk 50 yards, jog 50 yards, and continue alternating your pace. Over time, gradually increase the proportion of jogging. If you are overweight, over 50, and sedentary, start your fitness program with simple walking or some other type of exercise—not jogging.

Here are some tips for joggers:

• Wait an hour after eating heavily before you jog.

• Warm-up and cool-down are even more essential than with walking because of the extra stress to joints and ligaments.

• Buy good running shoes to protect your feet as well as to reduce the shock to the bones and ligaments in your ankles, knees, hips, and lower back.

• According to the American Heart Association, it is safe to run in winter when the temperature is as low as 10 degrees below zero Fahrenheit. In summer, it is *not* safe to run when the temperature is above 82 degrees.

• For safety and best results, run hard enough to sweat, 20 to 30 minutes three times a week. Give yourself the "talk test" frequently; if you can't carry on a conversation, you're running too hard.

• Wear a hat to protect yourself from sun or cold, and wear layers of clothing so that you can remove a layer as your body temperature rises. Never run in tight or nonporous materials such as plastic or rubber.

• Consider joining a jogging class or club where you can obtain expert supervision. You may also have more fun running with other people. However, jog with people who are at your pace; do not force yourself to keep up with people who run faster than you do.

• Drink plenty of water before, during, and after your run.

• Stay loose and have fun! Placing performance pressure on yourself reduces many of the benefits of exercise and may eventually result in deterioration of your joints and ligaments.

Swimming. Swimming provides the cardiovascular benefits of jogging without placing strain on body joints. A program of regular swimming will increase your body's flexibility as well as the volume of blood pumped through your arteries. Like walking, swimming improves your blood pressure and mental alertness. It can help reverse the cardiovascular effects of years of overeating and underexercising. The University of Texas Health Center in Dallas found that a systematic swimming-and-exercise program increased cardiovascular fitness (maximal oxygen intake) by 20 percent in inactive, middle-aged adults.

Swimmers look and feel better than sedentary people. Swimming will limber up your muscles and increase bone density, especially in the upper body, which is not strengthened by walking. But what if you never learned to swim, or your stroke is awkward and inefficient? Any vigorous activity in water will have similar effects—you don't have to be Mark Spitz to benefit. You can swim any way that's comfortable for you, or just bob, jump, walk, or jog through the water. Many adults take swimming classes to feel more at ease in the water. Classes are often available at community recreation centers, parks, local colleges, or gyms. Water-exercise classes, usually taught to lively music, combine the benefits of aerobic exercise and group support with the gentle cushioning of water. People with disabilities and joint problems, such as arthritis, can enjoy swimming without discomfort. The resistance of the water is the equivalent of exercising with weights so that your muscles develop a balanced strength.

Although swimming outdoors in warm weather is delightful, you may want to locate an indoor pool so that you'll be able to keep up your exercise all year long. When choosing a pool, make sure that it is long enough for the laps you plan to swim. If the pool is open to the public, visit during lap-swim hours to see how crowded it gets. New swimmers often feel intimidated sharing a lane with faster, stronger swimmers, so compare facilities with your own comfort in mind.

Equipment needs are minimal. Just make sure your bathing suit is lightweight, streamlined (even if you're still working to get that way!), and comfortable. Women who have had mastectomies and feel reluctant to appear in bathing suits can find well-designed suits at stores that specialize in fitting prostheses. Your local unit of the American Cancer Society can provide you with a list of stores. If you feel abashed about wearing the bathing suits available in department stores, you might choose from the wide selection of patterns and fabrics available at sewing stores and make one yourself. Or ask the store for the name of someone who can make a suit for you. Size and shape need not deter you from a swimming program. In fact, people with more body fat float better than thin people because fat is more buoyant than muscle and bone.

A swim cap will help keep water out of your ears; ear plugs work even better. People who are bothered by water up their noses use nose clips. In salt water or chlorinated pools, swim goggles keep your eyes from stinging. All of these items are available at a sporting goods store.

Start your swim sessions as you would any other aerobic exercise—with stretches and slow movement to warm up. These can be done in the water if you wish. Begin with one or two laps, or just a half lap, and increase your distance gradually until you can swim 20 to 30 minutes at your target heart rate. Take your pulse regularly to keep track of your heart rate. If your heart rate is too high or you need more air, swim slowly or float for a moment.

Varying your strokes is a good way to develop balanced muscle strength and pace yourself. Try a lap of vigorous crawl or backstroke alternated with breaststroke or sidestroke. Swimming on your back gives you a chance to catch your breath. As with any exercise, the important point is to keep moving, however slowly, and enjoy yourself. When you finish your session, swim slowly for a bit to cool down, and then stretch out again.

Before you plunge in, here are some additional considerations for safe swimming:

- Wait an hour after eating heavily before you swim.
- If you swim in open water (a lake, a river, or the ocean), always swim near a lifeguard. Collect information about weather, tides, currents, rocks, or undergrowth.
- In a public pool, educate yourself about policies on sharing swim lanes and using equipment (kickboards, fins, paddles, and so on).
- Never swim alone. Be sure a lifeguard is near, or else swim with a companion.
- Never drink alcoholic beverages or take drugs that affect your balance before swimming.
- Dive cautiously, checking beforehand to be certain that the water is deep enough and that other swimmers are at a safe distance.
- Do not swim under diving boards or in diving areas. Stay out of the fast swim lanes until you are also expert.

Cycling. "I'm 59 and in good health," says Rudy W. "I last rode a bicycle many years ago from my college dormitory to my classes. I'd like to resume cycling, but I wonder whether it's a good idea for a man my age." Whether indoors on a stationary bike or outdoors on a ten-speed, bicycling is especially good for older adults as well as for people who are overweight, because it is "nonballistic"; that is, we don't bounce up and down on our feet, punishing our joints, as we do in jogging or aerobic dancing. Cyclists seem to be less bothered by back and other problems, such as pulled muscles and sore tendons, that trouble runners.

If your doctor approves of your resuming exercise on a bicycle, you will be joining some 84 million Americans who cycle for fitness. For the over-50 group, bicycling is the third most popular sport. Only "general exercise" and swimming are more popular.

Cycling builds muscle strength in the lower body as effectively as jogging; upper-body exercises and stretching are good supplements. Like walking and running, bicycling improves cardiovascular fitness. Its advantage is that cycling causes virtually no stress on the joints. Stationary indoor bicycling produces the same benefits as road biking. Instead of watching the scenery, you can read, watch television, or listen to music while you exercise at home.

In addition to improving fitness, bicycling can also be an exhilarating way to travel, especially in a group. For information about biking clubs in your area, call a local bicycle shop. Some biking organizations organize tours ranging in distance from local rides to excursions worldwide.

Basic types of bicycles include the one-speed (starting at $150), ten-speed (starting at $200), and all-terrain (starting at $200). Adult three-wheeled cycles (about $400) are easier to balance than two-wheelers; good-quality three-wheelers have a low center of gravity. Consider one with a 20-inch wheel. Stationary exercise bicycles cost upwards of $100.

If you decide to buy a bicycle, visit a bike shop or sporting goods store where experts can tell you about the primary purpose and advantages of each type. You might wish to rent several models to try them out before you decide on a purchase. A good bike store can also give advice about operating the bike properly and will offer maintenance. To prevent injury, it's important to ride a bicycle that is adjusted for your height, reach, and leg length. The store that sells you the bicycle should be able to adjust it for your physique and ability.

When riding on public roads, wear highly visible clothing. You should *always* wear a safety helmet. Travel with the traffic, using the same rules of the road as motorists. Whenever possible, use bike lanes and bike paths; these are safer than roads used by autos because motorists often have trouble seeing and avoiding cyclists. Always ride as though motorists don't see you.

Clothing should be comfortable and tough enough to protect your skin if you take a spill. If you wear long pants, you can secure the cuffs with clips to keep them from tangling in the bike chain. Shoes should be flexible with heavy soles. Wear absorbent socks. As with any outdoor sport, layered clothing is the most adaptable for a range of temperatures and breezes.

A cycling exercise program should include:

- a safe place and a regular schedule for your rides
- at least three sessions per week
- warm-up for each ride, consisting of stretching and walking your bike or riding slowly for 10 minutes
- riding within your target heart-rate zone for 10 to 30 minutes each time, depending on how comfortable you feel
- cool-down for each ride, consisting of walking your bike or riding slowly for 10 minutes

Once you've accustomed yourself to regular cycling, you can use your bike for errands or recreation around the neighborhood or around the world.

Dancing. Dancing provides the cardiovascular benefits of walking or jogging, depending on the pace, with the additional fun of rhythmic movement to music and the exhilaration of being part of a group. In addition to developing flexibility and endurance, dancing makes people feel good while they're doing it—a natural high. Whether you go ballroom dancing, square dancing, or aerobic dancing, look for a class that includes older people and an instructor with experience and training. You can also dance at home to your own music, inventing your own routines.

- Warm up, using stretching and moderate exercise such as walking.
- Dance for at least 12 minutes at a time without stopping. Check your heart rate regularly, and slow down if you're exceeding your target range.
- Cool down by walking and stretching to slower music.

Other aerobic activities. Any physical activity will improve your fitness and burn calories if you can sustain it for 20 to 30 minutes while keeping your heart rate within your target range. If you live on a farm and do heavy work, you probably don't need any additional aerobic activity in your life, but if you're a city-dweller, you may try many additional kinds of exercise beyond the few examples we have suggested. For maximum benefit from any aerobic activity, follow the basic pattern of warm-up, exercise at target heart rate for 20 to 30 minutes (or as long as you're comfortable), and cool-down. Here are some possibilities you might like to investigate. Many of these activities can be even more fun when done to lively music:

- skating (either roller or ice)
- hiking
- jumping rope
- running in place (can be adjusted to any fitness level)
- rowing (machine or boat)
- walking on indoor treadmill
- cross-country skiing
- stair-stepping. Step up onto a stair or footstool, bring up the other foot, step down with the first foot, step down with the second foot. Alternate the foot you start with, and keep your back straight.

Fitness can also be attained through Eastern disciplines such as Tai Chi, which stresses rhythmic flowing body movements as a way to develop balance, coordination, and flexibility, and Hatha Yoga, which aims to improve flexibility, limberness, and muscle tone and control.

Modifying Exercise for Specific Needs

You may feel reluctant to start an exercise program because you feel your body "doesn't qualify" or because your bad back or arthritis or high blood pressure or diabetes has disabled you to the status of a sedentary observer. Good news! You, too, can do it. In fact, as we have mentioned previously, exercise has been shown to improve all of these conditions, if done appropriately and with qualified supervision. Local recreation centers, medical centers, and educational institutions may offer special activity classes for special needs. Many service associations can be helpful in recommending physical activity classes in your area.

You can also participate in standard exercise programs by adapting them for your own condition. Let your activity instruc-

ACTIVITY CLASSES FOR PEOPLE WITH SPECIAL NEEDS

These service organizations can recommend activity classes for people with special needs. Contact the national offices listed below or find local chapters in your telephone book.

American Cancer Society
1599 Clifton Road
Atlanta, GA 30329
(404) 320-3333

American Diabetes Association
1660 Duke Street
Alexandria, VA 22314
(703) 549-1500

American Heart Association
7320 Greenville Avenue
Dallas, TX 75231
(214) 750-5397

Arthritis Foundation
1314 Spring Street, N.W.
Atlanta, GA 30309
(404) 872-7100

National Association for the Deaf
814 Thayer Avenue
Silver Spring, MD 20910
(301) 587-1788 (voice and TDD)

National Multiple Sclerosis Society
205 East 42nd Street
New York, NY 10017
(212) 986-3240

tor know if you have a problem that will affect your response to exercise. *If you have one of the following conditions, it is essential to check your exercise plans with your doctor before beginning a new activity.* Be sure to discuss the modifications described below with your doctor to determine whether they are suitable for you.

Medication use. If you are taking medications, whether prescription or over-the-counter drugs, ask your doctor about the effect of these drugs during exercise. You may need to adapt your routine a bit. For example, several medications prescribed to lower blood pressure will affect your resting heart rate, so you will need to adjust your target heart-rate range. Diuretics ("water pills") do not affect heart rate, but they may make you more vulnerable to dehydration. If you are taking diuretics, be sure to drink plenty of liquid before, during, and after exercise, especially if the weather is warm. Some cold medications and diet pills will increase your heart rate.

Hypertension. If you have high blood pressure, avoid isometric exercises (movements in which the muscles strain against each other or a stationary object but do not move). These static exercises may stimulate a rise in your blood pressure. It is important to keep your joints and limbs moving or stretching when they are not at rest.

Warm up and cool down gradually and thoroughly. As much as possible, exercise with your arms held at shoulder level or below. Avoid working with hand weights above shoulder level. Arm movements above the shoulders will raise your blood pressure.

Keep breathing! Never hold your breath while exercising. Breathe normally to avoid cardiovascular damage from straining against a closed glottis (opening to the windpipe). You may need to tell yourself, "Inhale, Exhale," but if that's what it takes to remember, it's worth it.

Cardiovascular disease. If you are recovering from a heart attack, stroke, or surgery, exercise only in special programs run by qualified medical professionals such as physical therapists until your doctor approves another program.

Arthritis. People with osteoarthritis or rheumatoid arthritis can use the same exercise modifications. Emphasize movements that increase flexibility and range of motion while you develop strength. During aerobic activity, avoid movements that stress the joints. Instead of bouncing your weight on joints by jogging, aerobic dancing, or weight training, try water exercise or swimming. Be sure to warm up completely to lubricate joints before vigorous exercise. Build your exercise program slowly, and stop when any exercise causes unusual pain. Avoid working with weights, which increase stress on joints. During inflammatory episodes of rheumatoid arthritis, avoid exercise.

Obesity. A person who is very overweight has an increased chance of injury and overexertion during exercise, so it is important to start slowly and warm up thoroughly. Increase your activity gradually; if you are not accustomed to vigorous exercise, your muscles will need time to develop and support you properly. Exercise at a low intensity for longer periods of time, and try to exercise four to five times per week. Never exercise while wearing rubber suits or plastic wraps or in excessive heat.

Low-back pain. Often a result of poor posture, inactivity, or stress, low-back pain plagues approximately 80 percent of us at some time in our lives. Your exercise program should include stretches for the lower back muscles and hamstrings (back of the thighs) as well as movements to strengthen the abdominal muscles. However, abdominal exercises should be gentle movements such as curl-ups and pelvic tilts, not sit-ups and double-leg raises. Avoid jogging, jumping, running in place, or any other movement that jars the spine. Keep your knees flexed, both while standing and moving. Using hand and ankle weights may aggravate your condition, as will any twisting movement. Stop any movement that causes pain; instead, follow a plan of regular, moderate exercise to increase muscle strength and joint flexibility.

Diabetes. Physical exercise has an effect on the body similar to insulin. Along with proper diet and insulin (if required), exercise is an excellent way to maintain metabolic balance. If you have trouble with hypoglycemia, keep fruit juice or candy nearby when you exercise. Diabetics with poor circulation or numbness in the legs and feet should avoid weight-bearing exercise, such as jogging or walking, in favor of water exercise or swimming. Be sure to eat properly, but not heavily, before exercise, and if you use insulin, do not inject it over a muscle just before you use that muscle in activity. Doing so may increase the speed with which the insulin enters your bloodstream and bring on hypoglycemia.

Healthy Eating, Healthy Aging

Just as beginning an exercise program can improve health and reverse some of the effects we associate with aging, taking a good look at eating patterns can also improve well-being. Some researchers are discovering that eating patterns not only may keep us feeling better, they also may contribute to the health of the immune response and, therefore, to how long we live. As Jane Brody, nutrition writer for the *New York Times,* points out, "Dietary measures might eventually be used to slow the aging of the immune system and to extend the human lifespan by delaying the onset of diseases that result from immunological decline." Nutrients such as fish oils, zinc, selenium, iron, polyunsaturated fats, and certain amino acids and vitamins are being studied for their effects—both positive and negative—on the immune system's response to disease and injury. At this point, however, biochemical research has not produced firm recommendations for specific dietary changes. Until we know more, moderation is probably the key to a health-promoting diet and a healthy immune system.

Although we do not yet know exactly how diet affects our lifespan, we do know that, with age, we need fewer calories to maintain our body weight. *But we need all the same nutrients we ever did.* In fact, older people need more of some nutrients than younger people do. For example, the recommended daily allowance (RDA) of calcium for younger women is 1,000 to 1,200 milligrams. For postmenopausal women, who are more vulnerable to thinning bones, the RDA is 1,500 milligrams. Older people face the challenge of improving their food choices to eliminate unneeded calories while getting the nutrition they need for strong bones, cardiovascular health, good digestion and elimination, and resistance to disease.

Even when you decide to make changes in your eating patterns, you may find it more difficult than you expect. Many older people live alone, and it is harder to shop and cook economically for one person than for a family. It is also less fun. Hazel M., 78, often finds her refrigerator in a sorry state when she remembers to eat—a half-carton of old milk, a bag of flour, assorted jams and condiments, limp lettuce. It just feels like too much trouble to make shopping lists and cook for one. She depends on crackers, dry cereal, canned soups and spaghetti, packaged macaroni and rice casseroles, frozen dinners, and canned tuna for most meals. Food just doesn't taste as good to Hazel as it used to. For Hazel, eating alone contributes to a poor diet. Because a poor diet can result in poor health, lack of energy, and malnutrition, it's important to develop habits that make shopping and cooking more enjoyable.

Before shopping, Hazel should make a list of items needed. Although she should buy perishables in small amounts, she may save money by purchasing economy packages of lean meat, poultry, and fish, and then rewrapping and freezing them in meal-size portions. Many older persons rely on packaged fast foods because they don't like to bother preparing meals from scratch. But canned and frozen dinners are usually more expensive and often less nutritious than home-cooked meals. Packaged (processed) foods are usually much higher in sodium than fresh foods, and the increased sodium can aggravate hypertension. Older chefs can save preparation time by fixing small meals designed for couples or singles. Cookbooks with recipes for one or two diners are offered in bookstores and libraries. Leftovers from larger meals can be packaged in single servings, labeled as to contents and date prepared, and frozen for later use.

Many older people solve some meal-preparation problems by eating in groups, both for the pleasure of the company and for the improved nutrition. There are several ways to arrange to share your meals with other people. You can organize your own potluck meals with friends or neighbors down the hall, asking each person to contribute a dish to the meal once or twice a week. You can join other older adults at communal meals in senior centers and churches. You can arrange to eat with relatives on a regular basis, either at a restaurant or at home. And when you do prepare your own food, you can begin gradually to improve your dietary patterns.

Guidelines for Healthy Eating after 50

A simple way to plan daily meals to include the nutrients you need is to make sure you select from the four basic food groups. Two servings each from the dairy and meat groups, and four servings each from the grain and fruit-vegetable groups should make up the daily menu. Keep records for a few days, and check off your meals against this list.

Dairy group (two to three servings). This group is essential as a source of calcium and other nutrients. One serving consists of:

- 1 cup milk, buttermilk, yogurt, or soy milk*
- 1½ ounces cheese
- 1¾ cups ice cream, ice milk, or nonfat frozen yogurt
- ½ cup tofu (soybean curd)

Fish and meat group (two to three servings). Foods in this group provide concentrated protein. Many older people do not get enough protein, so you should make certain you select foods from this group daily. Although the group is identified by animal protein foods, dry beans and nuts also provide excellent protein, less expensively than from meat (and with less fat, in the case of beans). A protein serving consists of one of the following:

- 3 ounces cooked chicken, turkey, fish, or lean meat
- 2 eggs
- 1 cup cooked dry beans or peas
- 4 tablespoons peanut butter, almond butter, or tahini (sesame paste)
- ½ cup cottage cheese
- 5 ounces tofu (soybean curd)

*Soybean milk, which is sold under several brand names, is often used as a milk substitute by vegetarians and people intolerant to cow's milk. Soy milk has about half the protein and fat of whole cow's milk, and about 10 milligrams of calcium in each 8-ounce cup (cow's milk has about 300 milligrams per cup). Lactaid milk is an option for people with lactase deficiency, which is, unfortunately, a rather common condition in which milk products are poorly digested. When added to milk, over-the-counter Lactaid drops or capsules convert milk sugar into its digestible form.

Fruits and vegetables (four servings). These foods provide the fiber necessary for good digestion as well as the vitamins and minerals we need for all our metabolic processes. Be sure to include a fruit rich in vitamin C, such as a citrus fruit, every day. A serving might consist of one of the following:

- an average-sized raw fruit, approximately 1 cup
- a medium potato
- 1 cup raw vegetable
- ½ cup cooked vegetable or fruit
- ½ cup fruit or vegetable juice (unsweetened)

Grains (four servings). Cereal products provide carbohydrates for energy as well as vitamins and minerals necessary for normal metabolism. Using whole-grain products will increase the fiber that we need for elimination. Any of the following will satisfy the requirements for a single serving from the grain group:

- 1 slice of bread
- 1 tortilla or ½ pita
- 1 cup ready-to-eat cereal
- ½ cup cooked grain or hot cereal such as oatmeal
- ½ cup noodles, cornmeal, rice, or grits
- 1 small muffin or biscuit
- 2 graham crackers or 5 saltines

Other foods. Oils, butter, margarine, jam and jelly, cake, pie, candy, sauces, and alcohol do not fall into the four basic groups. These foods are "extras" that provide many extra calories but few essential nutrients. Use them sparingly if you are overweight, and be sure not to substitute them for the foods in the basic four groups.

Checking your daily meals against these four food groups is an easy way to ensure that you are meeting your basic nutritional needs. Many people don't need to be any more specific than this. Others, however, have special concerns for their diet, or they may have physical conditions that they can improve by changing the way they eat. *Before changing eating patterns, consult your doctor. It is especially important to get your physician's advice if you have any illnesses that might require changes in what or how much you eat.* Some drugs interact with certain foods that change their effects, and some drugs alter nutritional needs.

Losing Weight

While some people have trouble eating enough of the proper foods to get adequate nutrients and maintain a normal body weight as they age, others have trouble with too much body fat, or at least they think they do. Donald M. says, "I am 69 years old and in good health. I exercise moderately and am about ten pounds overweight. What type of diet should I follow to maintain this state of wellness? I don't want to get fat." Elaine Z. describes another quandary with aging and being overweight: "During all my 59 years, I've had a weight problem. I go from a size 14 to a size 10 and then up again, usually within six months. Recently, though, I've noticed that I've been unable to lose as rapidly, even though I watch my weight constantly. Is this because I'm aging? Do old people have more trouble losing weight?"

The answers to both of these dilemmas are similar. Although you may find you gain weight more easily with age, your body requires the same amount of most nutrients as that required by younger people. Day in and day out, not just while you're dieting, it's more important than ever to eat nutritious foods and cut down on sweets, salty snack foods, fats, high-calorie beverages, and alcohol. Eating patterns that emphasize fresh or frozen vegetables—especially the leafy green and orange kinds, fresh fruits,

MARITAL SABOTAGE

You've been following your new eating plan conscientiously for a week now, cutting down on sugar, salt, and fat and substituting high-fiber fruits and vegetables for sweet and salty snacks. But lo and behold, a chocolate cake appears in the kitchen during your absence at exercise class. "It just looked so good," says your spouse helplessly. "I couldn't resist." So you have a piece. And one the next day. Or your roommate says, "Let's go to the movies. You can skip your walk, just today." Three weeks later, you wonder where all your good intentions went as you notice yourself eating the same old stuff and gaining the pounds you lost. What happened? Intimate sabotage.

It's hard to make changes in any habits; changing ingrained eating or exercise habits takes time and effort. It also takes an environment that supports the changes—including the social environment. In other words, if you are with people who subtly undermine your efforts, it will be almost impossible to make permanent behavior changes. Are you doomed to yo-yo dieting forever?

Albert R. Marston, professor of psychology and psychiatry at the University of Southern California, notices that overweight partners sometimes sabotage others' fitness efforts as a way to avoid facing their own problems. On the other hand, normal-weight partners usually act as good models. Marston offers suggestions for coping with an overweight roommate or spouse who sabotages your changes:

- *Teach your partner to help you by praising your efforts, not by teasing or nagging you. For example, ask for praise and a pat on the back when you stick to your exercise program.*
- *Insist that chocolate cake be kept out of sight on a separate shelf. If your partner brings in foods you don't want to eat, maintain a separate space in the refrigerator and cupboard for them. Keep them in neutral containers that don't advertise their presence and tempt you; for example, take cookies out of their box and put them in a covered plastic bin.*
- *Keep your eye on your own goal. Don't set up a competition—even unconsciously—with your partner to lose weight faster or exercise more. You'll begin to sabotage each other. Instead, set up a mutual-support system, with praise and rewards for both of you as you reach your own goals.*

low-fat dairy or soy products, whole grains, and low-fat proteins such as beans, fish, and chicken will reduce the sugar, fats, and calories in your diet. As mentioned previously, exercise is more important than ever in keeping off extra pounds. A person who exercises regularly can eat more without gaining weight than a person who sits most of the day. Most experts today believe that a regular program of aerobic exercise is essential to maintain any weight loss.

As Elaine has noticed, "yo-yo" dieting—that is, constant fluctuations in weight—results eventually in slower weight loss and more rapid weight gain over the years the longer the cycle goes on. This up-and-down yo-yo process, losing weight on stringent diets and then regaining all the losses plus a few extra pounds, impairs the body's metabolic balance. Elaine's difficulty losing weight now has more to do with her yo-yo dieting than with aging. Fad diets—high-protein, high-fat, grapefruit, carbohydrate, macrobiotic, fasting, and so on—lack any scientific basis and will contribute to the long-term weight gain that results from yo-yo dieting.

Whether you want to maintain your weight or lose a few pounds, the most efficient method is to change your basic eating patterns and build a sensible nutrition and exercise plan you can live with indefinitely. It's a good idea to start by keeping records of your eating over a week or two and comparing your typical food choices with those we have outlined in the four basic food groups. Gradually add or substitute more nutritious choices. In addition to choosing a range of foods, you should also consider reducing your intake of fats and cholesterol-rich foods; increasing the fiber in your meals; ensuring that you are getting the proper amounts of minerals such as potassium and iron for maximum health; reducing your use of caffeine, sugar, and alcohol; and increasing the calcium content of your food to preserve stronger bones.

Cholesterol and Fats

A small amount of cholesterol—a fat-like substance that circulates in the blood—is necessary for many body functions. However, excessive amounts—deposited in the form of plaque—can clog the arteries, laying the groundwork for heart attacks and strokes. Because of this, the American Heart Association recommends cutting down on cholesterol-rich foods.

Cholesterol is found only in animal products such as meat, eggs, and milk; food of plant origin contains no cholesterol. A good target for a low-cholesterol diet is less than 200 milligrams of cholesterol per day. Read labels to see how much cholesterol is in the prepared foods you purchase. To give you a general sense of the cholesterol contained in foods, consider that 1 ounce of cheddar cheese has 30 milligrams of cholesterol; 1 egg yolk has 272 milligrams of cholesterol; 1 cup of whole milk has 34 milligrams; 1 cup of skim milk has 4 milligrams; a broiled hamburger patty has 90 milligrams; 3.5 ounces of skinned turkey breast has 69 milligrams; 3 ounces of baked halibut has 35 milligrams.

The American Heart Association also strongly recommends reducing the amount of fat in your diet, from the average American's 40 percent of daily calories to 20 to 30 percent. It is particularly important to cut down on saturated fats because the body converts them to cholesterol to a degree that varies from person to person.

Like cholesterol, saturated fat, which tends to be solid at room temperature, is found in animal products: meats, lard, eggs, cheese, milk, cream, and butter. In addition, some plant foods, although they contain no cholesterol, are high in saturated fat. Major sources of these foods are tropical oils such as palm oil and coconut oil. Again, read labels carefully. Keep in mind that a product can be cholesterol free and still contain artery-clogging saturated fat. Advertisements often deliberately blur this distinction.

Unsaturated fats—such as olive, safflower, soybean, and corn oil—may actually reduce cholesterol levels. These fats come from plant sources. Researchers have found some evidence that fish oils, especially from salmon, can lower serum cholesterol. However, a diet high in *any* fat is associated with obesity, which increases the risk of heart disease and diabetes. International cancer and diet statistics provide the strongest suggestion that excessive fat intake—which is typical of the American diet—may substantially increase the risk of colon, prostate, and breast cancer.

Even when you're using unsaturated vegetable fats, your good intentions may be sabotaged by a type of preservative processing called *hydrogenation*. Hydrogenated vegetable fats are just as damaging to the arteries as animal fats, so read labels carefully. If a fat keeps its firm consistency at room temperature, it is probably hydrogenated and, therefore, saturated. For example, hydrogenated peanut butter has a smoothly consistent texture that needs no refrigeration. Nonhydrogenated peanut butter or almond butter will separate at room temperature. You can tell when oils are still unsaturated because they rise to the top of the nut butter, so you have to stir them in and keep the jar refrigerated to maintain consistency. As a matter of fact, you should refrigerate most nonhydrogenated oils as well to prevent them from becoming rancid.

How can you calculate the percentage of fat in your diet? It takes a bit of arithmetic. One gram of fat has 9 calories. If you consume 1,500 calories per day, including 67 grams of fat, 40 percent of the calories in your diet will have come from fat (67 grams fat × 9 calories = 603 calories). If you want to reduce the calories from fat to 20 percent, you must reduce your fat intake to 33 grams per day. If 33 grams sounds like a lot, read the labels on foods you commonly use to discover the amount of fat per serving. Much of the fat we eat is hidden in common foods such as red meat (about 15 grams of fat in a 3-ounce serving) and whole milk (9.6 grams of fat per cup).

To reduce the total amount of fat in your diet, as recommended by the National Cancer Institute, choose poultry, fish, and lean cuts of meat with all visible fat and skin trimmed off. If you eat luncheon meats, choose those labeled reduced fat content. Eat fresh fish and shellfish, or those packed in water, not oil. Substitute fresh fruits and vegetables or air-popped corn for snacks of nuts, cookies, or pastries, all of which have high fat content. Try low-fat salad dressings. Season vegetables with herbs and lemon juice instead of fats and salt. Avoid frying foods in fats; instead, broil or bake on a rack, or fry in a pan with a nonstick coating.

The American Heart Association recommends avoiding all solid fats and shortenings, including meat drippings and ham hocks, as well as all other animal and hydrogenated fats. Other saturated fats, often used in bakery products, include chocolate, coconut, coconut oil, and palm oil. To reduce your intake of saturated fat further, use only margarines in which the first ingredient on the label is *liquid* safflower, sunflower, or corn oil. And monitor your use of eggs; keep your intake of egg yolks, including those in prepared foods, to four or fewer per week. Egg substitutes usually contain no egg yolks, so they do not contribute to the saturated fats or cholesterol in your diet, although they do contribute some fat—unsaturated or partially saturated. Read the label!

Fiber and Your Digestion

Florence and Herb E., a couple in their sixties, have been told that high-fiber foods are good for them, especially to retard cancer and heart ailments. They wonder whether "fiber" means what Grandma used to call "roughage," and how getting more fiber in your intestines could help your heart. Even if this mysterious substance called fiber is good for them, how much should they eat every day? Where does it come from? Are they doomed to bran flakes forever?

Dietary fiber comes only from plants, never from animal foods. Plant foods vary in the type and amount of fiber they provide, and some of the best sources are fruits and vegetables you might not expect:

apples	asparagus
bananas	beans and peas, dried
berries	corn
citrus fruits	eggplant
dates and raisins	white potatoes

melons	spinach and other dark leafy vegetables
peaches	winter squash
pears	yams and sweet potatoes

Looking at this list makes fiber seem pretty easy to take! Another important source of fiber is cruciferous vegetables, the cabbage family, which includes broccoli, bok choy, Brussels sprouts, cauliflower, and many more. These vegetables may have a protective effect against some cancers. Whole-grain products such as whole-wheat bread, brown rice, oatmeal, whole-grain pasta, bulgur, and kasha are well-known sources of fiber. So is the bran from whole grains such as oat, rice, and wheat.

Plant fiber comes in two forms, soluble and insoluble. Both types affect normal digestion and elimination, although in different ways. Insoluble fiber—present in vegetables, wheat, and cereals—increases the bulk of the stool and, thus, reduces constipation by allowing food residue to move through the intestine more normally. Soluble fiber, which we get from fruits, dried beans, and oats, has other important effects. Soluble fiber makes us feel full longer by delaying the stomach's emptying; slowing absorption of sugar, reducing blood-sugar highs and lows; and lowering serum cholesterol. Both types of fiber are valuable for helping digestive function and reducing risk of illness.

Colon cancer is less prevalent in cultures where fiber intake is high. The increased stool bulk may dilute the exposure of the colon to cancer-causing substances in the diet, or it may bind these substances and remove them more effectively from the body. High fiber intake may lower serum cholesterol, which can reduce the risk of coronary disease and heart attack. High fiber intake also helps prevent or treat diverticular disease, a common disease of the colon that can cause bleeding or painful inflammation. In diabetics, fiber often helps lower insulin requirements and stabilize blood sugar.

The National Cancer Institute estimates that the average American now consumes approximately 11 grams of fiber daily, far short of the 20 to 30 grams recommended for good health. More than 50 grams per day is not recommended, so use moderation. If your diet has been poor in fiber, it's best to increase slowly to let your intestine adjust to its new working conditions. Choose whole-grain breads and cereal more often, and substitute them for products made with refined flours—white breads, rolls, pastries, and cakes. Increase your consumption of fruits and vegetables, both fresh and frozen. Fruit juices have had much of the fiber removed, so eat the whole fruit whenever possible. Eat such fruits and vegetables as apples and potatoes with the skins. Cooked dried peas and beans provide high fiber content; add them to your diet gradually if you're not accustomed to them.

Another advantage of making these changes is that foods high in fiber are usually low in fat. Just don't sabotage your healthy gains by adding lots of butter or other cooking fats to your high-fiber meals! If you're concerned about weight control, making a systematic effort to increase your fiber intake to recommended levels will probably keep you so full that you won't feel hungry while you walk off those extra pounds. For specific guidelines, many books and pamphlets available in your local library or supermarket provide information on the amount of fiber contained in particular foods. And some package labels, such as those on breakfast cereals, carry information about the amount of fiber, sodium, fat, and calories in the product.

Water

Many older people have a decreased sensation of thirst, and so they forget to drink enough fluids and become dehydrated. All of us are vulnerable to becoming too busy to drink enough water.

Eight glasses (8-ounce glasses) of water or other liquid per day are recommended, because, first, water helps digestion and elimination. Most constipation is caused by insufficient fluids, insufficient dietary fiber, and lack of exercise. Second, by preventing dehydration, water helps to preserve muscle tone and prevent the sagging skin that often follows weight loss.

You can drink your eight cups of water in the form of soups, juices, and other beverages. Avoid coffee, teas, and soft drinks that contain caffeine; these beverages act as diuretics.

Sodium and Potassium

Sodium and potassium are two of the electrolytes that help maintain fluid balance in our cells; they are also essential to our nervous-system and cardiovascular function. However, as we age, we often develop problems with these two essential minerals. The typical American diet contains unhealthy amounts of sodium, approximately 2 to 7 grams daily, from many sources, including table salt. The Food and Nutrition Board of the National Academy of Sciences believes that an adequate and safe level of sodium is 1 to 3 grams daily. Your body only requires about ½ gram (500 milligrams) per day. The excess contributes to fluid retention and high blood pressure (hypertension). High blood pressure can lead to heart disease, stroke, and kidney failure. Since blood pressure rises naturally with age, restricting sodium to safe levels is important to improve this condition and reduce risk of cardiovascular disease. Reducing dietary sodium can also improve the effectiveness of drug treatment for hypertension, making a lower dosage possible or sometimes allowing medications to be avoided entirely. In its free booklet "Salt, Sodium, and Blood Pressure," the American Heart Association recommends these steps for reducing sodium in your diet:

- Use fresh foods (which already contain some natural sodium) rather than canned, salted, or packaged foods. Most food-preservative processes, except sundrying, add some form of sodium. Most canned foods have salt added. Even frozen foods are often blanched in salt water before freezing; some are packed in high-sodium, high-fat sauces. Cured meats contain high levels of sodium nitrite to keep that pink color.
- Read food labels carefully. The words *soda* and *sodium* and the abbreviation *Na* indicate added sodium. Table salt (NaCl) is 40 percent sodium.
- Reduce or avoid use of table salt.
- Avoid or eliminate use of monosodium glutamate (MSG). This seasoning is used as a flavor enhancer in many recipes and restaurant meals. When eating out, ask whether your restaurant uses MSG in cooking, and if so, ask to have your food prepared without it.
- Baking soda contains a high level of sodium. Limit your use of baking soda in cooking, and never use it as a remedy for indigestion. Your pharmacist can recommend much safer digestive aids that contain less sodium. Soy sauce also contains very high levels of sodium.

Cut down on salt slowly; like any other change, it works better if you take time to get used to it. You might start by taking the salt shaker off the table, and adding only half the amount you're used to in cooking. Making changes in small increments over time will get you down to safe and healthy levels of sodium intake.

In contrast to sodium, getting enough potassium can be a problem for older people. When diuretics are prescribed to eliminate fluids in people with high blood pressure, these water pills sometimes leach out the body's potassium along with the sodium.

If the problem is severe enough, your physician will prescribe a potassium supplement. However, in most cases you can overcome this deficiency by adding foods high in potassium to your diet. The following are good sources of potassium:

bananas	melon, honeydew
beans, cooked dried	orange juice
cantaloupe	potatoes, sweet and white
grapefruit juice	prune juice
greens, cooked	prunes
meat and poultry	tomato juice

Iron

Another essential mineral, iron, is critical to healthy blood cells and their ability to transport oxygen in your body. Although women often experience iron deficiency during their childbearing years, older people can suffer from iron deficiency because of poor diet. Take the following steps to ensure adequate iron intake:

- Use animal products for a portion of your daily protein. Lean red meats and dark meat from chicken and turkey are the best and most readily absorbed sources of iron.
- Combine animal and vegetable products to increase the amount of iron absorbed from the vegetables.
- Use cast-iron cookware whenever possible. Food cooked in cast iron absorbs iron from the pot.
- Emphasize iron-rich fruits and vegetables such as dark greens, beans and peas, berries, melons, and dried fruits. Eat them with other foods to increase absorption of iron.
- Drink coffee or tea separately from meals. Both beverages inhibit your ability to absorb iron from food.

Calcium and Osteoporosis

Thinning bones, or osteoporosis, produce many signs we associate with aging: shorter stature (from shrinking of the spinal column); spinal curvature ("dowager's hump"); fractures of the hip, wrist, or vertebrae; even periodontal disease (loss of the bone that supports the teeth), leading to loss of the teeth themselves. The typical American diet provides too little calcium in proportion to other minerals. Both women and men experience gradual loss of bone tissue over time, and poor calcium intake throughout life may contribute to this problem. In addition, reduced estrogen production after menopause accelerates bone thinning, so that women have an increased risk for osteoporosis. Women about to enter menopause as well as women who have completed menopause should consult their physicians about the advisability of estrogen-replacement therapy to slow bone loss.

At present, there is no cure for osteoporosis, but you can slow the process by making changes in your diet and exercise patterns. Weight-bearing exercise, such as walking (for the lower body) and swimming or calisthenics (for the upper body), helps retard the thinning process in the bones. Alcohol use and cigarette smoking increase the risk of osteoporosis. Many prescription drugs reduce absorption of calcium by the bones. To preserve your bones, your body needs adequate dietary calcium, in combination with vitamin D, every day. Otherwise, your tissues will extract from your bones the calcium needed for metabolic functions.

If you are at risk for osteoporosis, you may want to supplement your diet with calcium preparations. Some of the least expensive are sold as antacids; Tums and some Rolaids, labeled calcium-rich, contain calcium carbonate, which is 40 percent calcium. Standard Tums weigh 500 milligrams each, and therefore each tablet contains 200 milligrams of calcium (40 percent of 500).

GOOD SOURCES OF CALCIUM IN YOUR DIET

In later life, a recommended daily intake is 1,500 milligrams of calcium for women and 1,000 milligrams for men. You can get this calcium many ways in your diet, the richest sources being dairy foods. However, if you cannot tolerate dairy products, you can obtain calcium from other foods and from dietary supplements such as Os-Cal, Tums, Rolaids, and so on. If you are confused about how much of what adds up to enough calcium, figure it this way. One 8-ounce cup of milk (low-fat, nonfat, buttermilk, or reconstituted dried milk) or yogurt provides 250 to 300 milligrams of calcium. Other foods that provide the same amount of calcium as one cup of milk include:*

- *1 ounce hard cheese, such as cheddar, Gouda, Monterey Jack, mozzarella, Parmesan or Swiss*
- *½ cup ricotta*
- *½ cup raw, firm tofu (soybean curd)*
- *1½ cup ice cream or frozen yogurt*
- *4 or 5 canned sardines (with bones)*
- *4 ounces canned salmon (with bones)*
- *2 tablespoons blackstrap molasses*

Dietary supplements provide varying amounts of calcium. You have to read the label and calculate how much elemental calcium you're getting by taking 40 percent of the calcium carbonate content. For example, one tablet of calcium-rich Rolaids contains 550 milligrams of calcium carbonate, according to the label. Multiplying 550 × 40 percent yields 220 milligrams of calcium per tablet. By comparison, regular Tums provides 200 milligrams of calcium per tablet and Os-Cal provides 500 milligrams per tablet.

You can obtain smaller amounts of calcium from a variety of foods. Here are some examples, which should be eaten in combination with other foods for best absorption of the nutrients:

- *baked beans*
- *Brazil nuts, almonds*
- *broccoli*
- *cottage cheese*
- *dark green, leafy vegetables (especially collards, spinach, and kale)*
- *shrimp, oysters*
- *sorghum*
- *soy milk†*

**All food values taken from Jean A. T. Pennington,* Bowes & Church's Food Values of Portions Commonly Used, *15th ed.*

†Soybean milk, which is sold under several brand names, is often used as a milk substitute by vegetarians and people intolerant to cow's milk. Soy milk has about half the protein and fat of whole cow's milk, and about 10 milligrams of calcium per 8-ounce cup (cow's milk has about 300 milligrams per cup). Lactaid milk is an option for people with lactase deficiency, which is, unfortunately a rather common condition in which milk products are poorly digested. When added to milk, over-the-counter Lactaid drops or capsules convert milk sugar into its digestible form.

Read the label to make sure you are taking the appropriate amount to achieve the approximate target of 1,500 milligrams of calcium per day from both foods and supplements. Calcium from supplements is not always as well absorbed as calcium in foods, so rely on your diet for most of your needs. And always consult your physician or a registered dietician before adding any dietary supplements.

Although it is one of the scourges of aging, osteoporosis may be prevented or slowed by a combination of lifestyle changes. As with many illnesses and disabilities we once thought inevitable for older people, osteoporosis can be positively affected by healthy changes in our patterns of diet and exercise.

Whatever changes you choose to improve your health—increasing your level of physical activity, reducing your intake of fats and sodium, or including more fiber in your diet—enjoy the feeling that you are taking some control over the course of your own aging. "Old age is not for sissies," says the lettering on a coffee mug. And healthy aging is for those who take the responsibility for healthy choices.

Recommended Reading

American Heart Association. "Walking for a Healthy Heart."

An informative booklet that gets you started on a program for walking fitness. Also available: "Swimming for a Healthy Heart," "Running . . . ," "Dancing . . . ," and "Cycling . . . ," as well as other useful publications for people concerned about the cardiovascular benefits of exercise. Available free from your local American Heart Association, or from the American Heart Association National Center, 7320 Greenville Avenue, Dallas, TX 75231.

American Heart Association Cookbook, 4th edition. New York: David McKay Co., 1984.

A sample booklet of recipes from this cookbook, "Recipes for Low-Fat, Low-Cholesterol Meals," is available free from your local chapter of the American Heart Association. Also free are useful booklets with information about potassium, sodium, and cholesterol, as well as suggestions for healthy food choices, weight loss, and eating out without sabotaging your food plan. Available in bookstores.

American Heart Association Low-Fat, Low-Cholesterol Cookbook. Edited by Scott M. Grundy and Mary Winston. New York: Times Books (Random House), 1989.

Bailey, Covert, and Lea Bishop. *The Fit or Fat Woman*. Boston: Houghton Mifflin, 1989.

Brody, Jane. *Jane Brody's Good Food Book*. Toronto: Bantam, 1987.

Doress, Paula Brown, Diana Laskin Siegal, and the Midlife and Older Women Book Project. *Ourselves, Growing Older*. New York: Simon and Schuster, 1987.

League of American Wheelmen. *Tour Finder*.
A comprehensive listing of bicycle tour operators that offer excursions worldwide. Available for $4 from 6707 Whitestone Road, Suite 209, Baltimore, MD 21207, or call (301) 944-3399.

National Cancer Institute, National Institutes of Health. *Diet, Nutrition, and Cancer Prevention: A Guide to Food Choices*. Washington, DC: 1986.
Telephone 1-800-4-CANCER, the toll-free number for the Cancer Information Service, which can answer many questions about prevention and treatment and will send you a copy of this helpful booklet.

National Heart, Lung, and Blood Institute, and the National Cancer Institute, National Institutes of Health. *Eating for Life*.
Suggestions for eating patterns that reduce your risk of heart disease and cancer. For a free copy, send your name and address on a 3 × 5 card to Eating for Life, P.O. Box 7516, Young America, MN 55473-7516.

National Institute on Aging, National Institutes of Health. *Age Pages*. 1984. Superintendent of Documents, U.S. Government Printing Office, Washington, DC 20402.

National Institute on Aging, National Institutes of Health. Exercise/Nutrition.
Write to NIA at Building 31, Room 5C35, Bethesda, MD 20205, for a list of information sources and free or low-cost publications that describe exercise programs, or nutrition and aging.

President's Council on Physical Fitness and Sports. *Walking for Exercise and Pleasure*. 1985. Superintendent of Documents, U.S. Government Printing Office, Washington, DC 20402.

CHAPTER TWO To Your Good Health

We would like you to die at the age of 90 after having been shot by a jealous lover.

—an anonymous physician

A recent article in the *Los Angeles Times* began, "Marion and Myron Pinkston sometimes wonder what life will be like when they get old. At age 80, they have scarcely been sick in their lives. During his 40-year career as a salesman, Myron never missed a day. He still has most of his teeth and hasn't had a cold or a headache in five years." How do they do it?

At least part of the answer is what your grandmother told you: Eat right, get enough rest and exercise, and keep busy with satisfying activities. The Pinkstons do not use alcohol, tobacco, coffee, tea, or any other addictive substances. They stay involved with family and church activities, work in their vegetable garden and woodshop, and watch their diet. Marion and her husband are both healthy; neither uses any medications. They both amaze their physicians with their strong bones, regular heart beats, low blood cholesterol, and normal blood pressure. Marion's straight back makes her the exception to the 90 percent of women her age who have signs of osteoporosis.

Contrary to most stereotypes, aging itself—that is, growing older in the absence of disease—has few health consequences. Growing old does not imply illness or feebleness, especially if we have healthy patterns for eating, exercising, and keeping involved with life. Nevertheless, as we grow older, disability becomes more common because our bodies lose some of their ability to compensate for illness and environmental change, both of which stress the system. As a result, many illnesses are more serious and recovery usually takes longer.

For example, a 25-year-old who develops pneumonia may feel terrible for a week or two but respond quickly and completely to antibiotic therapy. An 85-year-old with pneumonia may develop kidney or heart complications because these organs, which were functioning adequately in health, cannot handle the stress of a serious infection. And unfortunately, people may become disabled by chronic conditions at any age. This variability between vigorous aging and frailty characterizes the older population. Some people, such as the Pinkstons, maintain virtually perfect health until the very end of life, while others become severely disabled in later years.

Illness tends to express itself differently in older people. Younger persons usually complain about specific symptoms, such as cough and fever when pneumonia is present, while older people usually develop general weakness, fatigue, confusion, or inability to function normally. As we age, we typically feel ill from a combination of problems or diseases rather than a single one. Although we often wish a magic pill would relieve all the symptoms, more often we must take care of several health problems simultaneously.

Our reactions to illness also change as we grow older. We may have lower expectations of what we can do, both physically and mentally. Perhaps as a result, mature adults generally complain less to their doctors in spite of having more illnesses. We mistakenly consider an aching back or knee just an inevitable part of getting old, with no solution possible. Or we might anticipate that our doctors will not take our symptoms seriously. We may fear that symptoms might lead to extensive tests, uncomfortable treatments, or even worse, placement in a nursing home. Because of these perceptions, most older persons aren't complainers.

In this chapter, we give practical advice about selecting a doctor and getting the most out of your medical visits. We offer tips on

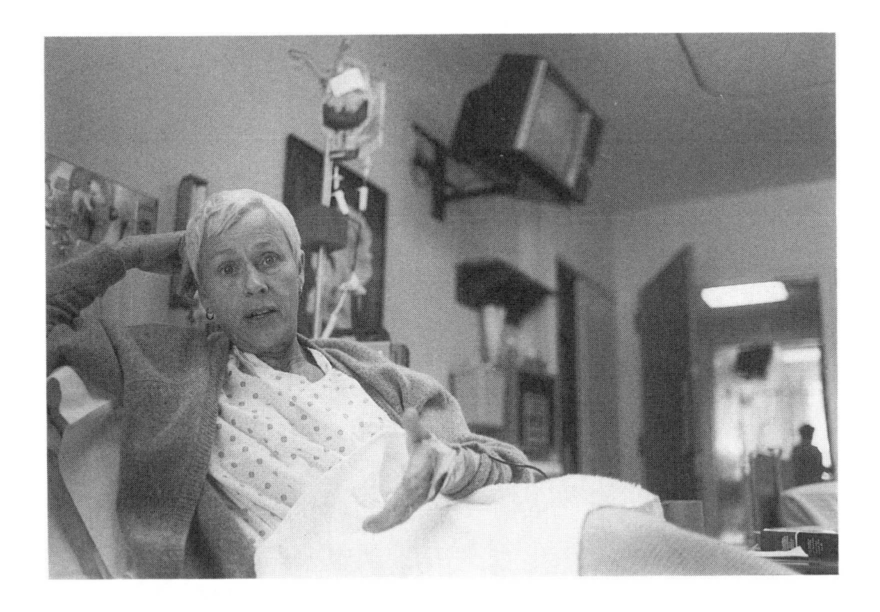

staying healthy (preventive medicine) and what to do when you get sick. We discuss the use of medications and your choices for refusing treatment. Finally, we present nitty-gritty medical facts as well as advice about some of the common medical conditions of aging.

Selecting a Physician

"I don't need to worry about that," you may say. "I'm perfectly satisfied with Dr. X. She's been my doctor for years. We're doing just fine, thank you." Although many of us have good, established relationships with health-care professionals, more and more older persons face the challenge of finding a new doctor.

Consider the situation of Pearl C., 68, who recently moved from New York to Florida. Although her arthritis was well controlled by medications, she needed to locate a physician in her new retirement community in case she became ill. Fortunately, Pearl's New York doctor had trained with a physician who lived in Florida near Pearl, and making a referral was easy. Carlos M., 70, had a different problem—his doctor of 25 years decided to retire. Although Carlos's physician handed on his practice to a younger person, Carlos didn't feel comfortable with him and found himself looking for a more mature physician. Tomiko A., on the other hand, had always relied on her obstetrician-gynecologist as her primary physician. Her obstetrician had guided her through pregnancy and childbirth three times, and in midlife Tomiko had found it simple to consult Dr. O. during her yearly exams for other small problems that came up. However, when in her sixties Tomiko developed high blood pressure and some intestinal problems, she found herself looking for a different kind of specialist.

When is the best time to select a new doctor? Before you get sick. Although you may be busy, and taking the time to select a physician may seem like an unnecessary burden, if you get sick you'll be better off with someone who already knows your health history and knows about you as a person. It's hard enough to select a new physician without having to do it in an emergency.

Most people select doctors from personal recommendations, usually from relatives, friends, or people in the health-care profession. That way, patients have an ally who is trying to match their personality to that of the physician. However, this method has something in common with a blind date. The outcome could be wonderful—or you could be stuck with a real loser. It is up to you to learn about the doctor's credentials, style of practice, and personality before you commit your medical care to this person.

Board Certification

All physicians must graduate from an accredited school of medicine or osteopathy and must have at least one year of postgraduate training (formerly called an internship) to become licensed to practice medicine. However, this minimum amount of training is not enough preparation to treat the often-complicated medical problems of older people. The prestige of the physician's medical school is relatively unimportant. Much more important is whether the physician is board-certified in a medical specialty. To become eligible for certification, a physician must complete post-internship training, called residency. Residency consists of two to six years of hands-on supervised experience. The physician must then pass a rigorous certifying examination to demonstrate competence in the specialty. Some physicians may be very capable without having certification, but board certification indicates that the physician has met at least the minimum standards of the specialty.

Ask a physician in what specialty he or she is certified. Most older people will want a physician certified in internal medicine or family practice to provide their primary medical care, perform check-ups, and manage medical conditions. People with certain conditions, such as heart disease or cancer, will also need a specialist such as a cardiologist or oncologist.

Do I Need a Geriatrician?

The medical specialty devoted to the care of older persons is called geriatrics. Physicians who are recognized as having special expertise in the care of older persons are called geriatricians. To become a geriatrician, a physician must first complete postgraduate training in a specialty, usually internal medicine or family practice. Then the physician accumulates experience in caring for older persons, either by at least two more years of intensive hands-on training (fellowship) or by extensive clinical experience.

Some internists or family practitioners may lack formal training in geriatrics, but have nevertheless developed a special interest in caring for older people. These physicians may have taken medical education courses or attended conferences, such as those sponsored by the American Geriatrics Society, that focus on diseases and health care associated with older people.

Recently, the American Boards of Internal Medicine and Family Practice have recognized the expertise of geriatricians by certifying geriatricians who meet these criteria and pass a challenging written examination. The first such examination was given in April 1988, when 2,407 physicians became the first certified geriatricians in the United States. As of 1991, more than four thousand physicians have been certified.

With all this expertise available, why shouldn't every older person be cared for by a geriatrician? First, there simply aren't enough geriatricians to go around. Currently, each geriatrician would have to care for more than thirteen thousand older persons. More important, most older people are too healthy to need these specialized services. Geriatricians typically focus their special skills on the frail older person with complex medical problems.

And finding one of these specialists may not be easy. The telephone book may list a few, but no inquiry about the doctor's credentials is made before a doctor is listed in the phone book. It's always important to inquire about the credentials and board-certification of any physician. The nearest teaching hospital or medical school with a division of geriatrics can probably refer you to a geriatrician in your community. Often this person will be a graduate of that hospital's training program.

Comprehensive Geriatric Assessment?

Sometimes, when an older person is particularly frail, the question arises whether a traditional medical evaluation is sufficient to manage the person's complicated health problems. Ron L. is concerned about his father: "Dad is living alone now, and we are worried that he's not eating enough or taking care of himself anymore. He's afraid of going into a nursing home. A friend suggested that my father be evaluated at a comprehensive geriatric assessment unit. What do these units do, and where are they located?"

Geriatric evaluation—or assessment—units have become available in the United States during the last decade. These units, often located in university teaching hospitals or in Veterans Administration hospitals, provide comprehensive evaluation, treatment, rehabilitation, and consultation for older persons who are especially frail and in danger of losing their independent functioning at home. Members of an interdisciplinary team specially trained in geriatrics—including physicians, social workers, nurses, dietitians, rehabilitation therapists, and pharmacists—work together to uncover medical, psychological, or family problems that interfere with the older person's functioning. The team assesses the resources available to the patient and designs a plan for care that will improve the person's ability to live as independently as possible. The most effective assessment units are inpatient facilities with links to good rehabilitation programs.

Effective assessment, rehabilitation, and planning can extend the patient's life and independent functioning. However, Ron may want to think over his father's need for this type of assessment, which is time-consuming and fairly expensive. People who are functioning normally do not need these services; on the other hand, people who are irreversibly disabled are unlikely to benefit from them. In addition, no matter how carefully the professional team evaluates the patient and plans for care, the patient will improve only if the team follows through with the treatment plan.

If Ron and his father decide to investigate local geriatric assessment units, they might begin by telephoning the nearest medical school for help in locating a unit. Community-service agencies, senior centers, and social workers who specialize in caring for older persons may also be able to provide the names of facilities in the area.

Preliminary Interview

Once you have identified a physician as a promising candidate to assume your medical care, schedule a visit. Customarily, on your initial visit the doctor will compile a complete medical history and perform a physical examination. On the other hand, you may want to follow the example of many young parents who interview several pediatricians before selecting the one who will care for their baby. When you make your first telephone call to a new doctor's office, specify whether you wish merely to interview the doctor or to make your first medical appointment. You will likely be charged either way, but possibly less if the visit is only for an interview.

Act carefully—your selection will have important implications for your future medical care. Get all your concerns about the physician's style out in the open before you make a choice. You may wish to write down a list of questions before you visit so you don't overlook anything. Here are some important questions to ask:

- Whom should I call if I get sick in the middle of the night?
- Who are the other physicians in this doctor's coverage group?
- Does this physician accept Medicare assignment (that is, bill only 20 percent of Medicare-approved charges) for all claims?
- If I need to make a visit between scheduled appointments, will I see the physician or someone else, such as a nurse practitioner or physician's assistant?

- If I am hospitalized, will my doctor see me every day, or will another physician make the daily visits?

In this initial interview you can also find out whether your personality and the doctor's are compatible. Will the doctor allow you to participate in medical decisions to the extent you want? Will the doctor answer your questions and communicate freely about your medical conditions? Do you trust this person with your health?

Getting the Most from Health Care

When you make your choice of a physician, you become that doctor's patient, whether or not you are sick. As a patient, you have certain rights and responsibilities that we'll discuss later. You are also a consumer of health care, and you probably want to get the most from your medical appointments. You can get your money's worth by being prepared, being a good listener, and asking the right questions.

Preparing for an Appointment

To make every appointment easier and more productive for both you and your doctor, take the following steps ahead of time:

- Be sure your past medical records have arrived at your new physician's office. Send a written request to your previous physician to have copies sent to your new physician.
- Try to focus on the one or two most important problems bothering you.
- Write down a list of questions you want to ask, so you don't forget something at the last moment.
- Compile a brief family medical history. Include the cause of

death of parents and siblings as well as your specific illnesses.

• Consider bringing a spouse or friend with you. This person can ask questions you might forget and help you remember details of the treatment program the doctor recommends.

• Bring all current medications in their bottles, including over-the-counter medications that you take regularly.

• Wear clothing that is easily removed because you will probably need to undress for your physical examination.

• Allow plenty of time to get to your doctor's office a few minutes before your appointment. Allow time for traffic and parking.

In the Doctor's Office

After you have checked in at your doctor's office, an aide or nurse will probably measure your blood pressure and weigh you. Probably you will have to wait to see the doctor. Doctors almost always run late.

Each day in the life of a doctor is a journey to the unexpected. Patients scheduled for routine check-ups may have medical problems that demand urgent attention. Although it is annoying to wait, you might feel less irritable knowing that your physician would spend extra time with you if you needed it. Doctors also run late because of patients who arrive late for their appointments; because of traffic snarls between the hospital and the office; and because of telephone calls from other patients and physicians, especially if your doctor has teaching responsibilities for physicians-in-training. However, these delays are usually brief. If you have to wait more than 20 minutes, ask the receptionist about the reason for the delay. Understanding the reason might reduce your anxiety, and you may decide to reschedule if the delay is going to be much longer.

When your doctor arrives, he or she may take a few minutes to look over your medical record. Some doctors review your record before meeting you, while others try to spend as much time as possible with you, so they review the chart in the examining room.

Next comes the real business of the appointment: the history, physical examination, and discussion of your concerns. The first time your doctor examines you, the history-taking and physical exam are likely to be extensive and may take an hour or more. Your doctor spends this time getting to know you and gathering background information for future visits. Later appointments may take only 15 to 20 minutes.

At every medical appointment, your satisfaction with the quality of care you receive depends on how effectively you communicate with your doctor. Here are a few tips for better communication with your physician:

- Be specific about your complaint. For example, if you have a pain, describe where the pain is, when it started, what type of pain it is (stabbing, burning, aching), and what makes the pain better or worse.
- Once you have described your complaint, expect the doctor to ask specific questions to help decipher what is causing the problem.
- Share the conversation. Neither you nor your doctor should do all the talking.
- Keep your questions simple and direct. If you have heard about a new treatment for your condition, mention the medication or procedure by name and ask whether it might benefit you.
- Ask questions until you understand the answers. Remember that anything unclear when you leave the office is likely to remain unclear at home.
- Don't get tangled up in medical jargon. If your doctor speaks

to you in terms you don't understand, request an explanation in language that you do understand.

Preventive Measures

Some people consider good health a matter of luck. They may be right, but this good luck is the kind you create yourself. You start with the right diet, add regular exercise (see chapter 1), and take sensible steps to prevent getting sick. Your doctor can be a consultant and guide, but you are the best person to keep yourself healthy.

Get your shots. If you are 65 years of age or older, or if you have a chronic illness such as diabetes, congestive heart failure, or lung disease, vaccinations against flu and pneumonia are important in your preventive care. Often available inexpensively at public health clinics or senior centers, immunizations against influenza (flu) must be given by injection each year. You probably need vaccination against pneumococcal pneumonia—the most common pneumonia affecting healthy older persons—only once during a lifetime.

Flu shots are usually given in the autumn; pneumonia vaccinations can be given at any time. You can have both injections at the same time. Although some people may have uncomfortable reactions, such as a sore arm or a fever, vaccinations do not cause the flu. While you're getting your flu and pneumonia shots, check to see whether your tetanus and diphtheria immunizations are up to date: You need a booster every ten years, or a full set of immunizations if you've never been immunized. Getting a few shots is a small inconvenience compared with getting sick or dying from a preventable disease.

Clean up your lifestyle. In addition to maintaining a healthy diet and exercise routine, you can prevent illness or reduce its se-

verity by taking a cold, clear look at your use of alcohol and tobacco. Both of these drugs contribute to the debilitating and painful diseases common in later life. Stopping alcohol abuse (see chapter 3) and tobacco use can be the best gift you ever gave yourself.

People have lots of reasons for not quitting smoking, such as "I've gotten away with it for this long," or "I'm too old to change my ways." According to the National Institute on Aging, it's never too late to stop. A recent study conducted by researchers from the University of Washington and the Mayo Clinic found, "No matter how old you are, no matter how long you've smoked, there's a benefit to quitting. As far as heart attack is concerned, the benefits begin to accrue within a few months." This research on smoking in people over age 54 included 807 people who had quit smoking within the previous year and 1,086 who continued smoking. All had undergone coronary bypass surgery. Within six years, 391 of the smokers had died, but only about half that number (210) of the people who had quit died.

Smoking tobacco increases your risk for several types of cancer, heart and lung diseases, ulcers, and osteoporosis. The benefits of quitting may take a little while to notice, but it is true that the more time that passes after you quit smoking, the better your health will be.

How does a person stop smoking? Many people just decide to quit and do it. Others look for support from clinics and organized groups. Many programs offer education and emotional support to help participants through their withdrawal from nicotine. Some people never feel withdrawal symptoms, but those who do report that the first few days can seem like years. Often, a gum containing nicotine may be used initially to control the symptoms of withdrawal. Organized programs also help you learn new patterns to take the place of the old familiar cigarette after a meal, with morning coffee, or during social gatherings. Situations that trigger the urge to light up can handicap your good intentions for months or years.

A variety of other programs, including group therapy, is available to help. Some programs are quite expensive, so investigate carefully before you enroll. For less expensive options, telephone your local affiliate of the American Lung Association, American Heart Association, or American Cancer Society for the names of stop-smoking programs in your area (see Resources). These agencies frequently sponsor programs at reasonable rates.

Keep your teeth. Getting old means losing your hair, your teeth, and your sex drive, right? Wrong. (See chapter 8 about your sex drive.) Although many older people have dental and oral health problems, these problems usually result from neglecting the teeth and gums, not from aging itself.

As we age, we produce less saliva, and irritations in the mouth occur more easily and take longer to heal. The further we advance in years, the more important it becomes to take meticulous care of teeth and gums. Dental care is a preventive measure for health because we are better able to eat a well-balanced diet if our teeth and gums are healthy. Someone who finds eating uncomfortable is less likely to eat a balanced diet.

Adults lose more teeth to gum disease than to tooth decay or any other cause. Caused by plaque that builds up on the teeth, gum disease can be prevented by brushing at least twice a day, flossing every day, and scheduling regular check-ups with your dentist. The signs of gum disease develop gradually and may go unnoticed. They are

- swollen or bleeding gums
- pus that appears when the gums are pressed

- loose teeth
- teeth that have changed their position, or a bite that has changed
- bad taste in the mouth, or bad breath.

Caries or cavities, the second most common dental problem among older adults, may also lead to tooth loss. Unfortunately, many older Americans do not have dental insurance, so they may avoid getting early dental treatment. Often they neglect their oral hygiene as well. As a result, over 40 percent of people 65 years of age or older have lost all their teeth. And because dentures are only one-fourth to one-sixth as efficient in chewing as natural teeth, people with dentures tend to eat softer food and suffer from inadequate nutrition.

Good dental health begins with regular check-ups with a dentist. Like selecting a doctor, selecting a dentist requires a close examination of credentials and making certain that your personalities are compatible. Telephone or visit a prospective dentist and ask about his or her experience with older people. If you are worried about the cost, investigate your local dental society's reduced-fee programs for seniors. Look in your telephone book or write to the American Dental Association for the address of the dental society near you (see Resources). Often dentists volunteer their services through community clinics or offer them at low cost through public health clinics.

Take Your Medicine

In spite of our best efforts, we sometimes require medications as treatment. As we age, Americans take more and more drugs, often medicating themselves with over-the-counter drugs. Older people use more drugs than younger people do, and they take them more often. For example, residents in one urban senior citizens' housing development used, on average, 4.5 prescription drugs plus 3.4 over-the-counter drugs daily, a total of 7.9 drugs per person, a much larger number of medications than those consumed by younger persons. The 12 percent of the population that is 65 years of age or older consumes 38 percent of all prescription drugs.

Although appropriate drug therapy can obviously be effective for many problems, both prescription and over-the-counter drugs may create problems as well. Older persons may develop several conditions that call for treatment with medications. Unfortunately, some of these medications may interact with each other, thus reducing their effectiveness or increasing their side-effects. The more drugs you take, the higher the chances you will have problems with drug interactions.

Side-effects can be more than just inconvenient. Juanita L., 75, had a major heart attack two years before her doctor prescribed eye drops for glaucoma. After beginning to use the eye drops, she became more and more short of breath over several weeks, complaining to her doctor that she could sleep only if she propped herself up on several pillows. The doctor deduced that the eye drops had weakened the strength of her heart contractions and precipitated congestive heart failure.

As we grow older, physical changes affect our bodies' ability to process and respond to drugs. For example, lean body mass, especially muscle, diminishes and is replaced by fat. Between ages 20 and 65, body fat increases on the average from approximately 18 percent to 36 percent of total body weight in men and from 33 percent to 48 percent in women. Thus, medications stored in fat cells will build up in the body and their effects will last longer. At the same time, medications not stored in fat will circulate at higher levels in the blood.

The two organs principally responsible for metabolism and

elimination of drugs—the kidney and liver—both function less effectively with age. Because of these changes, we may need smaller or less frequent doses of medication than a younger person.

Before you ask your doctor to prescribe a medicine or you decide to buy an over-the-counter drug, decide whether the risk is worth the cure. Frequently, your opinion is just as important as your doctor's. For example, an occasional backache may not bother you enough to accept the inconvenience and risk of a painkiller like ibuprofen, which may cause indigestion, gastrointestinal bleeding, kidney problems, or mental impairment. Also ask your doctor how effective a drug is likely to be. For some conditions, such as Alzheimer's disease, no effective treatment is currently available. Your doctor may be willing to prescribe a drug that may provide a small benefit, but you (or your caregiver) must decide whether you are willing to put up with the inconvenience and potential side-effects for the slight possibility of improvement.

If you and your physician decide that treatment with drugs is appropriate, ask your doctor to prescribe more economical generic drugs. For the most part, these drugs are as effective as their brand-name counterparts. With medicines that you will be taking over time—for blood pressure or diabetes, for example—mail-order prescription services can also save you money. You may want to have your first prescription filled at a local pharmacy and send a second prescription to be filled through the mail, which takes a few weeks.

Ask your doctor whether medications are available that have to be taken only once or twice a day. It's easy to confuse medications that you must remember to take several times a day, especially if you have more than one. If you are taking one medication every six hours and another every eight hours, you have to take something six times a day.

Take responsibility for informing yourself. If your doctor prescribes a new drug, make certain that you understand *why* it is being prescribed, *how* to take it correctly, and *what* side-effects are possible. Many people do not take the drugs prescribed for them, possibly because they don't believe that the medicine will help, or because the drugs cost too much. If you have reservations about taking a drug, talk them over with your doctor. A drug that stays in the bottle will not help you.

The American Association of Retired Persons (AARP) publishes leaflets with detailed medical information about more than 350 prescription drugs (see Resources). Here are some tips to help prevent problems with medications:

- Bring your current medications (including over-the-counter drugs) in their bottles with you when you go to the doctor, hospital, or emergency room.
- Remember that drugs you buy without a prescription may have side-effects and may interact with other drugs. If you are unsure whether an over-the-counter medication is safe for you, ask a pharmacist or your doctor.
- When your doctor prescribes a new medicine, ask whether it will interfere with the drugs you take already.
- When your doctor prescribes a new medicine, ask for samples or a prescription for just a week or two. Or you can instruct the pharmacy to give you half the prescribed amount, with a refill for the other half. This way, if the medicine causes side-effects or does not work, you won't have wasted a lot of money.
- If you notice unpleasant side-effects from a medication, call your doctor immediately rather than waiting until the next visit.
- Do not take other people's medicines, and don't give other

people yours. Drugs may look alike, but they have different purposes and effects.

Making Choices about Medical Treatment: Your Role and Your Rights

Keith J. worries about his father's medical treatment: "Dad's doctor wants him to have a bypass operation for his heart condition, but at age 83, Dad says he's too old for surgery. The doctor says his days are limited without the surgery, but Dad says his days are limited anyway, and he doesn't want to end them on the operating table. Should we urge him to have the operation, even though he doesn't want it?"

Annette G., 66, feels uneasy: "My doctor said I need to have my gall bladder removed, and I'm not convinced it's necessary. I'd like to get a second opinion, but I feel uncomfortable about sneaking behind my doctor's back. What would you recommend?"

Sometimes therapy with drugs is not enough, and we are confronted with the decision of whether to have surgery or another invasive procedure, such as laser therapy. The risk varies according to how extensive the procedure is and whether it requires general anesthesia. We need all the facts before making a decision.

On the one hand, several studies have found that age alone (older than 70 years) increases the risk for heart and lung complications during surgery. Furthermore, diseases common in older people, such as congestive heart failure, increase the risk. On the other hand, long-term results of surgery for lung and breast cancer appear to be as good for older people as for their younger counterparts. Before making your decision, there are several questions to ask.

- How serious is my condition? Are my health, ability to function, or life in danger if my condition goes untreated?
- How is my general health? Do other illnesses put me at higher risk for complications?
- Are other nonsurgical treatments available and effective? Is there any harm in trying these first?
- Does the decision about surgery need to be made right away? Is there any harm in waiting? Is this an emergency?
- Would it be beneficial to get a second opinion? (Some insurance companies require second opinions before elective surgery.)
- Am I mentally prepared for this procedure?

As a patient, your role involves much more than being prepared for medical appointments and communicating clearly with your doctor. You also have a role in making decisions about your health care. Although your doctor tries to understand your health problems and plan your care, "doctor's orders" are really only advice. You are free to accept or refuse this advice. You make the decisions about your care by weighing your doctor's advice along with other information and your personal beliefs. No matter how much the doctor believes that a test or operation is needed, it cannot be done without your consent. Refusing treatment is your option for everything from getting a blood test to cardiac catheterization to open-heart surgery.

If you have concerns about undergoing a procedure such as surgery that your doctor has recommended for you, clarify with your doctor the likely benefits and risks of the procedure. Find out if other ways could be tried first to treat your condition and what will happen if you don't have the procedure. Ask what the financial costs would be and whether they're all covered by your insurance.

Getting a Second Opinion

If you're still uncomfortable with the recommendation after getting answers to these questions, seek a second opinion. Remember that getting a second opinion is standard medical practice and that most doctors want their patients to be as informed as possible about their condition. It's important to make sure that the short delay caused by getting a second opinion won't be harmful. A second opinion should never result in delay or avoidance of emergency procedures.

To find another specialist for your medical problem, ask your physician for a referral or contact your local medical society or medical school. You can also find another specialist by telephoning the medical staff office of a nearby hospital and asking for names of physicians who practice in the specialty of interest to you.

Ask your physician to forward your records to the second doctor. Be sure to tell the second doctor the name of the procedure recommended and identify any tests you've had. If the second doctor agrees that surgery is the best way to treat your problem, he or she will usually send you back to the first doctor for the procedure.

What happens if the second doctor disagrees with the first? At this point, most people find that they have enough facts to make up their own minds. If you're confused by different opinions, you may wish to return to your first doctor for further discussion. Or you may wish to talk with a third physician.

Medicare will pay for a second opinion at the same rate it pays for other services, and most Medicaid (Medi-Cal in California) programs will also pay. If you have other third-party insurance or you belong to a health-maintenance organization (HMO), ask the patient-services representative about the company's policy on second opinions.

Remember, you're the patient, and it's your right to decide whether to undergo any procedure. Although your family and doctor may want to clear up possible misunderstandings about the risks of surgery and may have their own opinions about the value of the operation, you have the right to weigh your own options. And Annette has every right to secure a second opinion about the gall bladder surgery recommended for her. She need not feel she is slighting or betraying her doctor in any way. Each person must make his or her own decisions about treatment he or she wants or does not want.

Blood Transfusions

If you decide to undergo surgery that is not an urgent procedure but that may require a transfusion, consider storing your own blood in advance—a process called autologous transfusion. Usually, this process begins about three weeks before surgery (depending on how much transfused blood you are expected to need), and up to 2 pints of blood are taken from you each week. Recently, a hormone called erythropoietin has been used to improve some people's ability to store their own blood. Autologous transfusions, of course, eliminate the risk for transmitting diseases such as hepatitis or AIDS.

Extending Life

What if you become so seriously ill that you can no longer make your own decisions? Who should decide about treatment for you? When you are conscious and capable of making decisions, there is no question about who makes them—you do. Even if everyone in your family as well as your doctor agrees about what your treatment should be, the decision to have the treatment or not is yours and yours alone. However, if, for example, you should have a bad reaction to a drug in the hospital, and you are confused at the time an important medical decision must be made, you need a spokesperson. An excellent way to designate this spokesperson ahead of time—and you may need one at any time in life—is through a durable power of attorney or a durable power of attorney for health care (see chapter 5).

Do I want all available treatments used to prolong my life? Emily W. is mourning her 89-year-old grandmother, who is still living: "My grandmother is dying. I remember her as the spirit of the family and the inspiration behind my career. When I last visited her in the hospital on a business trip back East, she seemed frail but determined to live.

"Grandmother went home to my mother, but two weeks later, she was back in the hospital, this time in intensive care. The doctor asked my mother if he should place her on a respirator (breathing machine)—and of course, she said yes. She could not live with the awesome decision to end her own mother's life. But she did not really understand the consequences of Grandmother's disease. For three weeks, she visited her in the hospital, where Grandmother was sustained by a respirator to keep her body oxygenated because her lungs had failed, nourished by tube feeding, attached to a catheter and monitors, and unable to talk because she needed the respirator to live.

"When her lungs began to work again because of the medical interventions, Grandmother returned home, 38 pounds lighter, with her spirit gone and no hope of recovery. My beloved grandmother is facing a lingering death. She sleeps all day, will not talk except for calling my mother's name, is incontinent and bedbound. She continues to lose weight because she has no appetite."

When is enough, enough? Modern medicine has developed technologies to prolong life that were unimaginable fifty years ago. Devices are available that can virtually prevent anyone from having to die from lung or kidney failure. Pacemakers, mechanical pumps, and powerful heart drugs can sustain a failing heart for prolonged periods. All hospitals today, unless instructed to the contrary, give every patient all available treatment, including life-sustaining or resuscitation measures. It may seem almost impossible for patients to die peacefully unless they make their wishes explicit to physicians and health-care teams.

The decision is up to the patient, but obviously, it should be made before a crisis is at hand. In addition to the physician, someone in the family needs to know what the patient's real wishes are before a catastrophic event makes him or her incapable of expressing them. For example, if you suffer a heart attack and your heart stops beating (cardiac arrest), do you want emergency cardiopulmonary resuscitation (CPR) to be performed? Many heart-attack victims have been revived by CPR procedures—chest compression, artificial respiration, medications, and electrical stimulation of the heart. However, health-care facilities have extended the procedure to questionable situations. For example, several careful studies have demonstrated that CPR has no value for elderly patients living in nursing homes or with terminal cancer, kidney failure, or several concurrent serious illnesses. Furthermore, for some persons, such as those with advanced Alzheimer's disease or those who are in constant pain, it does not seem appropriate to try resuscitation. Nevertheless, without specific instructions to the contrary, hospitals and emergency medical personnel will apply all available treatments.

What's the harm in trying? Perhaps the worst case is that in which CPR partially succeeds. Sadie L., 95, who had advanced Alzheimer's disease, developed pneumonia and stopped breathing. Hospital doctors resuscitated her, and her heart remained strong. But she never regained consciousness. For nearly a month, until she died from an infection, she remained in a coma and hooked to a mechanical breathing machine.

At some point, your doctor may ask about your wishes if you should need CPR or some other life-extending measure, such as tube-feeding or use of a respirator. In some nursing homes these questions are asked of every new resident. However, you don't need to wait to be asked. Talk over these serious decisions with your family and your doctor so that your instructions can be entered in your medical chart. Regardless of your decision, it is important to know that *a decision about life-extending measures is reversible at any time.* (For more information about these issues, consult the section on using advance directives to express your wishes in chapter 5.)

You may have to face decisions about limiting other medical treatments as well. A person who has cancer may decide to stop chemotherapy, or a person with severe emphysema may decide not to be placed on a breathing machine. Your physician must accept these choices if they are your preference. As in the case of resuscitation, it is better to make these decisions when you are clear-thinking than in the crisis atmosphere of an emergency. You can always change your mind later, if you wish.

Common Health Problems in Later Life

The remainder of this chapter is devoted to medical problems associated with aging, the most common diseases and conditions that occur in older persons. For further information, consult the resources listed at the end of the chapter and your physician.

Cardiovascular Diseases

Joe D., 65, was on top of the world. He had earned his retirement. He had struggled to rise in the company and had retired with enough savings and pension to ensure that he would never have to work another day. Several months into his life of leisure, he was playing tennis on a hot afternoon when he noticed just a twinge of tightness in his chest. Although he couldn't really call the twinge a pain, he called it quits for the day. Several days later, the same thing happened. Joe was not a gambler. He scheduled an appointment with his doctor as soon as possible. A stress test confirmed that these twinges indicated serious coronary artery disease. The stress test results were so serious, in fact, that Joe's physician recommended a catheterization (a diagnostic procedure in which a tube is inserted in a blood vessel and threaded into the heart). This procedure revealed that one of Joe's primary arteries was almost completely blocked. Now Joe has recovered from his successful operation—percutaneous transluminal coronary angioplasty, or PTCA, using a balloon to open the artery—and has returned to the tennis courts without a twinge.

Coronary artery disease. Coronary artery disease resulting from atherosclerosis is still the leading cause of death for older Americans. It affects about 70 percent of persons by age 90, although about half have no symptoms. The symptoms of coronary artery disease fall into three categories: chest pain (or angina), heart attack, and sudden death. Angina, a short episode of chest discomfort, is often brought on by exercise, eating, or emotional conflicts; it is relieved by resting. These episodes of chest pain are caused by insufficient blood flow through the coronary arteries. A heart attack is more likely to be prolonged and is not relieved by rest. Heart attacks are almost always caused by a blood clot that suddenly blocks a coronary artery. Sudden death may also be caused by complete blockage of a coronary artery or by an abnormal heart rhythm.

Coronary artery disease often produces different symptoms in older persons than in younger persons. For example, crushing or squeezing chest pain becomes less common with advancing age. Instead, shortness of breath or a vague feeling of fatigue or confusion may motivate older people to get medical help. Commonly used diagnostic tests also must be interpreted differently with increasing age of the patient. Abnormal results from electrocardiograms (EKGs), for example, may be produced by causes other than coronary artery disease.

Physicians often recommend different treatment of coronary artery disease for older people when they have other illnesses that complicate the medical or surgical options. Surgical therapy (coronary artery bypass graft) is as effective in controlling symptoms in older as in younger persons, but the risks are higher for surgical complications and death. Still, the odds are good. Persons between 65 and 74 years old have odds of approximately 19 to 1 that they will survive bypass surgery; even if they are 75 years or older, their odds are 9 to 1. Of course, these odds vary depending on physical condition and other symptoms. However, some studies have found that coronary artery bypass surgery may be performed too frequently. If you are in doubt about your doctor's recommendation for surgery, get a second opinion.

As Joe's case demonstrates, PTCA, which uses a balloon-like device to open the clogged artery and increase blood flow, has been successful in older persons. In appropriate candidates, PTCA can control coronary artery disease in 80 to 90 percent of older patients. The odds of surviving this simpler procedure are much higher than those of surviving coronary artery bypass surgery—

49 to 1. However, it is common for the artery to become blocked again over the next few months.

Hypertension. Eleanor M. felt fit as a fiddle, but after her 65th birthday, she decided to see her doctor for a check-up, just on principle. After a thorough examination, her doctor told her that everything looked good except that Eleanor's blood pressure was elevated. Before initiating any treatment, the doctor wanted to check the readings over a few weeks. Eleanor left the office slightly dazed and worried about "the silent killer." At each examination, her blood pressure remained elevated. Eleanor's doctor recommended she begin taking a diuretic once a day. Her blood pressure responded well to this treatment, and the disease was controlled with a minimum of intervention. Eleanor began to learn more about hypertension, the disease that appears to have so few symptoms, but that can have such destructive effects.

Eleanor found that, in measuring blood pressure, two numbers are recorded. The higher number, which normally runs below 140 in younger persons and up to 160 in persons over 65 years, is called the systolic reading. The lower number, which normally is no higher than 90 for anyone, is called the diastolic reading. For example, a normal blood pressure might be 130 (systolic)/80 (diastolic), read as one hundred thirty over eighty. High blood pressure is especially common in mature adults, affecting up to 40 percent of people over 65 years. In isolated systolic hypertension, a form of hypertension that occurs almost exclusively in older people, only the systolic reading is elevated. Both types of hypertension increase the risk of problems such as stroke and heart disease. Researchers have demonstrated that it is important to treat ordinary high blood pressure to prevent stroke, and recently the benefits of treating isolated systolic hypertension have been established.

If you have high blood pressure, your doctor is likely to recommend some modifications in your lifestyle—weight loss for obese persons, exercise, and perhaps restriction of salt. The combination of smoking and hypertension in particular increases the risk for developing heart disease. If these changes in behavior are not enough to control high blood pressure, medication treatment usually begins with a diuretic (water pill). Now it is common to choose another kind of pill to start with—a beta blocker, a calcium-channel blocker, or an ACE-inhibitor. Your physician will consider your other medical conditions and medications in choosing methods to treat hypertension.

If your doctor prescribes medication for hypertension, be sure to ask about possible side-effects. Some blood-pressure medicines may cause dizziness when you stand up. Other medications may produce a dry hacking cough, swollen ankles, or dry mouth. Some blood-pressure medicines can disturb sexual function in men; if you develop a problem with impotence after starting a medicine, tell your doctor.

If you have high blood pressure, you should have your blood pressure checked regularly. Frequently, your doctor's office staff will do this for you at no charge. Pharmacies or senior centers will often check your blood pressure for free. Avoid electronic blood-pressure machines in malls and shopping centers; they are often inaccurate.

Stroke. Stan O. was playing with fire. He smoked, ate too much of the wrong types of food, and knew his blood pressure was high. Living in the fast lane, he rose to the top of the sales force and never gave a thought to his health. One morning during breakfast, his wife noticed that his speech was strange. His words made sense, but they were slurred as if he were drunk. And his face was uneven, the right side drooping a little. Frightened, Stan's wife called the doctor, who advised her to bring him to the emergency room. On the way to the hospital, the slurring of speech and facial droop gradually disappeared, and Stan returned to his usual self. Nevertheless, the doctor insisted on conducting tests, which revealed a narrowing of one of the major blood vessels to the brain. The doctor prescribed aspirin and strongly urged Stan to stop smoking, improve his diet, and take his blood-pressure pills. This time Stan listened, and the frightening episode has not recurred.

Strokes result from problems in the blood vessels that supply the brain. A clot may form in a vessel that has been previously narrowed by atherosclerosis or other disease processes, a clot may travel from the heart or another blood vessel, or a vessel may hemorrhage into the brain. Strokes are the third leading cause of death in older people and may cause various neurologic problems, including weakness or paralysis on one side, loss of vision or speech, and decline in mental functioning. Some strokes—as in Stan's case—are preceded by warning symptoms called transient ischemic attacks (TIAs) that usually last less than 30 minutes.

Physicians who suspect stroke usually hospitalize the patient and order medical tests to determine the cause of the symptoms. Typically, the patient undergoes a computed tomographic (CT) scan or magnetic resonance imaging (MRI). People who are having a stroke with increasing symptoms, or who have a heart condition that is the likely cause of the stroke, usually receive anticoagulant (blood-thinning) medication. Early complications of stroke include increased pressure in the brain, blood clots, and pneumonia. Stroke victims frequently have difficulty swallowing, so that foods and liquids may be diverted into the lungs, leading to pneumonia. Urinary incontinence and depression are other complications of strokes.

Most people recover to some extent after a stroke, but about 30 percent of stroke victims will die within one month, and survivors run a 25 percent risk of further strokes, heart attack, or death from vascular disease within two years. Approximately 80 percent of stroke survivors will eventually walk, but fewer than half return to fully normal function. Rehabilitation programs are extremely valuable in the post-stroke period; many stroke victims are transferred to rehabilitation facilities or "stroke units" after they become medically stable. Recovery may take months.

Men and women who have suffered a TIA are at high risk for having another stroke. Aspirin reduces the risk of stroke by 25 to 30 percent in these persons. Some people, especially those with a heart problem that can cause strokes, are treated with anticoagulation medications for the rest of their lives. Carotid endarterectomy, a surgical procedure that attempts to clean the blockage of a blood vessel that supplies the brain, is effective in some patients with severe narrowing of the vessel; the procedure's precise role in managing less severe narrowing is still uncertain.

Cancer

Gloria L., 57, knew that something was wrong. While showering she felt a lump in her left breast. She thought it might be just a small infection, but there was no redness or warmth. In fact, it did not even feel tender. Once she noticed the lump, she couldn't get the fear out of her head. She spent a week of restless nights and finally summoned the courage to see her doctor, who ordered a mammogram, a specialized x-ray of the breast. It confirmed the suspiciousness of the lump. Gloria's physician referred her to a surgeon, and the two of them decided that every attempt should be made to preserve her breast. After performing a biopsy, the surgeon removed the lump and the lymph nodes under Gloria's arm. Upon inspecting these tissues, the hospital's pathologist reported that, although the lump was positive for cancer, no malignant cells had appeared in the lymph nodes. Less than three months after discovering the lump, Gloria was back to jogging again.

Breast cancer. A common cancer of middle-aged and older women, breast cancer may be detected by three methods: breast self-examination, physical examination of the breast by a doctor or nurse, and mammography. These three techniques complement each other and should be used regularly. A woman should examine her own breasts carefully at least monthly. For women who are still menstruating, the best time is after the last day of each menstrual period. You can get the best instructions on performing this examination from a gynecologic nurse-practitioner, a surgeon, or the American Cancer Society (see Resources). In addition, a doctor or nurse should examine your breasts at least once a year if you are over 40, and the American Cancer Society recommends annual mammography for women age 50 and older. None of these methods is infallible, so it is important to use them all. The earlier the cancer is detected, the better the chance for cure.

In the past, the standard treatment of breast cancer was a modified radical mastectomy (breast removal) with removal of lymph nodes in the underarm area. Over the last two decades, large studies have shown a lumpectomy (in which only the lump and lymph nodes are removed) followed by radiation to be just as effective for most women. Older women with breast cancer that has not spread frequently receive hormonal therapy (tamoxifen), which appears to delay or prevent relapse. Women with breast cancer that has spread to the lymph nodes or other tissues are treated with hormonal therapy, chemotherapy, radiation therapy, or a combination of these. With current methods of medical treatment, many women with breast cancer survive for years despite widespread disease.

Lung cancer. Approximately half of the people who have lung cancer are over 65 years old. Smoking is the cause of almost all cases. The most common symptoms are a persistent cough, weight loss, and fatigue. Once lung cancer has been diagnosed, it is treated with surgery if the tumor has not spread and the person's health is otherwise good. Unfortunately, only a small percentage of persons with lung cancer meet these criteria. People with advanced lung cancer may be treated with chemotherapy, which prolongs their survival several months, but they undergo considerable side-effects. There are virtually no cures.

The best way to treat this devastating disease is by preventing it. Don't smoke, or stop smoking if you do.

Prostate cancer. As men age, particularly after 60, prostate cancer becomes very common. At one extreme, it may be a little cluster of tumor cells that cause no symptoms and are discovered and removed at the time of surgery for an enlarged prostate gland. At the other extreme, it may spread extensively to the bones or other organs.

Surgical removal of the tumor usually cures the smallest prostate cancers. With more severe disease, either surgery or radiation therapy is used, depending on the stage of the tumor. Prostate cancer that has spread to other parts of the body is not curable, but treatment that reduces the level of testosterone (a male hormone) in the body can control symptoms for long periods.

Overall, cancer is the second most common cause of death in older persons. Along with breast, lung, and prostate, colon cancer is the among the most devastating and widespread forms of cancer. For more information about all types of cancer, call a local chapter of the American Cancer Society (see Resources).

Arthritis

"Oh, my aching back!" Arthritis is the most common disease in people over 65. Almost half of older Americans are affected. Osteoarthritis, loss of the cartilage that lines the joints, is the most

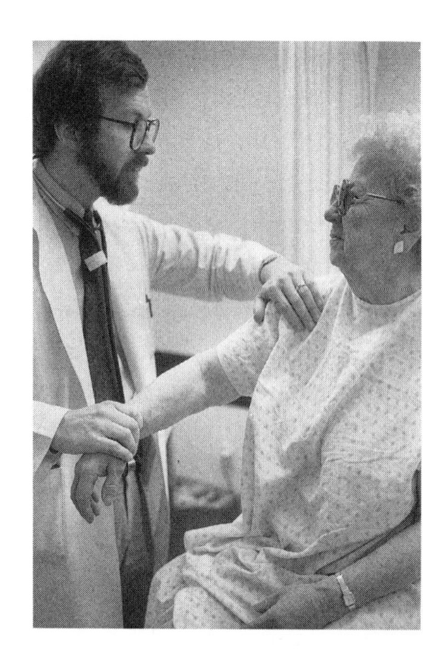

common cause of pain. New, abnormal bone may form, and existing bone may be destroyed or remodeled. The hands, knees, hips, and spine are most often affected.

The treatment of arthritis is aimed at relieving pain and preserving or restoring function. Pain can sometimes be controlled with acetaminophen or a group of drugs collectively known as nonsteroidal anti-inflammatory drugs, such as aspirin and ibuprofen. However, people respond differently to these drugs. What works for Millie's hip may not work for George's knee. A doctor may have to try several medications before finding the right one for each patient. Unfortunately, these drugs tend to have some serious side-effects, especially irritation of the stomach. Withdrawal of joint fluid and injections with a corticosteroid (a hormone) may help, but this procedure should not be performed too frequently.

Exercise, stretching, and physical therapy all help to manage symptoms and improve function. Surgery may help people who have severe functional impairment and who do not respond to simpler treatments. Total hip replacement has been a successful and safe option for many persons. Knee arthritis has been treated by removing cartilage using arthroscopy, performing bone surgery, or fusing the knee joint. Total knee replacement has been used but less successfully than hip replacement.

Diabetes

Sam K. had been gradually gaining weight for years, the result of too many dinner parties and business lunches and too little exercise. By the time he was 55 years old, he was almost 100 pounds overweight. Over the last three weeks, however, he had lost about 10 pounds even though he was still eating heartily. He was very thirsty and was urinating more frequently. Sam just did not feel right. He visited his doctor for a thorough check-up, which was unremarkable except for his obesity. The doctor sent some blood work to the lab and telephoned Sam the next day. His symptoms were the result of diabetes.

The prevalence of diabetes mellitus, a hormone disorder in which blood-sugar regulation is disturbed, increases dramatically with age. Almost half of the people with diabetes are unaware that they have the disease. Diabetes carries with it the danger of serious long-term complications, including eye damage (retinopathy), kidney and blood-vessel disease, and diabetic neuropathy (nerve damage). This nerve damage can produce burning pain or numbness in the feet, impotence, dizziness on arising, and diabetic foot disease. When diabetics neglect their feet, they may lose toes or legs to amputations as a result of diminished blood supply and nerve function.

Regular check-ups to detect complications early may allow treatment to prevent further damage and loss of function from diabetes. For example, early diabetic retinopathy can be treated with laser surgery; blindness can be prevented in many cases. Similarly, persons with diabetes who carefully inspect their feet each day can detect cracks in the skin, sores, or infections early, when treatment is easy and effective. Regular visits to a podiatrist are worthwhile.

Sam needs to change his diet to reach his ideal body weight, preferably by following a diet high in complex carbohydrates and fiber (see chapter 1). A nutritionist or dietitian can be very helpful in planning this type of diet and providing hints about how to stick to it. Exercise will improve Sam's ability to regulate blood sugar and lower the risk of coronary artery disease, which commonly accompanies diabetes. Before beginning an exercise program, Sam should check with his doctor. If diet and exercise do not adequately control his blood-sugar levels, oral medications may be necessary. These drugs vary in strength, duration of action, and cost. Diet, exercise, and oral medications can control blood-sugar levels in most older people with diabetes, but some must have insulin injections. Overmedication may cause hypoglycemia (low blood sugar), which may occur more frequently and may be more dangerous in older people.

You can find practical advice about dealing with diabetes from the local chapter of the American Diabetes Association (see Resources). Chapters often sponsor educational programs, and the association offers a helpful magazine, *Diabetes Forecast,* free to members.

Falls, Broken Bones, and Osteoporosis

Ed S., 72, complained that he was tripping over large objects that presented no problem for his wife. After his doctor referred him for an eye examination, Ed found he had severe cataracts in both eyes. Surgery to remove his cataracts improved his vision so that he no longer stumbles over objects he cannot see.

Approximately one-third of older people have at least one fall every year, and half of these people fall several times. Most falls are inconsequential, but sometimes a fall marks a decline in health or functional ability. It may also have severe consequences. Approximately 5 percent of falls result in a fracture, most commonly of the wrist; and 1 percent result in the most serious of consequences, a hip fracture. An additional 5 to 10 percent cause other injuries that may require medical attention or restrict activity. Falls may also have psychological impact: Older people who fall may avoid taking part in activities out of fear they will hurt themselves.

Medical conditions are an important cause of falling. For example, arthritis and neurologic problems—such as Parkinson's disease and disabilities from previous strokes—can affect balance and gait. Diseases that compromise overall health—such as heart and respiratory problems—may also contribute to falls. Medications—particularly sedatives and tranquilizers—increase risk of falling. Most commonly, falling results from a combination of disease, sensory impairment, medication, and the environment (like that loose rug or those poorly fitting slippers).

An occasional slip is nothing to worry about. But anyone who falls often should see a doctor so that the cause of the falls can be identified and treated. Gait and balance can be assessed, and the physician may suggest specific measures to improve stability—walking aids or physical therapy, for example. People who fall should first improve their home environment, correcting hazards such as throw rugs, loose carpet edges, cords, wires, or slippery floors, and installing hand rails, grab bars, and raised toilet seats as necessary (see chapter 6). Making these changes may help older people to remain independent in their own homes for as long as possible.

Osteoporosis. A loss of bone that accompanies aging, osteoporosis is a condition in which the bones lose calcium after menopause in women and during the later years of life in both men and women. In women, this loss results largely from the normal reduction in the hormone estrogen, but other factors also cause bone loss. For example, inadequate calcium and vitamin D may play important roles. Cigarette smoking and using alcohol (more than two drinks per day) are additional risk factors for developing osteoporosis. Black people, obese people, and those who regularly exercise to a moderate degree are less likely to develop osteoporosis.

This loss of bone tissue causes spinal problems, such as vertebrae collapse, making most of us shorter in old age and giving some of us a dowager's hump. The problem is that thin bone fractures easily. A slight fall may be enough, and spinal fractures may even occur spontaneously. The most common sites of fractures are the wrist, spine, and hip. Unfortunately, osteoporosis may not be diagnosed until a fracture occurs. Recently, screening techniques that measure bone density (densitometry) have become popular, but problems interpreting the test results and other technical difficulties must be resolved before the tests can be recommended for most older people.

The best approach to osteoporosis is prevention. Get adequate calcium and vitamin D (see chapter 1) and exercise regularly, especially with weight-bearing exercises such as walking. Women should ask their doctors about estrogen replacement during or after menopause. Each woman and her doctor must evaluate the relative risks of estrogen replacement. Estrogen alone is effective in preventing further bone loss, but estrogen treatment increases the risk of endometrial cancer (the lining of the uterus). Accordingly, women who take estrogen replacement medication must also take a progestin (Provera) or be monitored periodically with endometrial biopsies, a procedure that can be performed in the doctor's office. Several other drugs are used less commonly for osteoporosis. Calcitonin (a hormone) has been approved for the prevention of osteoporosis, but at present it is expensive and must be administered by injection or through nasal inhalation.

Hip fracture. The most severe complication of osteoporosis is hip fracture. Approximately 15 percent of white women and 6 percent of white men will fracture a hip during their lifetimes. Almost all hip fractures result from falls, usually at home. Approximately 15 percent of people with hip fractures from a fall have fallen before.

Surgery is the standard treatment, usually involving insertion of a pin or some other device to stabilize the bones. In some cases, the hip joint should be replaced. Sometimes surgery may be delayed for a few days to control medical conditions that might cause problems in recovery. Although the outlook for people who have hip fractures depends greatly upon how healthy they were before the fracture, a hip fracture is always a serious condition. As many as 25 percent of people with hip fractures will die within a year from complications of the fracture and loss of mobility.

Memory Loss, Dementia, and Delirium

Older Americans fear losing their mental abilities more than any other disability associated with aging. After middle age, many of us suffer increasing frustration with our memory: We block on people's names, find a word on the tip of the tongue, lose the name of that special vacation site or restaurant we thought we'd always remember. We worry silently, or we pass off the problems with a joke about early Alzheimer's. We are suffering from a common syndrome, minimal memory impairment of aging, in which forgetting names and a slight slowing of the memory process are the most prominent features. This slowing of memory differs from dementia (Alzheimer's disease is one form of dementia) in that other parts of mental functioning do not deteriorate, the memory loss does not become more and more profound, and functioning in everyday activities remains normal.

Dementia. It's reassuring to know that, although memory problems are common among older persons, dementia is not. In fact, dementia affects only 5 percent of persons aged 65 years or older; however, it becomes more common with increased age, affecting 15 to 40 percent of persons over 85. In contrast to the normal memory impairment of aging, people with dementia become more and more disabled, until they cannot recognize family members or remember common routines such as how to eat or dress themselves. Typically, at the onset of dementia, the person notices memory loss first, but often the family notices before the victim. The person may become defensive and use many strategies to cover up a failing memory, pretending to remember or becoming irritable when questioned.

Medical research and clinical practice have identified several types of dementia, the most common being Alzheimer's disease, a degenerative illness whose cause is unknown. Another type is multi-infarct dementia, caused by a series of strokes, usually in the deep parts of the brain. Parkinson's disease, chronic alcoholism, and vitamin B_{12} deficiency also cause dementia. Some mental illnesses such as depression may cause symptoms that mimic dementia—memory loss, irritability, and inattention—but when the depression is diagnosed and treated with antidepressant medications, intellectual function may improve.

Harriet T., 78, who is in the early stages of Alzheimer's disease, tells the same anecdotes about her deceased husband to everyone, every day. She talks about events of years past as though they had happened that week, and she honestly has no way of knowing when they did occur. When she sets out to the neighborhood market, she must always travel the same route, and sometimes, lately, she has been confused and gotten lost on the way home. She is angry because the state department of motor vehicles will not renew her license, and her family has taken away her car keys. Frequently she lashes out in anger, yelling at her adult children or throwing things at her household worker. In fact, it is difficult for her to keep workers. The burn-out rate is high for anyone who takes care of a person with dementia.

In addition to memory, Alzheimer's victims commonly lose other intellectual abilities, such as the ability to calculate. As in Harriet's case, they lose visual-spatial capacity, so they may get lost in familiar places. Personality and judgment deteriorate. Eventually they lose language, so that the little speaking they do seems irrelevant, disconnected from reality.

A medical evaluation for a possible dementia such as Alzheimer's disease includes three important steps: a complete history, a physical examination, and a mental status exam. The mental status exam consists of structured questions, the answers to which give hints about the person's intellectual functioning. Some of the questions (What day is it? Who is the current president of the United States? Where are you right now?) may sound a bit silly, but they provide valuable clues to memory loss and intellectual deficits. Generally, an experienced physician can diagnose dementia from these steps and will order laboratory tests primarily to exclude other medical problems that mimic dementia or cause it. Expensive tests such as CT scans and MRI usually do not provide much information about dementia. On rare occasions, a scan may detect a treatable condition that causes or mimics dementia.

At present, Alzheimer's disease and most other dementias are irreversible; we have no way to stop the memory loss. But even though none of the medications has yet been effective in reversing the intellectual losses of Alzheimer's disease, research and testing continue on drugs that may help (tetrahydroacridine [THA], choline, lecithin, and vinpocetine, for example). Other medications may be effective in managing some of the worrisome or dangerous behaviors that go along with dementia, such as wandering, hostility, aggression, agitation, and verbal and physical abuse. The medications most commonly used to help with these complications are major tranquilizers such as haloperidol (Haldol). Unfortunately, these drugs often have substantial side-effects and may actually increase confusion in some demented persons.

Thus, medical science may not have much to offer the Alzheimer's victim. It is important to focus on helping the victim and family cope with the progressive loss of intellectual capabilities as best they can. Usually, the first step is to adapt the demented person's environment, making it safer and simpler to manage daily activities. As dementia progresses, the family often enlists caregivers from community social services or nursing agencies to help with personal care—bathing, dressing, and feeding.

Today, many older persons find themselves becoming caregivers for a spouse or parent (see chapter 7), and the caregiver must take over more and more of the daily routine once carried out by the dementia victim. The attention needed by the demented person frequently reduces the caregiver's ability to function in other ways, and family crises begin to occur. Eventually, many caregivers begin to feel hopeless and depressed, become physically ill, or even burn out. Support groups and adult day-care are invaluable in maintaining the caregiver's mental health and the family's functioning. Local chapters of the Alzheimer's Association (see Resources) sponsor family support meetings and adult day-care centers and raise funds for research. Check your telephone book for a local address, or write to the national office for the address of the nearest chapter.

Delirium. Peter B., 75, was admitted to his local hospital for an elective minor operation under general anesthesia. All went well, except that Peter awoke from surgery confused and unable to recognize his wife or adult children. He also experienced some hallucinations, believing that he had been taken to prison and that the nurses were prison guards. His doctor examined him, ordered some blood tests, and adjusted his medications. Over the next week, he gradually became more lucid, and by the time he left the hospital he was back to normal.

The syndrome Peter experienced is called delirium (acute confusional state), and it usually results from acute illness, new medication, or surgery. Drug intoxication and withdrawal, infection, poor oxygenation, hypoglycemia, stroke, seizures, and heart disease may also cause delirium. The delirious person typically cannot engage in a conversation because of his or her disorganized thinking and inability to maintain attention. Often the person's level of consciousness fluctuates from more alert to less conscious. Some delirious people, like Peter, have temporary delusions and hallucinations.

Once the underlying cause of the delirium is corrected, the disorder will usually subside spontaneously, albeit sometimes slowly. A quiet, well-lit environment helps to reduce the stimulation that aggravates this condition. Having a familiar person nearby may also help. Occasionally, medications are needed to control the person's agitation and restlessness. However bad the symptoms may seem, though, the condition is temporary and reversible, unlike dementia. In some cases, however, delirium and dementia may coexist; in these patients, improvement may be limited.

Impaired Hearing and Vision

Annie R.'s friends thought that she was either becoming demented or depressed. She had become more and more withdrawn, seldom responding to invitations or attending social functions. She seemed suspicious and frightened, and she often forgot what her friends told her. She was no longer the immaculate housekeeper she used to be, and she was losing weight because she was not eating right. She seemed to be missing most of what was happening around her and, in fact, she was. Annie was suffering from sensory impairment; both her hearing and her vision had been deteriorating over the years. Her friends urged her to visit her doctor, who found she had cataracts in both eyes and progressive loss of hearing in both ears. Once she was fitted with hearing aids and had her cataracts removed, she was her old self again—back in the social swim.

Hearing. Hearing loss is the most common sensory impairment among older people. In fact, 28 percent of those over 65, and 48 percent of those over 85, report that they don't hear as well as they once did. Men have problems more frequently than women: Almost 20 percent of men over 85 are deaf in both ears.

Several conditions affect our hearing in later life. The gradual, progressive loss of ability to hear tones at the higher pitches is called presbycusis. Older persons may also lose some of their ability to repeat or write words they have heard, even when their hearing loss is mild. One important cause of hearing loss, affecting up to 30 percent of older persons, is simple to treat: excess ear wax impacted in the ear canal. Some antibiotics and diuretics commonly used in treating hypertension and heart disease may also produce hearing loss in older persons.

Because hearing problems are so common, it's important to have your hearing checked annually after you reach age 65. Hearing aids, which amplify sounds from your environment, can be extremely helpful, even with severe hearing loss. In general, wearing aids in both ears works best because you can localize the sound better and because two aids provide better amplification. The most popular aids are behind-the-ear models and all-in-the-ear models. Behind-the-ear aids have the advantage of being durable and easy to repair or service. In-the-ear aids are easier to insert but may be more difficult to adjust and may have more feedback (a high-pitched squeal). In-the-canal aids, recently developed, are the least visible and offer some improvement in hearing higher frequencies.

Whichever type of hearing aid you select, be sure to purchase it on a thirty-day trial basis, because not every kind of hearing aid will work effectively for every person. To get the best service, find a comprehensive audiologic center that offers assessment, service, and rehabilitation under one roof.

Try to begin rehabilitation counseling immediately when you purchase a hearing aid. This counseling includes education about the benefits and limitations of hearing aids as well as suggestions for communicating better with other people. Group counseling is most effective because it encourages hearing-impaired people to come out of their shell a bit and participate in give-and-take with others. It also develops camaraderie among people with a common problem. It may be helpful to involve family and caregivers in the counseling process so that they can understand how to support someone wearing aids.

Communicating with someone who has a hearing impairment can be challenging. But communicating with an older person whose hearing is limited may be easier if you follow these suggestions.

- Wait to speak until the listener can see you. If necessary, touch the person to get his or her attention.
- Speak a bit more loudly than usual, but avoid shouting.
- Avoid speaking directly into the listener's ear. Doing so will distort your message and hide your visual cues.
- Speak at a normal speed, not too fast or too slowly.
- Pause at the end of sentences.
- Make a point of pronouncing clearly—articulating—the ends of words and sentences. Don't swallow them or drop them. Avoid overarticulating.
- Speak at a distance of no less than 3 feet and no more than 6 feet.
- Focus light on your face so that the listener can see lip movements, facial expression, and gestures.
- Use gestures and write notes to improve communication.

- Remove objects such as gum, cigarettes, or food from your mouth to speak more clearly.
- Reduce background noise such as radio or television.
- If the listener does not understand, change your wording instead of repeating yourself.
- Try not to show frustration.
- Use portable amplifiers.

In certain public buildings, auditoriums, and churches, contained-area amplification systems are being installed to help people with impaired hearing. Special equipment is used to pick up the amplified sound, which is undetectable to others. Other communication aids include closed-caption (invisible without a decoder) television and specially equipped telephone sets for hearing-impaired persons. Chain stores such as Radio Shack and Sears offer special catalogs of telephones, earphones, and other electronic devices designed for people with hearing problems. Your local senior center or hospital audiology department can refer you to nearby resources for hearing-impaired people.

Visual impairment. Like hearing problems, vision problems increase with age. Approximately 13 percent of people over 65 report some problems with their vision, a proportion that increases to 28 percent among people over 85. More than 90 percent of older people need eyeglasses, and over 20 percent of people over 85 have poor vision even with glasses. Furthermore, we lose side vision steadily after middle age, creating a tunnel-vision effect in people who are most severely affected. Most of us have already encountered middle-age presbyopia, the far-sightedness that makes our arms seem too short when we try to read the newspaper. Changes in the eye's lens also scatter light and reduce resistance to glare, making night driving more of a challenge.

The most abnormal vision changes in later life are typically produced by four eye diseases: cataracts, macular degeneration, glaucoma, and diabetes. More than 40 percent of people over 75 develop cataracts, which are clouded or opaque lenses that cause a painless, gradual loss of vision. Cataracts may affect one or both eyes, and depending on location, may affect either distant or near vision. If vision loss is minor or if the person cannot have surgery, cataracts can be treated by use of special eyeglasses, contact lenses, and low-vision aids (products and devices that help visually impaired persons). For more serious vision loss, outpatient cataract surgery can replace the clouded lens with a permanent plastic lens that improves vision.

Macular degeneration is the leading cause of permanent loss in the eye's central vision among older people. A deterioration in the macula involves that part of the retina that receives and transmits central vision, colors, and sharp details. Macular degeneration comes in two varieties: dry (approximately 90 percent of cases) and wet (less common but more likely to cause blindness). *Dry macular degeneration* progresses to blindness in only about 10 percent of cases. Although no treatment is presently available, this type progresses so slowly that people may notice little distortion—perhaps just blurring—for many years. Patients must closely monitor their vision for sudden changes and deterioration using a device called an Amsler grid. Every day, patients should fix their vision on the dot in the center of the grid and call their doctors if any of the lines appear wavy or curved or if any of the squares appear missing. *Wet macular degeneration,* which can progress quickly, may be controlled with laser therapy in some cases.

Glaucoma, which affects about 3 percent of people over age 65, damages vision by increasing pressure inside the eye. Resultant pressure on the optic nerve, which transmits visual information to the brain, often reduces the visual field and leaves victims with tunnel vision. However, glaucoma is easily detectable at a yearly eye exam and can be treated with eyedrops or oral medications. Occasionally, laser surgery may be needed.

Among the other risks diabetics face is a higher-than-normal risk of vision impairment and blindness. According to the American Foundation for the Blind, approximately 3 percent of older Americans have suffered severe visual loss from diabetes, and the likelihood of developing diabetic eye disease increases with age. Diabetes can damage nerve endings and the structure of the blood vessels throughout the body, including those in the eyes. Unfortunately, many of these changes occur without perceptible symptoms, so it is very important for a person with diabetes to have thorough eye exams at least once a year. Laser therapy is often helpful in preventing vision loss once diabetic eye disease has been diagnosed.

The American Foundation for the Blind (see Resources) offers many helpful publications, including *Aids for the 80s, What They Are and What They Do,* a guide to devices from talking calculators to reading machines that can facilitate independence in daily activities. This foundation also publishes a *Directory of Agencies Serving the Visually Handicapped in the United States,* a state-by-state listing of community-service agencies and clinics that offer comprehensive evaluation of vision problems. You might find this directory in your public library, or you can write to the foundation. The Public Affairs Committee (see Resources) also offers many informative pamphlets on specific impairments: cataracts, macular degeneration, glaucoma, limited vision, blindness, and so on. Many public radio stations offer a radio reading service for people whose vision is impaired.

What can we do to make life simpler for a blind friend or family member? The American Foundation for the Blind offers the following guidelines:

- Let a blind person know you are talking to him or her by introducing yourself and gently touching the person's elbow.
- Meet someone who is blind at the door as the person enters an unfamiliar room.
- Briefly describe the environment as you lead the way through it. In an unfamiliar room, place the person's hand on a chair back so he or she can be seated.
- Let the person know when you are leaving the area. Leave the person in contact with a stationary object.
- Blindness does not cause deafness. You can speak in normal tones, and use the words you ordinarily do. Words like "look" and "see" are common to everyone, including blind people.
- If you wish to guide someone who is blind, it's simplest for the person to take your arm just above the elbow, and for you to walk about a half step ahead. However, many blind people do not need or want assistance except in unfamiliar places.
- Do not speak to a guide dog that is working. You may distract it from its job.

Incontinence

Kathryn I., 77, looked twenty years younger than her age. A bright and energetic person, she suddenly dropped her volunteer work at a senior citizens' center. When her friends and center staff telephoned, she adamantly denied being sick. Nevertheless, she became increasingly withdrawn. Her family finally convinced her to see a physician for a check-up. During a careful evaluation, the physician found that Kathryn was having urinary incontinence and was avoiding social activities because she was afraid that she would embarrass herself. After performing a few tests, Kathryn's doctor prescribed a medication that helps her control her bladder well enough to resume previous social activities without fear.

Urinary incontinence is the involuntary loss of urine in sufficient amount or frequency to be a health problem. The term incontinence also refers to fecal incontinence (involuntary loss of stool), but that is a less common condition and will not be discussed here. Although urinary incontinence is more common in nursing-home residents and in the acutely ill, up to 30 percent of older people in the community may also suffer from this problem. If it develops suddenly, it is usually related to an acute illness or a new medication and is easy to correct. If the incontinence develops over time and persists, it is probably one of four basic types: stress, urge, overflow, or functional.

Stress incontinence. Olga J., age 63, is the proud mother of eight children and the grandmother of fourteen. Healthy and active, she participates in aerobic exercise three times a week and works at a law firm. She does not even think about problems of aging. However, she has had one irritating complaint for the last five years. Whenever she coughs or sneezes, she loses a few drops of urine. Olga suffers from stress incontinence, or leakage of urine when abdominal pressure is increased, a disorder that occurs almost exclusively in women.

Pregnancy may relax the muscles supporting the bladder and urinary system. The result is that the normal mechanisms to contain urine can be overwhelmed when abdominal pressure is increased. Other possible causes include hormone deficiency after menopause and pelvic surgery. Separately or together, pelvic-floor (Kegel) exercises, hormones, biofeedback, and surgery may be helpful in managing this problem. To perform Kegel exercises, contract the muscles of the pelvic floor that surround the bladder outlet; repeat these exercises several times each day (see chapter 1). Biofeedback uses specialized equipment to help the incontinent person relearn to control contraction of the bladder and pelvic muscles.

Urge incontinence. Donna M., 68, suffered a minor stroke several years ago. She has improved greatly through physical therapy, hard work, and sheer courage. Now she is able to walk, though with a slight limp, and she enjoys quilting with a group of friends who meet three days a week. Although her walking is almost normal, she frequently cannot get to the bathroom in time. She just doesn't get enough warning. Donna's problem is common among stroke victims, but may also affect other people. Urge incontinence can also result from conditions such as cystitis or bladder stones. People troubled by urge incontinence have overactive bladder muscles that contract involuntarily when the bladder is not completely full. Hence, the actual amount of urine that is lost tends to be small. If a treatable cause is not found, bladder-relaxant medications or biofeedback may help in controlling urge incontinence.

Overflow incontinence. Don Q., 72, is a retired army captain who spends his golden years whittling away at his golf score. Lately he has noticed fullness in his lower abdomen and frequent loss of small amounts of urine. In fact, every time he urinates the amount is small, and he frequently has difficulty getting his urine flow started. Don has overflow incontinence from obstruction by an enlarged prostate gland. Overflow incontinence can also result from poor contraction of the muscles of the bladder. Prostate enlargement, diabetes, and drugs are common causes of overflow incontinence. If an obstruction is present, as in Don's case, surgery is usually indicated. If there is no obstruction, medications may help stimulate bladder contractions. Occasionally, a catheter (a long rubber or plastic tube inserted into the opening of the urethra and threaded into the bladder) is necessary to control overflow incontinence.

Functional incontinence. Joan L., 79, has had severe arthritis for twenty years and is presently confined to a wheelchair. When she has to go to the bathroom at night, she often does not want to waken her daughter or grandchildren, and so she wets the bed. This type of incontinence is really not a medical condition. Rather, it may be caused by dementia, misunderstanding, poor communication, emotional barriers, or environmental obstacles. Treatment for functional incontinence is supportive, including a regular schedule for using the toilet, a bedpan or bedside commode, and grab bars or other environmental changes that make the bathroom safer and easier to use. Replacing buttons and zippers with Velcro straps can help the person be ready to use the toilet immediately after getting to the bathroom. Many types of pads and adult briefs are available to manage incontinence. Catheters are rarely necessary for this type of incontinence.

Constipation

Leslie M. complained that her mother, Eve A., 85, made life miserable for everyone living with her. Although Eve was healthy, she complained incessantly about her bowels. Leslie, who cared for her mother in her home, had tried every laxative in the drugstore, as well as suppositories and enemas. Finally, someone told Leslie about a high-fiber cereal. After a few weeks of eating the new breakfast cereal, Eve virtually stopped complaining.

Constipation is a change in normal bowel habits—having bowel movements with reduced frequency or increased difficulty. In older people, constipation is likely to be painless and result from slow transit of feces through the large bowel.

People who suffer from constipation should first ask their doctors if any of their medications might be contributing to the problem. Many commonly prescribed drugs cause constipation as a side-effect. Stopping these drugs or substituting another drug can provide dramatic relief. The second step is to increase fiber in the diet (see chapter 1). Although numerous "bulk agents" are available at drugstores, a more palatable and natural way to get this effect is to eat high-fiber breakfast cereal and bread. Choose a cereal with at least 9 grams of fiber per serving, and start with a small amount to avoid cramps. Begin with a half bowl per day and gradually increase to a full bowl.

Regular elimination can also be encouraged if you keep regular meal times, drink plenty of fluids, and engage in regular physical activity. Stool softeners (such as dioctyl sodium sulphosuccinate) are commonly prescribed and may have some additional benefit. Some people find that elevating the feet when sitting on the toilet helps them have a bowel movement. Regular use of laxatives is *not* helpful and may actually damage the nerve supply of the colon, making the problem worse. Like many of the other problems of aging, constipation is best treated by making changes in eating and exercise patterns.

The many diseases and problems that frequently affect older persons make the road to healthy aging seem like walking through a mine field. In fact, good health habits, regular medical care to detect unrecognized disease early, and proper treatment once a problem is present can greatly increase your chances of healthy aging. As with other aspects of successful aging, the lion's share of the responsibility remains with you. Your assignments are to live a healthy lifestyle, select a good doctor who believes in preventive care, and attend promptly to the health problems that may arise.

Resources

AARP Mail-Order Pharmacy, American Association of Retired Persons, 1909 K Street, NW, Washington, DC 20049. Telephone: (202) 872-4700.
Write or call to locate the AARP mail-order pharmacy nearest you.

Al-Anon Family Groups, P.O. Box 862, Midtown Station, New York, NY 10019. Telephone: (212) 302-7240.
This national organization publishes books and other publications that are helpful to both alcoholics and their family members. These materials are also available through local chapters of Al-Anon.

Alcoholics Anonymous, General Services Board, 468 Park Avenue South, New York, NY 10016. Telephone: (212) 686-1100.
AA publishes books and other materials that are helpful to both alcoholics and their family members. To order, telephone a local chapter of AA or write to the national office.

Alzheimer's Association, 70 E. Lake Street, Suite 600, Chicago, IL 60601. Telephone: (800) 621-0379; in Illinois: (800) 572-6037.
This organization conducts research for the prevention and treatment of Alzheimer's disease and other dementias. It also provides support and assistance to both patients and their families. To locate the chapter nearest you, look in the telephone book or contact the national office.

American Association of Retired Persons, 601 E Street, NW, Washington, DC 20049. Telephone: (202) 434-2277.
Of special interest are *AARP Medical Information Leaflets,* which are available through the fulfillment office.

American Cancer Society National Office, Tower Place, 3340 Peachtree Road, NE, Atlanta, GA 30026. Telephone: (800) 227-2345.
ACS sponsors smoking-cessation programs and offers information, referrals, and support to people with cancer and their families. For more information, telephone your local chapter or write to the national office.

American Dental Association, 211 E. Chicago Avenue, Chicago, IL 60611. Telephone: (312) 440-2860 or (800) 621-8099.
Write for a copy of ADA's pamphlet, *Keeping Your Smile in the Later Years,* for information on maintaining your teeth or dentures. Also ask for the address of your local dental society.

American Diabetes Association, 1660 Duke Street, Alexandria, VA 22314. Telephone: (800) 232-3472.
ADA publishes brochures and other materials helpful for people with diabetes. These publications are available through local chapters or from the national headquarters.

American Foundation for the Blind, 15 W. 16th Street, New York, NY 10011. Telephone: (212) 620-2000.
Call or write for free publications on visual impairments, vision aids, and ways for the family and patient to cope with failing eyesight. The foundation can also refer you to local chapters or community-service agencies for visually impaired persons.

American Heart Association National Center, 7320 Greenville Avenue, Dallas, TX 75231. Telephone: (214) 373-6300.
AHA publishes materials helpful for people concerned about cardiovascular disease, healthy eating patterns, exercise, and the effects of smoking. These publications are available from your local American Heart Association or from the national office.

American Lung Association, 1740 Broadway, P.O. Box 596, New York, NY 10019. Telephone: (212) 315-8700.
The lung association sponsors smoking-cessation programs. It also offers assistance and services for people with pulmonary diseases such as lung cancer or emphysema. For more information, telephone your local chapter or contact the association's national headquarters.

Arthritis Foundation, 1314 Spring Street, NW, Atlanta, GA 30309. Telephone: (404) 872-7100 or (800) 283-7800.
The foundation conducts research into the prevention and treatment of arthritis and provides services and education for people with arthritis. For more information, call or write your local chapter.

Concern for Dying, 250 W. 57th Street, Room 831, New York, NY 10107. Telephone: (212) 246-6962.
This educational organization provides information about living wills (directions to physicians not to use artificial means or extraordinary life-support measures) and the right to die with dignity in case of terminal illness.

The Lighthouse, National Center for Vision and Aging, New York Association for the Blind, 111 E. 59th Street, New York, NY 10022. Call toll-free (800) 334-5497 or TTY (212) 980-7832.
The Lighthouse operates an information and referral service for older people with vision problems.

Narcotics Anonymous, World Service Office, P.O. Box 9999, Van Nuys, CA 91409. Telephone: hotline, (818) 997-3822 or (818) 780-3951.
Narcotics Anonymous offers support to people addicted to drugs, including prescription drugs, as well as to their families and friends. Based on Alcoholics Anonymous's twelve-step recovery program, NA has local chapters throughout the United States. If you know someone whom you suspect has a problem with prescription and over-the-counter drugs, NA may be able to offer guidance and resources.

National Association of Area Agencies on Aging, 600 Maryland Avenue, SW, Room 208, Washington, DC 20024. Telephone: (202) 484-7520.
Contact the national office to locate your local Area Agency on Aging.

National Council on Alcoholism, 1424 16th Street, NW, Suite 401, Washington, DC 20036. Telephone: (202) 206-6770 or (800) 475-HOPE.
This organization provides support and information to people with alcohol problems in the family. Write to the national office, or look in your telephone book for your local chapter. Many older people have found this group especially helpful.

Public Affairs Committee, 381 Park Avenue South, New York, NY 10016.
This educational organization offers inexpensive, informative booklets on a variety of topics, including mental and physical health problems. Write for a list of titles.

Self Help for Hard of Hearing People, Inc., 7800 Wisconsin Avenue, Bethesda, MD 20814. Telephone: (301) 657-2248.
This group provides information, referrals, and support to people who are hard of hearing.

Recommended Reading

American Heart Association. "Walking for a Healthy Heart."
Informative booklet that gets you started on a program for walking fitness. Free from your local American Heart Association. Also available: "Swimming for a Healthy Heart," "Running . . . ," "Dancing . . . ," and "Cycling . . . ," as well as other useful publications for people concerned about the cardiovascular benefits of exercise. American Heart Association National Center, 7320 Greenville Avenue, Dallas, TX 75231.

American Heart Association Cookbook, 4th edition. New York: David McKay Co., 1984.
Available in bookstores. A sample booklet of recipes from this cookbook, "Recipes for Low-Fat, Low-Cholesterol Meals," is available free from your local chapter of the American Heart Association. Also free are useful booklets with information about potassium, sodium, and cholesterol and suggestions for choosing healthy food, losing weight, and eating out without sabotaging your food plan.

American Heart Association Low-Fat, Low-Cholesterol Cookbook. Eds. Scott M. Grundy and Mary Winston. New York: Times Books (Random House), 1989.

Burgio, K. L., K. L. Pearce, and A. J. Lucco. *Staying Dry: A Practical Guide to Bladder Control.* Baltimore: Johns Hopkins University Press, 1989.

Doyle, Nancy C. *Involuntary Smoking: Health Risks for Nonsmokers.* Public Affairs Pamphlet No. 653.
Send $1 to Public Affairs Pamphlets, 381 Park Avenue South, New York, NY 10016.

National Institute on Aging, National Institutes of Health. *Age Pages.* This ongoing series provides information about common health concerns in the later years. To receive a list of past issues or to be placed on the mailing list to receive free single copies of future issues, write to the NIA Information Center, 2209 Distribution Circle, Silver Spring, MD 20910.

UCLA/USC Long Term Care Gerontology Center and UCLA Medical Center. *How to Talk to Your Doctor.* Los Angeles, CA: Regents of the University of California, 1985.
Single copies are available for $1.50 from UCLA Division of Geriatrics, Order Desk, 32-144 CHS, 10833 Le Conte Avenue, Los Angeles, CA 90024-1687.

UCLA/USC Long Term Care Gerontology Center and UCLA Medical Center. *Maintaining Continence: Bladder Control in Older People.* Los Angeles, CA: Regents of the University of California, 1985.
Single copies are available for $1.50 from UCLA Division of Geriatrics, Order Desk, 32-144 CHS, 10833 Le Conte Avenue, Los Angeles, CA 90024-1687.

CHAPTER THREE

Keeping Your Emotional Balance

Not everything that is faced can be changed, but nothing can be changed until it is faced.

—James Baldwin

Business, caregiving, volunteering, education, homemaking, medicine, writing, research, counseling, administration, art, music, construction, physical labor, crafts, sports, travel—the list of activities with which "retirees" occupy their time could easily fill this page. Using their long experience at coping with the vicissitudes of life, most older people handle their daily ups and downs with strength and wisdom. They stay active and use their later years to complete a life's work or to change directions. They have learned to nurture relationships with other people, care for themselves at dark moments, seek hope during hard times, and find peace of mind in reminiscence.

Older Americans worry less than younger people. They are three times more likely than young people to say they are never depressed. They are no more fearful than younger people of walking alone at night in their neighborhoods. Older people are less fearful of crime than they were just ten years ago. Ninety percent of older Americans say they are not afraid to die.

The *Los Angeles Times* found that people over 65 are generally pleased with their standard of living, in contrast to middle-aged and younger folks, even though most live on fixed incomes. In spite of the chronic health problems experienced by 86 percent of them, older people believe their age is the ideal time in life. The older people get, the happier they are, it seems.

How do we achieve this equilibrium in spite of the losses most of us experience by midlife? How do we lead productive and happy lives in our older years if our health is declining or we suffer the loss of our loved ones? Staying involved, staying active, coping flexibly with the stresses of life, and enjoying the moment are the answers given by older people who describe themselves as happy and fulfilled.

Wallace and Myrtle S., both age 72, recently sold their house and business in their hometown and moved to the Arizona mountains to build their dream home. They designed the house and drew their own plans. Now they are busy supervising construction and getting to know their new neighbors. They have already joined the local volunteer fire brigade and found some good friends. Wallace is doing the wiring in the new home, and Myrtle is planning the decor. Both are working on landscaping. Buoyed up by their project, they are exhilarated by their new directions and challenges, as well as by seeing a lifelong dream come true.

Bruce and Ruth R., also 72, are happy to stay in the home they built thirty-five years ago, although they take frequent trips to their boat in Puget Sound. Bruce keeps a hand in his aviation business, which he is gradually turning over to his son. Bruce says he has achieved the ideal balance between working as much as he wants and letting go when he feels like it. Bruce and Ruth are busy in community and church affairs, frequently socializing with friends and relatives. They love their town and their Northern California roots.

Bahran M., 66, was displaced from his native Iran by threats of a firing squad. With his family, he moved to the United States nearly ten years ago, attempting to rebuild his life in a foreign culture. An eminent scholar in Iran, he now teaches Persian literature at a U.S. university. Although he mourns deeply the loss of his library of twelve thousand volumes that included many original and historic manuscripts, he has found inner strength and resilience to start his life again. "Under any circumstances, at any age," he says, "I can build a new life because I feel . . . myself strong and young and vigorous."

Jorge and Rebecca N., 85 and 80, respectively, have built a community of friends and family in Miami since they immigrated from Cuba twenty-five years ago. Now retired from his accounting business, Jorge stays active in synagogue and social clubs. Even though Rebecca is battling ovarian cancer with regular trips to the hospital for chemotherapy, she attends as many meetings of her women's card club as possible. Other family members have taken over much of the cooking at get-togethers when she feels ill, but *Abuelita* (Grandmother) is still an important center of love and gossip in the gatherings. She teases and spoils her grandchildren, and they giggle at her stories about the family.

Emily A., 84, lives fifteen hundred miles from her nearest relative, a daughter in Michigan. Now retired from her lifework as an educator of young children, she lives alone in her condominium with an attendant to drive her car, clean house, and cook. She volunteers at a local day care center, where she plays with the children and teaches parenting skills. Her extensive network of friends and colleagues visit her and correspond with her often. Even after a series of health problems, she keeps up a salty, lively conversation, enjoying nothing more than a visit from friends.

Not all of us are as well balanced as these folks, however. Although most older people say they are maintaining a good emotional equilibrium, some are having trouble. For example, the suicide rate among white men over 85 is the highest for any group in the nation. Approximately 15 percent of older people suffer from depressive symptoms, often related to grief over loss of a loved one or reaction to physical illness. Older people use most of the drugs (prescription and over-the-counter) sold in this country. If they overmedicate themselves, perhaps because they become confused about dosage or timing of medications, they may become dependent on prescription drugs. Although alcoholism often goes unrecognized among retired people, elderly widowers have the highest rate of alcoholism of any group in the population. Is it too late, after 55, to deal with these problems? No. In fact, many old dogs are learning new tricks.

Today's older people were raised in a time when we paid more attention to our physical aches and pains than to our feelings. Until recently, most mental health professionals have ignored treatment for psychological problems in the elderly. But recent findings and clinical practice have demonstrated many ways in which longstanding patterns of unhappiness can be improved. In this chapter, we discuss some of the emotional problems older people might have as well as the help that is now available, including some ways that families and individuals can help themselves.

Depression: When We Just Can't Cope

Many of us are not prepared for the changes that come with aging in the United States today. Life has changed radically since our grandparents were aging. For one thing, in our grandparents' time, most people simply did not live as long as they do now. People died from disease and accidents more often than they do now, because there was little to be done to prolong the life of someone who had a chronic illness or disability. Another difference is that, in our grandparents' day, people tended to stay in the communities where they grew up, so that an older person had family, friends, and neighbors to turn to in difficult times. Today we live longer, and we move from one town, state, or country to another more readily. We may be alone, sick, and without financial resources, far away from our nearest blood relative. Growing older may bring many difficult adjustments:

- loss of spouse
- marital problems
- reduction in income
- retirement
- empty nest
- health problems
- hearing and vision loss
- changes in relationships with family and friends
- relocation, leaving home
- loneliness and isolation
- loss of mobility
- loss of independence

Any one of these changes can be depressing, and when several of them occur at once, people may find it difficult to cope. As pointed out earlier, most older people cope strongly with the adjustments of later life. But many of us have times when we could use extra help.

Unfortunately, because we were raised to be self-reliant and to consider asking for help as an admission of failure, we suffer our losses silently. We may hurt ourselves and our loved ones more than we need to because we're ashamed to admit that we're struggling and that we don't have the answers. We know we're not crazy, so we may refuse to seek professional counseling or support. In fact, the great majority of people in psychotherapy are not crazy. They just feel stuck and overwhelmed, and so they ask for professional help.

We may grow restless and depressed and hopeless, making the problem worse by refusing to get help. We may take a little wine to get through the afternoon, a couple of drinks to get through the evening. We may tell ourselves that no one notices, that alcoholics are those "bums" and "floozies" we see on city streets.

As a result of life changes, older people are more likely than younger people to suffer from depressive symptoms such as anxiety, sleep disturbances, and hypochondria. However, older people are less likely to seek help for these problems, except by taking medications and alcohol. That's the bad news. The good news is that most of the emotional problems of later life are treatable, and we now know enough about the causes and treatment for common problems to be able to help. Older people can feel and function better, sometimes better than ever before in their lives.

Symptoms of Depression

Robert W., 61, is troubled about his 81-year-old mother, Florence, who has been living alone in a neighboring state since the death of Robert's father four months ago. "She refuses to move," says Robert, "but she doesn't take care of herself or the house any more. She can't accept the fact that Dad is gone. She also has not been sleeping or eating well and has started to lose weight. She won't accept our suggestions to participate in the Meals on Wheels program or a senior center. We've thought of letting her get even more lonely until Mom agrees to move out of her house and get away from its associations with Dad."

Florence's symptoms are typical of depression, often a normal response to loss of a spouse. Some of the most common depressive symptoms include the following:

- sleep problems
- loss of appetite leading to weight loss (or overeating leading to weight gain)
- fatigue
- confusion
- difficulty in concentrating

- forgetfulness
- agitation
- lack of interest in previous activities
- tearfulness
- feelings of painful or overwhelming sadness

Usually, depressive symptoms triggered by a significant loss begin to lift after a few months, and the person slowly returns to the former level of functioning. Although Robert should expect setbacks in this process and be supportive about them, if his mother's depression lasts for a prolonged time, "letting her get even more lonely" will not cure it. Long-term depression endangers health and can even lead to suicide. Forcing a move to a new living arrangement means yet another loss, which will probably intensify the depression.

Robert could help his mother most by openly sharing with her his concern about her sleeplessness, weight loss, and lack of interest in life. He and other family members, if available, could help Florence by encouraging her to reminisce about Dad, allowing her to grieve over her loss openly and talk about her life without him. She—and the rest of the family—would benefit from sharing memories about Dad, perhaps over some old photos and scrapbooks.

Robert should strongly encourage his mother to see her doctor to rule out any physical illness that might be contributing to her problem. If none exists, Florence may need professional counseling, perhaps from a trained therapist at a senior center or a counseling agency the center recommends. She may be willing to see someone but unable to follow through, in which case she'll need assistance in getting to appointments. People who are depressed often respond to counseling and antidepressant medication.

Depression after Death of a Spouse

For a man or a woman, dealing with widowhood is painful. Whether a marriage was good or bad, the surviving spouse has lost a long-time companion. Other family members may feel reluctant to step in and fill the gap left by the deceased spouse. Friends may unconsciously ostracize the widowed person if that person reminds them that a similar loss could occur in their own lives. Also, people may not know what to say, and so they avoid the bereaved person after the funeral ceremony. It may be difficult for them socially to accept a single man or woman, no longer part of a couple. How people cope with widowhood depends on their life experiences, support network, and ability to work through grief, with or without professional help. Here are two examples of widows who have different ways of coping with their grief and depression.

Rachel Z. says, "My mother is in her nineties and in relatively good health. Since Dad died ten years ago, she's lived in an elderly persons' hotel that is considered one of the best in the city. I'm in my sixties and so is my sister. We take turns visiting Mom, but we always feel down when we leave. Nothing is quite right—the food, the other residents, even us. She's always irritable. It seems we can never please her. I've even thought of giving up visiting her because I feel so bad afterward, but I'd feel guilty if I didn't go to see her."

Sarah R., 55, has had a different experience with her widowed mother: "Recently Mom became a new person. For the past few years, since Dad died, she has been grouchy and demanding and always ill with one symptom or another. Now she's outgoing, chipper, and free of medical problems. All that happened is that she was treated for depression. She never seemed sad to me, just bitter. I don't understand the change, but it's wonderful. We have a whole new relationship now."

Although many older people exhibit the typical picture of depression—they are sad, lose interest in their usual activities, or have trouble sleeping and eating—some people experience a variation of depressive illness. These people become angry and irritable, and frequently complain of physical illness. For these people, too, antidepressant medications can be extremely effective in alleviating symptoms of depression. It is important to be aware that irritability may be a sign of depression, too, so that professional help can be sought.

Professional Help for Depression

The most common sources of depression in older people are significant losses, which may be real, anticipated, or imagined; physical illness; and side-effects of medication. Professional help is often needed to determine the cause and identify the most effective way to deal with the problem.

If someone you care about seems depressed, it's important to consult a professional specially trained in geriatric medicine or counseling. Although depression is the most common mental health problem of the elderly, its symptoms are commonly confused with symptoms of other mental or physical problems such as dementia or diabetes. Furthermore, drugs affect different individuals in different ways, and drug treatment for older persons differs from drug treatment for middle-aged or young people.

Often you can find a geriatric specialist by calling the nearest university teaching hospital or by contacting your local Area Agency on Aging (see appendix B). These agencies can refer you to a geriatric psychiatrist, psychologist, or social worker in your community.

If you are the adult child of a depressed person, especially if the behavior is part of a long-term pattern, getting help for yourself from someone who specializes in issues of aging is probably the best thing you can do. You may not be able to change your mother or father's behavior and attitudes, but you can learn to understand and handle your feelings toward your parent. Many family-service organizations offer support groups that focus on "you and your aging parent." There, you can meet with professional leaders and with other people coping with the same problems. To locate support groups in your community, telephone your community mental health center, senior center, Jewish Community Center, YWCA, pastoral counseling center, community hospital, or family-service association.

Treatment for Depression

Fred C. is 73 years old and living alone. For the past year he's felt as though he were in a trance. He mopes around the house and has no interest in doing anything. Recently he was hospitalized and treated for depression, but he couldn't take the drugs prescribed because they made him nauseated. His psychiatrist suggested shock treatments, but he refused them. Now he's in outpatient psychotherapy, but he still feels depressed. He is beginning to wonder whether anything can be done to help him.

Antidepressant medication. As Fred has discovered, antidepressant medication combined with psychotherapy is usually the treatment of choice for depression. Sometimes people need to be hospitalized briefly to stabilize their symptoms, especially if they are not taking care of themselves or feel suicidal. Unfortunately, the medications have side-effects that many older people cannot tolerate. These side-effects may include low blood pressure, difficult urination, constipation, nausea, dry mouth, blurred vision, confusion, and even delirium.

Sometimes the cure sounds worse than the disease! However, physicians have access to a variety of drugs, and a geriatric specialist is skilled in selecting and monitoring drugs for older people. Typically, older people begin on approximately half the dose prescribed for healthy middle-aged adults, simply because older

Common Antidepressant Medications

	Sedation	*Other Side Effects*
Tricyclics and Heterocyclics		
Amitriptyline (Elavil)	+ + + +	+ + + +
Desipramine (Norpramin, Pertofrane)	+	+ +
Doxepin (Adapin, Sinequan)	+ + +	+ +
Fluoxetine (Prozac)	+	+
Maprotiline (Ludiomil)	+ +	+
Nortiptyline (Aventyl, Pamelor)	+	+ +
Trazodone (Desyrel)	+ + +	0
Monoamine Oxidase Inhibitors		
Isocarboxazid (Marplan)	0	+ + +
Nardil (Phenylzine)	0	+ + +
Tranylcypromine (Parnate)	0	+ + +
Lithium		
Lithium carbonate	0	+ +
Psychostimulants		
Methylphenidate (Ritalin)	0	+ + +

Legend: + + + + = very marked + = slight 0 = none

bodies process any drug more slowly. The physician usually increases the dosage slowly, watching for side-effects, until the desired effects are achieved.

In Fred's case, it is important that he talk with his physician or other mental health professional about trying a different medication. If Fred doesn't do this, family members or friends should take the initiative. Several types of antidepressants may be used, each designed to work differently. It's also important for Fred to give the healing process time and remain in treatment, even though he feels frustrated with it. Antidepressant medications can take several weeks to achieve results. Psychotherapy can also take an extended period of time.

Psychotherapy. Psychotherapy—either in individual or group sessions—is also effective in treating depressive illness. Individual psychotherapy can be done with a social worker, psychologist, or psychiatrist. It is most likely to be conducted on a short-term basis. Weekly appointments of fifty to sixty minutes are likely to last ten to twenty weeks. The initial focus is likely to be on reducing the symptoms of depression, with later sessions devoted to learning more about the self. Fred, for example, might begin to understand many things about himself:

- His typical way of coping with loss. For example, Fred may need to develop new strategies for coping that are more effective.
- His typical way of thinking. Fred may need to learn what he can do for himself to improve his mood (increase his level of activity, challenge his own negative thinking, and so on).
- His typical way of approaching people. Fred may need to learn new methods for developing relationships with

people, so that he is less lonely and has support when life's crises come his way.

Armed with this new knowledge, Fred can begin changing his behavior and improving his life.

A therapist might also encourage the depressed person to join a self-help group. In that setting, group members share emotional support with others who are learning to cope with being alone. Toward the end of therapy, a good therapist will try to anticipate future problems and identify alternate strategies to prevent these problems from causing another bout of depression. Finally, the therapist might schedule follow-up appointments to see how the person fares as time passes.

Short-term psychotherapy following the death of a loved one is usually quite effective. Depression that has no specific precipitating event and that lasts for long periods of time may require longer treatment—or a different approach altogether.

Electroconvulsive therapy. Ed G.'s twin brother, Sherman, age 68, has been severely depressed for about a year and seems to be losing touch with reality. Sherman does not get out of bed or eat unless someone urges him. When he does get up, he just sits in his living room all day. Ed has found Sherman sitting in his armchair staring at a blank television screen, talking to Lucille Ball. Medications have not helped Sherman's condition. His doctor has recommended that he have electroconvulsive therapy (ECT). Ed remembers that Sherman had ECT when he got out of the Army after World War II and that ECT helped Sherman to get better. However, both Ed and Sherman remember how awful "shock treatment" was, and Sherman doesn't want to go through that again. Ed doesn't know whether to urge his brother to go for ECT or just to keep hoping Sherman will once again lead a normal life.

Many people have negative feelings about ECT, which was a popular and often overused treatment in the 1940s and 1950s before modern antidepressant drugs were developed. For some people, however, antidepressant drugs and psychotherapy do not work. In those cases, ECT is frequently the only treatment that does work. If the person's depression is severe and other types of treatment have failed, then a psychiatrist may prescribe ECT. ECT can bring prompt relief to seriously depressed people, including those who are suicidal. (Whenever people are unsure about medical advice, of course, they should get a second opinion.)

It is important for Ed and Sherman to remember that Sherman responded successfully to ECT forty years ago and had a long-term recovery. Moreover, methods of administering ECT have improved considerably since then. Equipment is far better and safer than it was forty years ago. Patients receiving ECT today are given anesthesia and muscle relaxants, so that the procedure is safe and pain-free.

Typically, a patient receives between 4 and 12 treatments up to three times per week. Side effects include headache immediately after treatment and some temporary confusion or memory lapse. Unless patients have medical complications, they can be treated as outpatients. There is no need to check into a hospital. Although it may sound frightening, ECT is often highly effective, with essentially no long-term complications. The terrifying image of permanent brain damage from ECT, dramatized in the movie *One Flew Over the Cuckoo's Nest,* is simply not relevant today.

Conditions Commonly Associated with Depression

Ellie S., 51, believes her 74-year-old mother, Jean, is a hypochondriac. "Ever since she moved to the retirement home after Dad died, Mom's doctor-shopping has been driving me crazy," Ellie says. "She comes up with a new ailment every few weeks, so I have to take her to the doctor. As soon as the physician catches on and tells her that her problem is psychological, she decides he's no good and looks for a new doctor. All she wants to talk about are her physical problems and the hard times she had during the Depression. I'm at my wit's end. What can I do with her?"

Hypochondriasis. Jean's problem is a frustrating one that has become Ellie's as well. While recognizing that her ailments are real to her mother, Ellie should at the same time avoid reinforcing the symptoms with unnecessary attention. Ellie could help her mother by taking her to enjoyable activities that might divert her from her preoccupation with illness. Ellie also can try to engage her mother in other subjects during the outing. Ellie should support her mother's development of a relationship with one doctor—an internist, family physician, or geriatrician—to oversee Jean's medical care. Each new symptom must be assessed medically because a physical disorder may exist. No one should assume that another person's symptoms have no medical basis. A doctor must assess each person's condition.

"Hypochondriasis" is the psychiatric term for excessive concern with health. The condition may involve frequent complaints of physical problems for which no doctor can find a basis, and it often forms part of depressive illness. Hypochondriasis may follow a major life stressor such as the death of a spouse, a disabling health problem, a move to a new environment, or financial difficulties. It may also be part of a lifelong pattern. The ailments, complaints, and visits to medical offices may be a lonely person's way of getting much-needed attention or communicating with other people. By escaping into the sick role, the hypochondriac may also be avoiding responsibilities, problems, or relationships.

A perceptive physician or geriatrician can sometimes lead a hypochondriac to examine the real reasons for seeking help. A psychotherapist trained with older people can treat the depression, help the person to mourn any losses, and encourage the patient to find satisfying activities outside the doctor's office. For various reasons, Ellie's mother may have found it more acceptable to focus on physical complaints than on her emotional problems. What she needs to do is talk with a professional about her fear, anxiety, and loneliness. For her own emotional needs, Ellie would benefit from individual counseling. She might also join a support group for children of aging parents.

Paranoia. Raul's father passed away two years ago. A year later, his mother, Benita R., 79, sold their home and moved into an apartment on her own. Although she's healthy in general, she complains frequently of headaches and says, "I just don't feel like myself." The biggest concern to her family is that she's becoming forgetful. Her family is undergoing a lot of upheaval because Benita has been accusing them and her friends of stealing keepsakes from her apartment. Raul suspects his mother puts these things away for safekeeping and then forgets where she put them.

Before assuming that Benita has lost her things, Raul should check the possibility that someone really has been stealing from her. If the keepsakes turn up in the apartment, then Raul could consider several possibilities that might be contributing to his mother's paranoia.

Within the past two years, Benita has experienced two major life changes—loss of her husband and loss of her home. Living alone may be giving her too much time to dwell on her losses. She may need to have someone around to provide a "reality check" or a diversion from unhealthy thoughts.

In older people, depression and dementia are often confused and misdiagnosed; both can contribute to paranoid thinking. Memory loss may be a sign of changes in the brain (dementia) or another disorder, such as toxic levels of medication. The paranoid behavior could be Benita's way of accounting for her forgetfulness, or it could be her way of getting attention. If Benita's hearing or vision are fading, she may think other people are taking advantage of her inability to hear conversations or see clearly.

It is important for Raul and the rest of the family to be supportive of their mother. They should not try to reason or argue with her because they will not be able to convince her that her things were not stolen. Benita needs a thorough assessment by a geriatric specialist to diagnose the source of her distorted thinking. A mental health professional skilled in geriatrics can help Raul to explore helpful ways to express his concern over his mother's problems and engage her in other activities and topics of conversation. The counselor or therapist can also explore with Benita her feelings about her situation as well as the consequences of her behavior. Any use of medication must be carefully monitored and coordinated between her doctor and her mental health professional.

Physical illness. People often become severely depressed as a result of the illness and pain that occur with age. A loss of physical ability can lead to a loss of the feeling that we are worthwhile and capable human beings. It is important to speak openly with loved ones and friends in this predicament, even when we are not sure we are saying the right thing. The only thing worse than being incapacitated or in pain is feeling abandoned. (In chapter 7 we offer more suggestions for helping people with serious illness.)

Hearing loss. Do people sometimes tell you that you're shouting in conversations? Do you often ask people to repeat what they've said? Is it easier to understand people when you're facing them? Do you have ringing or buzzing in your ears?

Hearing loss often comes on gradually as we age, without our being aware of the disability it causes for us or the problems it creates for our loved ones. Audrey S., 63, says, "I began to lose my hearing when I was in my fifties, although I kept denying it. I refused to wear a hearing aid because I didn't want to look and feel old. I even stopped going to church after I could no longer hear the sermon well or understand what other people were saying after the service. I became depressed. I was responding inappropriately in conversations, and people began to think I was stupid. I stopped going to club meetings or seeing my friends because it felt as though everyone avoided me. When I asked a friend to repeat a remark, she would often say, 'It doesn't matter.' I then felt *I* didn't matter to people any more. Finally, an old friend visiting from out of town helped me understand how foolish I was being. I visited an audiologist for an examination, and now I wear two hearing aids. I enjoy life again, I feel part of conversations, and I am doing all the things I used to love."

Older people sometimes suffer much more over not dealing with their hearing loss than they do from the hearing loss itself. Like Audrey, they may develop depressive and paranoid symptoms. Like Audrey, they may become more and more isolated. A person's refusal to get treatment may cause friends and family such frustration over their inability to communicate that they begin to drift away. As a consequence, relationships can break down or wither away.

If you know someone who is denying a hearing loss, you can help by speaking openly but supportively about the problem, as Audrey's friend did. Assure the person of your concern and affection, and help him or her to explore local resources for evaluation. Although some hearing loss is inevitable with aging, we often exaggerate our fear of deafness. Many older people suffer hearing loss from build-up of wax in the outer ear canal or have a condition that is correctable with medication or surgery, such as middle-ear infection. It is important to start with a medical evaluation and if hearing aids are needed, to follow up with a visit to a reputable audiologist.

Anxiety

Another common emotional problem among older people, anxiety often has its source in loss—threatened or real. As we grow older, we become more aware of physical disabilities, losses of many types, the rapid pace of uncontrollable change in our lives, and the reality of death. Sometimes it is difficult to cope with these fears constructively. Often we look back on childhood experiences and assume unconsciously that we will undergo the same difficulties our elders did. It helps to find a support group or professional counselor with whom to explore these fears.

Mabel W., 64, had been diagnosed with breast cancer and was undergoing radiation treatment following removal of a small lump in her breast. Although her doctor had assured her that the outlook for her recovery was excellent because the lump was removed at an early stage, Mabel was feeling afraid of so many things that she thought she was losing her mind. She could no longer stay alone in her apartment because she worried that the neighbors were planning to break in and rob her in her sleep. She was afraid to drive her car. When her family talked with her, she seemed distracted and often didn't pay attention to what they were saying.

Mabel's family helped her find a counselor experienced with reactions to physical illness and trained in working with older people. The counselor helped Mabel explore her beliefs about sickness, pain, and dying. Mabel remembered her mother dying of cancer at home, without enough medication for pain, and it took some work for her to separate herself emotionally from her mother's condition. Like Mabel's, most cases of anxiety can be successfully treated. Often a combination of psychotherapy and medication is the most effective.

WARNING SIGNS FOR SUICIDE

People with a serious intention of killing themselves usually leave clues. In older people, suicide is rarely impulsive. Typically, it follows a long period of consideration and preparation.

Stay alert to the following unusual behaviors that can indicate deeper problems:

- *Statements such as "I want to die," "My family would be better off without me," "I won't be around much longer for them to worry about," or "Life isn't worth living any more."*
- *Self-neglect, including neglect of grooming, eating, taking important medication, and so on.*
- *Sudden attention to putting affairs in order or drawing up a will.*
- *Giving away money or special possessions.*
- *Unusual interest or disinterest in religion.*
- *Behavior that indicates the person is going on a long and distant trip.*
- *Nonchalant or careless reaction to bad news from a physician.*

If you see any of these signals, whether verbal or behavioral, do not ignore them. Talk with your friend or loved one about his or her feelings; if you are still concerned, call your local community mental health center for professional help.

Looking silly if you're wrong is a small price to pay compared with the grief of mourning a friend's tragic self-destruction. You can help!

Self-destruction

Most older people express satisfaction with their lives. Yet, according to the study *Elder Suicide,* conducted by the American Association of Retired Persons, "Americans over 65 have a suicide rate . . . 50 percent higher than that of the general population and represent the age group most at risk for suicide. The elderly are not only taking their lives in disproportionate numbers, but they generally do it quietly, with few pleas for help."

Whether self-destruction is accomplished slowly (by refusing to eat or take proper medications, for example) or quickly (with a lethal instrument or drug overdose), older people are more likely to take their own lives. Data from the National Center for Health Statistics indicate that the 1986 annual rate of suicide in the general population was 12 per 100,000 persons. Among people aged 65 to 74, however, the suicide rate was 18.5 per 100,000; and among people 75 to 84 years old, the rate was 24.1 per 100,000, or double the rate of the general population. These figures take into account only deaths from a specific event; they do not include slow self-destruction from self-neglect.

Elderly white men are most at risk for killing themselves, especially if they are isolated or widowed. Among all American men over 85, the suicide rate is four times that of adolescents, the next highest group. Men in their sixties are four times as likely to kill themselves as women in that age group; by age 85, men are twelve times as likely to do so. This is partly because women are likely to choose a method of attempting suicide such as overdosing on medication, which can be reversed if someone intervenes in time to save them. Men are likely to use more violent and sure methods, such as shooting themselves.

People may become despondent and think about killing themselves out of grief over loss of a loved one, despair over poor health, fears about losing financial security or social status, anxiety over the rapid and uncontrollable pace of change in their lives, intractable pain, or simple loneliness. Some people may find suicide a rational answer to a hopeless situation, such as a long, painful terminal illness.

Depressed or isolated people often have self-destructive feelings. When someone expresses a desire to commit suicide, friends and family need to take these comments seriously. People who talk about not wanting to live may be asking for help. If someone you know seems despondent, encourage your friend to talk about his or her sad feelings. Discuss the subject openly, rather than hoping the feelings will go away if you ignore them. Often, just having a confidant—someone who cares—is enough to give the depressed person a sense of having something to live for.

If you are concerned that someone may try to hurt himself or herself, call your local community mental health center or hospital emergency room for advice and assistance. Suicide stemming from depression may be prevented if the person receives professional help in coping with depression.

Alcohol Abuse

Some experts estimate that 15 to 20 percent of older Americans abuse alcohol, and many alcohol counselors believe that the percentage may be higher if we include older people who drink quietly and alone and do not come to the attention of the health-care system. At present, we plan treatment in different ways for two types of older alcoholics: those with a longstanding alcohol problem and those whose abuse began later in life, perhaps precipitated by a crisis or in response to the stresses of old age.

Lifelong alcoholism. David W. recently telephoned a senior-service center for assistance in coping with a family problem. On a weekly visit to his father and mother, Joshua and Helen W., now in their sixties, David's wife Rachel had a traumatic experience. She returned home in dismay, reporting that Joshua had made suggestive remarks and tried to kiss her. When Rachel moved away from him and told him she wasn't comfortable with his behavior, he laughed and followed her, persisting. David's mother was present during the afternoon, but she acted as though she didn't notice her husband's activities. Rachel is now in counseling at a family-service center and for the time being has refused to visit her parents-in-law or to allow David to take their young daughter to visit. Rachel says she feels abused and needs time to work through her feelings.

David agrees that Joshua's behavior was out of line, but he says it probably will never happen again. Joshua has been depressed since he retired, and he has been sexually impotent since his open-heart surgery a year ago. He has had a drinking problem for years. Joshua often talks about not living long, and David doesn't want to upset the family any further. David and Rachel have had a cordial relationship with his parents in the past, even though his father has always been domineering. David doesn't see why Rachel is making such a fuss.

During a counseling session with David, the social worker—specially trained in geriatrics and alcohol treatment—recommended that David urge Joshua to see his physician to determine whether the change in his behavior might be a symptom of an underlying medical problem. She also recommended that David join a support group for adult children of alcoholics to help him learn how to handle his reactions to his father's drinking problem. The social worker supported Rachel's need to find help for her feelings about being molested. David was troubled about the problems in the family, and he wanted to know whether anything could be done to help his father.

The social worker suggested that if the family really wanted to make changes, and if they cared enough for Joshua's health to help him, they would have to confront him about his alcohol use. Once Joshua's physician determined that there were no other medical problems affecting his behavior, the social worker and the physician coordinated a family conference to help Joshua. As an important preliminary step, the family members educated themselves about the disease of alcoholism. Some of them attended Al-Anon, a support group for family and loved ones of alcoholics. They learned about typical family behavior that protects and hides the problem, enabling it to occur. They learned some of the ways that drinking was ruining Joshua's health as well as splitting the family.

Alcohol is a depressant, and when someone uses it to feel better, it actually deepens the depressed feelings. It also reduces inhibition and judgment, which is why people like to drink at parties.

A longstanding alcohol problem can contribute to cardiovascular disease and impotence.

The members of an alcoholic's family often behave as Helen and David did. They impose a code of silence to keep from acknowledging the household goings-on. However, at the family conference, each person explained to Joshua what he or she had seen and experienced as a result of Joshua's drinking. Joshua's partner from his former business was asked to participate; he told Joshua about his experiences with Joshua's drinking problem. Joshua's physician and clergyman participated as well. The social worker and physician encouraged the group to emphasize the concern that everyone felt. Both family and friends agreed that Joshua had gone too far for anyone to allow his behavior to continue. Either he had to quit drinking or his family would disintegrate. He would see very little of his son, his daughter-in-law, and his grandchildren. He would never be left alone with his grandchildren, for fear his impaired judgment would allow him to molest or abuse them.

When Joshua was forced to acknowledge the damage his behavior was causing himself and his family, he broke down and asked for help. His physician had arranged a stay at an inpatient alcohol treatment center, where Joshua was immediately admitted for a month to begin recovery under medical supervision. Joshua's family applauded his decision to stop drinking, and during the ensuing months, all the family found support groups to help them adjust to living with a new set of relationships. Joshua's mood lightened with treatment, and he began to feel he had something to live for. After his discharge from the detoxification center, he began attending meetings of Alcoholics Anonymous on a regular basis. He found many people like himself there.

Like many Americans, Joshua had found it difficult to accept

SIGNS OF ALCOHOLISM

Many clues point to the possibility that someone is an alcoholic. But some of these clues are subtle and could be signs of other problems. For example, early signs of alcoholism include marital problems, difficulties at work, changes in patterns of drinking, and on-and-off bouts of depression and anxiety. It may be difficult to tell whether emotional ups and downs result from alcohol abuse or from something else. An alcoholism specialist will take these signs into account as part of a whole picture.

Here are some other clues to alcoholism:

- *History of alcoholism in the family.*
- *Rigid drinking patterns. For example, allowing nothing to interfere with the cocktail hour or insisting on alcohol with sports programs.*
- *Inability to stop or control drinking, except for brief periods. Drinking patterns that have persisted over the years.*
- *Growing use of and preoccupation with alcohol. Drinking more often. Making certain that alcohol is always available at home or on social occasions.*
- *Sneaking drinks.*
- *Going on the wagon and then falling off. This usually happens more than once.*
- *Evasiveness or defensiveness about alcohol. Tendency to blame drinking on other people or on life's problems.*
- *Frequent mood swings. Personality changes that cannot be explained by causes or conditions.*
- *Increasing self-pity. Tendency to spend more time alone because of deteriorating relationships with family and friends.*
- *Blackouts. During an alcoholic blackout, the person may seem to function normally. However, later he or she cannot remember what happened during that time.*
- *Hiding a supply of alcohol. Hiding places may include the toilet tank, a file cabinet at work, the car, or out-of-the-way cupboards and closets at home.*
- *Missed appointments, work, or social occasions because of drinking.*
- *Neglect of adequate nutrition.*
- *Decrease in sexual desire and potency.*
- *Persistent drinking in spite of medical advice or family disruptions caused by alcohol.*

SIGNS OF LATE-ONSET ALCOHOLISM

Alcohol abuse has been closely linked to the stresses associated with aging. Most frequently, late-onset alcoholics are widows and widowers within five years of their bereavement. However, it is difficult to identify problem drinkers among the elderly because so many older alcoholics drink alone, quietly and secretly. Although an older person who develops a drinking problem late in life may show many symptoms common to a lifelong alcoholic, the signs of late-onset alcoholism are often more indirect:

- *odor on breath*
- *flushed face*
- *bruises or broken bones*
- *incidents of excessive drinking*
- *refusal to answer the telephone*
- *mail or newspapers piling up in or outside the home*
- *frequent trips to the hospital*
- *overly neat home or excessive self-grooming (because of overcompensation)*
- *legal difficulties (often because bills go unpaid)*
- *erratic eating and sleeping patterns*

Note that these signs may also indicate abuse of prescription drugs—a pattern that may result from emotional difficulties or from confusion and memory loss.

It is important to seek treatment from a center experienced with the problems of older people, such as a hospital geriatric center. Your local branch of the National Council on Alcoholism can also provide an outreach worker or referrals for treatment.

his alcoholism. People from the generations that suffered through the Depression and World War II are accustomed to using alcohol, often not recognizing that it is an addictive drug. They may think, "I've worked hard, and I deserve to relax a little and enjoy myself." They may think of alcoholics as "skid-row bums," believing that they are immune to this disease because they have a more affluent lifestyle. What these people may not realize is that, as we age, alcohol becomes more toxic to our bodies, and a few drinks do more damage to our judgment than they used to.

If you suspect that you or a loved one may be suffering from alcoholism, you can find information and help through local alcoholism-treatment agencies and hospitals. Medicare covers inpatient treatment for three to twenty-eight days. For long-term support, local chapters of the National Council on Alcoholism and Alcoholics Anonymous offer support groups and referrals for counseling. Check your yellow pages for agencies that can help.

Late-onset alcoholism. Gina C. needs advice about her 74-year-old mother. "Mother has been drinking heavily for more than a year, since Dad died. She doesn't care about her appearance, she isn't eating right, and sometimes she refuses to let me in her apartment. Yet she calls me at all hours crying and complaining about her aches and pains. What can I do?"

Gina can do four things to help. She can

- stop pretending with her mother and let her know that her drinking is a problem;
- get professional help for her mother;
- give her mother as much emotional support as possible; and
- seek emotional support for herself, so that she can cope with her mother's behavior.

Gina's mother is one of a large number of elderly alcoholics. Often older persons turn to alcohol after a loss such as dwindling financial assets, a decline in health, or the death of a friend. Women are most susceptible to late-onset alcoholism, especially between the ages of 45 and 55 (about the time their children leave home) and 65 and 75 (during retirement years when wives often become widows). Probably Gina's mother turned to alcohol to relieve her grief and loneliness, not understanding that the depressant effects would make her condition worse.

Gina's mother sees herself as helpless and hopeless. She is trying to cope in the only way she knows. She needs Gina's love and compassion to help her through this crisis. It is important for her to take part in activities that occupy her thoughts and energies. She may need a live-in companion to ease her loneliness and assist her with meals and bathing.

Treatment for late-onset alcoholism, in which a drinking problem begins late in life, differs from treatment for lifelong alcoholism. It focuses on identifying the emotional needs of the older person and finding ways to meet those needs, so that the person has something besides alcohol for comfort and relief of psychological pain. Treatment can also include providing support for Gina as she tries to help her mother without putting undue strain on her own life. A social worker skilled in long-term care and geriatrics can evaluate the psychosocial problems of the elderly alcoholic and find resources to help. A physician can be helpful in diagnosing the illness, arranging medical treatment (if needed), and treating other health problems.

Hospitals, senior-service centers, and geriatric treatment centers at colleges and universities can help you find treatment for an elderly, late-onset alcoholic. Your local chapter of the National Council on Alcoholism can also refer you to treatment agencies and professionals.

Self-Help Measures

Although professional help for painful reactions to life's crises is more accessible and effective than ever before, we can do a great deal to care for our own mental health. We have little control over the loss of a spouse or the onset of physical disability, but we can shape our responses to the losses and changes in life. We can gradually develop new patterns—or expand old ones—that will buffer us against the stresses we may encounter with aging. Learning to tell others about our needs and feelings, staying involved with other people, reminiscing, and practicing stress-reduction and relaxation techniques are all protective patterns that help keep us mentally healthy.

Telling Your Feelings

Murray T., 63, was told he had prostate cancer just a few years before he had planned to retire from his job of thirty years as an aerospace engineer. He had many friends and good relationships at work, but now he was spending his time in medical treatment and recovering at home. His wife, Bess, tried to keep his spirits up, but he became more and more depressed. His grief over his illness and his fear of dying were compounded by loneliness. When Bess contacted the American Cancer Society, a social worker at the agency offered some supportive counseling to the couple. When the worker asked whether Murray's friends had been coming to see him, Murray shrugged, "They called at first, but now I never hear from them. I guess they've forgotten me."

As the social worker pointed out, people are often at a loss to know how to respond to tragedy in a friend's life. Aside from the few rituals we still maintain in American society, such as attending funerals and sending flowers to hospital rooms, we haven't learned the right thing to do or say when someone we know is suffering. Many of us were raised to be self-reliant and to take care of our own problems, so we feel reluctant to "intrude" on other people's difficulties. And so we often let time pass without doing much. As in Murray's case, we "forget" about the person who has dropped out of our routine, especially if his or her condition reminds us of something we fear, such as serious illness.

What could Murray and Bess do to improve Murray's mood and reduce his loneliness? The counselor suggested that one of them call a few special friends from work to let them know how Murray is doing. Perhaps Murray could invite someone for lunch or for a visit on the way home from work. During the conversation, Murray could let his friends know that he missed their company and would welcome their visits and telephone calls.

Murray thought his friends knew how he felt, but unfortunately, few of us are mind readers. Although we like to believe that others know we love them without being told—and that they understand our needs and feelings—those beliefs are wishful thinking. Most people don't know what others need unless they ask or are told. And if we don't communicate our needs clearly, others may misinterpret our behavior.

Murray was probably misinterpreting his friends' silence to mean that they had forgotten him. His friends were probably misinterpreting his silence to mean that Murray was terribly ill or that he was doing fine and didn't need to hear from them. Without clear communication, both Murray and his friends were interpreting incorrectly.

It was difficult for Murray to take the step of letting his friends know he wanted to see them, but once he did, they responded right away. When Murray understood that his friends had been fearful of saying the wrong thing, and when his friends understood that Murray needed to know they hadn't forgotten him, the situation improved. Old buddies came by to visit, finding the same friend they had known for years and enjoying his company. They made it a point to call him regularly if they couldn't come to see him. Murray's depression and loneliness lifted.

Staying Involved with People

Although some people are lifelong loners, preferring their own company to others', most of us feel more balanced when we have a network of friends and acquaintances we can turn to for support. In fact, research has shown a strong connection between having a social network and a person's mental and physical well-being. For example, a study in California of seven thousand adults aged 30 to 59 showed that people live longer when they have a network of friends or family relationships, and when they visit these folks frequently or have other kinds of contact with them. Other studies have shown that older people who say they have a good social network live longer than people who describe themselves as isolated and alone.

We especially need our social networks during times of stress and loss, such as a death in the family, a serious illness, a separation, or a financial problem. During these times, other people may offer support by passing along important information, giving material help such as money or food, or providing emotional support. When we receive these things from others, even on a small scale, we know someone cares about us. Knowing someone cares enough to be there makes a big difference in how depressed or anxious we become during stressful times.

We maintain our social networks by giving support back to others. In fact, the most valuable way we pay back others for receiving help is by helping them. And because being generous and

helpful to others usually makes us feel good and gives us a sense that we are needed, we maintain our emotional and psychological balance by both giving and receiving support. Support works two ways. Modern behavioral science has gone to great lengths to rediscover some old truths. Both giving and having the grace to receive are critical to our mental health.

How do these generalizations apply to real life? Suppose our friends are gone and our family has moved to another part of the country? Suppose we've been relocated from a foreign land? Suppose we're bed-bound or too disabled to get out of the house? How do we connect with other people in a new place when we're 76 years old? How can we cultivate a social life when all our lives we depended on a spouse to make such plans? How do we start making new friends late in life?

You don't have to change your personality to find sources of support, but you may have to take a few risks, get rejected occasionally, or try out some unfamiliar situations. Here are two sources of new friends you may not have considered.

Volunteer work. Herb G., 72, volunteers twice a week at his local hospital, pushing wheelchairs and helping patients. Tom R., 68, a retired police officer, volunteers at his local Red Cross chapter. He teaches First Aid and CPR classes and helps disaster victims in the area. Gina M., 62, volunteers through her church as a companion to older people who are disabled or homebound. Harry M., 55, has joined the Gray Panthers. He organizes presentations at public hearings on issues important to older people. Frieda N., 66, is a volunteer member of the Service Corps of Retired Executives (SCORE), a group that provides free counseling to small businesses. They share their knowledge and experience to help people run their businesses or start new ones.

Gloria R. asks, "My husband and I are in our mid-sixties and in good health. We have retired comfortably and do volunteer work in the community. Sharing our experience and skills is important to us. We are interested in information about the Peace Corps. Do they accept older volunteers?" The answer to Gloria's question is yes. In fact, the Peace Corps considers age an asset. There is no upper age limit. Older people have accumulated a lifetime of knowledge and wisdom and years of experience in their trades or professions. No other single group has more to offer the people of developing countries. The number of volunteers over 50 years old and serving overseas is growing. Some older volunteers have found themselves more adaptable and more accepted than younger workers. The older volunteers may receive more respect in countries that hold their elders in high esteem. Joining the Peace Corps is a serious commitment as well as a way of trying out new possibilities in life.

When you follow your interests, you will find someone who needs your help. (Chapter 10 offers additional suggestions for volunteer activities.) As you become actively involved with others, you will find new friends and acquaintances, share your own skills and strengths with them, and warm yourself in the glow of knowing that someone else needs you and cares about you.

Groups. Are you a single person? A domino player? A quilter? A recovered alcoholic? A heart patient? A university alumnus? A singer or dancer? A group has formed for almost every interest and activity. Some groups are formal and highly structured, such as a bridge club, choral group, or bowling team. Others are less formal but sometimes more supportive, such as a neighborhood club or coffee group, a mutual support group for people with a particular disability or illness, or a self-help group for people maintaining their freedom from alcoholism or drug use.

Some people feel that joining a group is an admission of weakness, that all groups do is sit around and cry about their problems.

As any member of a healthy support group can tell you, just the opposite is the case. Joining a support group means that you're strong enough to ask for and receive help when you need it and that you're willing to help others with similar problems.

Some support groups are organized and led by their members; others may be organized by community-service agencies and led by professional facilitators. Some groups meet simply to share experience and support; others have a more specific aim of helping with emotional problems (group therapy). Choose your group by evaluating whether it meets your needs at the moment, whether it meets at a convenient time and safe place for you, and whether you have something in common with other members.

Elinor S., 75, was living alone and progressively becoming more withdrawn and depressed. At her doctor's urging, she joined a group for older people who live alone. In six months, the group had a profound effect on her life. She developed new friends and felt less depressed. Overall, she became more outgoing, as she used to be in her younger years. The group has helped many older people who felt isolated and lonely.

In a good group, individuals share their problems and group members share solutions. Learning to share difficulties and receive support from others helps members to find ways to overcome problems. Even when solutions do not exist, airing feelings and listening to others help make problems easier to live with. Your local mental health center or senior center would be good places to begin finding out about groups available in your area.

Reminiscing

Robert Butler, geriatric psychiatrist and founding director of the National Institute on Aging, has concluded that although the task of young people is to accumulate experience piece by piece, the task of older people is to "enjoy the finished product." Our image of "old codgers" sitting on store-front benches and chewing over the past is based on an effective technique for mental health: reminiscence. Reviewing the past—telling people about it or writing it down—allows us to continue to grow and adapt to new situations by using our own experience. The popular put-down of older people as dwelling in the past is no longer valid. Older people have been unfairly made to feel embarrassed and ashamed of reminiscing, telling themselves, "I'm boring everyone. I guess I've told that story before." We now understand that reviewing the past, making sense of our experiences by turning them over in our minds, is essential to keeping our emotional equilibrium as we age.

Even someone who is very depressed can get a lift by telling someone about a life experience. John T., 71, for example, was spending his last days in bed with an oxygen tank at his side. Although he had little physical pain, he was feeling depressed and lonely in spite of his wife and family's efforts. One day he showed a visitor some snapshots taken during his active life as a logger and sawmill foreman. The visitor commented on how interesting John's experiences had been and suggested he make a tape recording for his family. When the visitor returned, she brought a supply of blank tapes and helped John record his life. He could talk only for short periods, but he managed to make several tapes as a legacy to his family. From the time he began reminiscing, his mood improved. He smiled more and seemed less fretful. He was making sense of his life and leaving something important to his descendants.

Often people are comforted by reviewing their past experiences, but sometimes sadness or anger may well up. Even when tears or depression occur, they will usually pass within a short time. It's important to allow these feelings to come and go freely, without trying to force them. They are part of the process of integration—making a coherent whole out of a lifetime's experience.

So maybe it's time to start that journal or notebook. Write down those experiences that will never come again: the trips in the old cars, the Depression or war years, the first date, the first baby, memories of the farm or the city streets that have been permanently changed. Insert pictures from old magazines or photos and mementos. Take pleasure in the memories, and enjoy knowing that someday younger generations will learn from you the things they might never learn in any other way. At the Huntington Library, in San Marino, California, along with the first-folio Shakespeare, the Gutenberg Bible, and the Ellsmere manuscript of Chaucer is another valuable collection: diaries from men and women who crossed the United States during the frontier days. Many of these diaries have been published, and some of the most interesting are the daily records of ordinary people: pioneer women trying to make meals out of dried beans, flour, and brackish water; men hoping to make something of their lives by shoveling dirt in the California Gold Rush. These diaries are invaluable to historians and, more important, to the families and descendants of the writers.

If you are visiting someone in a nursing home, try spending time really listening to the old stories. Ask questions about old times, or take along some old photos to get the reminiscing started. If the conversation mostly turns to the person's failings in life, listen sympathetically until you're tired of the topic, and then turn the conversation around by asking questions with a positive orientation:

- What did you most like to eat as a child?
- Who was most important to you when you were growing up?
- What was the best day of your life?

Let the conversation flow as the speaker wishes, and be sure to stop while everyone is still enjoying the process. Children are a valuable addition to the group because they often ask good questions and because the stories may be new for them. Be flexible about time; people's energy varies, so the reminiscence may engross them for only a few moments one day and an hour the next.

Reminiscing is therapeutic for most of us. Whether you do it on tape, on paper, or in conversation, it is a normal and important part of healthy aging. Relax and enjoy it!

Coping with Stress

In teaching patients new habits to improve their cardiovascular condition, many physicians include instruction in daily relaxation and meditation right along with information on medication, diet, and exercise. Some physicians consider stress-management exercises (many of them adapted from yoga) to be a critical part of a program for improved cardiovascular health. The destructive effect of uncontrolled stress on our physical and mental health is well known. What do we mean by stress? And why is this topic especially important to older adults?

In the 1930s, researchers first demonstrated the stress reaction in animals. They found that when an animal is exposed to stressors such as cold, fatigue, or fear, its hormonal system responds to stimulate a faster heart beat, higher blood pressure, dilated pupils, and slowed digestion. Later researchers confirmed that people have the same internal reactions whether the stress comes from a physical threat, such as an auto accident, or a psychological situation, such as a heated argument. In the 1940s and 1950s, University of Washington psychiatrist Thomas Holmes and psychologist Richard Rahe studied the responses of five thousand people to discover the adjustment needed for various events in life. They found that the most stressful events were death of a spouse, divorce, separation, and death of a close family member—events that commonly occur in later life. However, many happy times were also found to cause great stress: marriage, birth, or moving to a new home. A high score on the Holmes-Rahe scale (representing several stressful life events or a few highly stressful ones) often precedes illness or accidents.

Although other researchers believe that stress is better measured in different ways, such as by the accumulation of daily annoyances or by the amount of control we feel over our problems, most agree that dealing with stress constructively is getting harder as times change. We are naturally constructed to cope with stress by taking physical action. For example, when we see a poisonous snake in the trail during a hike, our stress hormones (norepinephrine and epinephrine, formerly known as adrenaline) respond to the alarm by preparing our bodies to run away or to attack the snake. This automatic reaction is called the fight-or-flight response. Unfortunately, in modern life we often experience stress in ways that do not allow a physical response. When someone cuts us off on the highway, we may mutter something under our breath, but we can't run away or attack the other driver. When we encounter changes and losses in later life, we cannot solve the problems by attacking or fleeing them physically.

How can you stay healthy with all this unresolved stress? You can do many things to improve your responses to stress:

- Stay involved with other people. Cultivate your social network (see suggestions earlier in this chapter). Let others know how you feel about things. Be a good listener in return.
- Exercise regularly, at least twice a week, and emphasize positive thoughts while you do (see chapter 1). Exercise is a natural way to release tension, thereby reducing the effects of stress on your body and restoring emotional balance.

• Get some fun into your life. If you don't have enough people to laugh with, enjoy videotapes of comic movies or check out funny books from the library. Laughing—looking for the humor in your situation—helps you cope with the stressful times in later life.

• Do a daily attitude check: Focus on the positive aspects of your situation; avoid dwelling on failures; take some risks to make a change in your life.

• Keep in touch with the trees. Just looking at nature reduces stress and relaxes most people. If you can walk by the ocean or on a hiking trail, take advantage of your fortunate location. If you can't find a tree, put a few flowers in your room and take time to enjoy them frequently.

• When life seems out of control, choose something manageable to rearrange or clean up. Straightening your desk, cleaning out the garage, or working in the garden can relax you and give you a renewed sense of competence and control. Notice your improved outlook after you've pulled a few weeds!

• Learn a relaxation technique you can enjoy every day.

Relaxing yourself. When you deliberately relax your body, you benefit more than your cardiovascular and digestive systems, you also benefit your psychological balance. Depressed and anxious feelings lessen. You regain your sense of control and your understanding of what is really important.

Some people relax by using formal techniques such as yoga, meditation, self-hypnosis, meditative prayer, or progressive relaxation. Others relax by knitting, talking with friends, seeing a movie, reading, or gardening. It is important to have a relaxation period—(your nap doesn't count!)—once or twice a day. Here are some guidelines for the relaxation response technique developed by Herbert Benson, associate professor of medicine at the Harvard Medical School.

1. Choose a word or phrase that means something important to you. You might choose a religious phrase such as "shalom" or "I will fear no evil," or a word such as "love," "hope," or "peace." You can also use neutral words, such as "one" or "let go."

2. Find a quiet, private place.

3. Get into a comfortable position, either sitting or lying down. Let your arms and legs rest in an open position, uncrossed. Loosen tight clothing and shoes.

4. Gently let your eyes close.

5. Relax your muscles. One way to do this is by tensing and then releasing your muscles in groups, progressing through your body from foot to scalp. Another technique is to let your whole body melt into your chair, first noticing and then relaxing any tense spots.

6. Breathe slowly and naturally. As you do, repeat your focus word or phrase during exhalations. It is most effective to inhale through your nose, and then gently say your word as you exhale slowly through your mouth.

7. Let thoughts drift out of your mind. Don't worry about how well you're doing. When other thoughts come to mind, just let them drift away and return to repeating your word.

8. Continue for 10 to 20 minutes.

This relaxation exercise is most effective when done twice a day, preferably before meals instead of afterward.

As with exercise and diet, feeling better is mostly a matter of making small changes, repeatedly, over a period of time. Although we may need professional help occasionally for major problems, most of us can stay emotionally balanced by learning to cope with stresses in healthy ways. As we age, we all experience problems with physical changes and the loss of loved ones. We can add to the strategies that we've learned over the years, adapting to change and dealing with the challenges life brings—with a little help from our friends.

Resources

Alcoholics Anonymous, General Services Board, 468 Park Avenue South, New York, NY 10016. Telephone: (212) 686-1100.
Offers a wide array of services and publications helpful to both alcoholics and their family members. For information, call a local chapter of AA.

American Psychiatric Association, 1400 K Street, NW, Washington, DC 20005. Telephone: (202) 682-6000.

American Psychological Association, 1200 17th Street, NW, Washington, DC 20036. Telephone: (202) 955-7600.

Gray Panther Project Fund, 3700 Chestnut Street, Philadelphia, PA 19104. Telephone: (215) 382-3300.
Information is available on the Gray Panther networks operating throughout the United States.

Narcotics Anonymous, World Service Office, P.O. Box 9999, Van Nuys, CA 91409. Telephone: (818) 780-3951.
Narcotics Anonymous offers support to people addicted to drugs, including prescription drugs, as well as to their families and friends. Based on Alcoholics Anonymous's twelve-step recovery program, NA has local chapters throughout the United States. Look in the telephone book for your local chapter. If you know someone who you suspect has a drug-abuse problem, NA may be able to offer guidance and resources.

National Association of Area Agencies on Aging, 600 Maryland Avenue, SW, Room 208, Washington, DC 20024. Telephone: (202) 484-7520.
Contact this association to locate your local Area Agency on Aging.

National Association of Social Workers, 1425 H Street, NW, Suite 600, Washington, DC 20005. Telephone: (202) 457-0492.

National Council on Alcoholism, 1424 16th St., NW, Suite 401, Washington, DC 20036. Telephone: (202) 737-8122.

National Mental Health Association, 1021 Prince Street, Alexandria, VA 22314. Telephone: (703) 548-0010.
Write for free, informative booklets on "How to Deal with Your Tensions," "Coping with Everyday Problems," and other publications dealing with emotional and psychological problems.

Peace Corps, P-301, Washington, DC 20526. Telephone: (800) 424-8580, ext. 93.

Service Corps of Retired Executives, 1129 20th Street, NW, Suite 410, Washington, DC 20036. Telephone: (202) 653-6279.
Contact the national headquarters or the district office of the United States Small Business Administration.

Recommended Reading

Benson, Herbert, and William Proctor. *Beyond the Relaxation Response.* New York: Times Books, 1984.

Burns, David D. *Feeling Good: The New Mood Therapy.* New York: Signet, 1980.

Doress, Paula Brown, Diana Laskin Siegal, and the Midlife and Older Women Book Project. *Ourselves, Growing Older.* New York: Simon and Schuster, 1987.

Ford, Betty, and Chris Chase. *The Times of My Life.* New York: Ballantine, 1979.
In two chapters of this biography, former First Lady Betty Ford candidly describes her family's intervention in confronting her alcoholism. She also recounts her experiences during recovery.

Mann, Marty. *Marty Mann Answers Your Questions about Drinking and Alcoholism.* Revised edition. Orlando, FL: Holt, Rinehart & Winston, 1981.
Marty Mann is a cofounder of the National Council on Alcoholism, a self-help organization.

Milam, James R., and Katherine Ketcham. *Under the Influence: A Guide to the Myths and Realities of Alcoholism.* Toronto: Bantam, 1981.

CHAPTER FOUR

The Health Insurance Puzzle

There are many, many of these policies . . . available today and most of them with convoluted language even a legal scholar couldn't untangle.

—David Horowitz, consumer commentator, testifying at a hearing on catastrophic health insurance

Confronted with a dizzying array of health-care plans and skyrocketing costs, many consumers now approach health insurance in the same way they approach taxes: with a mixture of dread, resignation, and a sense that somehow they're being ripped off. These feelings are particularly strong among older men and women who worry that health-care costs and the costs of long-term care may deplete their savings.

These frequently asked questions illustrate a few of the complex health-insurance concerns with which older Americans are grappling:

- "Should I buy long-term-care insurance? If so, what policies are best?"
- "I'm considering joining a health maintenance organization (HMO). How do HMOs compare with traditional insurance plans?"
- "Do I need private insurance to supplement Medicare? How much extra coverage will be enough?"
- "My wife needs nursing-home care. How can I pay her expenses and still have enough money to take care of myself?"

The bad news is that there are no simple answers to these questions. Only you can choose the insurance you need. The good news is that once you have obtained accurate information, you can make intelligent choices to match your needs.

In this chapter, we give you the information you need to make choices about health insurance. We review Medicare and Medicaid benefits, compare the private health-care plans now available, provide tips for evaluating supplemental health-care policies, consider ways to cover costs of long-term care, and offer suggestions to help you trim health-care costs without cutting quality. First, however, let's look at an important difference that can affect insurance costs and coverage.

Group Plans versus Individual Plans

Helen S. is a 56-year-old widow with an individual health-insurance policy. Jerry K. is a 62-year-old engineer with group coverage provided by his employer. Helen and Jerry have the same personal physician, but there are major differences between their insurance plans—and thus between the costs of their health care.

Helen selected her insurer after shopping around extensively. By contrast, Jerry's employer chose his. Helen's policy is tailored to her particular needs, while Jerry's is designed to cover an average employee. When problems with billing or payment arise, Helen calls the insurer directly; Jerry contacts a group administrator. Helen's benefits cannot be changed without her approval; Jerry's can, at the direction of his employer. Helen is covered as long as she pays the premiums, but Jerry's benefits may stop when he retires or changes jobs.

You might think that Helen's insurance plan is the more desirable one—and clearly, individual health policies have advantages—but given the choice, Helen would rather be in Jerry's shoes. Why? Because group insurance coverage costs the consumer less than comparable individual coverage does. Moreover, many employers who offer group health benefits subsidize the premiums, so that workers pay even less for their coverage. For example, Jerry pays only $40 per month for health-care coverage, about one-fifth of the amount Helen spends. Another bonus is that many group plans provide more comprehensive coverage, including benefits for extras such as dental and vision care.

If your employer, former employer, or union offers group health insurance, you should almost always enroll in the insurance plan. You'll probably receive adequate coverage for hospital and medical care at comparatively low monthly premiums. If you do not have group coverage through employment, you may be eligible for group insurance through a professional association or fraternity. Before buying, shop around, though, because some association group rates are higher than those for comparable individual policies.

When you reach age 65, you will be eligible for Medicare, the nation's largest group insurance plan for older Americans, with thirty-three million members nationwide.

Medicare

Because Medicare coverage has been available since 1965, and because news about it often makes headlines, most older Americans are aware of this federal health-insurance program. Nevertheless, only one in five Americans aged 45 or older say they know "a lot" about Medicare, according to a 1987 survey commissioned by the American Association of Retired Persons (AARP). Three-quarters of those over age 45 admit they know "not much" or "only some" about what Medicare covers and how much it pays in reimbursement. Knowing a little about Medicare can be worse than knowing nothing, because knowing a little may lead a person to false assumptions about the program.

Alice J. figured she'd save a bundle on health care once she started receiving Medicare because she thought the program was free. She was dismayed when staff at the social security office, which administers Medicare locally, told her that *beneficiaries are required to pay premiums, deductibles, and coinsurance* (a percentage of some charges). Indeed, total out-of-pocket health costs for older people average about 15 percent of their income—the same proportion as before Medicare was enacted, according to the Senate Special Committee on Aging.

Although Peter L., sales manager for a small business, planned to keep working after he turned 65, he wanted to start receiving Medicare because its health benefits were better than those his employer offered. He assumed that he would automatically be enrolled in Medicare on his sixty-fifth birthday. Three months afterward, he called the social security office to find out why he hadn't received his Medicare card. He was told he needed to apply for benefits. *Enrollment is automatic only for retirees.*

Maria G. was determined to take care of her husband, who had Alzheimer's disease. But when Carlos started wandering at night, becoming belligerent when she tried to prevent him from leaving the house, Maria decided he needed the round-the-clock care and security of a nursing home. She knew Medicare would not foot the whole nursing-home bill, but she had heard it provided partial reimbursement. She was shocked to learn that Medicare defines the care Carlos needed as "custodial," and *Medicare does not pay for custodial care.*

Don't assume that you've got the scoop on Medicare. Get the facts! Medicare rules and regulations are not cast in stone. They may change rapidly, as many beneficiaries discovered when Con-

KEEP AN EYE ON THE FUTURE

These days, about the only thing you can count on in the health-care financing field is change—and plenty of it.

A case in point: When California Assemblyman Willie Brown drafted state legislation in 1989 requiring small companies to provide health insurance for their workers, he stipulated that the law would not take effect until January 1, 1993. Why the lengthy delay? "To give Congress time to enact a national health insurance plan and thus render the Brown plan unnecessary," reported the Los Angeles Times.

Brown is not the only one anticipating change. With at least 35 million Americans uninsured, and with hospital and medical costs climbing at about twice the rate of inflation, everyone from government decisionmakers to businesspeople to the man on the street agrees that something must be done to improve our present health-care system. Consequently, a flurry of activity at both national and state levels has attempted solutions. If enacted, any of the proposals described below could have a profound impact on your health-insurance needs—although it's too early to predict exactly how. Here's what the future might hold:

- National health insurance: *What do Chrysler chairman Lee Iacocca, Princeton economist Uwe E. Reinhardt, a national physicians' group, and former presidents Jimmy Carter, Gerald R. Ford, and Richard M. Nixon have in common? They all support some type of universal health-insurance plan to guarantee coverage for every American. Of course, they have yet to agree on the details. For example, should the plan be financed through existing funding sources, income and excise taxes, or new taxes on workers and businesses? Tune in to national news reports or check your newspaper for the latest updates.*
- Comprehensive long-term health care: *"The 1990s may very well be do-or-die time for long-term care," predicts Representative Edward R. Roybal (D-Ca.), chair of the House Select Committee on Aging. Other congressional leaders agree. Senator David Pryor (D-Ark.), chair of the Senate Special Committee on Aging, notes that the 1990s "will reveal what Congress has learned from the outcome of the catastrophic-care legislation, and how to apply that knowledge to the long-term health-care needs of older Americans." Despite growing consensus that the long-term-care problem demands a national solution, policymakers continue to seek the best answer. What benefits should be provided? Who should be eligible for them? Who will pay for them? If you have any suggestions, convey them to your representatives in Congress.*
- More accurate prediction of future obligations for retirees' health insurance: *A new accounting standard approved by the federal Financial Accounting Standards Board in 1991 may cut health-care benefits for retirees when it takes effect in January 1993. The rule change requires employers to calculate their future medical expenses for retirees and deduct that amount from the company's current earnings. At present, employers deduct from their profits only what they pay out for health-insurance premiums in any given year. The new rule "has companies scurrying to revamp their benefits and limit coverage," reports the* Wall Street Journal.

gress enacted the first major expansion of the program in 1988 and then turned around and repealed the catastrophic care benefits in 1989.

To help you separate fact from myth, we'll review some of the key features of Medicare programs. For more detailed information about eligibility, benefits, and reimbursement, consult *The Medicare Handbook*. To obtain a free copy, visit your local social security office or call toll-free (800) 234-5772.

How Do I Enroll?

Age 65 is Medicare's age of eligibility. Almost anyone 65 or older can enroll in Medicare, but if neither you nor your spouse has accumulated enough social security or government work credits to be insured for Medicare purposes, you'll have to buy into the system ($206.90 per month in 1991 for most enrollees). (If you're under 65 and have a terminal illness or are otherwise disabled, call your local social security office for information about eligibility and enrollment.)

In some cases enrollment is automatic; in others, you have to apply. If you're receiving social security or railroad retirement benefits, you will automatically be enrolled in Medicare on your 65th birthday. But if you plan to continue working past age 65, or if you have to buy into the system, you must take the initiative and apply. You should do this three months before your 65th birthday. For more information or to schedule an appointment, call your local social security office.

What Medicare Covers

Medicare consists of two parts. Part A, the hospital insurance, covers inpatient care, skilled home-health care, hospice care, and some convalescence in a skilled-nursing facility (see table 4-1).

Table 4-1. Medicare (Part A): Hospital Insurance-Covered Services per Benefit Period[1]

Services	*Benefit*	*Medicare Pays[2]*	*You Pay[2]*
Hospitalization	First 60 days	All but $628	$628
Semiprivate room and board, general nursing, and miscellaneous hospital services and supplies	61st to 90th day	All but $157 a day	$157 a day
	91st to 150th day[3]	All but $314 a day	$314 a day
	Beyond 150 days	Nothing	All costs
Posthospital skilled-nursing facility care	First 20 days	100% of approved amount	Nothing
You must be in a hospital for at least 3 days and enter a Medicare-approved facility generally within 30 days after hospital discharge[4]	Additional 80 days	All but $78.50 a day	$78.50 a day
	Beyond 100 days	Nothing	All costs
Home health care	Medically necessary skilled care, home health-aide services, medical supplies, etc.	Full cost of services; 80% of approved amount for durable medical equipment	Nothing for services; 20% of approved amount for durable medical equipment
Hospice care Available to terminally ill	As long as doctor certifies need	All but limited costs for outpatient drugs and inpatient respite care	Limited cost sharing for outpatient drugs and inpatient respite care
Blood	Blood	All but first 3 pints per calendar year	For first 3 pints[5]

[1]A benefit period begins on the first day you receive service as an inpatient in a hospital and ends after you have been out of the hospital and have not received skilled care in any other facility for 60 days in a row.
[2]These figures are for 1991 and are subject to change each year.
[3]Sixty reserve days may be used only once; days used are not renewable.
[4]Medicare and most private insurance will not pay for custodial care in a nursing home.
[5]To the extent the blood deductible is met under one part of Medicare during the calendar year, it does not have to be met under the other part.

Table 4-2. Medicare (Part B): Medical Insurance-Covered Services per Calendar Year

Services	*Benefit*	*Medicare Pays*	*You Pay*
Medical expense Physician's services, inpatient and outpatient medical and surgical services and supplies, physical and speech therapy, diagnostic tests, durable medical equipment, etc.	Medicare pays for medical services in or out of the hospital	80% of approved amount (after $100 deductible)	$100 deductible[1] plus 20% of approved amount (plus any charge above approved amount)[2]
Clinical laboratory services	Blood tests, biopsies, urinalysis, etc.	Full cost of services	Nothing for services
Home health care	Medically necessary skilled care, home health-aide services, medical supplies, etc.	Full cost of services; 80% of approved amount for durable medical equipment	Nothing for services; 20% of approved amount for durable medical equipment
Outpatient hospital treatment	Unlimited if medically necessary	80% of approved amount (after $100 deductible)	Subject to deductible plus 20% of approved amount
Blood	Blood	80% of approved amount (after $100 deductible and starting with 4th pint)	For first 3 pints plus 20% of approved amount for additional pints (after deductible)[3]

[1]Once you have had $100 of expense for covered services in 1991, the Part B deductible does not apply to any further covered services you receive for the rest of the year.

[2]You must pay for charges higher than the amount approved by Medicare unless the doctor or supplier agrees to accept Medicare's approved amount as full payment for services rendered.

[3]To the extent the blood deductible is met under one part of Medicare during the calendar year, it does not have to be met under the other part.

Source: Tables 4-1 and 4-2 are adapted from the *1991 Guide to Health Insurance for People With Medicare* by the National Association of Insurance Commissioners and the Health Care Financing Administration of the U.S. Department of Health and Human Services.

Table 4-3. How Medicare Assignment Works

	Actual Charge	*Medicare-Approved Coverage*	*Medicare Pays*	*You Pay*
Doctor Accepts Assignment	$500	$400	$320 (80% of approved charge)	$80 (20% of approved charge)
Doctor Does Not Accept Assignment	$500	$400	$320 (80% of approved charge)	$180 (difference between actual charge and Medicare payment)

Note: Both examples assume you have met the Part B deductible. Medicare law requires doctors who do not take assignment for elective surgery to give you a written estimate of your out-of-pocket costs if the total charge is $500 or more.
Source: *The Medicare Handbook,* 1990.

Part B provides medical insurance and helps pay for doctors' services, outpatient procedures, diagnostic tests, durable medical equipment such as wheelchairs, and many other services and supplies not covered under Part A (see table 4-2). Enrollment in Part B is voluntary and requires payment of a monthly premium ($29.90 in 1991), but you won't find comparable benefits at a lower rate. Consequently, this is one senior special you shouldn't pass up.

Medicare's participating providers. Medicare pays 80 percent of fees that it defines as reasonable; you are responsible for the remaining 20 percent of charges, called coinsurance. If your doctor, nursing home, or home-health agency charges more than the amount approved by Medicare, you will have to pay those charges as well as the coinsurance. Effective January 1, 1992, physicians are prohibited from charging more than 20 percent above the amount approved by Medicare. The limit will drop to 15 percent above the Medicare-approved amount in 1993.

One way to avoid out-of-pocket expenses is to use doctors and suppliers who have agreed to accept Medicare's approved amount as payment in full. Such doctors or suppliers can charge you only for the portion of the Part B deductible ($100 in 1991) you have not met and for the coinsurance (see table 4-3). At last count, about 40 percent of the nation's doctors accepted what is called Medicare assignment. Those who do can save you time as well as money because they submit the claim forms. For the names and addresses of participating doctors and suppliers, consult the *Medicare Participating Physician/Supplier Directory*, which is available free from your Medicare carrier, the insurance company that processes Medicare claims (these carriers are listed in *The Medicare Handbook*). The directory is also available for review in all social security offices and in most hospitals.

What Medicare Doesn't Cover

Medicare does not cover certain kinds of care, charges, or supplies. Most private insurance policies don't cover these items, either. Among the noncovered items are

- private-duty nursing
- care in a skilled-nursing home after 100 days each year (Skilled-nursing facilities have staff and equipment to provide round-the-clock nursing care or rehabilitation services prescribed by a doctor.)
- custodial services (for example, help in walking, getting in and out of bed, eating, and dressing), whether in a nursing facility or at home

- intermediate nursing-home care (such care may require the skills of a nurse but at a less intensive level than that given in a skilled-nursing facility.)
- physician fees above Medicare's approved amount
- drugs and medicines you buy yourself, with or without a prescription
- care received outside the United States, except under limited circumstances in Canada and Mexico
- dental care or dentures, check-ups, most routine immunizations, cosmetic surgery, routine foot care, and examinations for and the cost of eyeglasses or hearing aids

Medicaid

Like Medicare, Medicaid is a government insurance program that offers basic coverage for health and medical services. Despite these shared attributes and the often confusing similarity in their names, the two programs have important differences. In contrast to Medicare, Medicaid (Medi-Cal in California) is

- administered by state governments within broad federal guidelines,
- designed to provide health-care benefits to people with very low incomes and few assets, and
- required to cover extended stays in skilled-nursing homes and provide optional coverage for services delivered in intermediate-care facilities.

Even if you receive Medicare, you may be eligible for Medicaid, if not today, then possibly at some later time if you require long-term care. Paradoxically, while the notion of accepting such aid may insult your pride, if you need extended nursing-home care, one of the most prudent things you can do is to hasten the day when you qualify for Medicaid. To understand why, you first need to understand how Medicaid works.

Programs Vary by State

Medicaid is an extremely complex program that defies simple explanation. Because states have discretion in administering Medicaid, scarcely any two programs are alike. Services available, eligibility criteria, and reimbursement rates vary from state to state. They may even change from year to year within each state. Consequently, the best source for detailed, up-to-date information about Medicaid is the state or local government department that administers the program, typically the social services department, welfare office, or health department (check the government section of your telephone book).

Eligibility Guidelines

Medicaid is often considered a mixed blessing. When you need the benefits, you're relieved they're available. Unfortunately, it frequently seems as if you need Medicaid coverage long before you actually qualify for it. In most states, you qualify for Medicaid if you are at least 65 years old, blind, or disabled, and you meet the eligibility standards for supplemental security income (SSI), an income-support program for poor people (see chapter 5). How poor? In 1991, a qualifying SSI applicant must have had no more than $407 a month in income and $2,000 in assets. Recipients can keep certain assets and still be eligible for Medicaid. Commonly exempted items include

- your home
- your personal effects and household goods worth up to $2,000

- your automobile (regardless of its value, as long as you need it to work or to receive medical care)
- a burial fund of $1,500 or less

Fourteen states (Connecticut, Hawaii, Illinois, Indiana, Minnesota, Missouri, Nebraska, New Hampshire, North Carolina, North Dakota, Ohio, Oklahoma, Utah, and Virginia) use eligibility standards more restrictive than those we've described. It's best to check with your state's program about Medicaid eligibility.

If you have slightly more income or assets than your state's SSI program allows, you may still qualify for some relief under Medicaid. Since 1989, state Medicaid programs have been required to pay Medicare premiums, deductibles, and coinsurance for older and disabled persons with income and assets below a specified amount. In 1991, the cap for individual applicants in all but four states was $6,620 per year in income and $4,000 in assets, excluding the items listed above. Residents of Hawaii, Illinois, North Carolina, and Ohio have to meet somewhat tougher income standards: In 1991, income of no more than $6,289 per year was allowed for a single person. Income and asset allotments in all states increase each year. Although you will not receive full Medicaid benefits if you meet these eligibility requirements, you nevertheless will save money because your cost-sharing expenses under Medicare will be covered by Medicaid.

Income-Limitation Test for Nursing-Home Coverage

Medicaid is the principal source of public financing for long-term care. Not only does the program spend about 40 percent of its total budget on nursing-home care each year, but a majority of nursing-home residents—six out of ten—receive Medicaid assistance.

In many states, the Medicaid eligibility standards for people

MEDICAID NURSING-HOME BENEFITS

These states provide Medicaid nursing-home benefits to older persons defined as "medically needy."

Arkansas	*Nebraska*
California	*New Hampshire*
Connecticut	*New Jersey*
District of Columbia	*New York*
Florida	*North Carolina*
Hawaii	*North Dakota*
Illinois	*Oklahoma*
Iowa	*Oregon*
Kansas	*Pennsylvania*
Kentucky	*Rhode Island*
Louisiana	*Tennessee*
Maine	*Utah*
Maryland	*Vermont*
Massachusetts	*Virginia*
Michigan	*Washington*
Minnesota	*West Virginia*
Montana	*Wisconsin*

Note: List complete as of July 1990; check with your state Medicaid program for more current information.

Source: Data from National Governors Association.

who need nursing-home care are less restrictive than those described earlier, although few people would call them generous. According to the National Governors Association, thirty-three states and the District of Columbia cover nursing-home costs for "medically needy" older Americans—that is, people whose income minus their medical expenses results in net income below the state standard. In 1990, the state standards for a couple ranged from $192 per month in Louisiana to $750 in California.

For example, suppose that your mother enters a nursing home in California. Your parents' monthly income from social security and a small pension is $2,000. Your mom's nursing-home care costs $1,500 monthly. Will she pass the Medicaid income-limitation test? Yes, because your parents' income minus your mother's medical expenses is only $500 per month, an amount below the California standard. But if your parents lived in Louisiana, your mother would not qualify for Medicaid.

As a general rule, if you live in the District of Columbia or one of the thirty-three states that provide nursing-home benefits to the medically needy, you will pass the Medicaid income-limitation test no matter how high your income, provided it is less than or only slightly higher than the nursing-home costs. If you live in one of the other states, you will have to meet its income-eligibility standard to qualify for Medicaid nursing-home benefits. These standards vary, so check with your state's Medicaid program.

If you pass the income-limitation test for Medicaid nursing-home coverage, you have cleared only the first hurdle. You still must pass the tougher assets-limitation test to qualify for benefits.

Assets-Limitation Test for Nursing-Home Coverage

To qualify for Medicaid nursing-home benefits in most states, single persons must pass the SSI assets-limitation test described earlier—owning less than $2,000 in assets, excluding exempt items such as a home, car, and personal effects.

Let's suppose that you're a single person in need of nursing-home care. You've met the income-eligibility standard for your state's Medicaid program. You own a home worth $150,000, a $50,000 certificate of deposit (CD), stocks valued at $10,000, a checking account with a balance of $2,000, a car valued at $4,500, and personal effects and household goods worth about $2,000. That is, you owned these items before you entered the nursing home. But if your stay is extensive, you will have to spend the money in your CD and sell your stocks for cash—and spend all of that—before you can begin collecting Medicaid benefits. In fact, you won't qualify for Medicaid until all that's left of your nonexempt assets is the $2,000 in your checking account.

In the past, married couples had to meet equally restrictive standards in order for one spouse to qualify for Medicaid to cover extended nursing-home care. But in September 1989, the rules for married people changed. To protect the spouse remaining at home from impoverishment, states are required to total the couple's nonexempt assets, divide them equally, and allow the spouse living at home to keep half the assets or $13,296 (in 1991), whichever is greater, up to a maximum of $66,480 (in 1991).

Let's see how these rules would apply to our example. In this case, you and your spouse own the home, the CD, the stocks, and so on. Your spouse enters a nursing home. To find out how much of your combined life savings you, the spouse at home, can keep, total the values of both your nonexempt assets: the CD ($50,000), the stocks ($10,000), and the checking account ($2,000). (Remember, your house, car, and household goods are excluded from the assets determination.) Now divide the total by two. The result is $31,000, the amount you can protect. The rest (also $31,000) generally must be spent on nursing-home care for your spouse before he or she will qualify for Medicaid.

In most states, if the value of the divided assets is less than $13,296, then you can keep $13,296. If it exceeds $66,480, then you can protect only $66,480. You can keep any amount in between. (Both the lower and upper limits of the assets range will increase each year.)

Spousal-Maintenance Allowance

The 1989 Medicaid changes also allow the spouse living at home to keep more income than previously. Under the old rules, some surviving spouses—particularly women—were left with no income after everything went to the nursing home. Now, the spouse living at home can retain at least $856 a month in income (in 1991) up to a maximum of $1,662 a month. The minimum allowance may be higher in some states, and both minimum and maximum allowance will increase each year.

Later in this chapter we discuss ways to protect yourself against long-term-care costs. Some of the strategies involve shuffling assets to help you or a loved one qualify for Medicaid before going broke, so you may want to mark these pages for future reference.

Private Health Plans

Whether you're covered by a group policy, an individual policy, Medicare, or Medicaid, you may have to choose the type of health plan you want. The selection can be overwhelming. In the past two decades, the number of prepaid health maintenance organizations has skyrocketed (there are now more than 640 nationwide), and hybrid health plans combining aspects of HMOs and traditional fee-for-service insurance policies have multiplied.

While having many choices is usually considered a plus for consumers, it can also create confusion and—especially in health insurance—result in nasty surprises for unwitting buyers. To select the best health plan for yourself, you need to understand what's available.

As you read, keep in mind that not every plan will be open to you. For example, Medicare beneficiaries can only choose between fee-for-service plans and HMOs (in Medicare jargon, also called competitive medical plans). People who are independently insured typically also have limited selection. Employees of large corporations that offer health benefits usually have the most options. If you work for a company that provides health coverage, contact the personnel or employee benefits office to find out which plans are available to you.

Fee-for-Service Plans

Industry officials recently dubbed these "full-freedom-of-choice plans" because they allow you to choose your own doctor and hospital, an advantage for the many people who have long-standing relationships with family doctors and their affiliate hospitals. That option comes at a price, however.

Although their monthly premiums are often competitive with premiums in other plans, you'll pay a higher deductible and have to "copay" a share of covered hospital and medical expenses—usually 20 percent of each bill, up to a specified cap. In addition, you'll be responsible for any charges in excess of those deemed reasonable by the insurer. All these costs add up and can easily account for 25 percent or more of each bill. Consequently, some fee-for-service policyholders and most Medicare beneficiaries who choose this type of plan—and the vast majority still do—buy supplemental insurance policies to help defray out-of-pocket expenses.

Some fee-for-service plans charge lower premiums because they impose restrictions, such as requiring advance approval for hospital stays and elective surgery. Employers who provide health benefits are frequently choosing these "managed-care" plans to replace conventional fee-for-service policies.

Generally, fee-for-service policies cover hospital, surgical, and medical care as well as ancillary services including x-rays, lab work, diagnostic tests, and drugs provided by the hospital. Limited home-health services and mental health care may also be provided, but routine physical exams and other preventive services are not.

If you choose this type of plan, either you or your doctor will have to fill out claim forms. This task can be tedious, and if forms are completed improperly, payment may be delayed.

Preferred-Provider Organizations

Essentially fee-for-service plans, preferred-provider organizations (PPOs) are groups of health-care professionals under contract with insurance companies to provide services at discounted prices. As long as you receive care from participating doctors and hospitals (your insurer will give you a list), your deductibles and copayments will be lower than those of conventional fee-for-service plans. If you choose to use providers outside the system you will still be reimbursed, but at lower rates.

PPOs provide about the same health-care benefits as full-freedom-of-choice plans. They, too, focus on acute care rather than on preventive care. However, usually there are no claim forms to complete.

Health Maintenance Organizations

Health maintenance organizations are composed of hospitals, doctors, and other medical personnel who serve an enrolled group

HELP WITH INSURANCE FORMS

If insurance forms are making you sick, look here for help.

Writing about the ills associated with insurance claim forms, humor columnist Erma Bombeck quips, "The system has produced a new disease . . . Insurance Dermatitis . . . an allergy of sorts resulting from direct contact with forms (usually in triplicate) that causes people to break out in a rash, put off surgery, walk around with broken legs and consult Reader's Digest *instead of a doctor." It's going around.*

But help is often just a phone call away. For assistance with filling out Medicare claim forms, interpreting Medicare's "Explanation of Benefits," and resolving a host of other paperwork problems, contact the agencies and programs listed below. Don't wait! Although you always have at least fifteen months to submit Medicare claims, some insurance carriers won't pay claims older than that.

Medicare Carriers

The insurance companies that process and pay Medicare claims also answer beneficiaries' questions. Almost all of these companies have toll-free telephone numbers listed in The Medicare Handbook. *You can also obtain the number of the carrier assigned to your area by calling your local social security office.*

Senior Centers

Some senior centers set aside a few hours every week or so to provide help with Medicare paperwork to all comers. Others may provide telephone assistance. Call a nearby center to find out what's available in your area.

Social Security Offices

"We developed the forms; we should be able to help people fill them out," notes one social security representative. Staff may also be able to answer related questions. You can call toll-free, (800) 234-5772.

Medicare/Medicaid Assistance Program (M/MAP)

Administered by AARP and available in thirty-three states, this program matches trained volunteers with people needing assistance with Medicare or Medicaid claims. For the name and number of an M/MAP volunteer in your area, contact AARP at 601 E Street, NW, Washington, DC 20049, or call (202) 434-2277.

for a fixed fee, paid in advance. In other words, the HMO insures you and provides your medical services as well. While some HMOs use a group or staff model to provide care in a central location, others—known as individual-practice associations (IPAs)—contract with individual physicians or a group of physicians to treat patients in their personal offices and in community hospitals.

For many people, the lure of an HMO is the savings it offers. In return for prepaid premiums, the HMO guarantees to deliver all medically necessary services with nominal deductibles and copayments. Remember those steep out-of-pocket costs that sometimes accrue under a fee-for-service plan? Well, join an HMO and you can forget about them. Also, because services are prepaid, there are usually no claim forms to submit.

While you're saving money and time, you'll also be enjoying broader benefits. In addition to covering the basics (hospital, surgical, and medical care), HMOs offer benefits for a wide range of preventive health services, including regular physical exams, outpatient drugs, and, in some cases, eyeglasses, hearing aids, and exercise programs.

Sounds good so far. Before signing up, however, consider the trade-offs. Except in emergencies, enrollees must use the HMO's physicians and hospital facilities, and they may not always see the physician or specialist of their choice. This limitation can be troublesome, particularly when you consider that many HMO health providers have only limited experience in treating older patients. Fewer than 5 percent of HMO enrollees are 65 or older, according to AARP.

Another major drawback is limited selection. To qualify for membership, you must live within the HMO's specified geographic region or service area. If you receive Medicare, you can only select among HMOs that have contracts with Medicare. So even if you live in a large city, you'll have only a few HMOs from which to choose. This limitation might not be a problem if all HMOs were created equal, but they're not.

Some, including Maxicare Health Plans, Inc., one of the nation's largest for-profit HMOs, have encountered financial difficulties, which make them risky investments for consumers. Furthermore, 63 percent of HMOs do not provide home-health services, and some have come under attack for restricting the provision of durable medical equipment, such as wheelchairs and pacemakers. Charges have also surfaced that several HMOs have raised premiums, cut benefits, and dropped Medicare beneficiaries, underscoring the need for you to take a hard look before joining a plan. One way to do this is to talk with people in your age group who are present or former members of the HMO you're considering. Find out what they liked most and least about the plan, the health providers, and the care they received. Then visit the HMO and talk with the staff members. Often you can arrange a meeting through the member-service department, which is set up to answer consumer questions.

Choosing the Best Plan

Mavis R., 72, thinks the doctor she's had for the past twenty-seven years is worth his weight in gold. So even though she pays more to see him under her fee-for-service plan, she feels she's getting a bargain.

Five years ago, when his personal physician retired, Julius T., 75, joined an HMO after talking with other members and getting to know some of the staff. "I've never regretted the decision," he says, citing the money he's saved, the care he receives, and the extra benefits he enjoys.

When her employer offered workers a choice among three health-care plans, Jane T., 56, opted to enroll in the PPO. "It was cheaper than the fee-for-service plan and offered more selection among doctors than the HMO. It's the ideal compromise," she says.

As these examples illustrate, the best health-care plan is in the eye of the beholder. A plan that suits a friend may not suit you. If you have a choice among plans, base your selection on a thorough consideration of each in light of your current and anticipated health needs and your budget. Also, ask yourself these questions:

- What type of plan would work best for me?
- What benefits do I need in a health plan?

- Is it important that I choose my own doctor and hospital?
- Can I cover out-of-pocket expenses or afford a health-insurance supplement to help defray them?
- Am I diligent about completing and submitting claim forms?

If the plan you select doesn't meet your needs, you usually can switch to another. Medicare beneficiaries and individual policyholders can switch at any time; people covered by group insurance policies generally may change plans only during certain weeks or months of the year, when their employer or group association declares an open enrollment period.

Supplemental Insurance

You've got basic health-insurance coverage. You've selected your health plan. Now you'd like to forget about all this complicated insurance stuff, but the insurance companies keep nagging you.

"Every day, or so it seems, I receive mail from insurance companies offering to sell me health insurance that they feel I really can't do without," says Sally W., a 68-year-old Medicare beneficiary. "Then there are the health-insurance ads in magazines and newspapers touting the same message: 'Buy coverage for this, buy coverage for that.' Why, I've even seen television commercials marketing health-insurance policies! What benefits do these policies actually provide? And if I have Medicare, do I need the extra coverage?"

Sally is not alone. Many other older Americans ask similar questions when they find their mailboxes stuffed with flyers hawking health-insurance policies or hear another advertisement for coverage that supposedly will ensure that they're fully protected.

Frequently, the products being pitched are supplemental-insurance policies, of which there are four basic types: Medicare supplemental policies, hospital-indemnity policies, specified-disease policies, and long-term-care policies (discussed later in this chapter). *These policies are intended to provide additional health-care benefits to basic coverage. They should never be purchased in place of broader forms of coverage.*

Although many supplemental policies provide important health-care benefits, some offer more than they eventually plan to deliver. Unfortunately, the buyer has little recourse but to complain to state departments of insurance, which seldom take appropriate or sufficient action. Consequently, the wise consumer—that's you!—knows what he or she is getting before buying. Read on to find out what to look for in supplemental-insurance policies and, equally important, what to watch out for.

Medicare Supplemental Insurance

Often called medigap policies, these are designed to help fill some of the gaps in Medicare coverage. Which gaps? In accordance with regulations established by the National Association of Insurance Commissioners (NAIC), every medigap policy is required to provide coverage for the following items:

- Either all of the Medicare hospital deductible ($628 in 1991) or none of it. This either-or requirement makes it easier for consumers to compare Medicare supplemental insurance policies.
- The Medicare hospital coinsurance, plus 90 percent of per diem hospital expenses not covered by Medicare, up to a maximum of 365 additional days.

- The blood-transfusion deductible, unless the blood is replaced by the policyholder.
- The 20 percent copayment for physician services, after the policyholder pays the Part B deductible ($100 in 1991).

More than the specific details, it's important to know that minimum standards apply to every Medicare supplemental-insurance policy sold in the United States. This doesn't mean that all medigap policies provide the same coverage; some offer more benefits than the law requires. What it means, however, is that you'll generally never need more than one medigap policy; buying two only wastes money on duplicate minimum coverage.

Says one consumer advocate: "Anyone who tries to sell a person more than one [medigap policy] is trying to 'take' the customer." So far, more than 5.6 million older Americans have been taken, according to a 1987 study by the Health Insurance Association of America. That's how many people own two or more medigap policies.

Often they've been deceived. Horror stories of what consumer advocate David Horowitz calls "medicrap abuse" abound.

• An 88-year-old widow bought twenty-eight medigap policies. "Living alone and with her many ailments, I guess she was an easy mark for unscrupulous insurance agents," her nephew testified at a hearing before the Subcommittee on Health and Long-term Care of the House Select Committee on Aging.

• A couple in their eighties replaced their medigap policies with new ones that cost four times as much but provided the same coverage. An insurance agent misled them to believe that his policies covered custodial nursing-home care.

• An insurance agent tried to sell a 67-year-old man a new medigap policy by falsely claiming that Medicare approved only

50 percent of doctors' charges, and then peddling a policy that he said paid 100 percent of the bill—a statement that also proved false.

While the NAIC has drafted model regulations to crack down on such abuses, buyers should still beware. To help you protect yourself against fast-talking hucksters, you need to read between the lines of these commonly used, often misleading sales pitches:

• A social security or Medicare worker comes calling to sell you a medigap policy. Don't believe it. Representatives of these federal programs don't sell or service such insurance.

• A saleswoman explains that Medicare does not cover extended stays in a nursing home, then pitches a medigap policy. Her statement is true as far as it goes: Medicare helps pay for care in a skilled-nursing facility for only 100 days and does not cover stays of any length in intermediate- or custodial-care nursing homes.

But the agent has misled you by implying that medigap policies cover lengthy nursing-home stays. They don't. *Medigap policies do not pay for custodial or intermediate care at home or in a nursing home, the type of care older persons are most likely to need for long-term illnesses.* Consumers can purchase insurance policies that cover long-term care, but these are presently distinct from medigap policies and do not supplement Medicare hospital and physician benefits.

• A medigap insurance agent asks whether you'd be interested in a policy that helps prevent you from becoming a burden to your spouse or children. With your worst fears aroused, you have difficulty resisting the sales pitch. The implication is that medigap insurance offers coverage for long-term care. Once again, it doesn't.

If you're worried about what will happen if you ever need extended care, discuss your concerns with family members and explore options such as purchasing long-term-care insurance or buying into a continuing-care retirement community (see chapter 6).

- An insurance rep asks whether you'd like coverage for prescription drugs. You would, because your current medigap policy doesn't provide this benefit.

As noted earlier, some higher priced medigap policies provide more insurance than the law requires—for prescription drugs, physician fees in excess of Medicare-approved charges, or other benefits. Monthly premiums for these policies pay for the standard medigap insurance plus the additional coverage.

If you want broader coverage to supplement Medicare, upgrade your current medigap policy, if possible, or exchange it for one that fits your needs. (If you change policies, check for clauses on pre-existing conditions that may limit your coverage.) Don't buy an extra policy; you'll waste money duplicating insurance.

Before you buy any medigap policy, ask yourself whether you really need it. If you have group medical coverage through a current or former employer, you probably don't need supplemental insurance. Ditto for people who receive both Medicare and Medicaid (Medicaid providers are required to accept the Medicaid reimbursement as payment in full), and for HMO enrollees, who incur only limited out-of-pocket expenses.

Hospital-Indemnity Policies

These policies pay a flat rate (for example, $50) for each day the policyholder is in the hospital, regardless of benefits paid by other health insurance. Payments work like pocket money, to be used for whatever the recipient pleases.

Sold through agents or directly from insurance companies by mail, hospital-indemnity policies require careful shopping and close scrutiny. Because benefits are fixed, they also need periodic updating to keep pace with inflation. Some policies do not pay benefits until after a few days of hospitalization, and some pay nothing for outpatient visits. Weigh these considerations against shorter hospital stays for older patients these days (the average hospital stay for a 65-year-old was 8.7 days in 1985, down from 11.6 in 1975) and the increasing number of operations performed on an outpatient basis.

While everyone should think twice before buying a hospital-indemnity policy, some people should think three times. For example, HMO enrollees can probably do without this insurance because their out-of-pocket expenses are limited. Also, to the extent that these policies are designed to replace wages lost during hospitalization, you may not need one if you're living on retirement income and have adequate basic health coverage.

One common but ill-conceived practice is to buy a hospital-indemnity policy figuring you'll make money on it if you're hospitalized frequently or long enough. And you might. But if that's your idea of a good investment, then we must tell you about a large bridge we'd like you to buy.

Specified-Disease Policies

Also called dread-disease policies, these pay benefits for the treatment of a single disease, such as cancer, or a group of diseases specified in the policy. Typically such policies are not available to people who have been previously diagnosed or treated for the specified ailment.

On a scale of one to ten, with one representing a bad buy, we give dread-disease policies a quarter of a point for their next-to-nothing coverage. They're like shooting dice with the odds stacked against you.

So why do some people buy dread-disease insurance? Often because they mistakenly believe that such coverage will protect them from the high cost of long-term care. What should they do instead? First and foremost, explore their options. We discuss some of these below, including the option to purchase long-term-care insurance, another type of supplemental-insurance policy.

Protecting Yourself against Long-Term-Care Costs

Take a seat, because we're going to start with the cold, hard facts:

- Conservative estimates are that one in every three persons over 65 will enter a nursing home at some point in their lives.
- On average, a year in a nursing home costs between $25,000 and $34,000, according to industry experts.
- After only thirteen weeks in a nursing home, 70 percent of older persons living alone become poor; within a year, over 90 percent are impoverished, according to the U.S. House Select Committee on Aging. The outlook for married couples is only somewhat less bleak: One out of two couples becomes impoverished after one spouse has spent half a year in a nursing home.

Discouraging as they are, these statistics say nothing of the personal sacrifices and human suffering that lie behind them. To understand the feelings beneath the numbers, talk to someone like Frederick S.:

When my wife, Ruth, and I retired, our house was paid for, and it looked as though we had saved enough to enjoy our retirement years. At the very least we felt financially secure. . . .

Then, in 1980, my world turned upside down. My wife was diagnosed with Alzheimer's disease and Parkinson's disease. For the next four years I cared for my wife at home. During that time, her condition significantly deteriorated. She demanded the majority of my attention but I gladly gave it. Even though I was saving money by caring for my wife at home, the medical expenses caused a drain on our savings. In 1982, I was forced to sell our three-bedroom home and buy a one-bedroom condominium. . . .

On April 29, 1984—a date I will never forget—I left my wife unattended for a few minutes. I subsequently found her lying on the bedroom floor with a broken hip and shoulder. She had surgery, and after only ten days, the hospital wanted to move her to a custodial-care nursing home.

So, in less than two years, I paid over $70,000 to the nursing home, and our life savings were dwindling rapidly. To see my wife suffering so much from these dehumanizing diseases and to see our savings being eaten up at the same time caused me much emotional distress. . . .

Although I have bitter thoughts about what I have had to endure financially and emotionally, I still have one thing to be thankful for—I can visit my wife every day. I visit her daily at the nursing home between three and nine.

The story Lalah W. tells is equally agonizing:

I was visiting my sister and brother-in-law in Florida. During my stay, my brother-in-law, William, was hospitalized for internal bleeding caused by a stomach disorder. He was hospitalized ten days, then transferred to a custodial-care nursing home at the hospital's request.

After William entered the nursing home, my sister and I realized that he would probably spend his remaining years there. The symptoms of Alzheimer's disease were starting to creep up on him. Before he was institutionalized, my sister had been caring for him by herself. But with his stomach problems and the helplessness that he displayed with the Alzheimer's, it was becoming a tremendous strain for her to do so. . . .

> So far, my sister is managing to pay for her husband's nursing-home expenses from their personal savings. She will soon have depleted their money, however. . . . Her financial future is bleak, and I am afraid all she has to look forward to is life on public assistance.
>
> They worked hard all their lives and were diligent in planning for their retirement. They thought it would be the happiest time of their lives. Now they find themselves close to financial and emotional ruin because of a catastrophic illness.

Sound depressing? It's heartbreaking. But just feeling anguished by such stories is not enough. Eventually you need to start grappling with the questions these stories raise: What can you do to protect yourself against the high cost of long-term care? The answers are only partial ones and will continue to be so until we as a nation establish a comprehensive long-term health-care program, a goal toward which several congressional leaders are working. In the meantime, in addition to advocating that your legislators support such a program, you need to plan ahead to safeguard yourself against catastrophic health-care costs.

Develop a Medicaid Plan

If you need nursing-home care, chances are that either you or Medicaid will foot the bill. Don't count on Medicare because its nursing-home benefit is extremely limited. And don't pin your hopes on private long-term-care insurance. While such policies have improved over time, good ones are still hard to come by and then may be prohibitively expensive. Veterans Administration benefits? Don't expect much: The nursing-home coverage is limited and generally won't last longer than six months. That leaves you and Medicaid, and by the time Medicaid starts paying, you've already paid—and paid dearly. Remember the strict Medicaid eligibility standards we described earlier? Single nursing-home applicants can keep nonexempt assets of only $2,000 or less; married couples in which one spouse enters a nursing home can protect only $13,296 to $66,480 of nonexempt assets (in 1991).

Do these grim facts mean that you or your spouse will wind up virtually bankrupt if either of you requires nursing-home care? No, provided you plan ahead. So-called divestment planning is often used when one person wants to qualify for Medicaid nursing-home benefits as quickly as possible while preserving life savings. Typically, middle-income persons benefit most from divestment or Medicaid planning; people with very low incomes will quickly qualify for Medicaid if they need nursing-home care, while the more affluent can afford to pay the nursing-home tab.

One caveat to divestment planning is that it may help qualify you or a loved one for substandard nursing care. It's sad but true that the quality of nursing-home care provided to Medicaid residents is lower than that provided to private-pay patients. Consequently, most people prefer not to have to go on Medicaid. But if avoiding Medicaid is not an option for you, divestment planning is worth considering.

Although some people, most notably government bureaucrats, view divestment planning as reprehensible or even immoral, proponents staunchly refute such charges. "Is it immoral . . . to consider ways to avoid poverty? Absolutely not!" writes attorney Armond D. Budish in *Avoiding the Medicaid Trap: How to Beat the Catastrophic Costs of Nursing-Home Care.* "Isn't it far more immoral that our government forces its citizens to deplete their life savings on nursing homes? The goal of sound public policy should be to prevent this sort of financial devastation." We agree, and until that goal is reached, we recommend that you begin planning now to protect your best interests.

To help you, we will describe some of the most common

divestment-planning strategies (additional strategies are reviewed in Budish's book). Remember, though, as attorney Joel C. Dobris writes in the *Real Property, Probate and Trust Journal,* "Divestment is a dangerous game. Situations can change. Regional differences apply." While the suggestions below will help you identify your options, it's best to seek legal advice before implementing your Medicaid plan (see chapter 5 for tips on finding a lawyer).

Hold assets in exempt form. Two months after his wife, a stroke victim, entered Sunny Hills nursing home, Doug R. applied for Medicaid on her behalf. The public social-services worker told him that he and his wife had too much money in savings to qualify for Medicaid. "If I were you," the worker continued, "I'd pay off the mortgage on my house, maybe fix up my car, then reapply." Doug took her advice, and when he reapplied the following month, his wife qualified for nursing-home benefits.

As noted earlier, Medicaid applicants can keep certain assets (including their home and car) and still qualify for benefits. They can also legally use nonexempt assets, such as money in a savings account or CD, to buy exempt assets. This way, instead of paying the nursing home all of their savings, they've invested in their home, car, and household goods.

Keep in mind that it will do you no good to use nonexempt assets to buy new nonexempt assets. Cashing in your stocks to buy a second home by the lake won't help you qualify for Medicaid. The types and values of assets used to determine eligibility for Medicaid vary by state. You need to contact your state program for specific details.

Transfer assets thirty months or more before a nursing-home stay. Suppose that your widowed mother's health is failing. Right now, she's able to take care of herself, but she anticipates that someday she'll need nursing-home care. One way she can increase the likelihood of qualifying for Medicaid nursing-home benefits is to give a portion of her assets to you, your siblings, other relatives, or friends. If she does this at least thirty months before entering a nursing home, the transferred assets will not be counted in determining Medicaid eligibility. (If a person disposes of assets for less than fair market value within thirty months of a nursing-home stay, states can delay eligibility for Medicaid.)

The obvious drawback to this strategy is that parents may need the assets to support themselves. If they give life savings to children with the understanding that the assets will be used for the parents' benefit, they may be disappointed. There could be a parting of the ways between the parent or child, or the child could use the assets for other purposes. Furthermore, Medicaid may determine that such assets are actually available to the parent and count them in determining eligibility. Consequently, anyone considering this tactic should carefully weigh the pros and cons.

Shuffle assets between spouses. Because a couple's combined life savings are counted in determining eligibility for Medicaid, this strategy will not help the nursing-home spouse qualify more quickly for benefits. However, it may help preserve the couple's assets if the spouse living at home dies first.

Say, for example, that Mr. and Mrs. Smith own stocks worth $120,000 when Mr. Smith enters a nursing home. Mrs. Smith is able to protect $60,000 (half of $120,000) of the couple's investments. But most of those assets are in Mr. Smith's name. If Mrs. Smith dies first, the assets will revert back to her husband. Because he is now single, he can keep only $2,000 of nonexempt assets. Consequently, he may wind up spending down more of the family's life savings in order to qualify for Medicaid. On the other hand, if he had transferred everything to Mrs. Smith upon entering the nursing home, she could have distributed the assets to their children under her will. Mr. Smith would then qualify for Medicaid, and the couple's assets would stay within the family.

This example highlights two other important points. First, if one spouse enters a nursing home, not only should the couple consider transferring assets into the name of the spouse living at home, but that person should also give serious thought to changing his or her will. It may not be prudent to leave assets to an institutionalized spouse if those resources will only end up in the nursing home's till. Second, the example underscores the importance of executing a durable power of attorney (discussed in chapter 5). Without one a couple may not be able to transfer assets from the disabled spouse to the healthy spouse.

Seek a court order. One way for a spouse at home to retain more assets and income than state law normally allows is to seek a court order authorizing the additional support. Suppose that Mrs. Smith had used this strategy after her husband entered the nursing home. In Fulbright & Jaworski's *ElderLaw Newsletter*, attorney Marc Hankin notes, "The court order can go so far as to award her all of the community and even her husband's separate property. Whatever property the court order allocates to her need not be spent for her husband's nursing-home costs, and there is no limit on the amount that the court can award her. Similarly, the court order can require the husband to pay her spousal support even if it exceeds $1,500 a month [the usual Medicaid limit in 1989] and even if it comes from his social security or pension [benefits]." Some couples achieve similar results by divorcing after one spouse enters the nursing home. But as Mr. Hankin points out, seeking a court order is a less drastic alternative.

Set up a trust thirty months or more before entering a nursing-home. Simply put, when you establish a trust, you transfer ownership of certain property and other assets to a trustee, who agrees to manage the resources according to the terms of the trust document (see chapter 5). Before 1986, many couples set up trusts providing that if one spouse needed nursing-home care, he or she would receive minimal distributions from the trust. When made in advance of the Medicaid transfer-limitation period, this arrangement allowed the nursing-home spouse to qualify for Medicaid quickly while preserving most of the trust's assets for the spouse living at home. But Congress changed the rules in 1986.

The new rules are complicated, but the bottom line is that it is now more difficult—and trickier—to establish a trust so that its assets will not be counted in determining Medicaid eligibility. But it's not impossible, provided you get legal assistance. As with the other Medicaid-planning techniques we've reviewed, we recommend that you discuss this one with a lawyer.

Buy a Long-Term-Care Insurance Policy

Another method for protecting yourself against the high cost of long-term care is to buy private long-term-care insurance, which typically covers nursing-home stays and some home-health services. This option, however, is not for everyone.

For one thing, there's the cost—as much as $1,300 a year for a 65-year-old and considerably more for someone older. After analyzing long-term-care policies offered by forty-three of the estimated seventy companies selling such insurance in 1988, *Consumer Reports* concluded: "People whose income and assets are fairly modest should not buy long-term-care policies. They would quickly qualify for Medicaid benefits should they need to stay in a nursing home."

The other major concern is the policies themselves. Some are so restrictive that you wonder whether a good long-term-care policy is a contradiction in terms. Consider the policy a 67-year-old widower in Minnesota bought. "This policy covers everything," the sales agent said. "You won't have to worry about a thing." It turned out that the policy did not cover people with Alzheimer's disease and required a three-day prior hospital stay before entering a nursing home.

Lila K. purchased a long-term-care policy, but when she needed the benefits, the insurance company refused to pay. It claimed that the 81-year-old nursing-home resident needed only custodial care (help with routine activities such as walking and eating), which the policy didn't cover.

Harry B. entered a nursing home and encountered a similar problem. Although his long-term-care policy covered custodial care, it did so only if the policyholder first required skilled or intermediate care. Like most nursing-home residents, Harry did not need these higher levels of care. Consequently, he didn't collect a dime from the insurance company.

To help protect consumers from such costly surprises, the National Association of Insurance Commissioners has drafted a model law and regulations for long-term-care insurance. These standards are part of the model law:

- Require insurance companies to disclose information about the policy's benefits, restrictions, and renewability.
- Mandate that policies include a "free-look" provision, which allows the consumer to cancel the policy within thirty days for a full refund.
- Prohibit policy restrictions related to previous hospitalizations.
- Prohibit policies from covering only one level of care (for example, only skilled care).
- Prohibit policy restrictions related to previous levels of

care (for example, requiring that the policyholder receive skilled care before benefits will be paid for intermediate care).
- Require that insurance companies insure a policyholder for life as long as the premium is paid, and prohibit companies from raising premiums unless there is an across-the-board rate increase (in insurance lingo, this means the policies are "guaranteed renewable").
- Prohibit insurance companies from excluding coverage for policyholders with Alzheimer's disease.
- Require insurance companies to offer some policies with inflation-protection provisions (benefits under these policies automatically increase each year to keep pace with inflation).

By mid-1990, thirty-six states had adopted either the NAIC law or the NAIC regulations and three were about to do so. In states that haven't passed the NAIC model, the more restrictive policies may be sold. Consumers should be selective. To identify a good long-term-care insurance policy, *Consumer Reports* tells shoppers to look for one that

- Pays $80 for each day the policyholder is in a nursing home (most long-term-care insurance policies are indemnity policies, which pay a fixed benefit per day rather than a percentage of actual charges).
- Begins paying benefits at least twenty days after the policyholder enters the nursing home.
- Offers four years' worth of coverage for each nursing-home stay.
- Provides benefits for unlimited days for all stays.
- Pays full benefits for care provided in skilled, intermediate, and custodial-care facilities.

NAIC MODEL LAW OR REGULATIONS

These states have adopted the NAIC model law or regulations for long-term-care insurance.

Alaska	*Nevada*
Arizona	*New Hampshire*
Arkansas	*New Jersey (pending)*
California	*New Mexico*
Colorado	*North Carolina*
Delaware	*North Dakota*
Florida	*Ohio*
Georgia	*Oklahoma*
Hawaii	*Oregon*
Idaho	*Pennsylvania (pending)*
Illinois	*Rhode Island*
Indiana	*South Carolina*
Iowa	*South Dakota*
Kansas	*Tennessee*
Louisiana	*Texas (pending)*
Maryland	*Vermont*
Michigan	*Virginia*
Missouri	*West Virginia*
Montana	*Wyoming*
Nebraska	

Note: List complete as of July 1990.
Source: Data from National Association of Insurance Commissioners

- Does not have a requirement for a prior hospital stay.
- Covers home care without requiring previous nursing-home or hospital confinements.
- Specifically covers patients with Alzheimer's disease.
- Includes a waiver of premium feature that allows policyholders to stop paying premiums once they're confined to a nursing home.
- Is guaranteed renewable for life.
- Is offered by a reputable company.*

When shopping for long-term-care insurance, check with your current or former employer to find out whether such policies are available to employees and retirees. Although you'll have to pay the premiums, these may be lower than the rates for comparable individual policies. Keep in mind, however, that a cheap policy isn't a good deal unless it's what you need.

For a list of fifty-three long-term-care policies in order of estimated quality, consult the May 1988 issue of *Consumer Reports* ("Who Can Afford a Nursing Home?"). In addition to listing the best buys, the article provides a thorough analysis of the long-term-care insurance market.

Attach a Long-Term-Care Rider to a Life-Insurance Policy

Betty L., 56, has heard about the newest addition to the insurance industry's long-term-care products: "A friend recently bought a life-insurance policy that offers nursing-home coverage as well. She says that the policy's long-term-care feature offers an inexpensive way to insure against future nursing-home expenses. For

*This information copyright 1988 by Consumers Union of United States, Inc., Mount Vernon, NY 10553. Excerpted by permission from *Consumer Reports*, May 1988.

this reason, she recommends that I buy a similar policy. Is this a good buy?"

The jury's still out on that question. A small but growing number of insurance companies, including Continental Casualty, Security Connecticut, and First Penn-Pacific, now offer long-term-care riders for their universal life-insurance policies (see chapter 5 for a description of these policies). This arrangement allows all or a portion of the policy's death benefit to be prepaid in monthly installments to a living policyholder should he or she enter a nursing home.

Although payment formulas vary, monthly benefits for nursing-home care typically amount to 2 percent of the policy's face value (the dollar amount to be paid to the beneficiary when the insured dies) until about half of the death benefit has been paid. Suppose, for example, that your policy's face value is $100,000. Two percent of that amount is $2,000, the sum you will receive each month if you enter a nursing home. Under most policies, however, benefits will cease after twenty-five months, when half the policy's face value has been dispersed ($25 \times \$2,000 = \$50,000$, or half of $100,000). Benefits not used during the policyholder's lifetime pass to the beneficiary at death.

Because the company is simply advancing the death benefit, not paying out more money, long-term-care riders can cost as little as $100 per year on a $100,000 universal policy. By contrast, "stand-alone" long-term-care insurance policies may cost ten times that amount.

But determining whether the riders are worthwhile investments is complicated. Because most were recently introduced, there is too little actuarial information to indicate whether the long-term-care riders are over- or underpriced. According to one consumer advocate, they may represent an opportunity for in-

surance companies to tie something to the sale of universal life policies that is extremely profitable and on principle should be avoided.

Moreover, as of January 1991, the Internal Revenue Service (IRS) had not ruled on the taxation of nursing-home benefits payable under these riders. At issue is whether to treat them as health-insurance benefits, which are tax-exempt, or life-insurance proceeds, a portion of which may not be tax-exempt. Until this question is resolved, consumers should consult their tax counselors before making a decision regarding a long-term-care rider.

Also, evaluating and comparing policies can be extremely difficult when different types of insurance are bundled in one package. Shoppers may buy too much or the wrong kind of insurance.

Says one insurance expert: "It doesn't make sense to buy these policies for their long-term-care benefits unless you need the life insurance as well." Universal life policies, which accumulate a cash value from the premiums paid, are considered poor buys if surrendered during the first five to ten years of the policy. Older policyholders may pay enormous sales fees if they cancel their policies early.

Also keep in mind that long-term-care riders may cost less because they offer less than some stand-alone policies. For instance, if you anticipate needing benefits soon after the policyholder enters a nursing home, then look for a free-standing long-term-care policy. These concerns underscore the need for interested buyers to examine the new policies carefully.

Join a Continuing-Care Retirement Community

By some accounts, continuing-care retirement communities (CCRCs) offer the ultimate in retirement living. We're not just talking about comfortable quarters surrounded by attractive grounds, with an impressive array of services managed by a professional staff. The clincher offered by many CCRCs is guaranteed health care for the resident's lifetime.

Sound intriguing? Then turn to chapter 6 for more information about CCRCs, including costs (they're expensive), services, and limitations.

Cutting Insurance Costs: Dos and Don'ts

The following suggestions may help you save money on health insurance, select coverage that meets your needs, and protect yourself against insurance abuse.

What You Should Do

- Shop around for the best policy. Sure, it's a hassle, but it's also a wise investment because insurance benefits, premiums, and restrictions vary widely. The best deals aren't always offered by the insurance giants such as Blue Cross and Blue Shield. Lesser known companies may offer comparable (and sometimes better) coverage for lower rates.
- Take advantage of free-look provisions, which allow you time to examine the policy with the option of returning it for a refund if you're not satisfied.
- Complain to your state department of insurance if you believe you've been misled by an insurance agent or advertisement. In some cases, these regulatory offices can negotiate a refund.
- Review insurance policies annually to make sure they still fit your situation. Some policies, such as hospital-indemnity and most long-term-care policies, pay benefits in fixed amounts and may be outdistanced by inflation. Consider whether the policy should be updated or dropped.

• Familiarize yourself with changes in Medicare benefits and legislation affecting health-care insurance. Newspapers and your local social security office are good sources of information. Also contact the organizations listed at the end of this chapter for helpful consumer brochures.

• Ask insurance agents for their business cards. Not only may you need to contact them again, but you should know with whom you're dealing.

What You Shouldn't Do

• Don't buy a policy without first asking for, and then scrutinizing, the disclosure statement describing its costs, benefits, and restrictions.

• Don't buy insurance that duplicates benefits you receive under another policy. It's a waste of money.

• Don't replace a policy just because it's out of date. Switching may subject you to new exclusions (conditions that the policy won't cover) or waiting periods (the time until benefit payments begin). If possible, add new benefits to the old policy.

• Don't keep a policy just because you've had it for a long time. If it doesn't provide the coverage you need, drop it.

• Don't lie on insurance applications. If you don't mention that you have diabetes or a heart condition, you may not get paid when you need the money.

Money-Saving Tips

To lower health-care costs without sacrificing quality, consider taking the following steps:

• If you pay your own premiums directly, try to arrange to pay them on an annual or quarterly basis. It's cheaper than month-to-month because you can earn interest on the money between payment periods.

• Review all insurance bills and reimbursements. It happens—a company bills you for a service you never received or fails to reimburse you for a service you paid for out of pocket. If you have questions about a bill or payment, get answers! Contact your insurer, or if you have a group plan, your group administrator.

• Exercise your right to appeal Medicare decisions. The appeals process takes time, but it is often worth the effort if Medicare completely denies your claim or pays only a small fraction of it. Appeals procedures are described in *The Medicare Handbook.* For more help filing an appeal, call your local senior center or Area Agency on Aging (see appendix B) for a referral to a Medicare advocacy program.

• Buy generic drugs. Despite some clearcut variations in product quality, they're generally as safe and effective as brand-name medicines, and cheaper by as much as 40 to 50 percent. Your pharmacist can tell you which drugs are available in generic form and can answer your questions about them. Your pharmacist can also tell you which ones have been approved by the Food and Drug Administration (FDA) as being identical to the brand-name product.

• Get a second opinion whenever you have any questions about a recommendation for treatment or surgery, especially major surgery. Try to find a well-known expert who is not closely affiliated with the doctor making the recommendation; a second opinion is valuable only if it's independent.

• Exercise regularly, watch your diet, and get adequate rest. If you smoke, quit. A dollar's worth of prevention saves about $9 worth of cure. (See chapter 1 for tips on staying healthy.)

The Health Insurance Puzzle

Health insurance is a product you buy with the hope that you'll rarely have to use it. Should you need medical care, however, one of the last things you'll want to worry about is how to cover the expense. The best strategy for avoiding such a dilemma is to insure yourself adequately, not by purchasing a fistful of health-care policies, but by buying only the right policies—those that fit your personal needs.

Resources

The organizations listed below provide information about health insurance. Ask about free pamphlets that address your specific concerns.

Health Insurance Association of America, 1025 Connecticut Avenue, NW, Suite 1200, Washington, DC 20036. Telephone: (202) 223-7780.

Medicaid (Medi-Cal in California). For information about eligibility and benefits, contact the state department that administers Medicaid, sometimes called the department of public social services, human services, welfare, or health. Check the government section of your telephone book.

National Association of Insurance Commissioners, 120 West 12th Street, Suite 1100, Kansas City, MO 64105. Telephone: (816) 842-3600.

Social Security Administration. Visit a local office for information about Medicare or call toll-free (800) 234-5755.

State Departments of Insurance. Check the government section of your phone book for the address and telephone number.

Recommended Reading

Budish, Armond D. *Avoiding the Medicaid Trap: How to Beat the Catastrophic Costs of Nursing-Home Care.* New York: Henry Holt, 1989.

———. "Beyond Medicare." *Consumer Reports,* June 1989, 375–391.

Check your library for a back issue or request a reprint of the article from Consumers Union Reprints, P.O. Box 53016, Boulder, CO 80322. Be sure to enclose $3 when ordering.

———. "Paying for a Nursing Home." *Consumer Reports,* Oct. 1989, 664–667.
Check your library for a back issue or request a back issue from Consumers Union, P.O. Box CS 2010-A, Mount Vernon, NY 10551. Be sure to enclose $5 when ordering.

———. "Who Can Afford a Nursing Home?" *Consumer Reports,* May 1988, 300–311.
Check your library for a back issue or request a reprint of the article from Consumers Union Reprints, P.O. Box 53016, Boulder, CO 80322. Be sure to enclose $3 when ordering.

Inlander, Charles B., and Charles K. MacKay. *Medicare Made Easy.* Reading, MA: Addison-Wesley, 1988.

Polniaszek, Susan. *Managing Your Health Care Financing.*
Available for a nominal charge from the United Seniors Health Cooperative, 1334 G Street, NW, 5th Floor, Washington, DC 20005. Telephone: (202) 393-6222.

U.S. Department of Health and Human Services, Health Care Financing Administration. *The Medicare Handbook.*
To obtain a free copy, visit your local social security office or call toll-free (800) 234-5755.

CHAPTER FIVE

Planning Your Financial Future

When I was young I thought that money was the most important thing in life; now that I am old, I know that it is.

—Oscar Wilde

Sharon K. says she's lived too long to believe the adage, "If you've got your health, you've got everything." Notwithstanding a touch of arthritis, the 67-year-old retired teacher says, "I consider myself healthy and fit. Moreover, I expect to stay that way for several more years." But it's precisely because she's looking forward to living a good, long life that she needs to maintain her financial health as well. "Otherwise, let's face it," she says, "I could wind up out on the street." Although money can't buy happiness, Sharon notes it can secure something equally important—financial independence. "I'm retired now and want to enjoy my leisure," she observes. "So it's vital that my money work for me."

Is Sharon concerned about her ability to safeguard her financial future? Of course she is, and she's not alone. According to a survey by the Center for Mature Consumer Studies, 730 of 1,000 respondents (all over age 55) were worried about maintaining financial independence. Another study, conducted for a financial planning service, showed that six out of ten middle-class working Americans list "making sure I have a steady source of income when I retire" as their primary financial goal.

And so they should, say financial planners. "The number one concern of older Americans has to be maintaining a cash flow, not just for today, but over their lifetimes," stresses an officer of the Institute of Certified Financial Planners. An officer of the International Association of Financial Planners concurs. In fact, to play it safe, he advises clients to chart their financial futures until at least the age of 91. "It's an arbitrary number," he confesses, but the point is, you need to plan as if there will be a tomorrow.

Many older men and women do that, but not in the way these experts advocate. Rather than planning today with an eye toward tomorrow, they eye tomorrow as the day they'll start planning. The Foundation for Financial Planning dubs this the Scarlett O'Hara syndrome. "I won't worry about it today," says Scarlett, "I'll think about it tomorrow."

There are other excuses as well: the "pass the buck" affliction ("I'm no good with numbers," "I don't have a head for money") and the "ostrich" approach ("If I ignore the problem, maybe it will just go away"). If these evasions sound familiar, don't fret, but do recognize that they are self-defeating attitudes that can sabotage your potential for financial independence. And take heart from an investment advisor who contends that acquiring money-management skills needn't be the hardest part of being retired. Rather, learning to manage money is like learning a sport or any other task. It requires motivation, discipline, and practice, but the time you invest will pay off. Many people find that a commitment to financial planning yields results they can put in the bank.

In this chapter, we take you through the financial-planning process. You'll learn how to assess your net worth, set financial goals, and develop a budget. You'll also learn where to obtain reliable information and how to use it to make informed choices. To help you secure the financial future of loved ones, we guide you through the procedures for estate planning. And we review the legal tools available, including those that can help protect your interests if you become unable to do so. We also offer pointers on hiring financial and legal advisors.

Getting Started

Sam F., 63, is a purchasing manager for a large aerospace corporation. His wife Angie, 57, is a high school principal. "Both of us have worked hard over the years," says Sam, "but how hard is hard enough? At what point can we retire and feel confident we have enough money to live comfortably?"

Kay A. always relied on her husband to tend to the family finances. When he died suddenly of a heart attack, she had only the vaguest notion about how to manage money matters. "Fortunately, my husband understood my limitations and prepared his estate accordingly. Everything was in order when he died," says the 68-year-old widow. "But although the income from our investments supports me right now, I don't know whether it will sustain me over the long haul."

During the ten years following his retirement, John K. and his wife, Samantha, found time to realize some of their dreams: a trip to Europe, one to Japan and several trips to parts of the United States and Canada. These days, however, the couple, both in their seventies, stay closer to home, primarily because of John's health. John suffered a bout with cancer followed by a broken hip, which triggered an episode of depression. "John's recuperating and starting to enjoy himself again," Samantha says. "But if there's one thing that still nags him, it's worries about having enough money to cover future doctor bills. How can I assure him that if we need money it will be there?"

As these examples illustrate, many of the changes associated with growing older raise troublesome financial concerns. Although everyone wishes there were a simple formula for becoming a multimillionaire overnight, in fact, solutions to financial dilemmas vary because people's situations, attitudes toward money, and economic goals are so diverse. But the process—or steps—for achieving financial security are fairly constant and apply equally to Sam, Kay, Samantha—and you, whether you're at the height of your career or have retired and are living on a fixed income. Before answering questions such as whether you have enough money to retire, secure your financial future, or meet future health-care costs, you need to do three things: (1) calculate your net worth, (2) set financial goals, and (3) develop a budget. How will accomplishing these steps help? To find out, read on.

Assessing Your Net Worth

One financial planner describes his clients' concerns this way: "No matter what they say their problem is, what they're really concerned about is, What am I going to do when I reach the age of retirement and beyond, and how do I get there from here?"

To start, people first need to figure out where "here" is. Imagine, for example, that you're driving on an unfamiliar road to a vacation resort. Gradually it dawns on you that you're lost. You pull off the road to check your map. What do you look for first? Your location, naturally. Only then can you determine how to reach your destination.

Calculating your net worth serves the same purpose as finding your location on a map. It allows you to compare your assets (what you own) with your liabilities (what you owe). It provides a snapshot of your current financial position so that you can start charting your path to economic independence.

It also helps you set goals and manage money by forcing you to identify the types of assets you own, or perhaps more importantly, don't own. For example, when Sam and Angie calculated their net worth, they discovered that most of their assets were in cash accounts and income-producing investments such as certificates of deposit (CDs). They had very few growth investments (for example, real estate or stock) to provide a hedge against inflation, the enemy of retirees. Noting this deficiency, they started to research stocks with growth potential and a comfortable level of safety and to explore the possibility of buying a small house or condominium.

Financial planners recommend that you have assets in all categories because each type serves a different purpose:

- *Cash assets,* such as money in checking or savings accounts, provide income for everyday expenses and emergencies.
- *Income-producing investments,* such as CDs, treasury bills and notes, and bonds, help supplement retirement benefits.
- *Growth investments,* such as stocks or real estate whose values fluctuate with changes in the economy, help offset the effects of inflation.
- *Retirement assets,* such as pension benefits and funds in individual retirement accounts (IRAs), provide income when you stop working.
- *Personal assets,* such as your car and furnishings, contribute to your quality of life.

To find out how your assets are distributed and calculate your net worth, complete the Net Worth Worksheet that appears in this chapter. Keep in mind that a net-worth calculation is only helpful if it's honest and thorough. Don't sabotage your efforts by trying to accomplish the task in an hour; you'll need more time than that to sort through financial documents and obtain estimates for certain items. For example, you may have to ask a real estate broker to estimate the current value of your home, consult your employer to calculate your pension benefits, and call a stockbroker to find out what your investments are worth. It's time-consuming, but as-

NET WORTH WORKSHEET

Today's date: ____________

ASSETS (What I/we own)

For each asset below, list the current market value, or what a willing buyer would pay a willing seller in today's market.

	Current Market Value
1. *Cash in hand*	
Current checking account balance(s)	______
Current savings account balance(s)	______
Money market funds	______
Cash surrender value of insurance policies	______
Other assets	______
2. *Income-producing investments*	
Certificate(s) of deposit	______
Money-market instruments	______
Treasury bills, notes, and bonds	______
Municipal bonds	______
Corporate bonds	______
Notes receivable	______
Mutual funds	______
Investment trusts	______
Trust deeds/mortgages receivable	______
Other assets	______
3. *Growth investments*	
Real estate	______
Residence	______
Rental property	______
Stocks	______
Stock mutual funds	______
Business ownership	______
Partnership investments	______
Collectibles	______
Gold	______
Silver	______
Gemstones	______
Rare coins	______
Rare stamps	______
Antiques	______
Fine art	______
Other assets	______
4. *Retirement assets*	
Individual retirement accounts (IRAs)	______
Pension benefits	______
Keogh plan	______
Annuities	______
Employee savings plan	______
Deferred compensation plan (401(k))	______
Employee stock-option plan (ESOP)	______
Other assets	______
5. *Personal assets*	
Furnishings	______
Car(s)	______
Jewelry	______
Musical instruments	______
Stereo(s)	______
Television(s)	______
Camera	______
Video cassette recorder	______
Tools and equipment	______
Clothing	______
Other assets	______
TOTAL ASSETS	$______

LIABILITIES (What I/we owe)

List the following amounts.

	Amounts
1. *Short-term liabilities (due within one year)*	
Unpaid bills	______
Outstanding credit card balances	______
Unpaid taxes, including real estate taxes	______
Other short-term obligations	______
2. *Long-term liabilities (due in one year or more)*	
Mortgage loan(s) outstanding	______
Home equity loan(s) outstanding	______
Automobile loan(s) outstanding	______
Charge account(s)/installment loan(s) outstanding	______
Margin due (if any) on stocks	______
Life-insurance loan(s)	______
Other long-term obligations	______
TOTAL LIABILITIES	$______
NET WORTH	$______

(Total assets minus total liabilities)

sessing your net worth becomes easier with practice. When you do it regularly—some financial planners recommend every six months—calculating net worth allows you to measure your progress toward financial security, a step that's sure to bolster your sense of accomplishment and reinforce your commitment to prudent money management.

Setting Goals

With your current position firmly fixed on your financial map, you need to establish your future goals. Peer down the road. What lies ahead? A vacation? A new home? Retirement?

Instead of a flight into fancy, goal-setting should be an exercise in reality. To ensure that the goals you establish are feasible, a knowledgeable investment advisor recommends two strategies. First, think of common life events that cost money and affect you financially. For mature adults, such events may include

- career change
- retirement
- return to work
- unemployment
- relocation
- divorce
- widowhood
- remarriage
- disability or illness
- caring for a dependent spouse or parent

Determine which events might apply to you and set financial goals that will help you weather the transitions smoothly.

Second, use the Financial Goals Worksheet in this chapter to record your financial goals and (here's where reality sets in) the costs associated with them. Also include your financial plans for achieving your goals and the date on which you expect to accomplish them. It helps to distinguish among those that are short term (one to twelve months), intermediate (one to five years) and long term (more than five years).

Joseph and Carol L. used this process and found it an eye-opening experience. "One goal in particular—to retire within eight years—seemed to affect all the others," notes Joseph, a 57-year-old engineer. To maintain their current lifestyle, the couple figured they'd need an annual income of $40,000 in retirement. To achieve that long-term goal, Joseph and Carol decided they'd have to delay relocating and purchasing a new car, and would have to liven up the growth potential of their otherwise stodgy investment portfolio. Even with these changes, Joseph may have to postpone his retirement. "Still," he says enthusiastically, "I feel good that Carol and I were gutsy enough to confront these issues head on. With our heads out of the clouds, we have a better chance of realizing our dreams."

FINANCIAL GOALS WORKSHEET

Date ________________

	Goals	Estimated cost	Financial plan for achieving goal	Target date
Short-term (1–12 months)	________	________	____________	________
	________	________	____________	________
	________	________	____________	________
	________	________	____________	________
Intermediate (1–5 years)	________	________	____________	________
	________	________	____________	________
	________	________	____________	________
	________	________	____________	________
Long-term (over 5 years)	________	________	____________	________
	________	________	____________	________
	________	________	____________	________
	________	________	____________	________

Developing a Budget

Assessing your net worth and setting financial goals give you the big picture. But you'll miss the trees for the forest if you don't develop a budget. Unfortunately, when it comes to this step, many older men and women do what Karen C. does—nothing.

"Why take the trouble," argues the 69-year-old retiree, "when I know from experience how much I need to pay my monthly bills and how much I can afford to spend on clothes and entertainment?" But in almost the same breath, Karen admits that when her car breaks down or she has a medical emergency, she has to tighten her money belt until it hurts. She also concedes that she has trouble saving money, despite her need for a rainy-day fund.

Anne L. has a different problem. Observes the 62-year-old widow: "My expenses seem to fluctuate wildly, depending on whether I'm traveling, staying at home, or entertaining the grandchildren. I tell myself that everything will balance out in the end, but frankly, my finances feel out of control. What, if anything, should I do differently?"

Despite their different dilemmas, the solution for both women lies in developing a budget, a plan for coordinating monthly income and expenditures. A budget, financial planners say, can help you bypass money problems and steer you toward your financial goals by

- telling you whether you're living within your means;
- forcing you to make conscious decisions about expenditures;
- pinpointing any expenses you need to trim;
- helping you establish priorities; and
- allowing you to set aside a sum each month for savings.

Figure 5-1 Where's the money going? Consumer expenditures for people age 65 and over.

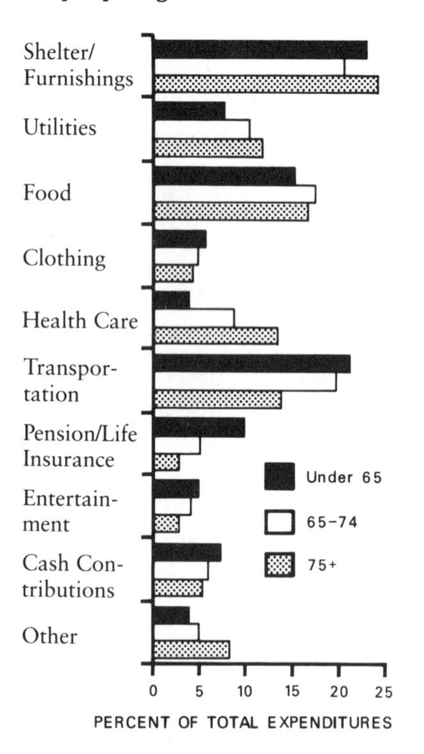

Source: U.S. Bureau of Labor Statistics, *Consumer Expenditure Survey: 1984 Interview Survey* (Washington, D.C.: U.S. Department of Labor, August 1986), Bulletin 2267.

Although budgeting is important for all ages, older men and women may find it particularly useful for two reasons. First, their income may drop virtually overnight following two events common in later life: widowhood and retirement. At such times, a budget helps you carefully monitor your spending pattern to ensure that it's consistent with your economic well-being.

Second, many older folks are house rich, but cash poor. For example, Karen owns a home worth $175,000, but lives on fixed social security and pension benefits. Like most older people, she spends about 60 percent of her monthly income on essentials such as food, utilities, and health care (see figure 5-1). She needs to keep a sharp eye on where her discretionary dollars are going, and a budget can help her do this.

Those who object that budgeting is time-consuming and complicated are often the ones who have never tried it. To find out how easy it is, use the Budget Worksheet in this chapter.

Living within Your Budget

What if your spending exceeds your income one month? Don't panic. It happens. The first month Marie C., 57, charted her expenses, she was shocked and dismayed to discover that between eating out and splurging on clothes she was $49.50 in the hole. The next month she declared a moratorium on outside meals and new outfits and managed to net a small surplus. And so it goes. If you overspend, just remember that you'll have to cut costs in following months to make up the deficit. These tips will help you trim expenses and live comfortably within your budget:

• Plan a regular savings program. Most financial planners recommend you set aside 5 to 15 percent of your gross income for savings and investing. Between age 50 and retirement, your sav-

THE RULE OF 72

To illustrate the value of compound interest with even modest amounts of money, financial planners apply the Rule of 72. According to this accounting tenet, 72 divided by the yield or interest rate earned on investments equals the number of years it takes money to double. For example, money earning 9 percent interest will double every 8 years (72 divided by 9 equals 8). So if you start with $5,000, you'll have $10,000 in 8 years, $20,000 in 16, and $40,000 in 32.

The same rule can be used to calculate the effect of inflation. In this case, 72 divided by the inflation rate equals the number of years it takes prices to double. For example, if the inflation rate is 5 percent, prices will double every 14.4 years (72 divided by 5 equals 14.4).

ings rate should jump from 15 to 20 percent. If you're tempted to shortchange yourself, remember this: With steady saving, even modest sums result in big payoffs over time.

- Create an emergency fund to cover unanticipated expenses such as those that would follow a major illness or loss of a job. For older adults, the fund should total six months' living expenses and should be readily available, say financial experts.
- Anticipate larger expenses in advance and set aside money each month to cover them. It often helps to go a step further and open a special account, sometimes called an impound account, specifically to cover fixed expenses that you pay quarterly, semiannually, or annually. These might include homeowners- and auto-insurance premiums, property tax, and federal and state income tax. Total the annual cost of these items and divide by 12. The result is the amount you should deposit each month to the impound account.
- Avoid fads and impulse buying.
- Limit purchases of expensive items by substituting similar but less costly ones.
- Take advantage of storewide clearance sales held at special times each year, such as after holidays.
- Make the most of senior-citizen discounts offered on airfare, hotel stays, travelers' checks, restaurant meals, and so forth.
- Read store advertisements and compare prices for the best deals.
- Avoid buying on credit. You may incur finance and interest charges.

Financial planners point out that the amount you spend ultimately is limited by how much you have to spend. For many people, spending income is defined by their salary. But as people grow

BUDGET WORKSHEET INSTRUCTIONS

1. List anticipated monthly expenses in column A. Some expenses, such as the rent or mortgage payment, are fixed. Others, including expenses for food, gas, and personal care, can change from month to month. For variable items, estimate the average amount you spend each month as accurately as possible.

2. For each line item in column C, calculate your income. Record how much you—or your spouse—anticipate receiving monthly in each category. Then total the amounts listed in column C.

3. Subtract total anticipated expenditures from total anticipated income (subtract the total from column A from the total of column C). Ideally, the result is a positive figure. If it's a negative result, you may be looking at trouble. Although you may find you overestimated your expenses or underestimated your income, it's best to play it safe and start planning now to (1) trim your expenses (discretionary funds for recreation, personal care, clothing, and the like will be easiest to cut); (2) boost your income; or (3) both.

4. At the end of each month, enter in column B all actual expenditures for each line, and then add the totals together. In column D, enter actual income for each line and total the amounts.

5. Subtract total actual expenditures from total actual income (subtract the total of column B from the total of column D). Ideally, the result is a positive figure. If you're in the red, however, read on.

EXPENSES	Column A Anticipated expenses	Column B Actual expenditures
Shelter		
Rent or mortgage payment	_______	_______
Property taxes	_______	_______
Property insurance	_______	_______
Maintenance	_______	_______
Gas, oil, electricity	_______	_______
Telephone	_______	_______
Water and sewer	_______	_______
Maid	_______	_______
Security system	_______	_______
Other	_______	_______
Food		
Groceries	_______	_______
Meals away from home	_______	_______
Other	_______	_______

EXPENSES	Column A Anticipated expenses	Column B Actual expenditures
Transportation		
Car payments	_______	_______
Gasoline, oil, etc.	_______	_______
Maintenance, repair	_______	_______
Auto insurance	_______	_______
Public transportation	_______	_______
Taxes and fees	_______	_______
Vehicle registration	_______	_______
Other	_______	_______
Clothing		
New purchases	_______	_______
Dry cleaning/laundry	_______	_______
Other	_______	_______

EXPENSES	Column A Anticipated expenses	Column B Actual expenditures
Health Care		
Health insurance	______	______
Physicians/dentists	______	______
Hospital costs	______	______
Drugs	______	______
Eye check-ups, contacts, glasses	______	______
Other	______	______
Personal Care		
Hair care	______	______
Toiletries	______	______
Pocket-money allowances	______	______
Other	______	______
Recreation		
Vacations	______	______
Recreational equipment	______	______
Recreational activities	______	______
Movies, theater	______	______
Parties hosted at home	______	______
Newspapers, books, etc.	______	______
Club dues	______	______
Other	______	______
Gifts and Contributions		
Religious and charities	______	______
Political causes	______	______
Family gifts	______	______
Holiday gifts	______	______
Other	______	______
Savings		
Savings accounts	______	______
Life insurance	______	______

EXPENSES	Column A Anticipated expenses	Column B Actual expenditures
Disability insurance	______	______
Investments	______	______
Employee savings plan(s)	______	______
Profit-sharing plan(s)	______	______
Pensions	______	______
Annuities	______	______
Individual retirement accounts (IRAs)	______	______
Retirement contributions	______	______
Other	______	______
Obligations		
Pet expenses	______	______
Credit card payments	______	______
Federal income tax	______	______
State income tax	______	______
Other debt payments	______	______
TOTAL MONTHLY EXPENSES	______	______

INCOME	Column C Anticipated income	Column D Actual income
All salaries and wages	______	______
Dividends/interest	______	______
Pension	______	______
Social security	______	______
Gifts	______	______
Other	______	______
TOTAL MONTHLY INCOME	______	______

older or retire, earnings from employment account for an increasingly smaller proportion of income. At the same time, benefits and payments from other income sources such as social security and pension plans become increasingly important. The following section on sources of income is directed to people who have not yet retired. We help you assess how decisions you make today will affect your financial well-being tomorrow.

Assessing Sources of Income

You're planning to retire early. You're considering a career change. You want to postpone retirement. You're getting divorced. You're thinking of taking a two-year sabbatical. You're preparing to return to the workplace after several years as a homemaker.

You're probably aware that any of these changes could affect your retirement income, but do you know how? Becoming informed will help you make better choices and avoid nasty surprises.

For example, suppose you want to retire at age 60. You qualify for social security benefits, but can't begin receiving them until age 62. If you start collecting benefits then, the amount you receive will be about 20 percent lower than if you wait until age 65.

Let's say you also qualify for your company's pension benefits, but the pension plan's normal age of retirement is 62. If you retire at 60, you'll still receive benefits, but they'll be reduced.

Should you postpone retirement to increase your benefits? The answer will vary depending on your personal circumstances. But clearly there are trade-offs, and it's best to weigh them before making your decision. "But," you might object, "I'm not a mathematical wizard. In fact, I find numbers mind-boggling. How can I make a sound decision?"

Tom U. felt the same way when, at age 57, he was offered a

Figure 5-2 Where's the money coming from? Income sources for people age 65 and over.

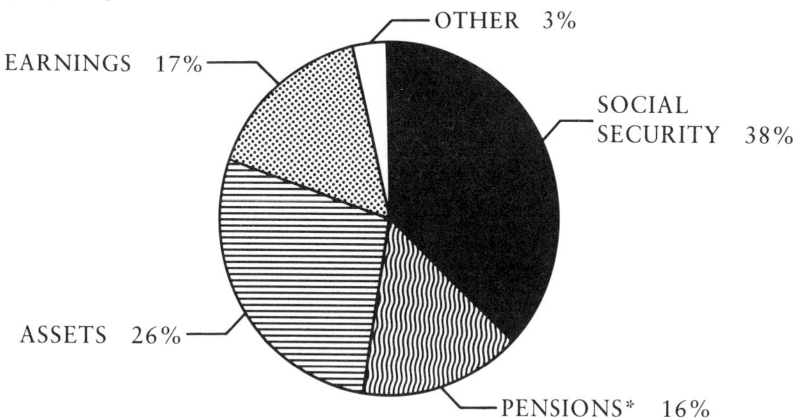

*Includes railroad retirement, which accounts for about 1 percent of income for aged units. (An aged unit is either a married couple with one or both members aged 65 or older, or an individual aged 65 or older who does not live with a spouse.) Railroad retirement has both pension and social security components.

Source: Susan Grad, *Income of the Population 55 or Older, 1986* (Washington, D.C.: U.S. Social Security Administration), Pub. No. 13-11871.

position at a new company. He wondered how accepting—or not accepting—the job would affect his plans to retire at age 63. Recalls Tom, "I knew if I took the new job, my pension benefits at the old job would be frozen at their current level until I retired. On the other hand, the new job paid more, and if I stayed there for at least five years, I'd qualify for benefits under their pension plan. Still, I balked at making a decision until my wife urged me to get more information. 'Why don't you talk with the personnel administrators at both companies?' she asked. 'Find out how the pension benefits are calculated under each plan and what your total benefits will be at age 63 if you take the new job and if you don't.' As usual, she was right. The more I learned about each option, the easier it was to choose between them. Ultimately, I decided to stay put, and I've never regretted the decision."

As Tom's story illustrates, making effective financial decisions has more to do with planning in advance and gathering accurate information than with computing complex mathematical figures and formulas. In the next section we discuss some of the most common questions about common sources of income in the later years: social security, supplemental security income (SSI), and employee pensions (including so-called "do-it-yourself" pensions). On average, benefits from these sources account for almost 60 percent of the older person's total income (see figure 5-2). To start, let's look at the benefits almost all older folks receive—social security.

Social Security

The most frequently asked questions about social security concern its retirement benefits. Beverly J. wants to know how early retirement will affect her social security benefits, and Frank R. wonders how late retirement will affect him. Karen D. wants to estimate her benefits so that she can plan for retirement, and beneficiary George A. wants to know what happens when he returns to work. In this section we offer some guidance to get you started. For more detailed information, visit your local social security office, or call toll-free (800) 234-5772. Ask about free booklets that deal with your specific situation.

Are social security benefits the only source of income I'll need when I retire? Definitely not! Since the program's inception in 1935, social security retirement benefits have helped protect millions of older Americans from destitution. But what was true then still holds today. *These benefits are not intended to replace all your earnings. Consequently, you should plan to supplement them with savings, pensions, investments, and other income.*

How do I estimate my monthly benefit amount? It's easy, so put your calculator away. If you're 60 or older, you can obtain an estimate of your monthly benefit by calling your local social security office. If you're under age 60, ask the office to send you a Request for Earnings and Benefit Estimate Statement. Complete this form and return it. In about six weeks, you'll receive a free statement estimating your future social security benefits, which you can use in preparing your retirement budget.

When and how do I apply for benefits? You should apply for benefits at least three months before you retire, and you can do so by telephone or in person at a nearby social security office. *Remember: you must take the initiative to apply for benefits; you will not receive them automatically.*

To save time, gather the following documents before you apply:

- Your social security card
- Your birth certificate or other proof of age
- Evidence of recent earnings, such as your last W-2 form or a copy of your self-employment tax return
- Proof of your spouse's or ex-spouse's death, if you are applying for survivors' benefits

If you're missing some of these documents, ask whether you can substitute others.

At what age can I receive retirement benefits? Most people qualify for full benefits at age 65, but there are also early and late retirement options. You can retire as early as age 62 and still receive social security benefits, but they'll be reduced by about 20

percent because you'll collect an additional 36 payments. Alternatively, if you delay retirement past age 65, you'll receive higher benefits. Persons who reach 65 in 1989 qualify for a 3 percent hike in benefits for each year they delay retirement. This credit will gradually increase each year until it reaches 8 percent in the year 2008.

Weigh these options carefully before selecting one. Decide whether you want reduced benefits starting sooner or larger payments later.

Starting in the year 2000, the age at which full benefits are payable will gradually increase from 65 until it reaches 67 in 2022. Reduced benefits will still be available at age 62, but the reduction will be larger than it is now.

Will a return to work affect the amount I receive in benefits? The answer depends on your age and how much you earn each year. If you return to work after you start receiving social security benefits, you will lose $1 in benefits for every $3 you earn above the annual exempt amount. In 1991, the exempt amount is $9,720 for people ages 65 through 69, and $7,080 for people under age 65. This amount will automatically increase each year. There is no ceiling on earnings for people age 70 or older. Starting in the year 2000, the age at which the earnings test applies will gradually increase as the retirement age rises.

Are my benefits taxable? In some cases, yes. Up to one-half of your benefits may be subject to federal income tax if half your benefits plus all your non-social security income exceed a base amount. In 1991, this amount was $25,000 for an individual and $32,000 for a couple filing jointly. The base amount changes each year.

If you have questions about your income tax, contact the Internal Revenue Service. Ask about free publications that address your specific concerns.

What about survivor benefits? If you are widowed, you may qualify for social security survivor benefits based on the earnings record of your deceased spouse. Even if you are divorced, you may qualify for benefits, provided the marriage lasted at least ten years.

You can receive full benefits at age 65, or at any age if you are caring for an entitled child of the deceased worker. Reduced benefits are available at age 60, or 50 if you are disabled. If you remarry after age 60 (or 50, if you are disabled), the new marriage will not prevent the payment of benefits.

To apply for survivor benefits, call or visit any social security office. You should apply as soon as possible after the death of your spouse or ex-spouse because the initial payment of benefits may be delayed for months.

Pension Plans

When Charles B. first accepted the job he's held for the past seventeen years, he was more interested in his earning potential than in the pension benefits the company offered. Now, while planning his retirement, he finds he has a lot of unanswered questions: By what type of pension plan am I covered? Am I entitled to any benefits at all? If so, how much will I receive at retirement? Will I receive regular payments or a lump sum? What about my wife? Is she protected?

When contacted, the personnel manager referred Charles to the plan administrator, the person in charge of the pension plan. She, in turn, offered to send Charles a summary plan description, a summary annual report, and information about survivor coverage. "Call me," she added, "if you need more information."

As questions about your pension benefits arise, you, too, should consult these materials. If you can't locate copies, do as Charles did—telephone your plan administrator or union representative and request them. And by all means, call again if you have additional questions or don't understand your entitlement. Make sure you receive answers to the following questions:

Am I in a pension plan? The answer, notes the Pension Rights Center, depends on (1) whether your employer has a pension plan, (2) whether the plan covers your kind of work, and (3) whether you meet the plan's membership requirements. Employers are not required to have pension plans, and those that do may exclude certain workers from participating.

Membership requirements vary from plan to plan. For example, Charles's pension plan allowed workers to participate if they were at least 21 years old and had completed one year of service. These requirements are typical of most plans; however, don't assume they apply to yours. Check your summary plan description or consult your plan administrator.

How does my plan operate? Most pension plans can be described as one of two types: defined benefit or defined contribution. If, like most employees, you're covered by the first, you'll receive a specified monthly benefit at retirement. In Charles's case, the plan promised to pay him $15 every month for each year of service. Other defined benefit plans may pay a fixed dollar amount, for example, $200 per month at retirement.

By contrast, defined contribution plans do not promise to pay a predetermined benefit. Rather, your employer contributes a fixed amount to your pension account (for example, 5 percent of your earnings annually), and at retirement, you receive the total contribution plus any investment returns, typically in a lump sum or an annuity.

Am I entitled to pension benefits? Participation in a pension plan doesn't necessarily mean you'll receive benefits from it. To earn a permanent right to all or a portion of your accrued pension—in other words, to become "vested"—you must work a specified period of time. For example, Charles was vested after working five years. Were he to leave the company today for a new job, he would still receive benefits from the plan at retirement.

Vesting requirements vary. Although in most plans you earn a right to your pension after you have worked five years, in others, full vesting may not occur until you've worked seven or even ten years. Also, if you leave a job before you've satisfied vesting requirements, you'll probably lose your pension credits and receive only contributions you paid into the plan. Consequently, if you change jobs frequently throughout your career, you might arrive at retirement with little or no accrued pension.

How much will my pension be? According to recent census estimates, the average pension benefit for retirees is about $630 a month. Your benefit may be considerably higher—or lower—depending on your type of plan, your years of service under the plan, and your age at retirement.

To compute the exact dollar amount of your pension, take a tip from Charles: Consult your summary plan description. Among other things it will tell you which years of service are counted in determining the amount of your pension, how your pension is calculated, and how much the payments will vary if you retire early or choose survivor coverage for your spouse.

Your summary plan description should also tell you whether your plan is "integrated," or coordinated with social security. Most private-industry plans are integrated, meaning a worker's pension is reduced by all or part of the amount he or she receives from social security. This adjustment can drastically reduce pension benefits, particularly those of lower paid workers. However, by law, integrated plans must leave employees with at least half their pension.

Most pensions are not indexed to keep pace with inflation. For example, if your plan promises to pay you $150 per month at retirement and you retire today, chances are that fifteen years from now, when prices are likely to have doubled, you'll still receive only $150 a month. As you chart your financial future, keep inflation in mind and plan accordingly.

When will I receive my pension? Full benefits are usually available at age 65, the normal retirement age for most plans. Some plans, however, pay benefits at earlier ages. For example, Charles's plan pays full benefits to retirees at age 60. Other plans may use a different age, so it's best to check on your own situation.

If you retire early, you'll probably receive reduced benefits because they'll be paid over a longer period. Under Charles's plan, for example, pensions are reduced 5 percent for each year that a worker retires before reaching age 60. Before you set your retirement date, find out how your age will affect your pension.

Is my spouse protected under my pension plan? Plans that pay annuities or monthly payments are required by law to provide survivor benefits. If you die, your spouse will receive lifetime survivor benefits, typically half the amount of your pension. Because the plan anticipates paying benefits over two lifetimes, your monthly payments may be lower than they would be if you were the only person covered. A husband and wife can reject survivor coverage if both persons give written consent.

Will I receive a lump sum or monthly payments? Most plans pay benefits in monthly or regular payments over a retiree's lifetime. However, some plans may pay benefits over a fixed number of years or in a lump sum. For example, if the total value of your benefits is $3,500 or less, the plan may require you to take them as a lump sum. If you leave a company before retirement, you may have the choice between regular payments that start when you retire or a lump sum immediately.

Given the choice, most people opt for the lump sum and then spend it rather than save it. If you have a choice, it's better to obtain professional advice before deciding. Although the lump-sum option allows you to invest your pension as you desire, your benefit will be immediately taxable unless you "roll it over" into an individual retirement account (IRA) within 60 days. Whether or not a roll-over is to your advantage is a question a tax accountant or other professional financial advisor should help you answer.

Individual Retirement Plans

Besides the two basic types of pension plans, employers may have other programs that help workers save for retirement. These "do-it-yourself" plans may be offered in addition to regular pensions, or, particularly among small businesses, serve as the primary retirement program. Moreover, you can create your own pension through contributions to a special account, regardless of whether your employer offers retirement benefits.

On the following pages, we offer brief descriptions of these individual retirement arrangements. Investment advisors recommend that, if these plans are available to you, you take advantage of them. In some cases, your contributions will be tax deductible. In every case, you can defer paying tax on the fund's earnings until you withdraw the money. And that means your nest egg will grow faster.

Individual Retirement Accounts. With an IRA, workers can contribute up to $2,000 a year and defer paying taxes on earnings from this money until they withdraw it. In some cases, all or a portion of the contribution is tax deductible. You can set up an IRA in addition to, or instead of, any pension plan your employer offers.

The rules for IRA distributions are strict. Premature withdrawals before you turn age 59½ carry a 10 percent penalty, in addition to any tax owed on the income. Penalty-free withdrawals of any amount can begin after age 59½. By age 70½, you *must* start distributions, and to avoid penalty, these withdrawals cannot fall below a certain amount. Typically, the minimum amount is calculated each year by dividing your life expectancy, as reported in IRS mortality tables, into the total amount in your IRA. The idea is that all of your IRA contributions will be distributed during your lifetime. If you want to stretch withdrawals over a longer period, you can calculate minimum distributions using the joint life expectancy of yourself and your IRA's designated beneficiary.

You can invest IRA funds in almost anything you wish: Stocks, bonds, mutual funds, money market funds, and certificates of deposit are some of the more common types of investments. You can also switch plan administrators—for example, from a bank to a stockbroker to a life-insurance company—to take advantage of changing economic conditions.

For more information, contact a qualified IRA custodian, such as a bank, brokerage firm, or insurance company. To find out whether your IRA contribution is tax deductible, contact the Internal Revenue Service.

401(k) plans. Under these plans, you can defer paying taxes on a portion of your salary by contributing it to a special account set up by your employer. Tax isn't due on the money until it's withdrawn, usually at retirement. Companies often impose a ceiling on contributions—for example, 6 percent of an employee's salary. The government sets another limit; in 1991 the limit was $8,475 annually.

What's especially attractive about 401(k) plans is that employers often chip in as well, typically 50 cents for every dollar you deposit. The only drawback—a small one—is that your investment options are determined by your employer. According to the *Wall Street Journal,* "A typical 401(k) plan offers three or four options: the employer's stock; a stock mutual fund; a 'balanced' fund combining stock and bonds; and a pool of guaranteed investment contracts that pay a fixed interest rate for a given period of time." You decide how to divide the money.

Rules for distribution are similar to those for IRAs: You can withdraw funds without penalty after age 59½ or at retirement, and you must start withdrawing by age 70½. For more information, contact your company's personnel or benefits department.

Employee savings plans. These are similar to 401(k) plans, except that you deposit after-tax dollars instead of pre-tax dollars to your special account.

Employee stock-ownership plans. Under an employee stock-ownership plan (ESOP), a company—through a trust it establishes—purchases shares of its own stock for employees. The trust holds the stock in individual employee accounts and distributes it to workers. If you're eligible for ESOP benefits, you may not have to pay tax on them until you receive a distribution from the trust, typically at retirement when your tax rate may be lower.

Knowing where the money's coming from is one thing; knowing what to do with it another. Since income from work is likely to decline as you grow older, it's vital that you develop strategies for making your money work for you. Investment planning can help you do this.

Investment Planning

George K.'s two favorite pastimes entail watching things grow. When gardening, the 72-year-old widower enjoys seeing the rosebuds blossom, the bean plants sprout, and the daisies flourish.

DOS AND DON'TS FOR INVESTORS

To make prudent investment decisions, meet your financial goals, and protect yourself against hucksters, you may find these suggestions helpful.

What Should You Do?

- *Invest with a purpose, keeping your financial goals in mind.*
- *Research investments adequately and obtain sound financial advice before acting.*
- *As a general rule, choose investments with low or no sales charges and a history of low expense fees.*
- *Deal only with reputable investment firms that you've had an opportunity to visit in person. Contact your local securities authority to find out whether the firm is registered to sell investments in your state. Also, call the local Better Business Bureau to find out whether other consumers have complained about the company.*
- *Avoid any deals promising unusually high returns with no risk. If it sounds too good to be true, it almost certainly is.*
- *Be wary of investments marketed by phone. The Federal Trade Commission says about* three-quarters of fraudulent investment schemes are pitched by telephone.
- *Report unscrupulous salespersons to the Better Business Bureau and to your state securities office.*

What Shouldn't You Do?

- *Don't invest in instruments you don't understand, even if a reputable advisor recommends them.*
- *Don't put all your eggs in one basket. Diversify your investments to spread your risk.*
- *Don't assume more risk than you can comfortably tolerate. If an investment is keeping you awake at night, it's time to unload it.*
- *Don't let tax considerations drive your investments. Remember that tax laws are subject to change. Your foremost considerations should be what you can afford and your financial goals.*
- *Don't use long-term investments to solve short-term financial problems.*
- *Don't shuffle investments in response to hot trends and tips. Stay focused on your true investment goals.*
- *Don't give financial advisors authority to invest your assets without your approval of each transaction.*
- *Don't pay cash for an investment.*

When investing, he takes pleasure in seeing his CDs mature, his dividends come up, and his stocks take off. Although gardening is his first love, he spends more time tending his investments. He responds to ads, chases leads in business publications, and watches financial news. He's got CDs, stocks, mutual funds, and municipal bonds. And, he says modestly, he's got "dumb luck" because most of his investments are winners.

George describes investing as "thrilling." But for every older person like him, there are more like Sue L. A former sales manager, Sue was always too busy to follow the stock market. Now retired, she knows her financial well-being depends largely on how astutely she invests her savings. But, she says, "I'm tempted to stash my cash in my mattress. I know that's the wrong strategy, but the alternatives are frightening. What if I invest in a company that goes bankrupt? What if I blow my money on a lousy stock tip?"

Says one financial planner: "Investing can be a frightening thing for older people. They know intuitively that they can't afford to lose much money or they'll hurt their standard of living." For many older folks, memories of the Great Depression bring bleak reminders of how tough things can get when the bottom falls out. Fears that the nest egg may not be safe are also fueled by more recent events such as Black Monday in 1987, when the stock market dropped more than 500 points, and stories about all the savings and loan failures.

Not surprisingly, many older men and women invest in only the most conservative instruments, those known as income investments: CDs, money market accounts, government securities, and certain mutual funds. Although such a strategy helps protect capital and provide income for living expenses, over the long haul it may undermine financial well-being because it doesn't provide a hedge against inflation. In order to preserve purchasing power, older folks need to invest in growth instruments as well. These include stocks and real estate, whose values rise and fall with changes in the economy. Although such investments are generally more volatile and risky than income investments, their potential returns are higher.

As a general rule, many financial advisors recommend investing a percentage equal to your age in income-producing instruments and the balance in growth investments. For example, the investment portfolio of a 65-year-old would consist of 65 percent income-producing investments and 35 percent growth investments. The split between income and growth investments for a 75-year-old would be 75/25.

For people who balk at the notion of risking any of their hard-earned savings, financial planners recommend slow, thoughtful action. Start with an ultraconservative portfolio and read all you can about investments. To help you begin, we describe below some of the most common investment instruments. You'll need to augment these brief overviews with information from other sources, such as your investment advisor, the business pages of your local newspaper, the *Wall Street Journal, Money Magazine,* and financial news programs such as the *Nightly Business Report* on public broadcasting stations.

In addition to understanding the purpose of your investment (do you want income or growth?), make sure you find answers to the following questions for each investment:

- *How liquid is it?* Liquidity refers to the ease with which an investment can be converted into its market value. For example, money in a savings account is very liquid because you can withdraw the full amount at any time. Your home, on the other hand, is considerably less liquid. If you wanted to sell it in a hurry, you'd probably have to price it below its market value. There's no rule of thumb regarding how liquid your investments should be, but keep in mind that you'll need enough income to meet your short-term obligations.
- *How risky is it?* Generally, the more risk you assume, the more you stand to gain. At the same time, of course, the more you stand to lose. People's tolerance for risk varies, so you need to assess your own.
- *What is its yield?* Yield is a measure of the investment's performance. It may be fixed and assured, as in the case of CDs, or it may fluctuate over time, as stocks do.

With these characteristics in mind, let's look at available savings and investment instruments.

Certificates of Deposit

Convenient, safe, and easy to monitor, CDs are sold by banks and savings and loan institutions in varying denominations, typically $500 and up. Deposits up to $100,000, including any interest earned, are fully insured by the federal government.

CDs pay a higher interest rate than savings accounts but charge penalties if you withdraw the money before a fixed term, anywhere from one month to a year or more. In general, the larger the deposit and the longer the term, the higher the interest paid. Interest earned on a CD is subject to federal and state income tax. Shop around for the best deal, because interest rates vary. To save time, check the business section of your local newspaper, which may publish weekly CD rates at major banks.

If you buy more than one CD, consider staggering the terms so that you'll have cash available if you need it. A long-term CD is not the place to lock up money you may need soon.

Money Market Funds

Available at brokerage and investment firms, money market funds can be opened with as little as $500 and allow you to withdraw your money at any time without penalty. These funds may also offer limited check-writing privileges. Although they pay higher interest than savings accounts, their rates are generally lower than rates for CDs. Money market funds are typically invested in low-risk instruments such as government securities. Though considered safe, these funds are not insured by the federal government.

Money Market Accounts

Available at banks and savings and loans, these accounts offer investment features similar to money market funds, but with one difference: Deposits to money market accounts are insured up to $100,000 by the federal government. However, there's a catch to that extra security. Minimum deposit requirements are higher, typically $2,500 and up, and if your balance drops below that amount you'll sacrifice your high interest rate, receiving instead the rate on passbook savings accounts.

Bonds

When you buy a bond, you're actually loaning money to the U.S. government, a state, locality, or private corporation. In return, the bond issuer promises to pay you a fixed rate of interest, usually in semiannual installments, and to repay the principal after the bond matures. You can usually sell bonds at any time for the prevailing market price, which may be higher or lower than the principal amount or the price that you paid because bond prices fluctuate with the interest rate and other factors. To monitor your investment, check bond prices, yields, and maturity dates in your local financial newspaper. Here are the types of bonds available.

U.S. Treasury bonds. "These," says one financial advisor, "are the definition of a no-risk investment." Sold in denominations of $1,000 and up with maturity dates ranging up to thirty years, U.S. Treasury bonds are issued by the federal government, an entity highly unlikely to default. Interest is paid every six months and is subject to federal, but not state or local, income tax.

You can buy bonds directly from Federal Reserve banks or, alternatively, from stockbrokers and commercial banks, which is usually more convenient but also more costly because they charge a commission. Some mutual funds specialize in treasury bonds.

You can also buy shorter term treasury bills and notes. So-called T-bills are available in varying denominations, starting at

$10,000, and they mature in three months to a year. Interest is paid when you buy them, typically within a week of purchase. Treasury notes are issued in denominations of $1,000 and up. They mature within two to ten years. Treasury notes pay interest semiannually.

Municipal bonds. Available through stockbrokers, these bonds are IOUs issued in varying denominations by states, cities, counties, and even school districts. Since 1986, new issues of these bonds have been severely limited, but the old ones are still plentiful. They are particularly attractive to investors in higher tax brackets because they're exempt from federal, and often state and local, income taxes. Although yields on municipal bonds are comparatively low, their tax advantages usually make up for the difference.

Keep in mind that municipal bonds are only as good as the issuer's ability to repay them. Consequently, quality is an important criterion for selecting a municipal bond. One indicator of quality is the bond's rating, ranging from high (AAA) to low (C). Generally, the higher the rating, the lower your risk and the lower your return. Ask your stockbroker for the ratings of bonds you're considering, and exercise caution with any rated BBB or below.

Corporate bonds. Corporations issue bonds when they want to raise money for special projects. As with municipal bonds, the quality of corporate bonds varies, so check ratings before investing. Dividends paid on corporate bonds are subject to federal, state, and local taxes.

Common and Preferred Stock

When you buy common stock, you purchase a piece of the company that issued it. In contrast to bonds, returns on common stock are not assured; as a part owner, you profit as long as the company does, a contingency partly dependent on the general economy's health and one that always carries a degree of risk. Although stocks are considered more risky than bonds, they generally outperform bonds in the long run. Ask your stockbroker about the track record of stock you're investigating. He or she can help you identify those that routinely perform well and pay regular dividends and those that are more volatile.

Preferred stock is generally considered safer than common stock. Although it, too, represents part ownership in a company, it guarantees a fixed return and in this way resembles a bond. Also, should a company go into bankruptcy, its preferred stockholders will be paid before common stockholders.

Mutual Funds

Some people say, "I don't have the time, inclination, or expertise to select and monitor my investments. I know I want income [or growth or a bit of both], but don't know which stocks and bonds suit my objectives. What I really need is a professional manager who'll make the tough decisions for me."

Behold the mutual fund. It allows you to diversify your assets by pooling them with those of other small investors. The fund is professionally managed with a clearly defined investment objective. For example, one fund may aim for long-term growth of capital, while another may focus on generating current income. To achieve its goal, the fund may invest in stocks, bonds, other instruments, or a combination.

Several financial magazines, such as *Money* and *Fortune*, routinely review and report performances of mutual funds. If you find a fund that interests you, obtain a copy of its prospectus, which describes the fund's objective, investment strategy, and track record. Also, check the prospectus to find out whether sales charges

(called loads), redemption fees, and administrative costs apply. Most financial planners recommend investing in "no-load" mutual funds to avoid sales charges. You can buy into the fund directly or go through your stockbroker. However, your broker may charge you additional sales fees or commissions (even on "no-load" funds), so clarify this issue before you place your order.

Annuities

Often purchased as a source of retirement income and available from life-insurance companies, annuities allow you to invest money, either as a lump payment or in installments, and receive, in return, a certain sum each month, usually for life. Generally, the older you are when you purchase an annuity, the more you pay for it.

There are two basic types of annuities: variable and fixed. With the first, the insurer invests your money in stocks, bonds, and other instruments whose values rise and fall with changes in the economy. Consequently, returns on variable annuities above a minimum floor specified by the insurer are not guaranteed. By contrast, a fixed annuity grows at interest rates set by the insurer. Earnings on both types of annuities accumulate on a tax-deferred basis until withdrawn.

Before buying an annuity, consider the drawbacks. If you turn in the annuity for cash early, you'll be subject to steep surrender charges that gradually diminish each year until they disappear, typically after five to six years. As with IRAs, if you withdraw sums before you reach age 59½, you'll have to pay a 10 percent penalty, plus any tax owed on the income.

Financial experts recommend that you shop around and compare yields and payment options offered by different insurance companies. Request a prospectus for each annuity you're investigating to determine surrender fees, sales commissions, management charges, and other expenses. If you don't understand the prospectus, ask the insurer.

When selecting a variable annuity, your foremost consideration should be its performance track record. The *Wall Street Journal* suggests that you look for annuities "that achieve consistently good returns without incurring excessive risk."

Real Estate

Your most valuable investment may be one that you bought decades ago: your house. Over the years, it has probably appreciated in value at the same time that it has been providing you with a substantial tax write-off. In addition, the equity you've built in your home can be used to secure a loan or provide income in retirement. How you manage this important asset can profoundly affect your financial future. That's why in chapter 6 we evaluate the pros and cons of selling or renting your home and review ways you can tap the equity in your home and take advantage of government programs designed for older homeowners.

Sometimes retaining money is harder than making it, particularly for people in high income tax brackets. When it seems your money's working harder for Uncle Sam than for you, it's time to get advice.

Income Tax Planning

Talk about income tax, and many of us prepare for the worst. Certainly, few people expect to hear any good news. If you're already cowering, surprise! The good news is that many older people are not subject to federal income tax at all. According to Internal Revenue Service (IRS) data, about half of all Americans over

FREE TAX-ASSISTANCE PROGRAMS

Through the IRS's Volunteer Income Tax Assistance (VITA) and Tax Counseling for the Elderly (TCE) programs, trained volunteers help low-income persons, the elderly, and disabled individuals complete their 1040 Tax Withholding forms. The free assistance is provided at VITA and TCE sites throughout the country beginning in February. To find the site nearest you, call the IRS on its toll-free line at (800) 424-1040.

In cooperation with the TCE program, the Tax-Aide Program offered by the American Association of Retired Persons assists those who need help completing their federal, state, or local tax returns or who wish to learn how to fill the forms out themselves. Trained volunteers provide the free assistance at about 8,600 Tax-Aide sites nationwide. Special arrangements are made to assist shut-ins and the disabled in a variety of settings, including hospitals and nursing homes. Again, call the IRS for the Tax-Aide site nearest you.

65 years do not owe federal income tax. The Senate Special Committee on Aging cites three provisions in the tax code of special significance to older adults:

- the exclusion of veterans' pension income and, for single persons with adjusted gross incomes less than $25,000 ($32,000 for couples filing jointly), the exclusion of social security and railroad retirement benefits from taxation;
- the one-time exclusion of up to $125,000 in capital gains from the sale of a home after age 55 (see chapter 6 for more information about this exclusion); and
- the elderly tax credit for low-income persons with few or no social security benefits.

Unfortunately, when there's good news, too often there's bad news around the corner. And taxes are no exception, because older folks who do pay federal income taxes tend to pay at a higher rate than other age groups. According to the Senate Special Committee on Aging, the effective tax rate in 1984 for older taxpayers was 17 percent compared with 14 percent for other taxpayers.

What can you do to ease the tax bite? Given the complexity and volatility of tax law, it's best to seek expert advice, particularly if you have a high income or a complicated tax situation. Accountants, certified public accountants, tax attorneys, and enrolled agents (who have passed a written IRS examination) all offer extensive tax-planning services for a fee. To find a qualified tax advisor you can afford, ask friends and business associates for referrals, and then interview at least three. The American Association of Retired Persons (AARP) recommends you find out the answers to these questions:

- Are you open all year long or only at tax time?
- What will you charge to handle my taxes?

- What is your professional educational background?
- Will you accompany me to the IRS if I am audited? What is the additional cost for this service?
- Will I get a refund from the IRS?
- Will you provide references from people in financial or business situations similar to my own?

If you do not itemize deductions and have few tax problems, free tax-assistance programs may be sensible alternatives to paying for advice.

What to Do When Financial Resources Fall Short of Financial Needs

Income tax planning. Investment planning. Retirement planning. Those steps are all well and good, you say, but serve no practical purpose in your life. You've been retired for years, have few savings left to invest, and are in the dubious position of wishing you had enough income to tempt Uncle Sam into taxing it. As it is, you can barely make ends meet. So what should you do?

To start, realize that it's never too late. No one is ever too poor to begin charting a path to financial independence. Make sure you follow the three steps we discussed earlier in this chapter: (1) calculate your net worth, (2) set financial goals, and (3) develop a budget and try to live within it. The results may not make you rich, but will likely make you more financially secure. If you have savings, particularly a small amount, be sure to invest it prudently, using the tips we provided previously. Also, find out whether you're eligible for income assistance through the federal supplemental security income program.

Supplemental Security Income

A more apt description of this federal program might be secret security income, because so few people have heard of it. According to a survey sponsored by the American Association of Retired Persons, almost half of the older persons eligible for SSI do not receive benefits because they are unaware of the program or do not know how to apply.

So what is SSI? It's an income-support program run by the Social Security Administration that provides monthly cash payments to low-income adults over 65 or to people of any age who are blind or disabled. Even if you are receiving social security benefits, you may also qualify for SSI.

Am I eligible for SSI? If you are age 65 or older, or blind or disabled, you may qualify for SSI provided you have a limited income (guidelines vary by state) and few assets (in 1991, no more than $2,000 for a single person, or $3,000 for a couple; your home and personal auto are not counted for this purpose). If you qualify for other income benefits such as social security or a pension, you must apply for them first. If you want to know whether you're eligible for SSI, telephone your local social security office for more information.

How do I apply for SSI? Your local social security office can explain the application procedure and tell you what information you must supply. Generally, you'll need your social security card; a birth certificate or other proof of age; and documents verifying your income and assets, such as payroll slips, copies of tax returns, bankbooks, and life-insurance policies.

How much will my monthly SSI payment be? It varies depending on what state you live in and your other sources of income. For example, in 1991, the maximum monthly federal SSI benefit was

$407 for a single person. If you lived in California, however, you could receive up to $650 a month. This is because California, which has a comparatively high cost of living, augments the federal payment. Twenty-six other states also supplement federal SSI benefits.

Although some SSI recipients qualify for the maximum benefits, payments may be lower if you have other income. Your social security office can give you information about levels of payment and how your income affects them.

Insurance Planning

No financial plan is complete until it addresses the "what ifs":

- What if I become seriously ill? How will I pay my medical bills?
- What if I need nursing-home care? How will I cover those long-term costs?
- What if I suddenly die tomorrow? How will my dependents support themselves?

Insurance planning helps you protect yourself against the unexpected. As situations change over time, your insurance needs also change. Many people, for example, need less life insurance as they grow older. At the same time, many feel they need more protection against potential long-term health-care costs. In this chapter we review the different types of life-insurance policies that are available and offer guidelines for selecting the coverage that is best for you. (For similar information on medical insurance, see "The Health Insurance Puzzle" in chapter 4.)

Life Insurance

Henry and Connie T. bought separate life-insurance policies when their kids were in diapers and the mortgage on their home was brand new. Now the children have graduated, married, and established careers. The house will be paid off this year. Henry wonders, "Do we still need life insurance?"

That question, say consumer advocates, is the first one you should ask when assessing your life-insurance needs. In *Your Financial Security: Effective Financial Strategies for Every Stage of Life,* financial advisor Sylvia Porter notes, "The only real reason to buy life insurance is if someone depends on your salary or services." Thus, if your children are self-supporting and your spouse would have sufficient income if you died, you may not need life insurance. If, on the other hand, you contribute to the financial well-being of others, you probably need coverage. It's best to discuss the needs of family members with them so that you can plan for unfortunate contingencies such as your own premature death.

Assuming you do need insurance coverage, how can you determine how much you need? The answer depends on your circumstances. *Consumer Reports* cautions against using rule-of-thumb estimates, such as five times your income, and recommends instead a three-step approach to calculating a dollar amount: First, determine your family's expenses. Then, "analyze your assets and the sources of income that you can use to cover the expenses. Finally, subtract the assets from the needs. The result is the amount of additional insurance that you'll need to buy."

Next, consider the type of policy that's best for you. In today's market, you can choose among five basic types of life insurance: term life, whole life, universal life, variable life, and variable-universal life. Several of these policies combine life insurance with a tax-deferred savings plan. Such policies can be a good way for people who need the death benefits to save for retirement. The *Wall Street Journal* notes that there are also pitfalls to these policies. "The biggest . . . is that insurance works as a retirement investment only if premiums are paid for many years. Further, financial advisors caution that insurance is more complex—and often less rewarding as an investment—than it first appears." In other words, let the buyer beware.

Before purchasing any life-insurance policy, make sure that you fully understand the provisions and have shopped around for the best deal. Also, ask about free-look provisions. Not every policy comes with one, but some allow you about ten days to examine the policy, with the option of returning it for a refund if you're not satisfied.

Term life insurance. These policies, which provide life-insurance coverage for a limited number of years, pay benefits in the event of death. However, in contrast to other types of policies, they build up no cash value (the cash value of a policy is the amount of money you can borrow from the policy at a rate of interest specified in the policy). Each dollar spent on term insurance is used to buy coverage, so at first these policies provide the largest death benefit for your insurance dollar. But as you grow older, premiums jump in proportion to benefits. Moreover, most policies cannot be renewed beyond a specified age, usually 65 or 70. After that, if you still want coverage, you'll have to buy or convert to another type of policy. If you buy a term life-insurance policy with a conversion clause, make sure you understand the conditions that will be imposed.

Whole life insurance. Also called straight or ordinary life, these policies combine life insurance with a savings account that accumulates a cash value on a tax-deferred basis. They offer coverage for as long as you live, regardless of your health or age, with no increase in premiums. Although premiums are initially higher than those for term insurance, they're comparatively cheaper as you grow older.

The cash value accrued in the later years of your policy can be used to supplement retirement income, in that you can borrow money from the policy at an interest rate specified in the policy. Any money owing at your death will be deducted from the policy's benefits.

If you surrender a whole life policy soon after purchase, your return will be sharply reduced by agents' commissions. These charges decline each year until they vanish, typically after five to ten years.

Universal life insurance. A flexible version of whole life, these policies allow you to modify the amount and timing of premium payments and control your cash-value growth. Your death benefits may also rise and fall, but they never will fall below a guaranteed minimum. As with whole life policies, universal life policies are considered poor buys if surrendered early.

Variable life insurance. Although these policies accumulate cash value, you—not the insurer—decide how to invest your premiums. Your death benefit and cash value may go up or down, depending on how your investments perform. Consequently, these can be particularly risky buys for novice investors. As with whole life insurance, you pay a fixed premium.

Variable-universal life insurance. These policies are a combination of variable and universal life policies. They allow you to vary your premium payments and death benefit and to choose your own investments. Again, unseasoned investors should cast a wary eye on these policies.

A Word of Advice on Seeking Advice

Everyone needs a financial plan, but not everyone needs help preparing it. Katherine O., a 76-year-old widow, manages her assets like a pro. Every morning she tunes into television news reports on early Wall Street activity. Then she flips to the business section of her newspaper to track her investments' performance and research new possibilities. Ask her, and she'll quote CD rates at every major bank within a ten-mile radius of her home. She claims she's not smart about money matters, but the facts indicate otherwise. Since she stopped following her stockbroker's advice twenty years ago, she's nearly doubled her net worth.

Katherine's friend, Nancy, on the other hand, is in the market for sound financial advice. "It will be snowing in hell before I learn to read a ticker tape; I simply have no investment sense," she confesses. Although she scans financial articles in newspapers and magazines, "the information confuses, rather than enlightens, me," she says. "I don't have a particularly large estate, but what I have, I want to protect. So, I'm shopping around for a good financial planner."

Like Nancy, many older men and women—lacking the time, inclination, or expertise to do justice to their financial plans—are turning to a relatively new breed of professional advisor: the financial planner. This person, notes the Foundation for Financial Planning, can help you focus on specific problems that stand in the way of your financial goals; he or she can prepare a written plan with specific recommendations to help you achieve financial security.

You don't need to be wealthy to benefit from the services of a financial planner. Often it's more important to seek help when every dollar counts. But consumer advocates caution that selecting a financial planner requires as much, if not more, thought and attention as choosing a doctor, lawyer, or accountant. Notes the Better Business Bureau: "Virtually anyone can hang out a shingle or place an advertisement in a telephone directory and be called a 'financial planner.' " While most who do are legitimate, some are less than scrupulous. According to a report by AARP, financial-planning fraud cost 22,000 investors more than $400 million in losses during 1986 and 1987.

To separate the good from the bad, you should interview a minimum of three financial planners and, for each, find out the answers to the following questions:

• *What credentials and education does this person have?* Some planners have taken special courses in their field and earned credentials such as certified financial planner (CFP), chartered financial consultant (ChFC), and master of science in financial services (MSFS). Others may be certified public accountants (CPA) or chartered life underwriters (CLU).

• *Is the planner registered as an investment advisor?* If someone is giving you advice on investments or use of the stock market, he or she should be registered with the Securities and Exchange Commission (SEC) or with a state agency.

• *How many years of experience does the planner have?* Experts recommend a minimum of twelve years.

• *With whom will you be working?* Don't assume that the person you interview will be the one who prepares your financial plan. He or she may delegate tasks to a colleague. In such cases, it's wise to interview this person as well.

• *Can the planner provide you with both professional and client references?* From your perspective, there is only one right answer: Yes. Be sure you follow up by interviewing them.

• *Can the planner provide you with sample plans prepared for other clients?* Again, this question demands an affirmative answer. Check to make sure the plans reflect the duties of a financial planner as outlined above.

• *How does the planner keep abreast of new financial developments?* It's important that your financial planner keep current on tax and investment strategies. Some do this by enrolling in continuing education classes or by joining industry associations that provide ongoing training and services.

• *How are fees determined?* Most financial planners earn commissions on annuities, tax shelters, and other investment products they sell. These planners may have an interest in selling you products that provide them with the highest commission. Consequently, a little healthy skepticism is in order when following their advice.

Always ask for a *written* estimate of fees and services, and then compare this with the estimates you receive from other financial planners.

For referrals to financial planners in your area, ask satisfied friends and business associates or contact the Institute of Certified Financial Planners or the International Association of Financial Planners (see Resources).

Estate Planning

Just as financial planning is fundamental to protecting your economic health, so is estate planning fundamental to securing the well-being of those you love. Too often, however, when it comes to this important step, we procrastinate. For example, Jack L. kept putting off the estate planning he should have done. Then one day, right in the middle of a tough tennis match, he felt a tightening in his chest, tingling in his left arm, and difficulty catching his breath. Certain he was having a heart attack, he forfeited the game and had his tennis partner rush him to the emergency room.

He spent the next couple of days agonizing while his doctor performed a series of tests; he spent the following weekend celebrating after he received a clean bill of health.

"My doctor suggested I shed a few pounds, but found no evidence of heart disease," recalls the 52-year-old corporate executive. "He speculated that the symptoms I had experienced were the result of overexerting myself on a particularly hot day and letting my imagination run wild."

Paradoxically, while relishing what he called his "new lease on life," Jack realized that now was the time to start planning his estate. "En route to the hospital that day, it struck me that I wasn't going to be able to take it all with me. So, I had better make sure that those I love benefit from the assets I've accumulated over a lifetime."

Estate planning is the process of setting forth binding instructions so that when you die, your personal property and other assets are distributed according to your wishes, and with a minimum of bother and expense for your heirs. Probably the biggest reason people avoid estate planning is that they don't want to think about dying. But as Jack discovered, preparing an estate plan isn't really for dying; it's for living. It allows you to extend a part of your life for the care of others. Thus, for many, it's a vehicle for a final act of love.

If you've been putting off planning your estate, perhaps now is the time to give it serious consideration. And even if you wrapped up this business years ago, you should review your plans periodically to make sure they still reflect your wishes, are up to date, and take into account any recent changes in your family or finances.

In the following pages, we review what you need to know before you start planning your estate, and then describe common legal tools available for distributing your assets.

The Preliminaries

Your net worth. Like financial planning, estate planning begins with a thorough and honest calculation of your net worth. If you haven't done so already, set some time aside to complete the Net Worth Worksheet in this chapter. The legal documents you select for distributing your estate will depend in part on your net worth, so it's important to calculate this figure as accurately as possible.

This step is often an eye-opener for older men and women who have accumulated assets they've forgotten about or overlooked. For example, when Jack completed a Net Worth Worksheet, he was surprised to discover he was worth almost twice as much as he thought after adding up the value of his house, which had appreciated considerably in recent years, and his pension benefits, life insurance, and other assets he hadn't previously taken into account.

Estate tax. In addition to knowing your net worth, it helps to be aware of estate tax rules so that you can take steps to minimize such tax if necessary. Under current federal law, your estate may be subject to tax if its value exceeds $600,000. In addition, your heirs may be liable for state inheritance and estate taxes as well as capital gains tax on assets sold at a profit. If you have an estate worth $600,000 or more, your best strategy for reducing estate tax is to seek advice from a lawyer.

The Tools: Wills, Trusts, Joint Tenancy

Your will. For many people, a will constitutes the foundation of their estate plan. Although it's not the only legal tool used to distribute property, it's the most common one and the one against which other options—such as a living trust (described later in this section)—are frequently weighed. Consequently, it's important that you understand this estate-planning device.

Your will designates how and to whom your assets will be distributed when you die. It also allows you to name an executor to carry out the terms of your will and to appoint a guardian for any dependent children. A properly drawn will makes it much easier for your heirs to settle your estate. In addition, it can save money in taxes and other estate settlement expenses.

To illustrate the importance of preparing a will, some legal advisors point out what happens if you die without one—called dying *intestate*. In such cases, the state intervenes with rules of its own that may not reflect your preferences. For example, suppose your spouse and two children survive you. Many states will divide your property equally among them. If you have no children, the state may give up to half your estate to surviving parents and siblings. In both cases, you might have preferred your spouse to inherit everything. Other drawbacks to dying without a will include extra legal expenses, burdensome proceedings that tie up your estate, and, particularly for large estates, missed opportunities to reduce taxes.

If you do no other estate planning, you should prepare a will. This rule holds even if your estate is small or your spouse has drawn up a will. You both need one.

For many people, a family conference is a prerequisite to preparing a will—or any estate plan for that matter—because it allows everyone concerned to discuss and coordinate wishes and to resolve any conflicts that may arise. Such conferences may be tense and difficult, at least initially. Recalls Alan W.: "When I gathered my wife and children to discuss my will, everyone shied away

SOURCES FOR LEGAL SERVICES

One of the best ways to find a qualified, affordable lawyer is the old-fashioned way—by word-of-mouth referrals from satisfied relatives, friends, co-workers, and business associates. You can also check the library. Although you probably won't find an attorney for hire there, the reference librarian can help you locate the Lawyers' Register by Specialities and Fields of Law, *which lists individual lawyers whom you can contact for information about rates and services. In addition, the organizations listed below can also help you find legal assistance at modest rates:*

• National Academy of Elder Law Attorneys, 1730 East River Road, Suite 107, Tucson, AZ 85718. Telephone: (602) 881-4005. Established in 1988, this association now includes 350 members, all of whom specialize in legal matters most needed by older Americans: long-term-care planning, income, housing, health, age discrimination and estate planning. Send a self-addressed stamped business envelope (No. 10) for a free list of member attorneys nationwide.

• State and local bar associations. Many of these sponsor legal-referral services to help consumers find affordable attorneys. For addresses and telephone numbers, check the yellow pages of your telephone book under entries such as "attorneys," "attorneys—referral service," or "legal services."

• Legal Services Corporation, 400 Virginia Avenue, SW, Washington, DC 20024-2751. Telephone: (202) 863-1820. This government-sponsored agency operates through approximately 330 local centers to provide legal help to low-income persons. To qualify, your 1991 annual income cannot have exceeded 125 percent of the poverty standard or $8,275 for a single person (the limits are $10,363 and $9,513, respectively, for residents of Alaska and Hawaii). People ineligible for services can request referrals to private lawyers. For the address and telephone number of a local center, check the white pages of your telephone book under listings starting with "legal aid," or contact the Legal Services Corporation.

• Area Agencies on Aging. Located in cities and counties across the country, these agencies administer legal assistance programs for Americans ages 60 and over. Services are typically designed for low-income persons. For information about legal assistance programs in your area, contact a senior center or your State Unit on Aging (see appendix B).

• Legal Counsel for the Elderly. This program of the American Association of Retired Persons operates hotlines in the District of Columbia and in Pennsylvania. Specially trained lawyers provide free legal advice or offer the names of lawyers in private practice who will charge reduced fees. The telephone number in Washington, DC is (202) 234-0970; in Allegheny County, PA, call (412) 261-LAWS; and for other Pennsylvania residents, call (800) 262-LAWS.

• American Bar Association Commission on Legal Problems of the Elderly, 1800 M Street, NW, Washington, DC 20036. Telephone: (202) 331-2297. This group publishes free booklets and brochures on legal topics of interest to older men and women. Call or write for a publications list.

from the topic until I explained that I needed and really wanted their help and input. Later on, my son and daughter started arguing over who should get what, particularly my collection of first editions. It took us over an hour to agree on an equitable distribution. It certainly wasn't the most enjoyable family discussion we've ever had. But I will say this: It was one of the most fruitful."

After compiling the names of your beneficiaries and a list of your wishes, you'll need to select an executor (also called a personal representative), who will be responsible for carrying out your will's instructions. You can appoint your spouse or another family member, your attorney, your bank, or a friend. The person you name should not only be someone you trust, but also someone capable of handling financial matters and willing to commit substantial amounts of time. Before drawing up your will, make sure the person you select as executor is aware of his or her appointment and understands the responsibilities involved. Executors are allowed to charge fees for their services, although family members frequently forego payment.

After accomplishing these preliminaries, Paul B., 56, wondered how to proceed: "A friend said I don't need to consult a lawyer, but could do my own handwritten will or use a form available in a stationery store. But are these legal and advisable?"

They're legal, but risky. A handwritten, or *holographic,* will may be ruled invalid if not properly prepared, and even if it passes muster, it may be easily challenged. A stationery-store form or other do-it-yourself device may not meet your specific needs and may create such serious problems that your family will need a lawyer to unravel them. (However, self-help advocates argue that these instruments are sufficient for people with basic, straightforward needs.) The safest way to ensure legality is to have your will drawn up by a lawyer. Fees depend partly on the number of consultations and the complexity of the will. According to the American Bar Association's Commission on Legal Problems of the Elderly, fees for a simple will start as low as $100.

Once the will is completed, your lawyer will retain a copy. You should keep another copy at home and inform family members of its location. Don't lock your will in a safety-deposit box because the safety-deposit box may be sealed at your death.

After you die, your will must be filed, typically by your personal representative, in a state probate court. Probate is the procedure used to ensure that the terms of your will are carried out and to transfer title to assets to your heirs. It is at this point that the court authorizes your executor to distribute the estate's assets.

Probate proceedings can be both costly and lengthy. Fees for a probate attorney and your executor are based on your estate's value. They vary by state, ranging from about 4 percent to 11 percent. Proceedings last several months, sometimes a year or more from initiation to completion. However, some types of property pass outside your will and do not go through probate. These include beneficiary-designated assets such as IRAs, annuities, and life-insurance benefits. Assets that you hold in joint tenancy with another person, such as a house or bank account, also escape probate if your co-tenant has a right of survivorship in the property.

Living trusts. "STOP PROBATE WORRIES! A living trust avoids a complex probate proceeding; allows quick distribution to your heirs; eliminates probate fees and costs, and saves substantial death taxes."

Sound too good to be true? Bud L. thought so when he read this advertisement in his local newspaper. He and his wife, Martha, both in their sixties, consider themselves traditionalists. Accordingly, in preparing their estate, they had both executed wills, just as their parents had done before them, and their parents' parents had done before that. With regard to living trusts, the Los Angeles couple figured that they were probably just another Southern California innovation, like creative financing for homes, which Bud and Martha wanted no part of. Still, Bud admits, "we were intrigued." And like a hundred or so other older people who spotted the advertisement that week, they were curious enough to attend the sponsoring legal firm's seminar on the topic. One type of trust used in estate planning, living trusts are growing in popularity. Although many participants entered the seminar as skeptics, several—including Bud and Martha—came out believers. That's because living trusts, while not for everyone, offer considerable advantages over wills.

To create a living trust, you transfer title to real estate, stocks, bonds, bank accounts, and other assets to a trust while you're still alive. You also designate a trustee, who is responsible for managing your assets. Most people who set up living trusts act as their own trustees, thereby keeping control and avoiding management fees. A less common alternative is to appoint someone else—for example, a family member, friend, bank-trust company, or professional trustee.

Trust documents also allow you to name a successor trustee, who steps in to manage and distribute your assets after you die or if you should become incapacitated. These documents also allow you to name beneficiaries, who will inherit the property in trust after your death.

If you set up a revocable living trust, you can change it at any time. By contrast, an irrevocable living trust cannot be altered unless the court determines that its provisions are unworkable or that they frustrate the trust's general purpose.

Unlike wills, living trusts do not go through probate; thus, your estate may be settled faster and with less expense. Living trusts also help you avoid the need for a conservatorship because you've already appointed someone, your successor trustee, to manage your assets if you cannot. Other benefits to these estate-planning devices include the possibility of saving on estate and inheritance taxes and the ability to keep estate information private. (In contrast to a will, which becomes a matter of public record, a living trust is kept confidential.)

Before establishing a living trust, consider the drawbacks. Transferring titles to homes, bank accounts, and business and other investments into the name of the trust can be cumbersome and time-consuming. Legal fees for setting up living trusts range from $700 to $3,000, which is considerably more expensive than those for preparing a will. When refinancing a home, some lenders require that the house title be taken out of a trust, although it can be placed back in afterward. And sometimes it's preferable to have your estate probated because probate restricts the time in which creditors can come forth with claims. Given these disadvantages, some financial and legal experts do not recommend living trusts for people with few assets. These experts argue that they're probably more trouble than they're worth.

Testamentary trusts. Another commonly used trust for estate planning, a testamentary trust is created by your will and becomes effective after you die. Lawyers point out that testamentary trusts offer many of the same tax-avoidance advantages of living trusts; however, they must go through probate. As with any type of trust, you should seek legal advice before establishing a testamentary trust.

Joint tenancy. Elizabeth H., a 78-year-old widow, is in a quandary: "I want to make sure my estate passes without hassle to my only son after my death. One friend has strongly advised me to hold title to my house, my largest asset, in joint tenancy with my

son. She said this would prevent the house from being tied up in probate court. Another friend, however, said joint tenancy can create all sorts of unanticipated problems. Who's right?"

Both friends may be right. With the most common type of joint ownership, joint tenancy with a right of survivorship, two persons own property—such as real estate, bank accounts, or investments—in both names. When one co-tenant dies, the other becomes sole owner of the entire property. The surviving tenant is entitled to the property without probate.

Although holding property in joint tenancy seems a convenient way to avoid probate, some legal experts recommend it be used selectively. In *Your Legal Rights in Later Life,* attorney John J. Regan writes, "Since either joint tenant usually may dispose of the property while both are alive, it is especially important to choose a person you trust to serve as joint tenant." Then, keep in mind the possibility that you and your co-tenant may have a parting of the ways, and your property may be sold out from under you.

Another drawback is that if a parent puts a child on the deed as joint tenant, the property becomes subject to attachment for the debts of the child. For example, if Mary names her son as co-tenant, her house—now *their* house—could wind up being used to pay her son's debts.

Furthermore, the first joint tenant to die cannot dispose of the property under his or her will, and the surviving tenant is under no legal obligation to share the property with other heirs. Because of all these factors, it's best to seek legal advice before placing large assets under joint tenancy.

Letters of Last Instruction

Regardless of the legal tools you select, you can facilitate the transfer of property to your heirs by preparing a letter of last instruction to be opened at your death. The letter should include the location of

- your will or trust instructions
- birth and marriage certificates
- insurance policies
- bank passbooks and numbers
- proof of ownership of property, checking accounts, credit cards, car(s), house(s), stocks, retirement benefits, and insurance policies.

Also list any memorial instructions:

- Do you want to be cremated or buried?
- Do you want the casket to be open or closed?
- Do you want a religious or fraternal memorial?
- Do you own a cemetery plot? If so, where is the deed?

Let your heirs know your wishes in your letter of instruction. Another effective tool for making your last wishes known is a durable power of attorney for health care, which is discussed in the following pages.

Perhaps equally important to survivors is an unusual document called an ethical will. It attempts to sum up what a person has learned in life, and it expresses his or her wishes for loved ones. A spiritual document, it is a "window into the soul of the writer" that transmits values, beliefs, and attitudes.

Advance Directives for Protecting Your Interests

Difficult as it may be to anticipate your death through estate planning, it may be even more disturbing to contemplate what may happen to you should you be incapacitated by a stroke or other disabling illness. Who will manage your financial affairs? Who will decide where you live? Who will provide consent for medical treatment? And, if necessary, who may withdraw that consent? You may think you have little control over who calls the shots when you can no longer do so. But by planning ahead for possible incapacity, you can protect your interests through advance directives. Let's look at what these are and how they work.

Durable Powers of Attorney

Simon D., a 63-year-old attorney, is like the rest of us. He wants to live a long, healthy life, and he hopes to make his own decisions and act independently right up to the very end. But he has read about the devastating effects of Alzheimer's disease, which progressively robs victims of their memory and ability to care for themselves. And he's had friends whose inevitable deaths have been prolonged by respirators and other forms of medical technology. He knows there's no guarantee that similar things won't happen to him. That's why the first legal document Simon prepared for himself, even before his will, was a durable power of attorney.

"An ordinary power of attorney," says Simon, "allows you to authorize another person, whom you select, to take action and make decisions on your behalf. The problem with these documents is that they lapse if you, the principal, become incapacitated, for example, by a stroke. A durable power of attorney avoids this pitfall because it remains effective even if you become disabled." He adds that, in some states, durable powers of attorney take effect only after the principal becomes incompetent.

A durable power of attorney allows you to transfer as much or as little power as you want. For example, you can authorize another person to manage all your property, or you can limit that person's power to selling your car. You can also stipulate how long you want the power of attorney to remain in effect, and you can cancel it at any time (it's best to do this in writing).

Traditionally, durable powers of attorney have been used in connection with property and commercial transactions. Indeed, New York state restricts the use of durable powers of attorney to financial matters. But in other states, say a growing number of legal experts, nothing in any statute or court decision suggests that these documents can't also be used to instruct someone to make health-care decisions on your behalf should you become disabled. Thus, if you live outside New York state and want to protect your right to receive maximum care in the event you become severely ill, consider executing a durable power of attorney. If you'd rather your doctor spared the heroics and let you slip quietly away, the prescription's the same: Consider a durable power of attorney.

The options are somewhat different for residents of a handful of states and Washington, D.C. California, Illinois, Maine, Nevada, Ohio, Oregon, Rhode Island, Texas, Utah, and the District of Columbia all have authorized the more specialized durable power of attorney for health care, which deals specifically with the kind and intensity of health care you want if you become incapacitated. If you live in one of these states, consider executing a regular durable power of attorney for financial matters as well as a durable power of attorney for health care.

Planning for incapacity requires some foresight on your part; only people who are competent may execute durable powers of attorney. Consequently, it may be too late for a person with Alzheimer's disease or another disabling illness to take this step. Also, be aware that durable powers of attorney are subject to abuse. In fact, most elder-abuse cases involve the misuse of a durable power of attorney. Consequently, when appointing an agent to act on your behalf, it's vital that you select a person you can trust, whether that is a spouse, a relative, or a close friend. You should also name an alternate in case the first person is unavailable.

Although short forms of durable powers of attorney are available in stationery stores, it's best to seek legal advice before executing these documents. Exceptions are durable powers of attorney for health care, which usually do not require an attorney's help. These documents are available from the Society for the Right to Die (see Resources) and from many hospitals and state or local medical associations.

Living Wills

Connie B., 64, spent twelve miserable days at the hospital while her husband, Cary, lay dying of cancer in the intensive care unit. He couldn't breathe, so a respirator breathed for him. He couldn't eat, so he was fed through intravenous tubes. Connie felt she should be grateful for these medical "miracles" keeping Cary alive, but she wasn't. The technology was merely prolonging her husband's death, and, she felt, robbing him of his dignity. She knew Cary wouldn't want that.

"I was heart-broken when he finally died," she recalls, "but at the same time, I was relieved that the ordeal hadn't stretched out for weeks. Later, I started wondering what I could do to ensure that when it was my time to go, I would die a natural death. A friend told me that a living will could protect my wishes. How does this work?"

Recognized by most states, a living will is a directive to physicians and family members that you not be given extraordinary treatment if it will only prolong your dying. In the event you are unable to express your wishes, your attending physician is legally obligated to carry out the terms of your living will. A physician who is opposed to taking such action is obligated to transfer you to the care of a physician who will carry out your wishes.

Some states require that living wills take a specified form, while others allow you to add instructions about wanted or unwanted treatment. To find out if you live in a state that authorizes living wills and to obtain a copy of the appropriate form, contact the Society for the Right to Die (see Resources).

While a living will helps you exercise your right to die with dignity, it has severe limitations. For example, in many states a living will is not binding unless the person signs it after having been diagnosed with a terminal or incurable illness. Thus, if your death is not imminent, your living will may not protect your right to refuse treatment. Also, the document's instructions may not apply to your particular situation because the circumstances of a critical illness and available treatment options are often unpredictable.

Although a living will is better than no directive at all, because of its limitations, many lawyers and physicians agree that a durable power of attorney (or a durable power of attorney for health care) is better. Of living wills, physicians Robert Steinbrook and Bernard Lo of the University of California, San Francisco, write: "On balance, this approach has not been successful. Few competent patients write such advance directives, and when they do, the wording is usually vague or ambiguous." They advocate instead the use of durable powers of attorney, calling them "preventive medicine for difficult decisions."

It's true that Americans are living longer than ever before. Paradoxically, having time on your side may work against you if you use longevity as an excuse to postpone financial and estate planning. As we said earlier, it's never too late to start charting your path to financial independence. Then again, it's never too early, either. Don't procrastinate. Take the steps we've outlined in this chapter and use the tools we've described. And don't forget to read on. In the next chapter you'll learn, among other things, how to make the most of what may be your most valuable asset: your home.

Resources

Institute of Certified Financial Planners, 2 Denver Highlands, 10065 E. Harvard Avenue, Suite 320, Denver, CO 80231. Telephone: (303) 751-7600.
Provides referrals to financial planners throughout the country.

Internal Revenue Service.
Call the IRS on its toll-free number, (800) 424-1040, or check the government section of your phone book for the number of your local office. Ask about free publications that address your specific concerns.

International Association of Financial Planners, 2 Concourse Parkway, Suite 800, Atlanta, GA 30328. Telephone: (404) 395-1605.
Provides referrals to financial planners throughout the country.

Pension Rights Center, Suite 704, 918 16th Street, NW, Washington, DC 20006. Telephone: (202) 296-3776.
This nonprofit organization publishes helpful booklets and other materials designed to educate workers, retirees, and their families about pension issues.

Social Security Administration.
Visit a local office or call toll-free, (800) 234-5772, for information about social security and supplemental security income benefits. Ask about free publications that address your specific concerns.

Society for the Right to Die, 250 W. 57th Street, New York, NY 10107. Telephone: (212) 246-6973.
Publishes free pamphlets about protecting your health care rights in the event you become incapacitated. Also available free are living wills for the states that have authorized them.

State Departments of Insurance.
These government agencies often publish pamphlets and brochures

designed to help consumers assess their life-insurance needs and purchase policies to meet those needs. Check the government section of your telephone book for the appropriate address and telephone number.

Recommended Reading

Before You Say Yes: 15 Questions to Turn off an Investment Swindler. Single copies are available free from the National Futures Association, Public Affairs Department, 200 W. Madison Street, Suite 1600, Chicago, IL 60606. Telephone: (312) 781-1300.

Consumer Budget Planner. Singles copies are available free from the American Financial Services Association, 1101 14th Street, NW, Washington, DC 20005. Telephone: (202) 289-0400.

Consumer Guide to Financial Independence. Single copies are available for $1 from the International Association of Financial Planners, Customer Relations, Two Concourse Parkway, Suite 800, Atlanta, GA 30328. Telephone: (404) 395-1605.

A Guide to Understanding Your Pension Plan. Single copies are available free from the American Association of Retired Persons, 601 E Street, NW, Washington, DC 20049. Telephone: (202) 434-2277.

Investors Information Kit. Single copies are available for a small charge from the New York Stock Exchange, c/o Don Jagoda Associates, 1 Underhill Boulevard, Syosset, NY 11791. Telephone: (516) 496-7312.

Porter, Sylvia. *Your Financial Security: Effective Financial Strategies for Every Stage of Life.* New York, NY: Morrow, 1987.

Regan, John J. *Your Legal Rights in Later Life.* Washington, DC: American Association of Retired Persons, 1989.

Riemer, Jack, and Nathaniel Stampfer (eds.). *Ethical Wills: A Modern Jewish Treasury.* New York: Schocken Books, 1983.

Tips on Financial Planners. Single copies are available for $1 from the Council of Better Business Bureaus, Inc., 1515 Wilson Boulevard, Arlington, VA 22209. Telephone: (703) 276-0100.

Weaver, Peter and Annette Buchanan. *What to Do with What You've Got:*

The Practical Guide to Money Management in Retirement. Washington, DC: American Association of Retired Persons; Scott, Foresman and Co., 1984.

What You Should Know about the Pension Law. Single copies are available free from the U.S. Department of Labor, Pension and Welfare Benefit Administration, Division of Public Information, 200 Constitution Avenue, NW, Washington, DC 20210. Also available free: *Often-Asked Questions about Employee Retirement Benefits.*

Your Pension—Things You Should Know about Your Pension Plan. Single copies are available free from the Pension Benefit Guaranty Corporation, Coverage & Inquiries Branch, Insurance Operations Department, 2020 K Street, NW, Washington, DC 20006-1806.

CHAPTER SIX A Place Called Home

We shape our dwellings, and afterwards our dwellings shape us.
—Winston Churchill

Older Americans, who spend more time inside their dwellings than younger persons, attach great significance to their homes. Not only is the physical space important, but the home represents memories and community. Seventy-five percent of older Americans own their homes, and in most cases it is their most valuable asset. For those on a fixed income who rent their living space, housing may be the biggest expense in their monthly budget.

Although most older Americans strongly prefer to spend their retirement years in their own homes, increasing numbers are choosing to move to a place that requires less upkeep, offers more companionship, or provides recreation and health care. Some people move because their current housing is prohibitively expensive, the neighborhood no longer feels safe, or they need more support services. While most older persons look for new homes near their old ones, some move great distances to be close to children or to find a warmer climate.

It is possible to make a home—a congenial environment—of any place you choose to live. For people thinking about housing today, the array of options can be overwhelming. Never before have we had so many choices.

In this chapter we explore living arrangements for different needs and situations. Some options, such as home modifications and social services, can increase the safety, supportiveness, and comfort of your present residence so that you can stay in it as long as possible. If you own your home, a reverse-annuity mortgage may allow you to tap the equity so that you can better afford to make repairs or pay for services. On the other hand, a retirement community may appeal to you if you are an active person looking for a different lifestyle or new friends. If you are concerned about available services and health care, you might consider shared housing or a continuing-care retirement community. If you require personal care or medical attention that can't be provided in your own home you may need to move to a board-and-care home or a skilled-nursing facility.

Decisions about housing—especially those that involve moving, drawing income out of your house, or sharing your home with another person—should be made only after a great deal of thought. You may find several ways to meet your needs. To help with these considerations, we offer basic information about such options as retirement communities, condominiums, cooperatives, rental living, mobile homes, living with adult children (including the option of accessory apartments), congregate housing, continuing-care retirement communities, and nursing homes. The more information you have, the better your choice will be for you.

Aging in Place

Beverly and Walter A., 66 and 81, respectively, were married in 1945. Their first home was a rental apartment above a restaurant in Detroit. In the 1950s, with the help of the G.I. Bill, and with two small children and a third on the way, they moved to their own home in the suburbs. In 1963, Walter changed jobs and the family moved to San Diego, California. They bought a comfortable ranch home large enough to accommodate four children (two in college by then), where they've lived ever since. Their hallway is a gallery of portraits chronicling their family history. Bev says, "The only change we've made so far was to accommodate our grandparent status—we bought a used crib. I love this house. We own it free and clear. I can't see myself living anywhere else. Our daughter wants us to move near her, and those grandbabies are so cute I'm tempted, but not right now."

Bev and Walter's preference for staying put is typical of most Americans. A 1987 study by the American Association of Retired Persons (AARP) found that 70 percent of people over age 65 agreed with the statement, "What I'd really like to do is stay in my own home and never move." But sometimes changes in health and finances challenge us to adapt to new circumstances. For starters, staying in your own house as long as possible often involves adapting it to your changing needs as you age.

Bev and Walter have not yet made changes in their home to adapt to their changing needs. Let's see how they might fix up their home to make it safer and more comfortable.

Home Safety and Modification

One housing expert recently noted that our nation is filled with "Peter Pan housing, designed for people who would never grow old." We do age, however, and the physical changes that accompany aging can make it difficult for us to carry out daily activities such as bathing, dressing, and cooking in the old homestead. When our physical condition and our home are not compatible, accidents can occur in the home. And accidents can lead to hospitalization and nursing-home stays. A good fit between ourselves and our homes is vital to remaining safe, active, and involved.

The American dream of owning our own home has cracks in it. As Ralph Waldo Emerson said in *Society and Solitary,* "A man builds a fine house and now he has a master and a task for life. He has to furnish it, watch it and keep it in repair the rest of his days." Indeed, almost 30 percent of older households have structural problems. The foundation may be cracked, and repairing it is

Figure 6-1 Adapt your bathroom to avoid accidents.

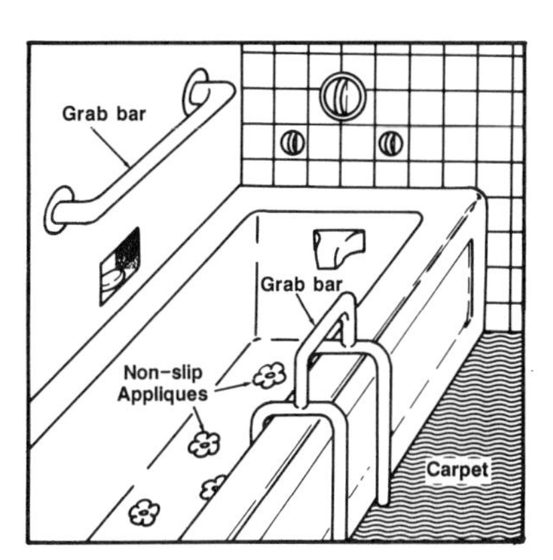

likely to cost more than an older person can comfortably afford. Another 12 percent of households have "dwelling-use" problems. For example, an 80-year-old woman who is crippled with arthritis may have trouble using the stairs of her apartment.

How can you adapt your home and lifestyle to meet your needs as you age? Here are some general solutions:

- Modify the structure of your house (for example, widen the doorway for a wheelchair).
- Install special equipment such as grab bars or handrails (see figure 6-1).
- Use assistive devices such as a walker or shower seat.
- Change the location of items in your house. Move furniture and take up throw rugs; transfer kitchen items that you use often to lower shelves.
- Replace household items with new ones that are more functional. For example, buy a chair with supportive arms, or rent a hospital bed.
- Change how or where you carry out activities. For example, take a sponge bath by the kitchen sink rather than soak in the bathtub, or convert a first-floor family room to a bedroom for someone who has trouble climbing stairs.
- Ask someone else to help you with activities that have become difficult, such as getting out of the bathtub or cooking.

Rose, 73, stood on a chair to reach a bowl on an upper shelf in her kitchen. The next thing she knew, the chair tipped. She broke her wrist and found herself seeing a physical therapist twice a week instead of joining her friends for a game of tennis. If we avoid changing our living patterns and our homes as we age, we increase our risk of accidents. Although anyone can have an accident, for older people the consequences of an accident can be serious—or deadly. The severity of injuries such as hip fractures increases with age, and injury is the fifth leading cause of death among older Americans.

Most injuries occur at home. About 600,000 older people end up in emergency rooms with injuries resulting from hazards that are overlooked and are sometimes easy to eliminate. Accidents, particularly around the home, can be avoided by taking precautionary measures.

In its research on products and environmental factors considered most hazardous to older Americans, the Buffalo Organization for Social and Technological Innovation identified floors and flooring materials as the most dangerous. The most troublesome areas for falls are the bathroom (especially while getting in and out of the tub), stairs, and kitchen. Get rid of those scatter rugs or secure them with tape, and save your bones!

Burns are also a problem. The most severe burns result from house fires. Cigarettes, cigars, and other smoking materials are often the cause of fires. Flammable clothing increases the severity of burns. The U.S. Consumer Product Safety Commission estimates that 70 percent of all people who die from clothing fires are over 65 years of age.

Fixing up the place to avoid accidents. Marion H., 68, was born in the beautiful two-story Victorian home where she has lived her entire life. Her family has owned this house for more than 125 years. Marion, who broke her leg in several places while running with her dog, spent six weeks in bed in traction. The ground-floor library became her bedroom. After she got out of traction, she found it difficult to climb up and down the stairs, but she disliked living in the library. At the suggestion of a friend, she installed a stair lift. Marion said, "I felt like a fool for breaking my leg in such a ridiculous way. Living in the library added insult to injury. The stair lift not only lifted my body, it lifted my spirits and restored my dignity."

Figure 6-2 Prevent falls by making your staircase safer.

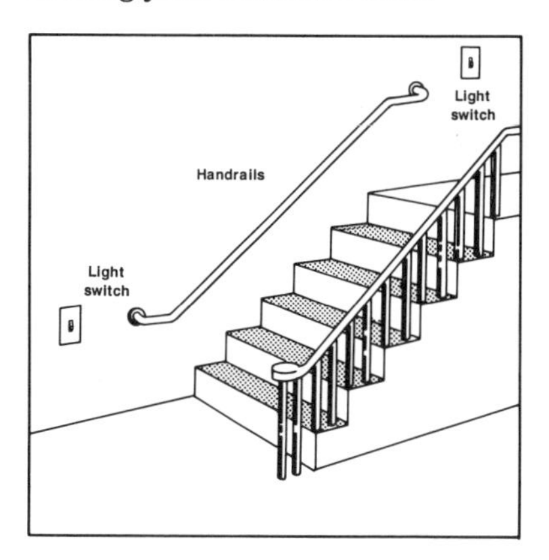

You can do many other things to make your life easier and more dignified. You can lower kitchen cabinets or move items to lower shelves so that you can reach things more easily. You can install a shelf outside the front door on which to put packages while you are unlocking the door. Some people with arthritis put lever handles on all their doors and water outlets because the twisting motion required for using round handles has become difficult. Depending on your needs, you might consider buying a raised toilet seat, adding grab bars in the bathroom, using a handheld shower, buying easy-to-hold tableware, constructing ramps, widening doors, or installing light switches at the top and bottom of the staircase (see figure 6-2).

You may feel reluctant to add such features because you associate their institutional appearance with hospitals or nursing homes. The truth is that many of them should be in all our homes. Fortunately, many of the products available today have been specially designed to complement the home environment. Browse through home-appliance catalogs and you'll be amazed at the array of attractive devices that promote independence (see Resources at the end of this chapter).

High-tech help. Technology in the home has enormous potential to enhance our lives by creating environments that are safe, accessible, comfortable, and easier to control. Many new products that make our homes more functional are available through medical supply companies, mail-order firms, hardware stores, and department stores. You can buy washers and dryers that have controls that you push rather than turn. Telephone panels now come with oversized numbers. Irons automatically switch off or give

INCREASE YOUR SAFETY AT HOME

• Post emergency numbers on your telephone.

• Position at least one telephone in a place that would be accessible if an accident left you unable to stand.

• Install smoke detectors and make sure they work. Some fire departments will help you obtain and install them.

• Wear clothing with short or close-fitting sleeves while cooking.

• If your electric sockets are overloaded, add new outlets or circuits. Don't use extension cords or multi-socket adapters.

• Install night lights in halls, bathrooms, and bedrooms.

• In the bathroom, install grab bars. Add nonslip appliques to the tub and shower. Use nonskid mats on the floor. Consider buying shower seats and raised toilet seats.

• To avoid a fire, don't tuck in an electric blanket or place covers on top of it. Never leave the blanket turned on when no one is using the bed. Safest of all, use a down comforter and eliminate electric bedcovers.

• Make certain your home has light switches at the top and bottom of stairways. Handrails should run down both sides. The top and bottom steps should be marked with bright, contrasting tape.

• Eliminate glare and shadows by installing window shades and improving lighting.

• Remove or secure all rugs and runners that slide. Buy double-faced adhesive carpet tape and apply it to the back of your rugs, or place rubber matting under them.

• Turn your water heater down to 120 degrees Fahrenheit (or lower) to prevent burns.

voice to warning messages. Inexpensive lamps turn themselves on and off in response to a sound. In the next few years, look for voice-activated appliances that won't even require you to push a button or clap. If you are especially concerned about security or falls, you might consider buying or renting an emergency-response system such as Lifeline. These electronic systems connect you directly with an agency or a hospital. If you qualify, Medicare will reimburse the costs of this technology.

New technological advances are being integrated into the Smart House, a home of the future. The Smart House is intended to monitor and control heating, air conditioning, lighting, and security systems—automatically. The system depends on specially installed wiring and equipment that is linked to a computer. While several similar systems are already on the market, they are quite expensive. The fully integrated Smart House will be available several years from now.

Obtaining home-repair services. You or members of your family may be able to make simple modifications to your house. If you have physical limitations that require environmental changes, you may want to ask your doctor or a home-health agency to arrange for an occupational therapist to assess your home. With prior written authorization from a physician, home visits by an occupational therapist—as well as purchase and installation of medically needed items such as grab bars, handrails, and raised toilet seats—are reimbursable through Medicare and Medicaid. Medical supply companies that sell these products can also install them.

Medicare and Medicaid generally do not pay for safety repairs such as fixing broken steps or installing safer wiring. You will have to dig into your own pocket for other changes you might want to make in your home: installing new locks, adding insulation, putting in a hand-held shower, widening doorways, lowering shelves, or building ramps. If you have a limited income, check your senior center for community-service organizations that operate home-repair and safety programs. Some agencies will send someone to make such changes in your home and will provide safety checks regardless of your income.

Some cities and towns also provide home-repair services that range from fixing a broken window or leaky pipe to more extensive jobs such as installing a ramp for a recent amputee or weatherproofing a house to conserve energy. Private contractors, handymen, retired workers, or trainees often do the work. Qualified homeowners may be asked to pay a small fee for services or furnish the necessary materials.

But what if you don't qualify for such a program, or the program does not cover the changes you want? Locating reliable help for construction or repairs can be a challenge. Your neighbors and local newspaper may be good sources of referrals. However, before agreeing to have anyone do work in your home, check references and inquire with the Better Business Bureau about the company's records. Make sure the contractor provides a written estimate of what you will have to pay, when the work will be done, and the time it will take. If changes are required from the orginal contract, get cost estimates. *Never* pay contractors or repair workers large deposits before they complete the work.

Under Title I of the federal Housing and Community Development Act of 1974, low-income homeowners can borrow against the equity of their homes. The loan typically carries a below-market interest rate and is secured by a lien against the house. Cities usually administer this program. Payment on the home-equity loan is deferred until the house is sold. The loan is for home repairs or remodeling.

Government departments of aging and social services often help low-income homeowners and renters with their utility bills. Some communities make assistance available only during the coldest or warmest months. In addition, public utility companies may set up special payment schedules during peak months, as well as provide weatherization assistance to qualified customers. Many utility companies offer other free conservation consultations to help residents use energy economically.

Services in Your Home

Even after you make the necessary changes in your home, you might need some assistance from an outside source to continue living there safely. If your spouse has died and you never had much interest in cooking, getting help with meals can make the difference between maintaining your health at home and developing nutritional problems that could put you in a hospital or nursing home. If you are caring for a disabled spouse, consider getting help

SERVICES TO HELP YOU STAY AT HOME

• ***Information and referral*** *helps you find what you need. Your senior center, community social services department, or State Unit on Aging are good places to begin.*

• ***Adult day health care*** *is an organized daily program of therapeutic, social, and health activities for adults with physical or mental impairments. The program is designed to help restore or maintain the clients' greatest capacity to care for themselves. Adult day health care can be a short-term transition from a hospital or home-health program to personal independence. It can also be a long-term alternative to institutionalization when 24-hour skilled-nursing care is not medically necessary, or when institutionalization is undesirable.*

• ***Home chore workers*** *typically clean house, do errands and grocery shopping, and prepare meals. Some chore services include yard maintenance and snow shoveling.*

• ***Home-delivered meals*** *bring nutritious meals to people unable to prepare their own. Some programs provide 5 meals per week; others bring lunch and supper as well as weekend meals. Meals are usually delivered once a day, often by volunteers.*

• ***Home health care*** *brings certain medical services to your home. These may include skilled nursing, occupational therapy, physical therapy, speech therapy, nutrition counseling, medical supplies and equipment, a homemaker, or a home health aide. A home health aide has been trained to assist with bathing and dressing, transferring a disabled patient, meal preparation, light cleaning, and laundry.*

• ***Emergency response systems*** *are electronic devices designed to summon help during an emergency. They are programmed to telephone an emergency response center, where the staff have relevant information and can respond quickly. These units, usually worn around the neck, can be leased.*

• ***Friendly visitors*** *offer social contact to people who are isolated or homebound and who have no regular contact with relatives or neighbors. Volunteers from church groups or social agencies usually visit weekly.*

• ***Hospice*** *provides services at home or in a health facility. It offers support for terminally ill patients and for their families, using a plan of care approved by the family physician. Hospice care focuses on relieving disease symptoms and pain.*

• ***Protective services*** *provide legal and financial assistance or conservatorship to confused persons as well as to people unable to manage their affairs or protect themselves from injury or exploitation.*

• ***Senior center or nutrition sites*** *offer low-cost group luncheon meals. Seniors can enjoy each other's company and participate in social activities before or after the meal. Many programs provide transportation.*

• ***Social day-care centers*** *primarily offer social programs. In addition, many centers provide some medical supervision, establish links with medical facilities, or provide transportation to health-care services.*

• ***Telephone reassurance*** *provides daily contact for people who live alone, who are anxious about their security, or who have life-threatening health problems.*

• ***Transportation and escorts*** *are often available through senior centers or public transportation systems. Physical assistance is also provided to people who need help traveling to medical appointments and shopping.*

with home chores or enrolling your spouse in an adult day-care program a few days a week so that you can get the respite you need to keep healthy, too.

Supportive services such as meals on wheels (low-cost, home-delivered meals for homebound seniors), transportation, and home-chore workers are available in most communities. Check with your local senior service center or your hospital's home-health agency for providers of services like these. Your State Unit on Aging (see appendix B) can direct you to local senior centers or your Area Agency on Aging.

Keeping Up with the Cost of Your Home

Even when home services are reimbursed by insurance or provided by community agencies, it still can be difficult to make tax payments and pay for home maintenance. Living on fixed incomes, some of us are faced with choosing between repairs to the roof and food on the table or heat in the winter. Most of us have less income in retirement than we had during our working years, so our ability to keep up with rising property taxes is correspondingly reduced.

Property-tax relief. Carol O., a retired teacher living alone, says, "I bought this house in 1933 for under $7,000. Now, the county says it's worth over $200,000. I could never afford to pay property taxes on that amount." Many states have responded to the plight of people like Carol with property-tax benefit programs. Here are three of the most common:

- Circuit-breaker tax relief is tied to need. The amount of tax relief for which you may qualify is based on a comparison of your income with your property-tax liability. In some states, renters are also eligible for this program.

Figure 6-3

HOME-EQUITY CONVERSION

• A homestead exemption subtracts some of the home's value from the total assessment before the tax rate is applied. All homeowners receive the same amount of exemption, regardless of income.

• Deferral allows homeowners to delay paying all or part of their tax until the owner sells the home or dies. States may charge below-market interest rates on the debt.

Contact your state department of taxation and revenue to learn about tax-relief programs in your state. You might also want to consider a home-equity conversion, an innovative program that will allow you to obtain money based on the value of your home.

Turning home equity into cash. An elderly couple in New Jersey is now financially secure in their home for at least ten more years. A widow in California calls it a miracle that she is free from bill collectors. A 73-year-old widower doesn't have to sell his home of thirty-five years in order to make ends meet.

Like other older Americans, these homeowners found themselves in a common financial dilemma—house rich and cash poor. According to Jane Bryant Quinn of *Newsweek,* "The value of their houses may be rising sharply. Yet their cash incomes often fall behind the rising cost of fuel, property taxes and other expenses. It's like living in a bank vault, dead broke."

Estimates are that older Americans own more than $600 billion in equity in their homes. A relatively new financial tool, home-equity conversions, enables homeowners to keep their homes (see figure 6-3). Providing both a lump sum of money and monthly income, these programs are often available to homeowners whose monthly income is too low to qualify for a conventional mortgage loan. A home equity conversion can help you avoid being forced to move or to make loan payments from your monthly income.

Drawing on home equity, you might use the money to put in

ramps, handrails, elevators, or bathroom fixtures that allow you to continue living self-sufficiently. Some people use equity loans to meet medical and health-care expenses. Some even use the money to travel!

Two types of equity-conversion plans are available today: reverse mortgage and sale lease-back. It's wise to *seek legal advice* so that you understand the options and risks of both plans (see Resources). The following overview will get you started.

Reverse mortgages. Under a recent program of the Federal Housing Administration (FHA) and the Department of Housing and Urban Development (HUD), 25,000 insured home-equity mortgages are available through 8,000 HUD-approved lenders in thirty states (although not in every city and locality). This government program is available until September 1995.

With a reverse mortgage, homeowners age 62 and over may continue to live in their homes until they move, sell, or die. They may sell their property at any time, retaining any proceeds that exceed the amount needed to pay off the mortgage. Homeowners cannot be forced to sell their homes to pay off the loan. HUD will insure lenders against the risk that the mortgage may grow to exceed the value of the property.

According to HUD's Office of Policy Development and Research, the insured mortgages offer three payment options: (1) a tenure option, which provides monthly payments to homeowners as long as they occupy the home as a principal residence; (2) a term option, which provides monthly payments for a fixed period selected by the homeowner; and (3) a line-of-credit option, which permits homeowners to draw funds as they need them, up to a maximum amount. In addition, the homeowner may draw a lump-sum payment, combine a line of credit with monthly payments, or change the payment plan if needed.

One financial planner cautions that although a home-equity loan can be a beneficial tool to consumers, consumers need to be careful. Home-equity loans are a tool and, like other tools, should be used only when you know how to use them. Fortunately, part of the new HUD-FHA program includes consumer education and counseling.

Before setting up a home-equity conversion, a counselor must discuss other options with you, including mortgages and social services. Other financial options might include sale lease-back financing, deferred payment loans, and property-tax deferral. You must be informed of the tax consequences of home-equity conversion. Many older people are concerned that equity conversion will prevent them from leaving their homes to their children. Financial counselors are required to discuss the impact that home-equity conversion will have on your estate and heirs as well as the effect it will have on your eligibility for other federal and state assistance.

Sale lease-back. Sale lease-back plans were first introduced in 1978 by the Fouratt Corporation to help an elderly California resident. According to Rick Watson of Fouratt, the woman owned her home free and clear. She did not want to move, but she was living in desperate conditions because of inadequate income.

In most sale lease-back plans, the owner sells the home to an individual buyer or an investment firm, and then leases it back for lifetime occupancy. If you enter into this type of arrangement, you become, in essence, a renter in your home. By contrast, most reverse mortgages enable homeowners to borrow against their home equity and repay the loan, usually within ten years.

The purchase price usually is paid as a lump sum plus fixed monthly amounts, based on the seller's life expectancy. According to Watson, the buyer also purchases a deferred annuity for the seller. This annuity begins paying out when the loan ends. If the seller dies before the full loan is repaid, the loan balance is paid to the estate. Sale lease-backs can be risky if the monthly payments are not from a secured source of funds such as a guaranteed annuity.

Moving Out

The U.S. Census Bureau estimates that, while 20 percent of the population moves each year, only 5 percent of older people do so. In fact, most older people do not change their residence until their mid-seventies. In general, older people move because of widowhood, increased frailty, loss of income, or family changes, although a growing number of new retirees move to enhance their lifestyle. Most people don't go far, though. About 80 percent of moves are local or within the same state.

For those willing to go farther, Rand McNally has compiled a list of what it calls America's retirement "Edens" based on cost of living, climate, personal safety, housing, social services, leisure, and recreation. Here are the top ten from their list:

1. Murray, Kentucky Lake, Kentucky
2. Clayton, Clarkesville, Georgia
3. Hot Springs, Lake Quachita, Arkansas
4. Grand Lake, Lake Tenkiller, Oklahoma
5. Fayetteville, Arkansas
6. St. George, Zion, Utah
7. Brownsville, Harlingen, Texas
8. Bloomington, Brown County, Indiana
9. San Antonio, Texas
10. Port Angeles, Strait of Juan de Fuca, Washington

Did you find your dream locale on this list? People often find a place special for their own reasons. For example, Anita and Joe M.

planned on retiring to Florida, where they had friends. Joe, a pharmacist, studied hard for the state license and made special trips to Florida to take the exam. He passed on his first try. But instead of moving to Florida as planned, he and Anita moved to California, where their two children lived. Family ties were more important than career and friends in choosing a place to retire.

For five years Edna and Eddy W. visited friends in Florida each winter. When the couple decided to give up living in Queens, New York, however, they didn't head for Florida, but for Cape Cod, where they had maintained a summer home.

These days, Pearl and Lou S. spend winters in Arizona. In fact, Pearl and Lou never gave any other place a second thought. About ten years before Lou retired, a relative came back from Arizona, singing the praises of retirement in the sun. The outgoing couple knew it was the place for them. Summer finds these two snowbirds packing up and heading for Minnesota, along with relatives and friends.

Many older Americans have found Florida, California, Arizona, and Texas attractive; according to the U.S. Census Bureau, those states welcome the largest numbers of mature migrants. You may want to consider some of these questions before you make that big move:

- Can I afford to rent for a few months so that I can learn about the area before I commit myself?
- What kinds of housing are available in this area?
- Are good-quality social services and health care available?
- What cultural and leisure opportunities are there?
- How far will I live from the post office, bank, shops, place of worship, and recreation activities?
- Is public transportation available?
- What costs will be incurred in the move?

- What will be the monthly costs of maintaining my new residence and lifestyle?
- How will I make new friends?
- How do I plan to spend my time after I move?

Selling Your Home

Once you have worked through the decision to move, you may have a house to sell. In that case, you'll find some good news and some bad.

The good news. You may qualify for a once-in-a-lifetime tax exclusion on up to $125,000 of profit generated by the sale of your principal residence. You qualify if

- you were age 55 or older on the date of the sale or exchange,
- you owned and lived in your main house for at least three years out of the five-year period ending on the date of the sale or exchange, and
- you or your spouse did not exclude gain on the sale or exchange of a home after July 26, 1976.

Let's see how it works. Isabella and Peter H., 56 and 58, respectively, sold their home in December 1988. They had owned the home for 10 years when they decided to move to a new rental development a few miles away.

Isabella and Peter figured the sale on their home the following way:

Selling price of the home	$150,000
Selling expenses:	– $ 10,000
Amount realized on sale	$140,000
Cost basis of old house	
(original costs plus improvements)	– $ 70,000
Gain realized	$ 70,000

The bad news. The catches to using the tax exemption could trip you up. If you are not careful, you could lose the benefit. For example, if you have recently remarried and have now decided to move and exercise your $125,000 exclusion, you may be out of luck if your new spouse has used this exemption before. People often wonder whether to use the $125,000 exclusion or save it for the future. This decision depends on your health, your future housing plans, and your financial situation. Discuss your situation with your accountant, and obtain a copy of *Tax Information for Selling Your Home* (Publication 523) from the IRS (see Resources).

Making Relocation Easier

After you've sold your home and are beginning the move into your retirement spot, you'll be faced with sorting out your household—the physical furnishings of your life. You begin going through the closets, sending your adult children "care packages"—old report cards, pictures, books, and household treasures. As you neatly pack the boxes, memories flash by, and you begin to wonder: Am I making the right move? Did I pay too much? Will I make new friends? Will I like it? Can I really leave my home and its memories after all these years?

Even when you have made your own choice to do it, moving can be stressful. Gerontologists sometimes refer to "relocation trauma" or "transplantation shock," a common problem that affects all of us when we move. The hardest moves are involuntary ones in which there is a big change, such as a move from your own home into a nursing home. However, even in these situations, a drop in morale is usually only temporary.

The more control and predictability in the move, the smoother it will go and the more secure you'll feel about it. Learn as much as you can about your new area and neighborhood. Orient yourself as quickly as possible. Where are the shops? Is the post office nearby? Once you've adjusted, you are likely to find a pleasurable new adventure waiting for you.

Now, let's explore some of the housing options you might wish to consider. Your interest in any of these choices will be determined by your finances, health, personal preferences, and family situation.

Living Abroad

Although most people find new homes close to their old ones, increasing numbers of mature Americans are experimenting with living in a foreign country. Geri and Reuben P., retired managers for an international company, collect their social security checks in Spain. They are among 300,000 social security recipients abroad, according to Peter A. Dickenson in *Travel and Retirement Edens Abroad.*

Living abroad can be exciting and enriching. Most people who choose this lifestyle have previously lived abroad or traveled extensively. Many have family roots in other countries, as did Rose W., who had been a war bride. After World War II, Rose and her husband lived in Chicago for thirty-seven years. Then they retired early and moved to Lake Como, Italy, where Rose's family had a country home. Rose says, "Italy was always in my blood. Even after I moved to America, we visited at least once a year. Now the grandchildren visit us here."

In what countries are American retirees likely to be most comfortable? International Living's Quality of Life Report surveyed health services, recreation, environment, cost of health care, cost of living, culture, and freedom in many nations. By their criteria, in 1988 the ten best countries were the United States, Canada, Australia, Switzerland, New Zealand, Sweden, Italy, Germany, the Netherlands, and France.

If you are considering living abroad, first visit the area and explore its environment, shopping, health care, support services, cost of living, and leisure activities. If possible, take an extended vacation and live in the country for a few months to see how you like it. Investigate the effect of your move on taxes and health-care coverage. Talk with your insurance agent about health-care coverage abroad, and look into resident alien benefits in the country you are considering. The IRS publishes a brochure, *Tax Guide for U.S. Citizens and Resident Aliens Abroad* (Pub. No. 54), that explains your new tax situation.

Exploring the facts and identifying your options will give you more control. You may not want to live abroad for the rest of your life, but maybe it's time for a new adventure.

Retirement Communities

For the past thirty years, Mildred T., 82, has made Sun City and Sun City West her home. Mildred and her husband, Clarence, a postal department employee, had spent their lives in Wisconsin. When Clarence retired in 1960, he wanted to move to Florida. They visited the state at Christmas, but Mildred didn't like the humidity. At Easter they visited Arizona, and both agreed it was for them. Six months after Sun City opened, they moved in.

When Clarence died in 1974, Mildred was lonely and felt her house was "overwhelmed with sadness." She decided she needed a change, and so in 1978 she moved to Sun City West, a new retirement community nearby. Mildred still rises daily between 5:00 and 5:30. By 6:00 A.M. she's out taking her two-mile walk. Then it's breakfast and off to the clubhouse for crafts, pinochle, or her volunteer work. Over the last six years, Mildred has arranged ninety-six tours for Sun City residents. She's almost too busy to stop and talk because she's making plans for an upcoming trip to Epcot Center in Florida.

The largest residential retirement community in the nation,

FEATURES OF A RETIREMENT COMMUNITY

- *Suburban or rural location*
- *Orientation toward leisure and recreation*
- *Garden apartments, townhomes, or private homes*
- *Middle- and upper-income residents*
- *Young-elderly residents, initially in good health*
- *Many couples*
- *Self-contained community*
- *Organized group activities*
- *Age restrictions*
- *Moderate climate*

Sun City is home to 46,000 men and women. The community celebrated its thirtieth year of operation on January 1, 1990. Today, Sun City boasts 26,000 homes with seven recreation centers, eleven golf courses, and a 355-bed hospital.

Sun City and Leisure World (in Laguna, California) are the two best-known retirement communities in the United States. Hundreds of smaller ones are scattered across the country, with the largest concentration found in the sunbelt.

Retirement communities are growing in popularity, especially among newly retired couples. Residents generally report a high degree of satisfaction with their lifestyle. People often say they enjoy living in a community with others who share similar backgrounds and experiences. They feel that their neighbors are there to help if needed and that the community is interdependent.

However, some people in their eighties do not enjoy the same good health as Mildred. Therefore, as residents age, established retirement communities must provide services for residents who may become sicker or poorer. *Arizona Trends* reports that 10 percent of Sun City's residents now live below the poverty level.

Newer retirement communities are generally smaller than Sun City. For one thing, land costs have risen, and large tracts of land are not so readily available. Also, today's retiree typically wants a smaller community with special amenities.

Many retirees want more specialized communities. For example, one community boasts of its art collection, music room, and cultural events. Another brags that it has no golf course for residents to maintain. Yet another promotes its Christian atmosphere. Some of the new communities feature the latest in home design, such as big kitchens with high-technology appliances and modern bathrooms. If you're interested in retirement community living, chances are there is a place just right for you.

Retirement communities generally offer a variety of housing units for a range of prices. Residents usually pay a membership fee for use of the facilities. Home ownership fees vary from about $30,000 to $300,000 and up. Many communities also offer rentals.

Before moving to a retirement community, housing expert Leo E. Baldwin, author of *Housing Options for Americans,* recommends that you consider the following:

- present costs and projected future fees;
- location, especially the distance from transportation and your family;
- services and facilities available;
- ability of the community to be flexible in meeting your needs as they change over time; and
- community management and the extent of residents' participation in it.

Condominiums

"When we sold our home after nearly thirty years, we moved to an apartment. In the apartment, we had no equity, and I didn't have any say in how things were operated. So six months later we moved to this condominium," says Harry S., an energetic 70-year-old who lives with his wife and dog in Del Rey Beach, Florida. "That was seven years ago. I've been a board member for the past two years. My wife, our dog, and I are happy here. We have the advantages of home ownership but none of the burdens."

In a condominium development, you hold title to your own residence but share ownership of the common space with other resident-owners. Common space generally includes hallways, entrance areas, grounds, and recreational facilities. Residents pay the expenses of their own units as well as a monthly fee that covers maintenance of the property held in common. Usually a board of directors from the homeowners association oversees the operations; sometimes the board hires a management firm to handle the day-to-day operations.

Condominiums are popular among older people accustomed to the benefits of home ownership. Condominiums offer the tax advantages of home ownership (residents can deduct real estate tax and mortgage interest), but leave the burden of property maintenance to the management association. Most condominiums serve people of all ages, although some cater to older people by including features that emphasize safety and convenience, such as single-level units, emergency alarms, tub and shower bars, and easily turned door levers instead of knobs.

While Harry S. and his family are pleased with their condominium, it is not quite the same as owning their own home. Conditions, covenant restrictions, and association by-laws govern life in the condominium complex. Read these documents carefully so that you understand them before you buy a condominium. Also, try to attend a meeting of the condominium association to get a sense of how the community operates.

Condominium conversion—it could happen to you. A popular housing option in the 1970s, condominium fever swept the nation, particularly in large cities. In the rush of conversion from apartments to condominiums, some older people found themselves displaced or, like Mary S., "having to come up with $60,000 to buy the apartment that I'd lived in for seventeen years." Today, many cities have laws regulating condominium conversions.

Betty K., a retired legal secretary and the noontime speaker at a senior citizen center, asks, "What can you do if your apartment is going to be converted to a condominium?" Betty already knows the answer. Seven years ago when her apartment was undergoing condo conversion, she sprang into action. She learned about the laws her city had passed regarding conversion, and armed with that information, she organized the tenants in her building. "Although I am not a favorite of my landlord, who wanted to make a bundle," Betty says, "my neighbors and I saved our homes."

If you live in an apartment building about to be converted to a condominium complex, consider the following steps:

- Hire a lawyer—individually or with a tenant group—who specializes in conversions.
- Become familiar with the laws that govern condominium conversions in your city.
- Consider buying your apartment. Sometimes in an effort to get tenants to agree to conversion plans, landlords offer big discounts to tenants.
- If you cannot stop the conversion, consider renting from someone who buys condominiums as an investment. You'll probably pay more rent than you are accustomed to.
- If you have to move, investigate compensation. Some cities require landlords to pay dislocated tenants partial compensation. Check with your locality to see how much you are entitled to. If there are no local laws covering conversion, negotiate with the landlord. The last thing the landlord wants is adverse publicity—it's not good for sales!

Cooperatives

Many people think of cooperatives as 1960s-style group living. Yet, cooperatives have been popular in urban areas since 1945. Cooperative apartments offer essentially the same tax benefits as single-family home ownership. Cooperatives are corporations set up to operate residential units. The owner of a cooperative unit owns shares in the building. The unit's location, size, and layout are among the factors considered when the shares are allocated. Each owner usually has one vote, even though a resident with a larger unit may own more shares. The purchaser of a cooperative apartment has a proprietary lease that outlines the owner's rights and responsibilities, as set forth in the corporation's by-laws and the house rules developed by the cooperative's board of governors. Cooperatives usually have rules concerning subletting and permanent guests. The board of directors typically reviews prospective co-op owners and must pass favorably on them before a unit can be sold. Like condominiums, cooperatives offer residents tax advantages with none of the headaches of maintaining a private home.

Consult a lawyer before you purchase a cooperative so that you understand the kind of equity arrangement involved. Check with your state about its regulations on cooperatives. Also inquire whether there have been any complaints filed against a cooperative in which you're interested. Speak with the co-op's residents and find out how the board of directors operates.

Rental Living

David and Sarah A. have made apartment dwelling a way of life. Joan and Mike W. have just sold their home and moved across town to a new apartment complex. Dan, a widower, needed a change of scenery after his wife died and found a rental unit with plenty of neighbors. Cary S. lived in a rural area until she gave up driving at age 87. Then she moved to a suburban rental unit with access to public transportation.

Today's wide array of rental housing includes plenty of options. With some advance planning and careful legwork, you're likely to find a rental unit—whether it be a house, apartment, or condominium—that suits your needs and fits your budget. Begin your search by asking yourself

- What are my priorities?
- Is access to public transportation important?
- Does price limit my choices?
- Must my dog or cat come along with me?

State Farm Fire and Casualty recommends that you evaluate your new residence according to these criteria:

- location and convenience
- condition and appearance
- layout and design
- special services and amenities
- price and value

As in other settings, look for features such as call buttons and grab bars that will allow you to remain in your home if you become physically frail.

Mobile Homes

Joe S., 70, bought his first home—a mobile home—in the 1980s for $17,500. He was fond of saying he came from the same town as former President Reagan. "We both lived in Pacific Palisades; I in a mobile home overlooking the ocean and he in an estate several miles from the ocean."

Like Joe, many mobile-home owners say that joining a mobile-home community was the best thing they ever did. According to a HUD report on the Manufactured Housing Program, 83 percent of mobile-home residents report that their "house" is an excellent or good place to live. Three out of four owners would recommend purchasing a mobile home to others.

You may be saying, "I'll never live in a mobile home," but consider the cost advantage. The average price of a single-width mobile home (990 square feet) is about $20,000, and double-width homes are available for about $30,000. The national average cost for a three-bedroom home is about $100,000. Most older persons in mobile homes own them, and the majority of mobile home owners pay for their homes in cash. You may want to re-examine your attitude.

With the present high cost of housing, mobile homes have become more attractive for young and old alike. In *Where We Live: A Social History,* Irving Welfeld estimates that "during the 1980s, an average of 257,000 new mobile homes were purchased annually and placed in use."

According to Welfeld, the 1940 U.S. Census considered "trailers" in the same category as caves—not even counted as housing units. However, these images have given way to a new housing hybrid. Since 1976, federal legislation has required mobile homes to meet minimum standards for safety, design, and manufacturing. Today's mobile homes come in a wide array of sizes and offer a choice of floor plans. Some come with three bedrooms, several bathrooms, a porch, patio, carport, customized windows, and all the modern appliances—dishwasher, garbage disposal, and air conditioner. And most mobile homes are in fact placed permanently on land owned by the resident.

Many owners choose to live in mobile-home parks, where monthly lot fees range from about $100 to $700. The fee generally includes the hookup to utilities and the use of park facilities, perhaps a swimming pool and a recreation center.

More than 60 percent of mobile homes are located in rural areas, with high concentrations in Arizona, Montana, Nevada, and Wyoming. Thus, Joe S.'s Pacific Palisades location is an exception. Zoning regulations in most cities and suburbs exclude mobile homes.

If you are considering a mobile home, buy one that has been manufactured under HUD guidelines and standards. Unlike traditional homes, mobile homes usually do not increase in value, so negotiating a loan may be more difficult. Check with your bank and inquire about FHA and Veterans Administration loans. Most mobile homes are located in rural areas, so be sure you have good access to services.

If you are buying the site on which you'll locate your mobile home, or if you plan to live in a mobile park community, you should exercise the same care and thought you would in considering any other housing option. If you are considering a used mobile home, have it inspected. An inspection is especially important if you plan to move the mobile home to a new site.

As a mobile home owner, you receive the benefits of the largest housing-related government subsidy—deducting interest payments from your taxes. A discussion of several other popular federal housing programs follows.

Housing and Urban Development Programs

Since the 1930s, the federal government has played a role in housing, particularly for people with low incomes. Among those programs most used by older persons have been Section 8, Section 202, and Public Housing, all administered by the Department of Housing and Urban Development (HUD).

Section 8. This program helps low-income renters by paying the difference between what they can afford and the fair-market rent for a unit. The tenant's share is usually about 25 to 30 percent of his or her income. While some Section 8 units are found in newly constructed or rehabilitated housing, the great majority are in existing structures. In all cases, landlords must agree to participate in the program, tenants must meet eligibility requirements, and the units must be judged up to certain standards.

Section 202. Section 202 housing provides low-interest loans to nonprofit sponsors. The program finances construction of residential housing exclusively for older people. These projects generally have many social and recreational services that make them appealing places to live. Section 202 projects often provide meals and easy access to support services. The newer ones are intended for low-income persons who qualify for the Section 8 program.

Evelyn S. has lived in 202 housing in Malden, Massachusetts, for ten years. She says, "It's located in the center of everything. I like living with friends and neighbors who share my experience and concerns. And we see plenty of young people too—they visit their grandparents, or I see them in the market or at church."

Public housing. Developed and managed by a local housing authority, public housing projects range from fewer than ten units (usually in rural areas) to more than nine hundred units. While some older people live in projects that include families, many others live in complexes especially designed for them.

Celia M. says of her apartment in a public housing complex, "I came to America when I was 14, I married at 16, and this is the first new apartment building I've ever lived in. Next to getting my citizenship, this is the best thing to happen to me. At 81 I feel I've made it in America!"

Some experts estimate that more than 45 percent of all public housing is now occupied by people over 65. Older persons in public housing pay approximately 30 percent of their income for rent. In the last decade, most new public housing has been designed for older Americans, not because others aren't in need, but because, as Abner Silverman writes in *Everybody Loves Momma,* "The elderly don't make waves. They don't have children to overuse project facilities. They generally get along with their neighbors, irrespective of religion and social status or color. They try to take care of these dwellings. They live by middle class standards."

Section 8, Section 202, and public housing have long waiting lists. During the Reagan administration, the federal government drastically reduced outlays for new construction programs, thus intensifying the shortage. If you are interested in these programs, put your name on the list as soon as possible. Check with your local or state housing authority for a list of Section 8, Section 202, and public housing developments in your area.

Living with the Children

Poet laureate Robert Frost wrote, "Home is the place where, when you have to go there, they have to take you in." Most older people who move in with their families do so for financial reasons or because their health has declined.

Take the case of Steve and Sarah S., both in their forties. He's a professor; she's active in community affairs. Together with their 13-year-old son, they live in a comfortable home in a college town in upstate New York. For years they talked about building a house in the country after their son entered college. Two years ago their plans changed. Steve's father required hospitalization twice within a few months. Steve realized that his father could no longer live alone.

Steve and Sarah invited his father to move in with them for six months. He's still there. There have been no more hospitalizations. Says Steve, "My dad has made a life here he never had in New York City. He's connected with people. He's a computer whiz in the college course he's taking, secretary for the Little League, and an active member in local environmental groups."

The move is now permanent; none of the family talks about change. Steve's dad helps with household chores, watches his grandson, and insists on paying a small amount for room and board.

Of course, there have been changes. Instead of buying land in the country, Steve and Sarah enlarged three bedrooms and added a new bathroom to give themselves more privacy. They completed the remodeling just in time. Soon after, Sarah's widowed mother, who had suffered a stroke, moved in with them as well.

Experience has taught this multigenerational family what to expect. Sarah's mother is getting counseling to help her with the transition. Says Steve, "She's having a harder time adjusting. She was very much a force in her own community and an active church member for years. Her physical problems have been difficult for all of us, but we are learning."

Steve and Sarah have no complaints about the choices they've made. However, many families could not make such a comfortable adjustment to living together. How can you predict whether a multigenerational living arrangement will work in your family? Experience suggests that if you have an open, honest relationship and enjoy each other's company, you have a good chance of working out the problems of living under one roof. Trust your hunches and feelings. If you have old, longstanding differences, or if you watch the clock whenever you visit your adult children, living together may cause your relationship to further disintegrate. If you're considering combined households, make a list of the pros and cons of living together. Then, parents should ask themselves these questions:

- Will I feel like a guest in my child's home?
- If my adult child lives far from my present residence, how will I maintain my friendships and other social contacts?
- What will loss of privacy and, perhaps, increased dependence mean for me?
- How will I handle conflicts in lifestyle and values?
- How will I contribute to family expenses?

Adult children should ask themselves these questions:

- How will I maintain my lifestyle?
- What impact will this change have on my spouse and children?
- What changes will our home need to accommodate an older relative?
- What contribution—financial or other—do I expect from my parent(s)?
- What contribution do I need from other family members, such as my brothers and sisters?
- How will I handle conflicts and new demands on my time?

Many families use other approaches to provide closeness, support, independence, and privacy for an older relative. Two other options are accessory apartments and granny flats.

Accessory apartments. A completely private, self-contained apartment within a single-family home will probably cost between $16,000 and $25,000. Families often have little trouble deciding to remodel their home to accommodate a relative. Lila E. says, "When Momma needed a different place to live, I knew my home would be perfect with a little remodeling. That was the easy part. Choosing a contractor and then dealing with him became major problems for me."

Sally C., a 54-year-old widow, solved the endless problems and decisions of remodeling by employing a professional advisor. To create an accessory apartment in her home for her divorced daughter and young grandchild, Sally hired an architect to design the space they needed. Sally then interviewed five contractors and got bids on the project from three. Feeling somewhat overwhelmed by her choices, she rehired her architect to help her choose a contractor and supervise the project. Sally says, "My home is better than ever. My daughter and I can maintain our own lifestyles. The rent she pays allows me more freedom to travel, and I don't worry about my property because she's there. I also enjoy being part of my granddaughter's life."

If you're considering building an accessory apartment, check first into local zoning restrictions. Then hire an architect or contractor to evaluate whether your home's design can accommodate such an apartment. Finally, consult Patrick Hare's book, *Creating an Accessory Apartment,* for useful advice (see Resources).

Granny flats. An elder cottage housing opportunity (ECHO), colloquially called a "granny flat," is a self-contained home built for temporary use on the property of an existing residence. ECHO housing is removable and resellable. According to Edward Gunion, 85 percent of the granny flats his company produces are installed on the lots of adult children. The other 15 percent are bought by older people for property they own. A one-bedroom unit costs about $25,000, plus delivery and hookup.

Gunion also points to a new program in Pine Grove, Pennsylvania, where 184 granny flats are being developed in a small-village atmosphere. Purchase of such a large quantity has lowered the granny flats' unit price by about 20 percent. Most ECHO units range from 280 to 900 square feet. ECHO housing can be prefabricated, built on site, or manufactured (that is, a mobile home). Units can be designed so that the exterior is compatible with the home on the lot.

The lower cost of ECHO housing means that you won't have to sink your entire nest egg into the unit, especially if you are moving from a traditional home that you've owned for many years. Mary F., of Frederick County, Maryland, lives in ECHO housing on her son's property. She sold her home of twenty-five years, and even after purchasing the granny flat, found herself with a profit of $56,000. She says, "I now have money to buy Christmas and birthday presents for my eight grandkids."

The biggest obstacle for people interested in ECHO housing is local zoning laws. These laws restrict any increase in the dwelling-unit density that would change the character of a neighborhood. Although elderly advocates support zoning for granny flats, they are often opposed by civic and homeowner associations with concerns about adding low-cost housing to their neighborhoods.

If you want to build ECHO housing, you must submit a formal request, typically for a conditional or special-use permit, to your local zoning authority. If ECHO housing is not permitted, try working with the zoning authority and local civic association to introduce legislation that would permit such housing. You may have the best chance in California and Hawaii, which have the most progressive legislation.

Living Alone

Sally M. expresses concern about her mother: "Both my sister and I are willing to have Mom come and live in our homes, but she refuses. Is this common?"

Pride and independence are important to older people. In a 1986 survey for the Commonwealth Fund Commission on Elderly People Living Alone, Louis Harris found that although 75 percent of older people who live alone say they have grown children with whom they could live, 99 percent of those prefer their independence. One of their greatest fears is being a burden to their children and other relatives.

Shortly after the death of her mother, Stacy M. and her father, Edward P., jointly decided he would come to live nearby. They also discussed living together, but they concluded that, while the 71-year-old retired executive loved his daughter and granddaughters, he would quickly tire of the stream of school-age girls who made his daughter's residence their second home.

After several months of searching, they found a condominium about three miles from Stacy's home. Edward's youngest granddaughter now proudly tells her friends, "We don't have a babysitter anymore. My grandpa watches us." Edward says, "Although I haven't yet recovered from the death of my wife, living near my family gives me a sense of privacy and independence I cherish; here I feel I'm needed and I belong."

Many who live alone are not as fortunate as Edward. The Commonwealth Fund Commission on Elderly People Living Alone found poverty rates nearly five times higher for older Americans who lived alone than for couples. About one in three older people live alone, and the majority are women over the age of 75, generally widowed, and frail, physically.

Living with New Friends

Shared housing. Thomas Fuller wrote in 1732, "Better one's house be too little one day than too big all the year after." Many older people today are still overhoused—living in large homes they find difficult to maintain. One solution is sharing the family home with others.

What is shared housing? Generally, it is an arrangement in which two or more unrelated persons share a house or an apartment. Each usually has a private bedroom, but shares common living space in the kitchen, dining room, and living room. In addition to the economic advantages, successful shared-housing arrangements foster friendship and companionship. Here are examples of three people who find housesharing to be successful:

- "Having someone around is like medicine for loneliness," says Jennie S., 91.
- Rose B., 89, says, "Here I have people who care like a family. I couldn't ask for anything better."
- Bill K., 74, says, "With someone to share the expenses and help with the yardwork, I think I'll be able to live here forever."

Two models of shared housing presently found in communities across the nation are *match-up* and *group-shared residence.* In match-up programs, a homeowner or renter shares his or her home with a tenant. The tenant may pay rent or provide services—such as yardwork, housecleaning, or errands—in exchange for part of or all the rent. Work in exchange for rent is a popular option offered by older people looking for younger ones to help them maintain the independence of living in their own homes.

Group-shared housing is a by-product of the 1960s campus

movement for cooperative housing. According to the Shared Housing Resource Center in Philadelphia, the typical group-shared home has eight persons, usually unrelated, living cooperatively. Today, most such residences for the elderly are organized and operated by nonprofit organizations. These residences charge a monthly fee for a private room, meals, general maintenance, and professional management.

In Los Angeles, Alternative Living for the Aging (ALA) provides both group and individual matches. Director Janet Witkin explains, "The purpose of our program is to help people remain independent through their interdependence with others." A visit to ALA's co-op houses (group-shared housing) is proof that Witkin is on to something. Residents of each co-op house have private bedrooms and baths. They prepare most of their own meals in the house kitchen. However, five evenings a week, residents share dinners prepared by a professional cook. The common areas are homey, warm, and comfortable; the residents' bedrooms are repositories of history and personality. Bill S., 86, describes his experience: "I came here to get away from loneliness. I didn't realize how much there was to go to."

The key to successful house sharing is finding compatible personalities. Just because two people grew up in the Bronx and both like bagels or salsa, they're not necessarily ideal roommates. To avoid conflicts, agencies screen potential roommates and look for areas of compatibility, such as hobbies and other personal interests. They encourage people to talk about potential concerns—for example, which items or areas will or will not be shared—before moving in together. Successful residents in group-shared homes tend to be highly flexible and tolerant of others.

Shared housing has received increased attention in the past decade, partly because of consumer demand for affordable housing. Maggie Kuhn, a founder of the Gray Panthers, advocates shared housing. Kuhn became involved in shared housing years ago while caring for her elderly mother. Today, she owns and lives in a multigenerational home in Philadelphia.

The 1990s will see an increase in shared-housing programs as more older homeowners find themselves living alone, paying high property taxes and maintenance costs in homes designed for families. At the same time, single elderly renters, who often pay more than half their income for housing, will be looking for more affordable shelter.

Across the country, about four hundred shared-housing programs can help you find a housemate, check references, clarify mutual expectations about rights and responsibilities, set up rules, and develop a lease. The Shared Housing Resource Center is a good place to start looking for information about programs (see Resources). If shared housing is for you, consider your preferences in a housemate, including age, smoking or drinking habits, and pet ownership. If you advertise independently for a housemate, use a post office box to avoid publicizing your name and address. Be sure to check references of all potential housemates (see figure 6-4).

Figure 6-4

Congregate housing. Congregate housing is a residential complex that combines apartment living with services such as meals, cleaning, laundry, scheduled transportation, and a 24-hour emergency-response system. Congregate housing comes in several styles. Some projects are aimed at active older persons with comfortable incomes. Newspapers are full of advertisements for these complexes that emphasize a safe environment, social opportunities, and the convenience of services that can be purchased separately. In many such projects, residents who become disabled can contract privately for health care if needed at home, but operators encourage disabled residents to leave if their condition compromises their independence.

The Massachusetts Department of Elder Affairs reports the case of Mrs. W., who lived alone in a large house after her husband died. She said, "I knew I couldn't stay alone, really. But I was terrified that when I moved, it would mean being a burden in my daughter's house or living in a nursing home. I was scared that for the rest of my life I would have to live in someone else's place and be dependent on them. Moving into this congregate house showed me that my fears were unfounded."

Residents like Mrs. W. set their own schedule, but know that the facility has a variety of support services available when they are needed. Mrs. W. can have an active social life while maintaining her own private unit. Although congregate facilities may have similar goals, services, physical layout, and population, each complex takes on the unique characteristics of its residents and surrounding neighborhood.

Developed and managed by private companies, most congregate housing is fairly expensive. Some nonprofit and public sponsors are trying to make these options available to people with moderate and lower incomes as well. However, the relatively high cost of development has impeded this effort.

Another type of congregate housing, often referred to as "assisted living," is designed for older persons who need more help. In such projects, the basic monthly fee includes the cost of health care, with assistance available to help residents with personal care such as bathing and taking medications. Again, privately run facilities, which are also the most readily available, tend to be expensive. Check with your State Unit on Aging (see appendix B) for information on congregate housing and assisted living in your state.

Board and Care. They go by many names: old folks home, rest home, adult foster care, and domiciliary care home. Generally, board-and-care homes provide residents with a private or shared room, meals, and help with activities of daily living. Most provide laundry and housekeeping services. Larger facilities sometimes offer an activity schedule with music, exercise, group discussions, games, or outings.

Thousands of board-and-care homes in this country serve more than one million residents, most of whom are older persons living on supplemental security income (SSI). These homes also serve disabled people. Most homes are licensed for fewer than twenty residents. The majority of board-and-care homes are businesses that make a small profit. Often they are located in residential neighborhoods, sometimes in converted buildings originally designed for another purpose. Board-and-care homes are licensed by the state in which the facility is located. However, most states have minimal standards for licensing, and enforcement is lax. Some grievous cases of fraud, neglect, abuse, and even murder have taken place in board-and-care homes.

In 1989, the nation learned of a case involving Dorothea Puente, a boarding-house operator who was charged with nine counts of murder. As the television cameras rolled, seven bodies were dug from the backyard of Puente's home in a residential neighborhood in Sacramento, California. Police investigators discovered that the common denominator among the victims was their social security income. Dorothea Puente had put herself in control of at least eleven social security checks. Puente's friendly appearance belied her lengthy criminal record, including convictions for forging social security checks and drugging older people to rob them.

Unlike Puente, most board-and-care operators try to provide a safe, caring environment. But the Puente case highlights the need for caution when placing any person who may be frail or dependent in someone else's care. It also highlights glaring weaknesses in state licensing and supervision of care facilities.

In evaluating a board-and-care residence, consider the following questions, adapted from recommendations by AARP:

- Is the home's manager bonded?
- Can the home provide the services you need?
- Is the location safe and convenient to transportation?
- Are financial records kept current and in order? How often will you be permitted to review them?
- Does the building appear safe?
- Is the home licensed?
- What do current residents think of the home?
- Do the house rules suit your lifestyle?
- What scheduled activities does the home provide?
- Is someone available to help you remember to take medications?
- Will you share a room? What if you don't get along with your assigned roommate?
- Is the food to your liking?
- Is the bathroom close to the bedroom?
- What are the home's discharge policies? Will you be readmitted if you need to spend time in a hospital or nursing home?

Before deciding on a board-and-care facility, contact your state's continuing-care licensing office, which should provide you with a list of licensed facilities in your area. Compare size and location. Telephone several likely prospects to get answers to your preliminary questions. Ask the licensing office to show you the complaint files on any facility that you are seriously considering. When strict supervision of public licensing is not in place, it is up

BEFORE YOU JOIN A CCRC

The National Consumers League recommends that you obtain answers to these questions before joining a continuing-care retirement community (CCRC):

- *What is the entrance fee?*
- *Under what circumstances can it be refunded?*
- *What are the monthly fees and how are they calculated?*
- *What expenses will be my responsibility?*
- *What is the community's financial reserve?*
- *What medical services are provided as part of the community health plan?*
- *Are a nursing staff and physician on call around the clock?*
- *Can I be removed from my residence? Under what circumstances?*
- *What happens to my personal property if I move within the community?*
- *What is the policy for residents who find themselves unable to meet the monthly fee?*

to each consumer to check the background of any residential facility—*before moving in.*

Another group-living option is continuing-care retirement communities (CCRCs), which have been around since early in our nation's history.

Continuing-care retirement communities. In the past, church groups and other social-service organizations created retirement communities to provide shelter and health care for poor people. Older persons would sometimes be required to turn over their assets in return for services. Today, continuing-care retirement communities appeal to those who want to plan for future health-care needs and don't want to be a burden to their children. Each year the American Association of Homes for the Aging (AAHA) receives many calls from prospective CCRC residents.

The typical CCRC is home to between three hundred and four hundred people, most of whom entered when they were about 75 years old. Attractive campus settings feature residential units, community spaces, and health facilities. Living units range from studio apartments and small garden houses to separate townhouses spread around the grounds. Common areas include dining rooms, libraries, craft and music rooms, auditoriums, guest quarters, barber and beauty shops, banks, and convenience stores. An activities director arranges trips, special events, a regular calendar of classes, and local transportation.

CCRCs require an endowment (not an equity investment), an entrance fee, and a monthly maintenance fee. Monthly fees typically change over time, reflecting increases in operating costs. Most CCRCs require people who enter the community to be fairly healthy and to have Medicare, both Part A and Part B, as well as supplemental health insurance. Entrance fees range from $20,000 to $350,000, with monthly fees varying from about $400 to $2,000.

WHAT CAN YOU EXPECT FROM A CCRC?

Although the services provided vary among different facilities, most CCRCs include the following in their basic fees:

- *Residences consisting of studio or 1 to 2 bedroom units, with small kitchens, private bathrooms, and heating and air conditioning*
- *Two or 3 meals daily on a fixed schedule, with special diets available*
- *Light housekeeping and linens*
- *Social and recreational activities*
- *Tray service*
- *Community facilities*
- *Health and nursing-home services; additional fees may be charged for nursing-home care*

At entrance, these fees are ordinarily tied to the health-services guarantee chosen by the resident. A person moving into a median-priced one-bedroom apartment under an all-inclusive contract that guarantees full health benefits at no additional cost would typically pay $58,600 plus $870 in monthly charges, according to AAHA. Under a modified contract, which entitles residents to limited medical services, a similar unit would cost $42,300 plus $720 per month. Residents willing to foot their own health-care bills would pay $34,700 plus $580 per month.

Experience shows that only one in four residents ever needs nursing care on a permanent basis. Those who don't want to subsidize someone else's bill might prefer to take responsibility for their own health-care costs. Some communities are now experimenting with fee-for-service nursing-home care to reduce costs and attract more residents. For many older people, choosing among contracts boils down to anticipating future health-care needs—and putting a price tag on peace of mind.

Thelma and Lou lived in Leisure World, California, for twelve years after Lou retired from an insurance company. They had no children, and Leisure World was wonderful for them. Lou played golf regularly; Thelma joined a gardening club. Their evenings were spent with friends, playing bridge or enjoying the company. In 1985, Lou died at the age of 79. For the first time in fifty-three years, Thelma lived alone. Her friends continued to call and visit, and she was invited to the same social events, but she felt different. After grieving for Lou, Thelma began to think of her own future. At 77, she wondered who would take care of her if she became ill or frail. So Thelma did what a growing number of older Americans are doing—She moved to a CCRC. Thelma says, "At this stage of my life I wanted to know where I was going to be and how I would be cared for. The CCRC gives me a sense of security I need."

ADDITIONAL COSTS AT A CCRC

Be careful to plan extra funds for these items, which most CCRCs do not include in their fees:

- *Drugs and prescriptions*
- *Dental and eye care, including eyeglasses*
- *Personal companions*
- *Private-duty nurses*
- *Health-insurance premiums*
- *Personal laundry*
- *Apartment furnishings*
- *Entertainment, newspapers, and magazines*
- *Personal costs such as telephone, clothing, and toilet articles*

Continuing-care retirement communities provide many of the services that professionals think should be available to all older people. However, because of their cost, mid- to upper-income retirees are often the only ones who can afford them. Most residents of CCRCs have incomes above $50,000 per year.

New communities are springing up all the time. Currently, about seven hundred CCRCs are operating, with many more in the planning stages. Although voluntary groups are still involved in CCRCs, increasing numbers of proprietary organizations, hospitals, and nursing-home chains are entering this market.

If a full-service CCRC can tailor living arrangements and services to your situation, is it right for you? People who have joined these communities say that these were the most important reasons they did so:

- guarantee of a full range of services, particularly health care
- enhanced ability to maintain independence because of services available
- desire not to be a burden to family members
- protection against the costs of long-term care
- a setting that is safe and secure
- freedom from home maintenance such as painting, lawn mowing, or home repairs
- assistance with meals, shopping, and light housekeeping
- living with people the same age.

Consumer protections. More than twenty states regulate CCRCs. State regulations have been developed because of public concern over the poor management of some facilities and the vulnerable position in which older residents have been placed. One of the most vivid examples, nonprofit Pacific Homes in California, used poor actuarial data in developing their fee structure. But perhaps their biggest problem was that their written contract guaranteed life care but did not permit them to adjust monthly fees to cover costs. Needless to say, the company went bankrupt, leaving residents without the money they had invested or the services they believed they had purchased.

Regulations vary from one state to another. Most have been developed since 1983 and require CCRCs to

- hold residents' fees in an escrow account
- keep a reserve fund
- provide full financial disclosure to residents and potential residents
- provide specific contract assurances

If joining a CCRC appeals to you, visit a few in the area where you might want to live. Many have special guest quarters where you can spend a few days viewing life in the community, eating the meals, touring the facilities, participating in activities, and talking with residents and staff.

Whatever your feelings about the communities you visit, don't sign a contract on the spot. Take it home and meet with your lawyer and accountant. Make sure you understand specifically what you are getting and what you are not. Also, explore carefully the financial obligations you will be undertaking, how much you can afford, which services are not provided, and what is provided for an extra fee. Will your income and assets cover the costs over time?

Life Care—One Woman's Perspective

The same precautions that apply to signing up with a CCRC apply to a life-care community. Both provide similar facilities, except that life-care communities typically require a large single payment that guarantees life-long housing, meals, and health care. Anne V. lives in Canterbury Woods, a life-care community run by the Episcopal Homes Foundation in Pacific Grove, California. When she and her husband moved in ten years ago, Anne was 71. The unit they chose from among six models cost $54,000. Today, a similar unit costs about $100,000, with maintenance costs about $1,200 per month.

In the 1970s, Anne and her husband had watched as Canterbury Woods was built; afterward, they visited a friend who lived there. Soon after their youngest child married, they went to sign up. On a waiting list for three years and three days, Anne says, "It was well worth the wait."

When her husband became ill, Anne cared for him for more than six years. In the last two months of his life he became an invalid. At the urging of the medical staff, Anne finally placed her husband in the community health facility and visited him daily, often staying until 10:00 P.M. and then walking back to her residence nearby.

Three weeks after her husband died, she slipped late at night and found herself unable to get up. Alone in her two-room unit, she dragged herself to the telephone. Within a few seconds a security guard and a nurse were at her side.

An avid reader, Anne may be found at night curled up in bed with her latest book. She makes good use of the community's two small libraries. She also takes advantage of the many activities available. Says Anne, "It's been an ideal community to live in. It has a marvelous ambience. I'm not ever going to be a burden on my children, and I feel safe and secure."

Whether you choose a life-care community or one of the more numerous CCRCs, be careful to explore the guarantees and financial stability of the institution. Before you turn over any money, be certain you are buying what you need and that the company that owns the facility must hold your money for the facility's use.

Nursing Homes

Connie and Phil M. cared for her father, Sam, when he could no longer live alone because of Parkinson's disease. They remodeled their house so that Sam could have his own private space. For several years, the family's arrangement worked well. Connie continued her career and arranged personal care for her dad. Then her teenaged son was diagnosed with testicular cancer.

Connie and Phil had to commute to a cancer center in another state. All the family's attention focused on the boy, leaving their younger daughter and Sam to shift for themselves. Finding herself physically and emotionally drained, to say nothing of being away from home quite often, Connie decided that she could no longer take good care of her father.

Six months after her son's diagnosis, and after visiting several nursing homes, Connie and Sam agreed he would enter one run by a voluntary agency. Connie continued to visit regularly. When her son died two and a half years later, she thought about inviting Sam to live with the family again, but friends convinced her that she needed time to rebuild her own life and to attend to her husband and daughter. Besides, her father had made a new life for himself.

Rose and Bill J., both 76, lived in a small house in the country. Rose was active in her church, keeping her fingers busy knitting scarves and sweaters for the annual bazaar. Bill was a retired truck hauler who enjoyed woodwork and visits from his three children and ten grandchildren, all of whom lived within a three-hour drive. Though they were not wealthy, Rose says, "The cards were stacked in our favor." Then one day, Bill had an auto accident en route from the grocery store. Hospital examinations revealed that

A Place Called Home

Bill had had a massive stroke. Completely paralyzed on the right side of his body, he had lost the use of both his legs and hands. His speech was slurred, and he couldn't feed himself. The hospital staff recommended that Bill be discharged to a nursing home.

Bill's illness threw the family into crisis. Rose felt like a failure because she couldn't care for her husband. Furthermore, the family could not afford to maintain Bill in the nursing home closest to their residence.

Myths and reality. Moving into a nursing home often feels like failure or betrayal to both the family and the patient. This step is almost universally feared by both young and old. Ann M., 67, says, "I took care of my mom at home until she died. I wonder if my kids will do the same?" Maggie L., 35, says, "I have three kids. I hope they'll be good insurance against ending up in a nursing home." Robert W., 16, observes, "I visited a nursing home for a school project and found it scary and depressing." Nursing homes bring us face to face with our own mortality, and most of us would rather avoid them.

Some people believe that all older people are abandoned by their families and dumped into nursing homes. To the contrary, most older people live in the community, and 80 percent of the care they need is provided by family, friends, and neighbors—with little support from formal systems. Let's look at some facts about nursing homes:

- At any given time, less than 5 percent of older Americans live in nursing homes.
- We run about a 35 percent risk of needing a skilled-nursing facility at some time in our lives.
- Women are more likely than men to enter a nursing home—primarily because they live longer.
- Most nursing-home residents are 85 or older.

- Most nursing-home residents (84 percent) are without a spouse at the time of entrance.
- Most nursing-home residents (63 percent) have children.

At present, nursing homes in the United States fall into two general categories: skilled-nursing facilities (SNFs) and intermediate-care facilities (ICFs). The patient's need for medical care determines which type of facility is most appropriate. Sometimes both types are housed in the same building, either in separate wings or on different floors.

Skilled-nursing facilities. SNFs employ licensed nurses on shifts around the clock for people who need a high level of personal and medical care, such as those convalescing after a hospital stay or with a long-term illness. SNFs provide care similar to the care in a hospital, where the professional staff carry out physicians' orders. Although these facilities are identified by their medical nursing care, they also offer other specialized treatment, such as speech, physical, and occupational therapies. If they receive Medicaid and Medicare reimbursements, they are required to maintain a social service staff and provide daily social activities for patients.

Intermediate-care facilities. ICFs accept residents who are not fully capable of living alone or caring for themselves, yet who do not require full-time nursing care. These nursing homes provide medical and nursing care, social rehabilitation, and room and board. Residents are usually able to feed and dress themselves. They need less intensive nursing care than that provided by SNFs.

Finding a Nursing Home

A nursing home is the most restrictive and costly type of housing discussed here. Before you or someone you love moves to one,

be sure to explore the housing options discussed earlier in this chapter. Obtain the advice of your physician, hospital social worker, or a care manager (see chapter 7) to decide what level of care is most appropriate and affordable.

There are no perfect institutions. Bertha W., 87, visits her 93-year-old husband in a nursing home every other day. She says, "It's a good place for him. They provide wonderful care and are kind, but he can't get used to the cooking. So I always bring him something special from home to eat."

Even the best institutions—no matter how homelike, warm, and caring—run on schedules and provide care differently from home. To keep your expectations realistic, visit at least three nursing homes before you make up your mind. You'll find great variation in the quality of care and in the physical and social environment. And you'll find that one family appreciates characteristics that another family rejects. In selecting a nursing home, be sure to include the prospective resident as much as possible. The adjustment will be safer and less emotionally painful if the patient can visit the facilities, have a tour, and contribute—even minimally—to choosing the new residence.

Your family physician may be able to recommend some nursing homes. However, some physicians have financial interests in nursing homes, so you have a responsibility to compare facilities available in your area for yourself.

Your hospital's social service department deals with nursing homes regularly and can refer you to homes with openings. Friends, neighbors, and clergy may be able to recommend facilities. Your state licensing office should be able to provide you with a list of local facilities.

Your selection will depend partly on whether the stay will be short while the patient recuperates from an illness or surgery, or whether the home may become a permanent residence. If the stay will be short, you may be more concerned with the home's rehabilitation program than its homey environment. If the stay will be long, the nursing home becomes the resident's world; and while the shifts of workers change three times daily, the environment should provide consistency, activity, and as much social stimulation as the patient can enjoy.

Advance screening. With your list of possible facilities in hand, begin the screening process over the telephone. Find out what level of care the home provides. Is it certified for reimbursement by Medicare or Medicaid? Most people enter nursing homes paying their bills privately and may later need government assistance; the facility's participation in Medicare and Medicaid may have a long-range impact on your family finances. (Nursing-home care costs more than $25,000 per year. See chapter 4 for ways to protect yourself against long-term-care costs.)

Is the facility within easy traveling distance? Location is important because visits from friends and relatives become a main link to the outside world for someone in a nursing facility. Is the home accepting new residents? If not, how long must you wait for an opening? Unfortunately, many good facilities have waiting lists and prefer patients who pay privately. However, don't eliminate a facility you like because you're concerned about the waiting list.

Susie and her mother, Vera, 76, had to place her father Dave, 82, in a nursing home because a severe stroke coupled with Alzheimer's disease had completely overwhelmed their ability to provide care at home. In the difficult times after Dave's stroke, Susie and Vera remembered the nursing homes they had visited almost nine months earlier when they were planning for Dave's advancing Alzheimer's disease.

Susie says, "It came much quicker than my mother and I were

prepared for. We hoped he'd remain at home for several more years. And when I called the nursing home my mom and I thought was best, we couldn't get him in. We were quite desperate. He had to leave the hospital, and home was no longer a possibility. So, somewhat reluctantly, we placed him in another home recommended by the hospital. We visited him daily. Three months later, when an opening became available at the home of our choice, we moved him. It's hard to tell whether he notices the change, but my mom and I feel we've done the right thing."

Site visit. When you find at least three suitable nursing homes, telephone the administrators and make an appointment to visit. Try to visit in the afternoon, a good time to see the facility in action. Allow yourself one and a half to two hours for the visit. The nursing-home administration should be able to answer questions about the philosophy, financial arrangements, admission procedures and general operation. Ask to meet with the head nurse, social worker, activities director, and president of the residents' council. Ask them about their jobs and perceptions of life in the home.

If you can arrange to see a meal served, do so. Do residents eat in the dining room, or do they get tray service in bed?

Nursing home checklist. When evaluating a nursing home, let your eyes, ears, and impressions be your guide. What works for one person may not suit someone else, and nursing homes vary in style, philosophy, and services. Use the Nursing Home Checklist in this chapter as a guide to find out basic information. You might want to take a copy of this form with you when visiting a nursing home. You can use our checklist as a foundation and add questions about your specific concerns.

Adjusting. Plan to cope with emotional ups and downs after the move of a loved one to a nursing home—a time that can be

NURSING HOME CHECKLIST

Record the names of the three nursing homes you visited and rate your satisfaction with them.

1. ______________________ 2. ______________________ 3. ______________________

Nursing Home
1. 2. 3.

ADMINISTRATION

1. Is the home certified in the Medicare and Medicaid programs?

2. Does it have a license from the state?

3. How long has the administration been with the facility? Does the administration have a state license?

4. Does the administrator have a degree or special studies in gerontology?

5. How have the new Nursing Home Reform Amendments been implemented? What changes will have to be made?

____

____

____

6. If a resident is hospitalized, how long will his or her bed be held in the home?

7. What role does the resident council play?

FINANCIAL

8. What services are covered in the basic charges? What services are not?

9. Are services such as speech and occupational therapy provided? Does the home pay for them?

10. How are advance payments handled if the resident leaves or dies?

11. What happens if a resident spends down personal resources and needs government assistance (Medicaid)?

12. Who owns the home?

13. What are the conditions and provisions of the contract?

Nursing Home
1. 2. 3.

SOCIAL WORKER

14. How are roommates selected? Under what circumstances are they changed?

15. How many hours per week is the social worker on staff? (forty hours is best)

16. How does the social worker handle problems? (for example, those that might occur among roommates, family, and staff)

SOCIAL AND RECREATIONAL ACTIVITIES

17. What techniques are used to involve patients in activities?

18. Are there some activities that encourage the family's involvement?

19. Is there an ample supply of equipment for the activities program?

20. What is the activity director's background? How long has the activities director been with the facility?

HEALTH SERVICES

21. In a skilled-nursing facility, is a registered nurse on duty seven days per week?

22. What is the ratio of nursing staff to patients on each shift?

23. How are drugs stored, monitored, and distributed?

24. Does the facility have its own pharmacist?

25. What typically happens to the resident in a medical emergency?

(a) Is emergency transportation easily available?

(b) Is a physician available on staff or on call?

Nursing Home
1. 2. 3.

26. What policies and programs does the home have for attracting, training, and retaining nurses and aides?

YOUR OBSERVATIONS

27. Does the outside of the building look well maintained?
28. Is the environment homey and welcoming?
29. Is the facility generally free from odor?
30. Do the hallways have special handgrip railings?
31. Does the cleanliness of the home meet your standards?
32. How do the staff treat the residents? Do they call them "dear" or by their proper names?
33. Are residents up and dressed? Do they look well cared for? Does the staff show interest in them?
34. What is your impression of the dining room, activities room, library, lounge, and lobby?

MEALS

Since meals tend to be a source of great concern to the residents, ask to eat a meal at the facility with residents.

35. Is the meal the same as described on the menu?
36. Is there an ample supply of food? Is it attractively prepared? Is the temperature correct? How does it taste?

Nursing Home
1. 2. 3.

37. How are people treated who need help eating?
38. Do the residents seem to enjoy the meal?
39. Are seats assigned, or do residents choose their own?
40. Are snacks and special diets available to residents?

INDIVIDUAL ROOMS

41. How close is each room to the nursing station?
42. Are a chair and reading light provided? Is there ample room for personal belongings?
43. How many people share a room? Is there a curtain for privacy?
44. Are there private places where residents and families can spend time together?
45. Is there a telephone readily accessible for the resident? Is there a TV in the room?
46. Is a pleasant garden or other outdoor space available to the resident?
47. Are there grab bars around the toilet and nonslip bathtubs?

FAMILY CONSIDERATIONS

48. Will other family members and friends feel comfortable visiting someone here? Is the facility near the homes of family and friends?

difficult for both the resident and the family. Anna F. says, "After my mom moved to the nursing home, I found myself crying at odd times. I was ashamed to admit to myself and my friends that I couldn't care for her any longer."

Tim R. states, "Pauline and I were married for fifty-three years. I think we were only apart when she went to the hospital to give birth. She's been in the home for two years now, and I still have trouble sleeping at night."

Jacob S. reports, "It isn't living here that's so bad, it's just that I still miss my garden and the many things I collected over the years."

Ruth B. explains, "The hardest thing about living here is not having any privacy or any say about who my roommate is."

For most people, the adjustment to nursing-home life is slow and often difficult. In exchange for medical care, supervision, and security, the resident gives up some degree of control and independence. Residents whose thinking is still clear may object to sharing a room, dining in a group, or living with people who are confused or demented. Even in the best nursing homes, it is hard to balance individual preferences with the institution's functions.

If you are moving to a nursing home, talk with the social worker or someone else you trust about your fears and concerns. If someone in your family is moving, try to help your relative explore these feelings. If someone is giving up a home, he or she should be the one to decide which possessions to take and which to give away. Pay attention to the pet or special treasure that he or she is especially concerned about leaving. Little things can take on symbolic significance when a person is in crisis, and moving to a nursing facility is usually a crisis for both the new resident and the family. Be patient and open about your own feelings so that guilt will not drive a wedge between you and your loved ones.

Reactions. When Mary told her brother Bill that she could no longer care for her dad at home, Bill asked, "How can you do that to Dad after he has done so much for you?" However, Bill did not volunteer to have his father move in with him.

Sally M. and Gloria C. are good friends. When Sally M. placed her mother in a nursing home, Gloria said, "I don't know how you did it. I could never have done that to my mom." Gloria C. never had to face that decision because both her parents were killed in a car accident.

Kathy B. has taken care of her depressed grandmother for ten years. It has affected her social life and career. One day a colleague asked Kathy, "Haven't you done this long enough and at great sacrifice?" Kathy felt guilty for even thinking of putting her grandmother in a nursing home.

Unfortunately, guilt often accompanies the decision to place someone we love in a nursing home. Though well intentioned, other people often project their own guilt onto us and make us feel worse. If you're overwhelmed with your feelings, seek professional help. Your feelings may get in the way of providing the best care for a frail older person. In many instances, a nursing home is the most appropriate environment.

Said Marie B., an 87-year-old nursing-home resident, "I hated the idea of coming here, but now that I've been here over a year I've made a new life for myself. I no longer wait for the phone or the mail. I wheel myself to the activity room nearly every day. I've made friends with a lady who was in elementary school with me. In my spare time, I crochet clothing for my great-grandchildren's Barbie dolls."

The most important thing you can do to ease the adjustment process and your feelings is to visit regularly. Visits, even brief ones, assure the resident that he or she is still an important part of the family and community. Encourage your relative to talk about both the present and the past. Take along some photo albums or scrapbooks to reminisce over (see chapter 3). Take the grandchildren when you can. You will be crucial to the nursing-home resident's emotional health.

Problems and complaints. Before signing up with a nursing home, check with your state's nursing-home ombudsman office (an ombudsman is required by federal law). Find out whether complaints have been filed against the home you are considering. The ombudsman is mandated to investigate and resolve complaints made by residents or their families. (See appendix C for a complete list of state ombudsmen.)

Later on, if you should have a complaint that the nursing-home ombudsman cannot resolve (most do not have formal legal power), file your complaint with your state department of health. Be specific, and list steps you've already taken to resolve the issue, such as talking with the nursing-home administrator. After you've filed your complaint, follow up to make sure that someone is assigned to your case and is investigating your concerns.

Improving quality of care in nursing homes. The federal Nursing Home Reform Amendments of 1987 call for a nursing home to "care for its residents in such a manner and in such an environment as will promote maintenance or enhancement of the quality of life of each resident." These laws touch on self-determination, personal and privacy rights, abuse and restraints, right to information, visits, transfer and discharge policies, and protection of personal assets.

This legislation has stirred controversy and generated a number of lawsuits. Scholar Rosalie A. Kane, member of the Institute of Medicine committee that produced the study on which the legislation was based, points out: "Although, in Shakespeare's phrase, these outcomes are 'a consummation devoutly to be wished,' an adequate quality of life for nursing-home residents cannot be legislated into being; it will, I hope, come about, but only through gradual and continual refocusing and reordering of priorities."

It will be important for all those interested in the welfare of nursing-home residents to watch how the new rules are implemented in the 1990s. A public concerned about nursing-home life is the best guarantee that nursing homes will continue to improve.

Like any other home, a nursing home is important in defining who we are and what we feel about ourselves. And like the process of aging itself, moving to another home requires adjustments.

Today's society offers many options for safe and independent living for the increasing proportion of older adults. Fortunately, we live in a time that offers more opportunities for a fulfilling and pleasurable later life than any generation ever before us.

Resources

American Foundation for the Blind, Customer Service Division, 15 West 16th Street, New York, NY 10011. Telephone: (800) 232-5463; (212) 620-2000.
The foundation offers books and other materials for visually impaired persons, including product catalogs, films, lists of low-vision services, a lending library, and other self-help information.

Geri-Wear, P.O. Box 780, South Bend, IN 46624.
Geri-Wear markets apparel with adaptive closures of Velcro, snaps, and ties to make dressing easier.

M&M Health Care Apparel Co., 1541 60th Street, Brooklyn, NY 11219. Telephone: (800) 221-8929, (718) 871-8188.
Ask for their catalog of apparel with adaptive closures of Velcro, snaps, and ties to make dressing easier.

National Association of Senior Living Industries, 1814 Duke of Gloucester Street, Annapolis, MD 21401. Telephone (301) 263-0991.

Self Help for Hard of Hearing (SHHH), 7800 Wisconsin Avenue, Bethesda, MD 20814. Telephone: (301) 657-2248.
This association offers information about and publications on products, technology, and environments that increase the independence of hearing-impaired persons.

Vis-Aids, Inc., P.O. Box 26, 102–9 Jamaica Avenue, Richmond Hill, NY 11418. Telephone: (718) 847-4734.
This company sells aids and appliances for persons who are blind, visually impaired, hearing impaired, and physically disabled.

Recommended Reading

American Association of Homes for the Aging. *The Continuing Care Retirement Community: A Guide Book for Consumers.* 1129 20th Street, NW, Washington, DC 20036-3489. Telephone: (202) 296-5960.

American Association of Retired Persons. *A Home Away from Home: Consumer Information on Board and Care Homes.* 601 E Street, NW, Washington, DC 20049. Telephone: (202) 434-6030.
Also, ask for a copy of *Home Made Money: Consumers' Guide to Home Equity Conversions,* which is available from the Home Equity Information Center, Consumer Affairs Section.

American Bar Association, Commission on Legal Problems of the Elderly. *Home Equity Conversion* (brochure). 1800 M Street, NW, Washington, DC 20036. Telephone: (202) 331-2297.

American Health Care Association. *Thinking about a Nursing Home: A Consumer Guide to Choosing a Long Term Care Facility.* 1201 L Street, NW, Washington, DC 20005. Telephone: (202) 842-4444.

Andrus Gerontology Center. *Home Evaluation Checklist.* University of Southern California, Los Angeles, CA 90089-0191. Cost: $5.

———. *Home Modifications Resource Guide.* See address above. Cost: $5.

Arthritis Foundation. *Guide for Independent Living.* 1314 Spring Street, NW, Atlanta, GA 30309. Telephone: (404) 872-7100. Cost: $6.

Costal Colony Corp. *Elder Cottages.* 2935 Meadowview Road, Manheim, PA 17545. Telephone: (717) 665-6761.
Ask for information about manufactured elder cottages.

Internal Revenue Service. *Tax Guide for U.S. Citizens and Resident Aliens Abroad* (Pub. 54); *Selling Your Home* (Pubs. 523 and 2119). Internal Revenue Services, Washington, DC 20224.

National Center for Home Equity Conversion. *A Financial Guide to the Individual Reverse Mortgage Account (IRMA).* 110 E. Main Street, Madison, WI 53703. Telephone: (608) 256-2111.

———. *Sale Leaseback Guide and Model Documents.* See address above.

National Consumers League. *Life Care.* 815 15th Street, Washington, DC 20005. Telephone: (202) 639-8140.

Patrick Hare Design Associates. *Accessory Apartments and Granny Flats.* 1246 Monroe Street, NE, Washington, DC 20017.

———. *Creating an Accessory Apartment.* See address above. Cost: $15.

Shared Housing Resource Center. *Is Homesharing for You? A Self-Help Guide for Homeowners and Renters.* 6344 Greene Street, Philadelphia, PA 19144. Telephone: (215) 848-1220. Cost: $2.

State Farm Insurance Companies, Public Relations Department. *Apartment Guide.* 1 State Farm Plaza, Bloomington, IL 61710-0001. Telephone: (309) 766-2311.

U.S. Consumer Product Safety Commission. *Home Safety Checklist.* Washington, DC 20207. Toll-free hotline: (800) 638-CPSC; in Alaska and Hawaii: (800) 638-8270; in Maryland: (800) 492-8104.

———. *Safety for Older Consumers.* See address and telephone numbers above.

U.S. Department of Commerce, National Bureau of Standards. *Guidelines for Stair Safety.* Washington, DC 20234.

CHAPTER SEVEN

Changing Family Roles

Intergenerational relationships are more important . . . today than they have been at any point in history.

—Vern L. Bengtson, gerontologist and professor of sociology, University of Southern California

Our families are the people we usually turn to first when we are in need, and our families usually respond, even if family members must change their patterns and roles. When war, famine, or financial difficulties strike, necessity may pull in older and younger generations—as well as more distant relations—under the same roof. But within a few generations, as economic conditions allow, young couples and grandparents move out to live independently.

Though modern adults of any age generally prefer separate households, family members usually maintain close ties with one another, and older adults play an important role in this connection. For example, one study of three generations of Canadian families confirms what many of us know from experience: Older women take the role of keeping the family connected, circulating family news, and giving coherence to the family group by alerting everyone when gatherings are needed for celebration or mourning. Older men typically assume roles more connected with the workplace and the financial well-being of the family, often acting as career mentors for younger generations. Family members carry on the same important roles today that they have for generations, in good times and bad. Within this larger pattern, however, individual family roles can change drastically and unexpectedly.

"When the kids grow up," we say, "we'll have time and money to do the things we've dreamed of." We'll travel. We'll go back to school or change careers. We'll put our feet up and watch the baseball game. We'll have the children and grandchildren around the

Thanksgiving table, just as our grandparents did. As we mature, we dream and plan for our independence from the responsibilities of work and young families. But sometimes, our expectations are upset.

Just as we settle into a relaxed, mature relationship with our parents, perhaps they become disabled, and the relationship turns upside down. Now we feel like parents to our parents, and they are struggling unhappily with feeling dependent and childlike. We plan to enjoy our grandchildren, but perhaps when Tina is three, her parents divorce. Her mother later remarries and moves far away, so that we lose the granddaughter we adore. The couple next door, who planned to sell their house and spend ten years in a Winnebago seeing the world, may find their plans disrupted by chronic illness. Instead of being able to enjoy the relaxed days of their mature relationship, they find their world turned upside down, as one spouse now becomes the caretaker for the other. At the office, a co-worker tells us that his divorced daughter and between-jobs son both have moved back home, bringing along new challenges for family relationships and for beliefs about the age at which adult children should become independent.

Today's longer life expectancy makes older men and women demographic pioneers. Increasingly, they have the opportunity to define, by their examples, what it means to be an adult child, parent, grandparent, and great-grandparent—maybe all at once. With longer life expectancy, family ties can bind members from four and even five generations. While belonging to a multigenerational family can feel warm and secure, it can also feel confusing and frustrating. We sometimes feel like the "sandwich generation," mature adults helping our children begin their independent lives while at the same time helping our parents as they lose some of their independence.

Demographics show that our expectations of support from a traditional family structure will be further challenged in the future. In the 1980s, for example, half of American families were either single-parent families or blended families (parents who have remarried, bringing children from previous relationships together in a new family). Where do the grandparents fit in? How do grandparents maintain relationships with grandchildren who have blended into another marriage? How do we all adjust if Grandpa decides to remarry?

How do older adults balance competing demands for energy and resources? How do we reconcile family needs with personal limitations, or with personal needs for growth? How do we learn to get along with Mother again, after living separately for forty years, when she needs to move in with us? How can we help Father remain in his hometown after his heart attack, even though he's living alone? Thanks to modern medical technology, people are living longer with illnesses that once would have ended their lives in middle age. How do we cope with the long illness of a spouse or parent? How does the family support a parent who wants to remain independent but has increasing disabilities over a period of years? When is a nursing home the best choice?

Even if we have no one in our own family we can look to as an example in our new situation, we can benefit from the experience of other people. Although it is a new discipline, gerontology (the study of mature and older adults) has quickly accumulated information about the effects of longer lives on older people and their families. In this chapter, we offer examples of and information about the changes taking place in today's family relationships: grandparenting; adult children returning home; caregiving for a disabled spouse or parent; and coping with a long illness or placing a disabled person in a care facility.

Grandparents

The recent increase in life expectancy has resulted in a profoundly different relationship between grandparents and grandchildren. Although the age at which we become grandparents—forties and fifties—has stayed pretty much the same over the generations, we are living longer, and so we are more likely to see our grandchildren grow up. At the turn of the century, American children were likely to lose most of their grandparents by the time they reached age 15. By 1976, though, a 15-year-old had a 90 percent chance of having at least two grandparents living and a 50 percent chance of having three grandparents living. These cold statistics simply quantify what many of us have seen in our lifetimes: When today's older generation was young, our parents were more likely to die in middle age, thus missing the chance to enjoy their grandchildren's growing years.

The grandparenting role has changed over time, too. Since World War II, travel has become much easier, and most people have telephones. A child can talk to Grandfather on the phone, even when Grandfather is 300 miles away in Miami. Even when "over the river and through the woods to Grandmother's house" means a 200-mile trip, we can easily drive the interstate highway or fly that distance to enjoy family gatherings. It's no longer a two-day ordeal with old cars or wagons, dust, and rough roads. Families find it physically easier to be together; grandparents can develop close relationships with their grandchildren.

A child born today may have four middle-aged grandparents and several older great-grandparents who will live long enough to enjoy the new family member's growing-up years. With falling birth rates, however, there are likely to be fewer grandchildren around to capture the attention of grandparents. As Andrew Cherlin and Frank Furstenberg point out in *The New American Grandparent,* "In past times, when birth and death rates were high, grandparents were in relatively short supply. Today, as any number of impatient older parents will attest, grandchildren are in short supply." Soon the grandparents will outnumber the grandchildren. The Bureau of the Census estimates that by the year 2000, there will be more people over age 55 in the United States than children under age 14.

Because older people as a group are more financially secure today than before World War II, they have more leisure time and money to spend on grandchildren. And since they are living past the age at which their energies are absorbed by raising the last of their own children, they may have time to pay attention to the small ones, to build relationships with the future generations of their families.

Styles of Grandparenting

When Mimi and Harry D. were in their sixties, they had raised five children of their own and welcomed twelve grandchildren to the family. Mimi and Harry retired from San Francisco to a walnut ranch in rural Northern California, where the grandchildren often gathered in twos and threes during summer vacations. Mimi spent her days cooking and playing card games, at which she and Harry were expert. They expected the children to amuse themselves, although they were welcome to join the card games when they grew old enough to play. During hot summer afternoons, Mimi would read aloud from Charles Dickens's novels while Harry and the grandchildren listened, sitting outside under the live oaks. Often they played dominoes or did crossword puzzles together. Once or twice a week, Harry would gather all the resident grandchildren into the car and drive them to a nearby lake for a swim.

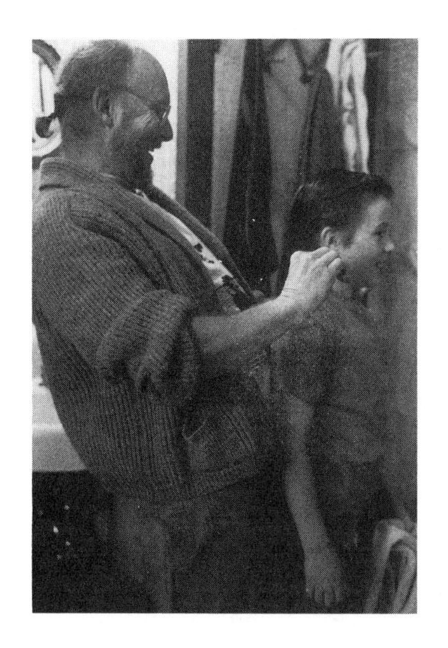

After Mimi and Harry died, their grandchildren shared fond memories of the Dickens novels, the swims, and the large gatherings at mealtimes, but they remembered little about their grandparents as people. Born at the turn of the century, Mimi and Harry felt children should be enjoyed briefly but not encouraged to participate in adult conversation or family decisions. They loved their grandchildren and they were kind and firm, but they maintained their distance, retaining a traditional style of relationship between grandparent and grandchild. In many families, grandchildren report even more distant relationships with grandparents, especially if the grandparents did not speak English or came from a culture that discouraged closeness between elders and children.

On the other hand, today's grandparents, even in blended families, often develop friendlier relations with their grandchildren than they ever had with their own grandparents. For example, Joan A., 53, has four grandchildren from her three children and their six marriages. Although the grandchildren live with different parents at different times, Joan systematically makes opportunities for her grandchildren to stay with her, even though she has an active social life and a full-time career. Joan works at maintaining friendly relationships with all the children's parents, offering to babysit when she can. She enjoys the children's company, treating them respectfully and affectionately and taking pleasure in watching their changes as they grow. Her grandchildren feel free to speak openly with her, telling her their concerns and feelings and joining her in games, crafts, and storytelling. They know they can call her with their problems and triumphs. Joan tries hard to refrain from interfering in her adult children's decisions. Although she often feels her experience could be useful to them, she knows they will ask if they need her help.

Both Joan and her ex-husband stay in touch with all their

grandchildren. Joan's fiancé, Russ, is developing a friendship with Joan's grandchildren. Russ's own grandchildren from a former marriage live in a distant city, but they come to visit Russ and Joan during summer vacations. It takes a lot of energy to maintain close relationships in nontraditional families, with couples separating and family units reforming, but certainly the benefits of these relationships make the effort worthwhile.

Grandparents and Divorce

Some divorcing parents cut off not only each other, but the spouse's family as well, an event that can hurt both the grandchildren and the grandparents. Chances are good that modern grandparents will have to cope with such changes in the traditional family. At today's divorce rate, 40 percent of children experience a divorce between their parents. Unfortunately, the family of the noncustodial parent (most commonly the father) frequently loses contact with the grandchildren. Edith W. says, "My husband, Fred, and I are in our early sixties. Our only son and daughter-in-law divorced about a year ago. We are heartbroken because our two beautiful grandchildren have moved with their mother to a city 100 miles away, and we've only seen them once over the past year. Our son has visiting rights and lives about twenty-five miles from us. How can we communicate with our grandchildren more often?"

Edith's and Fred's problem is a sad but common one. Statistics show that only 5 percent of all grandchildren see their grandparents at least twice a week, and about 80 percent see their grandparents from once a week to as little as once a year. This trend may result from today's high divorce rate and job mobility.

Because their son has visiting rights, Edith and Fred could talk with him about possible arrangements for seeing more of the grandchildren. When the children visit their father for the weekend or a vacation, the grandparents could arrange a family get-together, including some activities that are especially fun for children. Perhaps Edith or Fred could volunteer to drive to their son's home to see the children instead of waiting for him to bring them to visit. He might welcome the offer of some babysitting during his working hours.

Probably the most important thing Edith and Fred can do to increase the amount of time they spend with their grandchildren is to mend their relationship with their former daughter-in-law. They can let her know they support her as a parent, invite her to join in family gatherings along with the children, and perhaps offer to care for the children once in a while.

Grandparents who travel could offer to take the grandchildren along on an occasional outing or trip. They should first discuss this idea with both the parents and grandchildren to find out how they feel about it. Between visits, the grandchildren and grandparents can exchange letters, photos, and telephone calls to maintain their close feelings for each other.

When marriages break up, parents often call on the grandparents for emotional and financial help. Grandparents may feel pulled back into a parental role when they find themselves babysitting while the children's mother works every day, or raising grandchildren from a broken marriage. It can be difficult to adjust to becoming a parent again, especially when the relationship can be changed at any time by another marriage.

Managing Grandchildren's Behavior

With changing families, blended families, and older grandparents, knowing how to communicate your expectations for children's behavior can be a problem. Often the way we raised our children differs from the way they are raising their children. How do we handle these differences? Does a grandparent have a right to intervene in the parents' management of their children?

In general, relationships will be stronger if grandparents let their children come to them for advice, and otherwise maintain a tactful distance from these issues. Grandchildren need support and love from their grandparents; they do not benefit from a family divided by quarreling over how to discipline the children. Children can adjust to having one set of expectations at home and another elsewhere, so grandparents should feel free to expect behavior they approve when grandchildren are visiting in their homes. Sometimes steering a course between managing the grandchildren, maintaining friendly relations with the children's parents, and preserving your mental health can call for great diplomacy and creativity.

Jeff and Rita M. are in their late sixties. Their married daughter and her family live 200 miles away. Jeff and Rita adore their two grandchildren, ages 4 and 7, but the children are very active and not well disciplined. "We enjoy seeing them," Rita says, "but after a weekend visit to our place, we need a week to recover. Should we say something to our daughter? We don't want to cause hard feelings."

It's important for grandparents to let their own children know what they're feeling. Jeff and Rita should approach the problem in the least threatening way possible, and not as though they were teachers of correct child management. They might tell their daughter that it is sometimes difficult for them to keep up with the children's energy level. While discipline is primarily the responsibility of the parents, Jeff and Rita should not be afraid to set limits in their home that the children's parents should help enforce.

To cut down on the chaos, the grandparents could suggest

some outdoor activities such as going to the park or on a hike. Children often respond well to being taken out separately to do something they choose with one grandparent or the other. Making an effort to spend time separately with each child will reinforce their feelings of being worthwhile individuals, give everyone a chance to know one another better, and improve the children's responsiveness to adults' limits and requests.

If Jeff and Rita still feel too worn out to have the young grandchildren visit their home, they might plan visits to their daughter's home until the children are older. This strategy would allow them to arrange the visit to suit their energy level, including the length of stay and times they arrive and leave.

One of the dangers of grandparent–grandchild relationships is that grandparents may step over the boundaries and assume the role of disciplinarian and decisionmaker, a role that belongs solely with the parents. Because of family changes caused by divorce and working parents, grandparents often play a greater role in children's lives, and the boundaries become blurred. For example, Martin S., 62, has four grandchildren. Recently, he says, "I said something to my 7-year-old grandson that upset him greatly. His mother, my daughter-in-law, became furious, and we had a terrible fight. She even cursed at me over the telephone. What should I do? I'm not thrilled with my daughter-in-law, but I don't want to jeopardize my relationship with my grandchild."

Probably Martin was out of line, if he made both his grandson and his daughter-in-law so upset. He should talk with his daughter-in-law about what happened, perhaps asking for her suggestions about how he should have handled the situation with his grandson. Her cursing may have represented her frustration and anger with him at the moment. However, other problems may be contributing to tense feelings in this situation, and these should be worked out to improve the relationship with both the daughter-in-law and the grandchildren. Perhaps a third party could act as mediator.

Grandchildren look to grandparents as mentors, caretakers, role models, and family historians. From them, children learn about the "good old days," what their parents were like as children, and about their own roots. Sometimes grandparents feel more interest in the upbringing of their grandchildren than they did with their own children, and this intense interest may evoke harsh judgments of the grandchildren. By all means, Martin should call his grandson and apologize. A 7-year-old boy is no match, whatever the circumstances, for a 62-year-old grandfather.

Pediatrician T. Berry Brazelton, author of *Families: Crisis and Caring,* sees grandparents as having the opportunity to develop a special, important relationship with grandchildren, one in which the children receive unconditional love and minimal criticism. While parents must acquaint the child with the harsher realities of life and its rules, grandparents can indulge themselves and the children with special times—small gifts, outings, telephone calls, and cards—and enjoy the more pleasurable side of the child's company. Like other writers, Brazelton sees this special relationship as invaluable to the child. And if the grandparents stay out of family disputes and refuse to take sides between parents and children, they help stabilize the family and liberate themselves: "Grandparents no longer need to be parents, nor are they teachers. That's the lovely freedom of the role. Just sit and rock in the midst of chaos. Let them come to you."

Misunderstandings

Misunderstandings between generations arise easily, often as a result of differences in parenting style and cultural expectations.

Sometimes these misunderstandings have their roots in the exhausting, emotionally laden days of a new child's arrival. Jeanne S., a new mother, says that since her son's birth eight months previously, her grandmother has been a regular visitor, bringing presents, laughter, and love into their home. On the other hand, her husband's grandmother seems much less interested in her first great-grandchild. She rarely visits or calls. Jeanne feels hurt that her husband's grandmother doesn't seem to care about this marvelous new person, their first baby. Is she misunderstanding her baby's great-grandparent?

In the past, four-generation families were uncommon. Today, about 40 percent of people over 65 have great-grandchildren. A recent study of 450 great-grandparents between the ages of 71 and 90 found that nearly all of them enjoyed their status as great-grandparents, particularly their sense of personal and family renewal. Although they found emotional fulfillment, 78 percent said they had only limited contact with their great-grandchildren. Their reasons included age, poor health, lack of patience with small children, and a feeling that the child's family was too busy. These men and women lived farther from their relatives than those who felt more involved with the family. Nonetheless, all but two indicated they still felt emotionally close to their great-grandchildren.

Although this study's findings cannot be generalized to all great-grandparents, they do suggest a number of reasons why Jeanne's husband's grandmother has not become more involved with the new baby. Lack of interest is probably not one of them. Jeanne and her husband might clear up the misunderstanding by speaking openly about their feelings. Perhaps Great-grandmother would enjoy having the baby brought to see her, particularly if she is not able to travel easily herself.

Sometimes grandparents have hurt feelings because they feel

pushed away by the new parents. For example, Anna M., 62, anticipates the birth of her first grandchild in a few months. She lives in the same city as her son, Julio, and daughter-in-law, Gloria. Gloria's mother, who already has five grandchildren, lives 2,000 miles away. Anna is crushed because Gloria has asked her own mother to come and help out for a week after the baby is born. Anna says, "I know it's her mother, but my daughter-in-law and I have a close relationship, and she knows how important this first grandchild is to me. Should I say something?"

No. Even though Anna's feelings are understandable, she should respect her daughter-in-law's decision. Since the two of them have a good relationship, the choice was probably difficult, and in the end Gloria chose the mother who nurtured her. Research has shown that a special closeness exists between adult women and their mothers, especially at the time of childbirth.

Anna could talk with Julio and Gloria about how she can best help after Gloria's mother goes home. As new parents, they are likely to be physically and emotionally exhausted, needing time to bond with their child. Anna could praise them for their efforts and offer to help with shopping, washing, cooking, or cleaning. During the week that Gloria's mother is helping out, Anna could call to see how the new family is doing and ask when it would be convenient to come by for a short visit.

When psychologist Lillian Troll reviewed research on grandparents' adjustment to their new roles, she found that grandparents enjoy contact with their grandchildren (and great-grandchildren), but that they do not usually want constant contact. She concludes, "It is more accurate to view grandparents as family watchdogs who stand ready to jump in when their children or grandchildren are in trouble, but who otherwise are happier when all goes well so that they too can go about their own affairs." Treating grandparents, parents, and children with respect as individual persons—without getting lost in stereotypes—helps all of us avoid intergenerational misunderstandings.

When Grandparents Remarry

Difficult as it is to adjust to blended and reblended families with assorted grandchildren from various marriages, it is often as much of a shock to the family system to have a widowed or divorced grandparent remarry. The traditional concept of "until death do us part" has taken on new meaning in an era of longer lifespans. Marriages once ended in the death of a partner after twenty to thirty years; now they have the potential to last forty to seventy years—or to end in divorce after any number of years. We are all different at age 60 than we were at 20, and young people whose personalities blended when they were young may grow incompatible as older adults. When children leave home and retirement brings a couple into intense daily contact, marital conflicts that once could be ignored may become unbearable.

It is difficult at any age to accept the divorce of one's parents, perhaps more so when they are elderly. It is painful to lose a parent in death. It may be even more difficult to accept the role of "new wife" assumed by Mother if at age 72 she wishes to be married for a second time in a white dress with a veil.

We may worry that Mother's new husband will take advantage of her, that she'll end up nursing a sick man someday, or that she is endangering the inheritance we believed would come to us. We may mourn again for Father, wondering how Mother could "forget" him. We may wonder about our responsibility to this new parent, knowing that we cannot assume a child's role again. We may resent his intrusion in the family life, anticipating changes in beloved rituals and holiday celebrations. Or we may see that

DEAR ABBY

The following letter, reprinted from syndicated columnist Abigail Van Buren's The Best of Dear Abby,* *vividly illustrates the discomfort of adult children when aging parents decide to upset the applecart of a long marriage. Imagine the writer's feelings if Dad and Mother, in addition to seeking divorce, decide later to remarry someone else!*

DEAR ABBY: I am absolutely beside myself with the news my parents gave me this morning. They drove over here and calmly announced that after forty-four years of marriage they are getting a divorce! I honestly believe they have taken leave of their senses.

They have had their differences like all married couples, but they have never separated—not even for one day. I can't imagine what has come over them.

Dad says that since he is 70, if the good Lord gives him another five years he wants to live them in peace. Mother, who is 69, says she feels the same way.

I suggested a larger apartment with two bedrooms, frequent separate vacations, a trial separation—anything but a divorce. But they insist they have thought it over and this is what they both want. Abby, they have children and grandchildren who love and respect them. How can parents disgrace their families that way?

—THEIR DAUGHTER

DEAR DAUGHTER: Your parents have a right to make their own decisions, for their own reasons, without loss of love or respect from their children and grandchildren. And if they terminate their marriage after forty-four years, where is the "disgrace"? Perhaps they stayed together as long as they did out of consideration for you. They need compassion, not criticism.

**Taken from the DEAR ABBY column by Abigail Van Buren. Copyright 1988 Universal Press Syndicate. Reprinted with permission. All rights reserved.*

Mother's loneliness without Father has been relieved by this new relationship, that the sparkle in her eye and readiness of her smile are worth the disruption to our old assumptions about our parents.

What contributes to successful marriage in later life? It has been found that late-life marriages have the best chance for success under the following circumstances:

- The children encourage the marriage.
- The couple has known each other at least eleven years.
- The couple has sufficient income for their needs.
- The couple pools their resources.
- Both people are fairly satisfied with their lives.

The adjustment in family roles and expectations can be smoothed by open communication. The new couple should not only make clear their financial expectations for each other, they should rewrite their wills to make appropriate arrangements for each other and their new family. Often, it helps to speak candidly with adult children about financial arrangements, responsibilities in case of illness or incapacity, and division of the estate. Everyone's feelings should be respected, and the financial stability of the older couple should be a primary concern in the allocation of assets. It may take time and tact for everyone to adjust to the idea that the old home may be sold to support the new couple, or that the family inheritance may be divided differently than everyone had expected.

Multigenerational Households

One of the myths of American society is that the family is disintegrating, that older people are abandoned by their families when they become sick and disabled. Many people believe in some utopian past with several generations under one roof, all living in harmony and mutual support. By investigating old parish records and census reports, historians and sociologists have found that multigenerational families—both past and present—lived together primarily for economic reasons. When they can afford independence, older people have typically preferred to live separately, although they keep in frequent contact with their families. Those with children maintain close relationships by calling, writing, or visiting. Young adults typically want to establish independent households. However, changes in the demography and economy of the nation may interfere with that independence. When people become disabled or financially overwhelmed, they look first to families for support, whether they are young or old.

The Empty Nest Refilled, or Guess Who's Moving Back Home?

Georgia and Tony G., a couple in their early fifties, have raised four children to adulthood. Their youngest daughter, age 23, still lives with them. Teresa works at a full-time job, attends college to learn to work in the travel business, and saves money for trips to the places she's always wanted to see. Paying rent in even a small apartment in their community would eat up her small salary and keep her stuck in her dead-end job. Georgia and Tony are happy to help Teresa get a start on the career she wants, and they enjoy having her live with them. They miss the company of a large family. They have been happy to help out when their two sons have needed a temporary place to live between jobs, too. But they felt different when their older daughter, Stella, 29, needed to move back in with them after her divorce.

"She can't work, support her 2-year-old, pay for daycare, and pay rent in a decent place," says Georgia. "We're glad to help her get back on her feet, but she's an adult now, with her own ways of doing things. Often we disagree about how to discipline Jimmie. And sometimes I resent doing the laundry and housework for two more people. After all, I go to work every day, too. We love each other, but I don't know how long we'll be able to live together."

Tony and Georgia are part of a national phenomenon. Their children—"boomerang kids"—are being forced back home because of rising housing costs, low entry-level salaries, loss of jobs, divorce, a return to school, or the need to save money. Economists predict that the generation of people presently between the ages of 18 and 34 is one of the first generations that will not do as well as their parents. This is partly because secure, entry-level jobs are not as available as they were in the past, and partly because of the rise in the cost of living and housing coupled with a reduction in real income. As in past centuries and other cultures around the world, the family home has become a roof for parents, grandparents, great-grandparents, and children. According to the Bureau of the Census, 19 million people between the ages of 18 and 34 now live with their parents, an increase of 53 percent since 1970. How do we learn to live together again after the children have become adults? How do we cope with the loss of privacy, the increased financial burden, and the increased responsibilities when we have grown accustomed to independence from the responsibility of a young family?

Family counselors find that this transition can be successful if the family renegotiates ground rules, preferably before the adult child moves back home. Without a prearranged contract, everyone risks falling back into the old family roles, with Mom and Dad picking up the mess and paying the bills, and the adult children resenting their parents. The parents should talk over the situation carefully together, identifying the responsibilities they would like their adult children to assume. They should lay out the house rules with respect to such matters as cleaning, use of alcohol or drugs, visits from friends, sex in the family home, maintenance of automobiles, pets, payment for rent or food, responsibility for finding work, use of the bathrooms—whatever might have been an area for conflict in the past or might become one in the future.

After the parents identify their concerns and wishes, they should talk these over openly with their adult children. If everyone's needs and feelings are respected, the family can agree on arrangements that all can live with as long as necessary. Some families write up a family contract, while others find this step unnecessary. But most families realize that the agreement will need to be renegotiated from time to time as circumstances change and the multigenerational family finds new ways to accommodate living in one home.

Family Caregivers

As we've discussed, the American family has changed substantially in composition since the turn of the century, expanding into more generations because more people survive into old age, and shrinking within generations because of lower birthrates and smaller families. In other words, the living members of today's family are likely to range from infancy to old age, but there will be proportionately fewer young folks than in the past and a larger number of older people. Among people over age 65, 10 percent have living children also older than 65. Of people over age 70, 70 percent have living brothers and sisters.

Because the generations are becoming smaller, some older people worry whether anyone will be available to take care of them. Florence F. says, "I am a 78-year-old widow. Years ago when my mother was no longer able to care for herself, my husband and I took her in to live with us until her death at age 92. Now I'm concerned about who will care for me if something should happen. One of my children lives out of state, and the other is divorced and has a full-time job. I feel strongly that it's the responsibility of children to care for their aged parents. What's happened to the notion of family members being there for each other?"

Florence has already set an example for her children by caring for her own mother, but she needs to approach them with her concerns. It's a good idea to talk with them about her fears, difficult as that can be. Many adult children do think about how they will care for their parents, should the need arise, but they are reluctant to discuss these issues for fear of insulting their parents or infringing on their independence. Probably Florence's children will help in any way they can. The notion of family members "being there for each other" has not died. However, the responsibilities may be harder to fulfill when today's smaller families are separated by distance or divorce.

Regardless of overall demographic changes in family composition, children usually go out of their way to aid their older parents. Only 5 percent of older adults reside in nursing homes or other care institutions. The other 95 percent live independently, with friends, or with relatives. Families provide the bulk of the financial resources and daily assistance needed by sick or disabled older people. According to the U.S. Center for Health Statistics, family members (spouses, adult children, brothers, or sisters) provide 80 percent of all the home care for frail older people, far more in terms of financial value than all the services provided by public agencies. Family members provide transportation, perform home chores, help with financial and legal matters, and coordinate services and appointments. It would be impossible to place a dollar value on the emotional support families provide, without which many of us would have given up long ago.

Most frequently, care of older relatives falls to women, usually wives, daughters, or daughters-in-law. According to the Older Women's League (OWL), women today can expect to spend 17 years caring for children and 18 years assisting a parent. Nearly 2 million women are caring for children and parents simultaneously. In the late 1970s, researcher Elaine Brody interviewed 161 three-generation families to assess the amount of care given by middle-aged daughters to their mothers. She found that daughters helped their mothers an average of 8.6 hours per week, an amount that increased to 28.5 hours if the mother lived in the daughter's home. Although more than 54 percent of women are employed outside the home, they still become the primary caregivers for frail parents. Many studies have found that sons usually become caregivers only if no daughter is available.

Adult children with frail parents face a dilemma. Most of them continue to care for their parents until that care exceeds their physical, financial, and emotional resources. Only then, when the caregiving adult child (or that child's spouse or children) becomes overwhelmed, ill, or otherwise incapacitated, is the parent requiring total care placed in a long-term-care facility, such as a nursing home. And typically, the adult child is plagued by guilt, remorse, and self-reproach after taking this step.

Caring for a Parent Who Lives Alone

Peter V., 56, expresses a common dilemma for adult children of frail parents: "My widowed mother is 78; she lives alone. She is failing physically to the point where she needs help with shopping, keeping house, and getting in and out of the bath. The problem is, who is going to take the responsibility for her care? We three children have our own families to care for, and we work full time. We would feel guilty about having someone come in to help Mom, yet we have our limitations. Where do we start?"

Many people over age 75 become functionally impaired to some degree and require assistance to live at home. Because so many people are reaching this age at a time when fewer of the traditional unpaid caregivers—wives and daughters—are available because they now work outside the home, it is often necessary for alternative arrangements to be made for a parent's care. In order to plan properly for the care of a parent, a family conference might be called, with everyone involved considering the following questions:

- What kind of relationship do you have with your parent and siblings?
- How much caregiving, if any, are you willing and able to provide?

- What types of services are you willing to perform? Shopping? Homemaking? Personal care? Paying bills and coordinating appointments?
- What financial resources are available to pay for the parent's care? Savings, pension, contributions from family? (Medicare pays only for limited home-health services.)
- How much help is your parent willing to accept from family and others? Children often have the best intentions, but the parent may have different preferences.

Information on services—health care, homemakers, personal care, transportation, meal programs—is available from counselors at local senior centers as well as local government offices on aging. If an Area Agency on Aging is located nearby (write or call your State Unit on Aging, listed in appendix B, for a referral to a nearby AAA), you might visit the office in person to obtain a list of services available to you. The office can also refer you to people who can help you plan parent care. The United Way, Family Services of America, and religious social service organizations also offer referrals and information. A professional care manager (see the "Care Management" section in this chapter) can help you and your family understand the process of aging and the different community resources and types of financial support available. A care manager can also help you anticipate future needs and potential problems.

When an Aging Parent Lives Far Away

Gladys S. says, "I live in Ohio and my 79-year-old mother lives in Florida. If something should happen to Mom, how can I get help for her? Are there any agencies that specialize in working with long-distance relatives to plan for their care?"

Today, people of all ages are increasingly mobile. As a result, many retired people live far away from their children. At a minimum, Gladys needs the following names and telephone numbers:

- Mother's closest neighbors and friends
- people who can be called on to make a daily telephone check, do grocery shopping, or provide transportation to a medical appointment
- Mother's physician and hospital
- Mother's local church or synagogue

If Gladys's mother does not have an established support system, or if she suffers from a chronic medical condition, a social worker at the local senior center, or one referred by the local Area Agency on Aging, can provide information about help available in the community for her. Another excellent source of assistance is the local church or synagogue. If Gladys's mother has been hospitalized, the hospital social worker or discharge planner can provide information about home-care services and other support in the community.

Care Management

For families who live at a distance from a frail parent or who simply need more help arranging care within their own community, free or low-cost care-management services are available from senior centers and family-service agencies run by religious groups. A geriatric care manager specializes in advising and assisting older persons and their families in long-term-care arrangements. In nonprofit and public agencies, care management is usually offered to the client either free or for a small fee. For a higher fee, private care management is also available from a variety of professionals, most often social workers and nurses in private practice. When

PRIVATE VS. PUBLIC GERIATRIC CARE MANAGEMENT

Typical fees for private care management may be approximately $150 to $300 for the initial assessment, family conference, and care plan, with services thereafter costing about $50 to $60 per hour. Before spending a sum this substantial, you need to consider carefully whether public (nonprofit agency) or private care management is what you need.

A booklet written by InterStudy, a consulting agency in Minnesota, provides guidelines to help you evaluate the relative advantages of private and public-agency care managers. Here is a summary of InterStudy's conclusions:

Public-agency care managers

- *may provide free or low-cost services, depending on your finances*
- *may have established connections with many service providers*
- *are usually better supervised and monitored*
- *may understand eligibility requirements and procedures for public assistance better than someone who works primarily with private clients*
- *typically use existing community resources and are less able to customize services*

Private-practice care managers

- *may be available nights, weekends, and holidays*
- *serve fewer clients and so can provide more personalized service and attention*
- *may be more flexible, innovative, and creative in developing a care plan because they are not subject to the organizational requirements of a large agency*
- *may be more responsive and quickly available because they do not have to fill out long forms or complete lengthy agency intake procedures*

Both public and private care managers can help you fill out Medicare and Medicaid forms. For a list of private care managers in your area, contact the National Association of Private Geriatric Care Managers, 1315 Talbot Towers, Dayton, OH 45402. Telephone: (513) 222-5794.

choosing private care management, it's important to work with an agency staffed by licensed or certified workers. The field is fairly new, and care-management agencies are not regulated.

You can find a care manager by contacting the agencies that offer information and referrals for senior services or by telephoning county social service agencies. Hospital discharge planners and social workers, visiting nurse associations, and public health nursing agencies can also refer you to sources of care management. You can also find sources of care management under "social services" and "social workers" in the yellow pages of your telephone book.

What can a care manager do for you? Many care managers

have a master's degree in gerontology, social work, nursing, or counseling. Their expertise helps them evaluate needs and locate the services required to help older people stay independent and active as long as possible. They can be especially helpful when an older parent lives at some distance from the family or when the family and the parent are estranged. A care manager can help you

- identify the need for services—both present and future—and assess eligibility for public assistance
- screen, hire, and monitor persons to help in the home or provide other services such as yard work, transportation, and so on
- coordinate medical, legal, and financial matters and recommend specialists for immediate help or for future planning
- monitor how things are going and alert the family to any problems
- assist a parent who needs to move to a retirement complex or nursing home, or move out of a hospital or nursing home
- offer counseling and support for the family and the parent
- help to resolve a crisis
- provide consumer education and support

A care manager can do as little or as much as the family and the parent wish. Care managers do not replace family members; they merely help do the things an adult child would do if he or she were more available.

Geriatric care managers have extensive knowledge about the availability, costs, and quality of services in their communities. Thus, a geriatric care manager can usually connect you with the services your parent may need. These knowledgeable persons can keep you informed and provide you with professional opinions and advice. They can save you time, money, and worry.

Before you begin to work with a care manager, be sure to check his or her credentials carefully. What degree and professional license does the person have? Because the field of care management is unregulated, your best protection against unethical behavior is your state's licensing regulation for related professional specialties such as clinical social work, nursing, or psychology. Ask for references, and check them carefully. Ask whether you may talk to other clients (the care manager can provide clients' names only if the clients have offered to waive their confidentiality to speak with you). Call local agencies to check the reputation of the care manager. If you are in a community where a choice of care managers is available, compare the fees and services of at least three potential managers. Be particularly cautious if you are planning to ask the care manager to become your relative's conservator or guardian. It is important to find people with high ethical standards to safeguard the financial well-being of a disabled person.

Caring for a Parent or Spouse at Home

Time-consuming and difficult as it can be to arrange for care in another city, the wrench of becoming "parent" to a declining spouse or frail parent in your own home brings even more painful adjustments. The change in roles may happen gradually or abruptly. Because women tend to live longer than men, and because women also take on the role of caregiver most frequently, the most common arrangement is for a middle-aged woman to take care of her elderly mother. However, men also find themselves in the dilemma of becoming late-life caregivers. When men become ill, it may be more difficult for them to accept help because many men have learned that their role is to take care of the family and household.

Bob and Sue R., 75 and 73, respectively, worked all their lives and felt they deserved their comfortable retirement in a small Pacific coast town. They had experienced several problems with health in the past decade, but nothing that substantially interfered with their activities of gardening, fishing, painting, and travel. Their marital relationship had often been troubled by conflicts, but their commitment to family, common values, and financial interests kept them together. Then Bob had a stroke. After a stay in a convalescent hospital, he was ready to come home. At first, Sue waited on him conscientiously, preparing and serving meals he could chew easily, feeding him, cleaning him, and changing him. After a few days of caring for a bed-bound, semi-paralyzed husband, Sue's back gave out, and so did her patience. Bob's temper flared easily, too; he hated feeling helpless. Sue realized she had no intention of spending her own old age caring for a sick old man, even one she cared about. When she hired a live-in nurse, Bob felt angry and betrayed that his wife would not care for him. At first, he refused to cooperate with the nurse, and Sue had to try several before they found one who could coax Bob into a good humor. Then Bob became seductive with the nurse, and later he became childlike.

When Frieda M. was diagnosed with possible Alzheimer's disease at age 58, her husband, Chuck, promised to care for her. For a while he managed by hiring a caretaker to come to their home while he continued working as an aerospace engineer. His income was important because their medical insurance did not cover personal care and housekeeping. After three years, Frieda's forgetfulness and confusion had increased to the point that it became difficult to keep attendants. Frieda would forget who they were from day to day, and her suspicion of these "strangers" made her act aggressively with them. Chuck retired early to care for his wife.

He took on all the household tasks—fixing meals, encouraging Frieda to eat, helping her dress, and cleaning up after her. As she began to stay awake at night and wander away from the house, though, Chuck found he needed help again. The local Alzheimer's day-care center offered a program of activities designed to keep people functioning as normally and safely as possible. Chuck found the day-care fees well worth the relief of respite from constant care. At the center, a support group for caregivers helped him cope with his stress and his grief over seeing the wife he loved disappear before his eyes. As he said, "It's as if Frieda doesn't live in her own body any more." He still feels guilty that one day, when he can no longer provide what she needs, he will have to put Frieda in a full-time care facility.

Several years ago, Elinor W.'s widowed mother, Elsa, aged 83, gave up her driver's license because of poor vision. She began to have noticeable memory problems and difficulty taking care of her affairs. Elinor and her husband built a small apartment adjoining their home so that Elsa could live close to them but maintain her own household and stay as independent as possible. However, Elinor had to assume responsibility for managing Elsa's money, accompany her to medical appointments, and keep the household running. It seems to Elinor that mother and daughter have reversed roles and that their previously good relationship is deteriorating. "The more I do for her, the more she resents me," says Elinor. "She says I'm trying to 'take over.' " Elinor is stumped for ideas about how to handle the transition from daughter to caregiver.

Such changes in lifelong relationships demand constant adjustment and respect for everyone's feelings. Losing the ability to function independently stirs feelings of anger, helplessness, and fear. Even when it is clear that a frail parent or spouse needs as-

HELPING A CONFUSED OLDER PERSON

Confusion in older people can be the result of organic brain disease, depression, deafness, or vision problems. The most common cause of persistent and progressive confusion is Alzheimer's disease. A range of distressing symptoms is typical as the disease advances:

- *memory loss, forgetfulness*
- *difficulty understanding something seen or heard*
- *impaired judgment*
- *difficulty using words correctly*
- *disorientation to time and space—inability to keep track of time or tell where one is*
- *difficulty learning any new information, however minor*
- *mistaking one person for another*
- *change in personality*
- *restlessness and panic, an urge to get away*

As a person with Alzheimer's disease approaches the end of life, all resemblance to the earlier personality disappears. The American Health Care Association points out that most of us have trouble accepting these changes in someone we always considered strong and alert. We are especially uncomfortable if the person is alternately confused and aware. Although our natural response may be to pull away from such strange behavior, it is more important than ever to stay involved. People who are confused need support. According to the AHCA, you can help in the following ways:

- *Touch and hold the person. Dress him or her daily, in attractive clothing and comb the hair in a pleasing style. Don't forget the dentures.*
- *Talk to the person as an adult, even if he or she doesn't seem to understand. Discuss family or neighborhood life. Some people find it helpful to bring out photos or scrapbooks to help the conversation.*
- *Reorient the person frequently to time, place, and identity of the people around him or her. Also remind your relative of the date, season, and weather.*
- *Include your loved one in family and neighborhood activities so that he or she feels included and wanted. Activity also provides mental and social stimulation, which helps maintain normal functioning as long as possible.*
- *Keep your household routine orderly and the same from day to day. Keep the home arranged the same way, remembering that a confused person has trouble adapting to anything new.*
- *Continue to visit with your loved one, even if you feel he or she does not recognize you or cannot participate in the conversation. We do not know how much people can understand when they no longer talk, but we know that their health and mood benefit from social and mental stimulation.*

sistance, you must ask yourself whether you're doing some things for them that they could still do for themselves. For example, when you accompany Father to the doctor, do you answer questions instead of letting him explain? Do you remember that it may be Mother's frustration at her clumsiness or forgetfulness that causes her to display feelings of irritability or anger?

It's important for people to have as much control as possible over decisions that affect them and to do as much for themselves as they realistically can. Urge Mother or Father to tell the doctor about recent changes in health so that the doctor can determine whether a physical problem is contributing to any mental problem the parent is having. Encourage a spouse with paralysis or intermittent dementia to express his or her feelings about being able to do less, and ask what kind of assistance he or she prefers. If you communicate your commitment to help the disabled person be as independent as possible, your relationship with that person should improve. If it doesn't, seek counseling or join a support group led by a professional skilled in working with older adults. Senior day-care centers, community mental health centers, and many hospitals offer support groups and counseling for caregivers.

Caring for the caregiver. Although the natural focus of attention is on the sick person, professionals who work with long-term illness know that most caregivers neglect their own needs and often exhaust themselves. A social worker at the American Cancer Society says, "If you don't make sure the caregiver has respite and support, pretty soon you have two sick people—the cancer patient and the caregiver—and no one is left to care for the patient." Her observation was validated by researchers who compared older adults who took care of spouses with Alzheimer's and a group of older adults who were not caregivers. The caregiving spouses had a high rate of depression during their caregiving years—about 30 percent of them had at least one episode of depression, compared with 1 percent of the control group. Caregivers also developed infectious diseases at a much higher rate, a particular risk when the caregiving spouse is an older adult who could die of infectious disease such as pneumonia or influenza. Caregivers also had a lower immune response than the control group.

Financial strain can be a particularly painful stress for caregivers.

During a long-term illness, only medical and skilled-nursing services are adequately covered by Medicare. Like most other medical insurance (see chapter 4), Medicare does not cover housekeeping, meal preparation, personal care, transportation, or help with financial affairs. Nursing-home care for an Alzheimer's patient can easily cost more than $30,000 per year, none of which is covered by Medicare. Often, spouses find it necessary to separate or spend down their assets to qualify for Medicaid or for local programs that provide long-term-care services to frail older adults. This process can produce tremendous emotional conflicts—anger at the frail spouse or parent, frustration because of loss of lifestyle and independence, guilt over feelings of anger and frustration, and anxiety over what will be left to support the remaining spouse in his or her later years.

If you are providing care to a frail parent or spouse, you can only be helpful to them if you make a determined effort to take care of yourself, as well.

- Identify people who can provide you with respite. The daily maintenance that Dad needs will not be covered either by Medicare or private insurance, so you and Dad may decide to employ a family member, friend, or aide to help out. Training on how to provide safe personal care is available; check with geriatric centers at local hospitals, or contact a home-health agency or visiting nurse association for assistance.
- Find a support group. Meet regularly with other caregivers or children of aging parents to help each other with guilt, frustration, grief, and other feelings. You can also share valuable tips on solving problems, take turns caring for each other's loved ones for short periods, and offer respite to each other in emergencies.
- Maintain your own health. Eat a balanced diet (see chapter

1), make time for relaxed meals, get regular exercise, and take care of your own medical problems promptly. You may have to leave another caregiver in charge of your parent or spouse so that you can take care of your own health.

• Do only what must be done. Be realistic and set priorities for each day. You will not always be a caregiver, so put off the less important tasks for the future, when you will have more time.

• Prepare yourself for the day you can no longer be the caregiver. Turning the responsibility over to someone else—admitting you no longer have the energy, strength, skills, or resources to provide what your parent or spouse needs—can be an act of love. Give yourself credit for all you have done, and give guilt a swift kick when it sneaks into your thinking.

• Be creative about finances. Perhaps you can offer a service to a friend, neighbor, or member of your church in exchange for keeping your parent company. Many service agencies loan equipment free or at a reduced price to people suffering from illness. Check your local senior newspaper classified ads for used sickroom equipment.

Hiring help at home. The physical and emotional strain of providing continuous care for a loved one can be exhausting unless you have some relief. Although it is difficult to bring a new person into the home to take over tasks you are accustomed to doing yourself, you can ease the process by following a few simple steps.

Over a period of a week, keep a list of tasks you perform and your attitudes. Do you need strictly personal services for your spouse or parent, or will there be some housekeeping duties as well? How do you feel about eating with an attendant? Once you have an idea of your basic needs, develop a job description that includes the duties to be performed and qualifications you are seeking. Of particular concern for you are tasks with which your spouse or parent needs assistance. These responsibilities should be clearly spelled out, along with the work hours that will be required.

When choosing an attendant, first screen the person over the telephone. If he or she sounds promising, arrange for a personal interview. If you place an advertisement in the newspaper, list only your telephone number, not your address. During the interview, discuss in detail your needs and the type of work involved. The job description can be used as a tool to focus the discussion. Check job references to verify employment history, inquire about personal work habits, and ascertain why the person left previous jobs.

Two-way communication is important in both hiring and keeping attendants. Initially your new attendant may want to know how you're feeling about his or her performance. Be honest in providing both praise and criticism, and be patient with someone who may be trying to fit into your household. If you have trouble recruiting a private attendant, you may find it useful to call a professional home-health agency.

Making the Decision to Put a Loved One into a Care Institution

When you can no longer provide the care your loved one needs, you will enter a painful period of readjustment. You might feel that you are admitting defeat or that you are giving in to hopelessness and death. When Anthony H., 72, had to admit that his wife Emma, 67, could no longer remain in their home because he could not keep up with her daily care and night-time wandering while still maintaining his own health, he went through a period of self-criticism and depression. Emma resisted moving to an assisted-living facility for demented older people. She seemed to feel her husband was abandoning her, although the new home was well-managed, friendly, and caring.

For several months, Anthony suffered emotionally while Emma adjusted to her new surroundings and he adjusted to her absence. It took him a while to recover from the strain of five years of caring for her. Fortunately, the couple had many friends who visited Emma and made a point of involving Anthony in their social activities. Eventually, Anthony was able to accept his decision as the only one that would allow him to maintain his own health and the one that actually was better for Emma. In her new home, she was able to roam the halls and gardens, but the facility was secure enough that she could not get into the nearby streets or wander away and get lost, as she often had at home. Furthermore, the assisted-living facility was associated with an excellent nursing home, so that as Emma's condition progressed, she could receive nursing care in a familiar environment.

In *Helping Your Aging Parents,* psychologist James Halpern suggests some guidelines for making the transition from home care to institutional care:

- Share your feelings with other family members and work to reach a joint decision that respects everyone's feelings, including your own. Make plans for sharing financial responsibility and add up the financial resources available, including Medicare and insurance payments.
- Hold a family meeting, which can be useful to resolve friction between siblings. A family meeting can also provide support to the caregiver who can no longer cope with the burden of care and help to deflect the guilt that an older parent may attempt to impose.
- Include the older parent or disabled spouse in the decision process if possible. Your success in placing a family member in a care facility depends greatly on having the

person involved in the decision. Let the person visit various facilities with the family and ask where the person feels most comfortable.

- Shop around for a community-care facility in advance. Evaluate the programs, activities, food, medical care, and other facilities. Trust your hunches—if the place feels cold and uncaring to you, look elsewhere.

People with a wide range of disabilities live in care facilities, and these facilities vary in the types of services they offer. Your parent or spouse may happily adjust to a board-and-care home or senior retirement home. On the other hand, he or she may need more supervision but minimal medical care, as Emma did, and may fit in well in an assisted-living facility. A nursing home provides only one alternative to home care, so investigate cheaper, less restrictive possibilities in your community (see chapter 6).

Giving up to the care of strangers a spouse with whom you shared your life or a parent who nurtured you may bring on strong feelings of abandonment—of your old self as well as of your loved one. Adjusting to the loss of your caregiver role, to living alone, to awaiting the inevitable progression of a loved one's illness will be easier to handle if you have support from family and friends. Many hospitals and care facilities hold information sessions and support-group meetings for family members. You may also find that accepting changes in your own life becomes easier if you share your experiences with others who are undergoing something similar. You can also share your solutions; helping others has always been an effective way for people to ease their own pain. As in the other life changes of older adulthood, friends can be good medicine.

Resources

Children of Aging Parents, 2761 Trenton Road, Levittown, PA 19056. Telephone: (215) 945-6900.
CAP offers information and referrals for services throughout the United States.

National Association of Area Agencies on Aging, 600 Maryland Avenue, SW, Suite 208, Washington, DC 20024. Telephone: (202) 484-7520.
NAAAA makes referrals to household-assistance services in your area.

Older Women's League (OWL), 730 11th Street, NW, Suite 300, Washington, DC 20001-4512. Telephone: (202) 783-6686.
Local chapters have organized in many communities to lobby for the well-being of older women.

Recommended Reading

Brazelton, T. Berry. *Families: Crisis and Caring*. Reading, MA: Addison-Wesley, 1989.

College of St. Scholastica. *Family Caregiving: A Manual for Caregivers of Older Adults*. Duluth, MN: 1988. The College of St. Scholastica, 1200 Kenwood Avenue, Duluth, MN 55811. Telephone: (218) 723-6000.

Doress, Paula Brown, Diana Laskin Siegal, and the Midlife and Older Women Book Project. *Ourselves, Growing Older*. New York: Simon and Schuster, 1987.

Halpern, James. *Helping Your Aging Parents: A Practical Guide for Adult Children*. New York: Fawcett Crest, 1987.

Jarvik, Lissy, and Gary Small. *Parentcare: A Commonsense Guide for Adults and Children*. New York: Crown, 1988.

MacLean, Helene. *Caring for Your Parents: A Sourcebook of Options and Solutions for Both Generations*. Garden City, NY: Doubleday, 1987.

Mace, Nancy L., and Peter V. Rabins. *The 36-Hour Day: A Family Guide to Caring for Persons with Alzheimer's Disease, Related Dementing Illnesses, and Memory Loss in Later Life*. Baltimore, MD: The Johns

Hopkins University Press, 1981. Distributed by the Alzheimer's Disease and Related Disorders Association, 70 East Lake Street, Chicago, IL 60601-9880.

Miles Away and Still Caring: A Guide for Long-Distance Caregivers. A publication of the American Association of Retired Persons, 1909 K Street, NW, Washington, DC 20049.

National Council on Aging, Dept. 5087, Washington, DC 20061-5087. Write for *Ideabook on Caregiver Support Groups,* a directory of nearly 500 support groups. Publication number 2010. Cost: $7.

Neidrick, Darla J. *Caring for Your Own: Nursing the Ill at Home*. New York: Wiley, 1989.

Seskin, Jane. *Alone Not Lonely: Independent Living for Women Over Fifty*. Glenview, IL: Scott, Foresman, 1985. A publication of the American Association of Retired Persons, 1909 K Street, NW, Washington, DC 20049.

Silverstone, Barbara, and Helen Kandel Hyman. *You and Your Aging Parent: The Modern Family's Guide to Emotional, Physical, and Financial Problems*. New York: Pantheon Books, 1982.

Who Cares? Helpful Hints for Those Who Care for a Dependent Older Person at Home. Available from University of Southern California Andrus Volunteers, University Park/MC-0191, Los Angeles, CA 90089-0191.

CHAPTER EIGHT Intimacy

Sexual expression and the power given to it by society are, for most, young or old, a connection with vigour and life, a relationship—and a symbol of reaffirmation of self.

—Ruth B. Weg, gerontologist, University of Southern California

When was the last time you saw a steamy movie with a gray-haired heroine? What is the average age of sexy models in billboard and magazine advertisements? If these questions can honestly be answered "never" and "21," it is because our culture generally assumes that sexual desire fades with hair color and that older people have lost interest in sexual expression—or they should have. With few exceptions (*The Cosby Show, The Golden Girls, Empty Nest,* for example), television dramas depict mature adults as people without interest in sex. Sadly, many of us succumb to this theft of our sexuality.

Some people, after a lifetime of unrewarding sexual relationships, sigh, "Thank God I don't have to worry about that anymore." And many of us are alone, perhaps mourning the loss of a lifelong sexual partner, with few opportunities for finding new partners. Some of us suffer from disabilities that make traditional sexual intercourse painful or difficult; we may feel disqualified for a sexual relationship because we think our disabilities make us physically unattractive. But for most older people, the coals are still warm, even if the fire's been dampened by loss of relationships or health.

Ask yourself a few questions to assess your level of interest in this subject: How do you feel about sex? Do you currently have an active sex life? If not, would you like to? What aspects of sensuality and sexuality are important to you—intercourse? touching? cuddling? oral sex? tenderness? masturbation? caring?

By raising a few basic questions, we begin to see the many possibilities for sexual expression. While most older adults continue to have sexual interests and feelings, they don't have to engage in intercourse to be normal or happy. As Thomas Walz and Nancee Blum point out in *Sexual Health in Later Life,* "Sexuality is something that takes place more often between the ears than between the legs."

As mature adults, we have feelings about sex that have been shaped by lifelong experiences with family, friends, and teachers, and by social and religious institutions. But don't buy the popular notion that older adults are sexless. Research shows that people lead active, satisfying sex lives well into their nineties, and if you choose, chances are you can be one of them.

By now you're aware of the lifestyle choices that help maintain good health into your later years. Along with not smoking, exercising regularly, eating a balanced diet, reducing stress, and maintaining a social network, another important influence on our well-being—largely overlooked and too often scorned—is exercising our sensuality and sexuality.

The changes we experience with age can affect our sexuality and our relationships. For example, older men usually require more direct stimulation to get an erection. Both older women and older men may become widowed and find themselves learning to reenter the dating scene. In this chapter, we offer information about some of the issues of late-life sexuality and options for improving the quality of our intimate relationships.

Age Brings Changes

Let's review the major physiological changes that occur with age and that affect sexual response.

CHANGES IN SEXUAL FUNCTION: THE OLDER MAN

What physiological changes can an older man expect that will affect his sexual activity? The most common changes include the following:

- *an erection that takes more time to complete (a few minutes more after stimulation)*
- *an erection that is not quite as large, firm, or straight as in earlier years*
- *reduction in lubrication before ejaculation*
- *shorter warning period—or no warning at all—prior to ejaculation (or longer warning period because of a spasm in the prostatic urethra)*
- *reduction in the amount of seminal fluid and a decrease in the need to ejaculate*
- *ability to delay ejaculation and make love longer*
- *decrease in the force of ejaculation*
- *rapid loss of an erection following orgasm*
- *increase in the refractory period (time it takes to achieve another erection after orgasm)*

The Older Man

Bernie K. is 61 years old. He works full-time as an insurance salesman, and he's an avid cyclist and swimmer. He and his wife of thirty-four years have always enjoyed their sex life. But these days Bernie's worried. It takes him longer to get an erection, and when he does, his penis isn't as firm as it was in his younger years. He's afraid that he's "losing it" and that impotence (incapacity to have an erection sufficient to carry out sexual intercourse) is around the corner.

Bernie's fear is common, and the changes he's experiencing are normal. According to the late Alex Comfort, author of *The Joy of Sex,* "Potency doesn't 'go' with age, if you mean that loss of function is to be expected. Function does, however, change; the sex drive does get less urgent, and response is slower. The result should be more miles per gallon, however, not loss of function."

Older men who have experienced satisfying intercourse over the years will usually maintain a firm erection once they're fully excited. Gentle manual stimulation of the penis is helpful. By ejaculating only once for every two or three times they make love, older men can extend intercourse for the enjoyment of themselves and their partners.

A pattern of regular sexual activity helps preserve sexual ability. Remember, too, that all men are impotent at times because of fatigue, stress, illness, or alcohol use. When this occasional impotence occurs, your partner might help by using the approach recommended by one 63-year-old woman:

- Be understanding.
- Help in the ways he suggests.
- Reassure him it's okay.
- Be very loving in a truthful, caring—not patronizing—way.

According to geriatrician Robert Butler and gerontologist Myrna Lewis, co-authors of *Love and Sex after 60,* most sex therapists don't consider impotence or erectile dysfunction a problem unless it occurs in 25 percent or more of sexual encounters with the same partner. In that case, it helps to view the problem as a physical or psychological difficulty that's usually treatable. Causes of impotence and treatment methods are discussed later in this chapter.

The Older Woman

Marge G. is a 61-year-old divorcee. Several months ago she met 59-year-old Henry S. through a video dating service. The two took a romantic trip to Hawaii, where they first had sexual intercourse. "I was so turned on by Henry," said the vivacious, attractive redhead. "Part of me was enjoying the pleasure of the moment, and the other part was in pain. Though I felt very excited, my vagina was dry and the thrusting hurt. Also, I've always enjoyed reaching orgasm by having my clitoris stimulated manually. I found that it, too, was dry and tender."

Rather than ignoring the problem, Marge talked about it with her partner. "The next day we made a trip to the drugstore for some K-Y jelly. That evening we missed the dinner show!"

Women generally experience little loss of sexual capacity from age alone. As in Marge's case, changes women notice are usually delayed for many years after menopause and can be traced directly to reduction in the ovarian hormone, estrogen.

How can these postmenopausal changes be minimized? The cure may indeed be pleasant. Butler and Lewis report evidence that regular sexual activity (including masturbation) helps preserve functioning, especially lubricating ability, and may even stimulate estrogen production. Sexually active women also seem

CHANGES IN SEXUAL FUNCTION: THE OLDER WOMAN

What physiological changes can an older woman anticipate that will affect her sexual functioning? The most common changes include the following:

- *reduction in vaginal lubrication*
- *vaginal lubrication that takes more time (from under one minute to up to five minutes)*
- *thinning of the vaginal lining*
- *a narrowing and shortening of the vaginal canal and reduced elasticity of vaginal tissue*
- *increased possibility of infection in the vagina and bladder*
- *possible irritation of the bladder and urethra during intercourse*
- *slight reduction in the size of the clitoris in very old women*
- *less firm vaginal lips*
- *thinning of the fatty tissue covering the clitoris*
- *reduction in the intensity of vaginal contractions following orgasm*

to have less vaginal atrophy. If you haven't engaged in sexual activity for a while, you may feel tight or dry at first, but you can help overcome this with Kegel exercises (see chapter 1), followed by gentle and slow resumption of sexual activity, using a water-soluble lubricant as Marge did.

Women who have severe problems may be treated with estrogen-replacement therapy (ERT), which reduces or eliminates vaginal atrophy. Before estrogen is prescribed, a doctor usually orders an endometrial biopsy (from the lining of the uterus), a pap smear, and a mammogram. These tests check for any pre-cancerous conditions that would rule out using estrogen. Many doctors believe that most of the risks associated with estrogen are related to inappropriate dosage or to giving estrogen without balancing it with a progestin.

Although there are risks associated with ERT, it also has clear benefits that, for most women, outweigh the risks. In addition to alleviating vaginal atrophy, ERT may reduce or eliminate depression and hot flashes (sudden rise in skin temperature, heavy sweating, and sleep disturbance). In the long run, the most important benefits of ERT are a reduction in heart disease and osteoporosis (thinning of bones that leads to fractures). Estrogen can be administered vaginally, orally, or by a skin patch.

You may be pleased to find that your sexual appetite and pleasure increase after menopause. In their study of sexuality among 800 older adults, Bernard Starr and Marcella Bakur Weiner found that 87 percent of female respondents said that sex after menopause is "better" or "the same." Commented one 60-year-old participant, "I'm freer—no worry of pregnancy—not as hurried, no kids around, better knowledge and appreciation of partner. Some sensitivity, not as strong. But real enjoyment."

While the intensity of an orgasm may lessen, the desire and

enjoyment can be as intense as in younger years. Each woman can teach her partner what she finds pleasurable. Even women who have never had orgasms can learn to have the experience. Many women have found masturbation useful to find out how an orgasm feels (see section on masturbation later in this chapter).

Effects of Illness and Drugs

If you suffer from arthritis, hypertension, heart disease, or diabetes, you're not alone! Most older adults have at least one chronic condition, and many have several. Chances are, too, that you're taking medication to treat any such disorders, and with drugs come side-effects. These common health problems and treatments can affect your sexuality.

Many prescription and over-the-counter drugs can cause sexual dysfunction. A 1983 study in the *Journal of the American Medical Association* reported that 25 percent of sexual problems in men were caused or complicated by medications. Tranquilizers, antidepressants, and some drugs for high blood pressure can cause impotence; other medications can lead to failure to ejaculate in men and reduced sexual desire in women.

Other drugs that can cause sexual problems include corticosteroids (taken for arthritis) and analgesics (for pain). Narcotics such as morphine and heroin, and other abused drugs such as cocaine, marijuana, and alcohol, may also cause sexual dysfunction. Most sexual impairment caused by drugs is reversible by lowering the dosage or using an alternative drug or other treatment. Never take any of these steps without first consulting your physician.

Physical Impairments

As mentioned, many medical problems can affect sexual functioning. Among these are Parkinson's disease, low back pain, radiation therapy, and chemotherapy. A common condition that affects 40 million Americans is arthritis.

Rheumatoid arthritis and osteoarthritis are the two major forms of the disease, and they may cause pain during sexual activity. Pain during intercourse may be minimized by experimenting with different positions. For example, rather than the usual position, with the woman on her back and the man over her, you and your partner might use a side position, in which you face each other. Some couples find it is more comfortable if both partners stand. The man enters from behind. The woman uses furniture to support herself. Other positions you may want to experiment with are described in the Arthritis Foundation's *Living and Loving: Information about Sex* (see Recommended Reading). The Arthritis Foundation also recommends taking a warm bath or shower before sex, and timing pain-relief medication so that it's effective during intercourse.

It's important to communicate openly with your partner about which sexual activities and expressions of intimacy are pleasurable and which are painful. What time of day is best? People with rheumatoid arthritis often feel more pain and stiffness in the morning, while for those with osteoarthritis, morning is usually the best time.

Health and grooming aids designed to help people with arthritis look and feel their best may be found in various home-health catalogs. One readily available source is Sears. Also, many communities have self-help groups for people who suffer from arthritis. For further information, contact your local chapter or the national headquarters of the Arthritis Foundation (see Resources).

Impotence

Jokes abound. In an effort to woo an attractive therapist, womanizer Sam Malone of the TV show *Cheers* fakes an impotence problem that requires counseling. Actor Ted Danson, playing it for all it's worth, says: "Lately I haven't been able to get the ol' Evinrude cranking." While many viewers roar with laughter, for some it's not funny.

An estimated 10 million American men suffer from chronic erection problems or impotence. In the past, most men were reluctant to discuss the problem, and many doctors were uncomfortable with the topic as well. Now impotence is more commonly understood, and doctors are finding new ways of treating it.

The myths about impotence, along with a lack of accurate information, can make things seem worse than they are. Let's set the record straight on two counts. First, although difficulties in achieving erection increase with age, they are not part of normal aging; second, impotence can often be improved or reversed.

What should you do if you believe you are impotent? Consult your physician. To recommend the best treatment, your doctor needs to determine whether the problem is physical, psychological, or both. He or she will take a thorough medical history and give you a complete physical examination. Some people also benefit from the expertise of a urologist who specializes in potency, sometimes in consultation with an endocrinologist (a specialist in hormones) and a psychologist or sex therapist.

Your doctor may recommend some tests to help determine the cause of impotence. For example, one test monitors a man's erections each night while he sleeps. If nocturnal erections are minimal or absent, physical impotence may be the problem. Other tests can determine whether blood flow to the penis is impaired or whether the body is producing too little or too much of certain hormones.

Mechanics of Erection

To understand the many ways erectile functioning can be disrupted, it helps to know how an erection takes place. An erection is an involuntary response to sexual stimulation and excitement, which cause the brain, nerves, heart, blood vessels, and hormones to work together, producing a rapid increase in the amount of blood that flows into the penis. Two spongy chambers in the shaft of the penis trap and hold the blood. As the chambers rapidly fill with blood, they expand, and the penis becomes firm and elongated.

Unlike their experience earlier in life, most middle-aged and older men need tactile stimulation of the penis, in addition to erotic thoughts, before erection occurs. An erection cannot always be willed. Often, erectile problems are caused by a combination of physical and psychological problems. In older men, the causes are much more commonly physical.

Physical Causes of Impotence

Physical impotence occurs when disease, surgery, or an accident damages certain blood vessels or nerves or upsets the hormonal balance. Other possible causes include use of alcohol, tobacco, and some medications, particularly those used to treat high blood pressure and depression. Six physical causes of impotence that are of common concern are diabetes, heart disease, prostate surgery, alcohol, tobacco, and drugs (see figure 8-1). Emotional concerns may also contribute to physical causes of impotence.

Figure 8-1 Common causes of physical impotence.

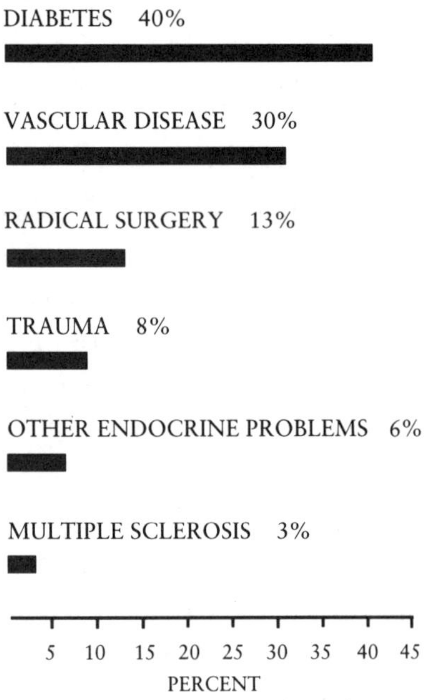

Sources: American Diabetes Association, American Heart Association, National Cancer Institute, American Cancer Society, and Bureau of Health Statistics.

Diabetes. At age 54, Victor C. began having trouble maintaining an erection. It was obvious after several months that the problem wasn't going away. Although he was embarrassed, Victor summoned the courage to discuss his erectile problem with his doctor. His doctor ran a series of tests and discovered that Victor had diabetes. Once that condition was under control, Victor was able to resume a full sex life.

Victor's story is not uncommon, because impotence is sometimes the first symptom of diabetes. Once the disease is diagnosed and controlled, however, potency may be restored. But when impotence persists in men whose diabetes is well-controlled, it may be permanent. Impotence occurs because the disease disrupts both the nerve messages and blood supply to the penis.

For information about the possible effects of diabetes on potency, the American Diabetes Association provides reprints of their article, "Impotence" (see Recommended Reading).

Heart disease. Howard L. and his wife had enjoyed an active sex life throughout their long marriage. Then, at age 61, Howard suffered a heart attack. The couple resumed having sexual relations a month later, but Howard had chest pain that frightened him and prevented him from having an erection. "Am I going to die in bed?" he wondered. "I kept thinking about how embarrassing it would be for my wife!"

Howard solved the problem by discussing it with his physician, who prescribed nitroglycerin, to be taken before intercourse to improve circulation and reduce pain. However, heart disease leads many other adults to give up sex because they are afraid sex will cause a heart attack. Yet the risk of death during sexual intercourse is very low. You need to consult your doctor to get recommendations for your specific case, but generally sexual activity can be resumed three to four weeks after a heart attack.

The time and place for sexual relations become more important for someone recovering from a heart attack or heart surgery. For example, some people find that early morning, immediately after a good night's sleep, is best. Similarly, many people feel more relaxed in their own beds than in unfamiliar surroundings. It is best to wait one to three hours after eating a full meal because large amounts of blood are required for digestion. A publication with useful advice is the American Heart Association's *Sex and Heart Disease* (see Recommended Reading).

Stroke sometimes affects sexual function by damaging physical abilities. However, it's unlikely that sexual exertion will cause another stroke. Using different positions or medical devices that assist body functions, such as those described in the section on treatment for impotence, can help make up for any weakness or paralysis that may have occurred.

Prostate surgery. For many people, any lower-body surgery (such as removal of the prostate, bladder, or rectum) can increase anxiety about sexual desirability and potency. Such was the case with Ed B., who had a prostatectomy (removal of part or all of the prostate gland) at age 58. After his surgery, Ed was able to maintain an erection and experience an orgasm, but he could not ejaculate seminal fluid. "I thought it was the beginning of the end," said the good-natured postal worker. "I became so upset about not ejaculating that I couldn't get an erection. It was a vicious cycle."

The cycle was broken when, in desperation, Ed discussed the problem with his doctor. He was relieved to discover that his experience is the norm. After most types of prostate surgery, semen is sometimes pushed backward into the bladder and voided with the urine. Penile ejaculation may return following some regrowth of the prostate.

Prostatic surgery rarely affects potency. According to Butler

and Lewis, 80 percent of men return to their presurgery sexual functioning, 10 percent have improved sexual functioning, and 10 percent have some loss or total loss of the ability to achieve an erection. The perineal approach, sometimes used in the surgical treatment of cancer or in other serious situations, is the primary physical cause of impotence following prostatic surgery, because critical nerves may be cut. Today's techniques have reduced the frequency with which this problem occurs. Overall, the most common cause of postsurgical impotence is psychological, usually resulting from lack of information about what to expect after surgery.

Alcohol. Earl G., 69, has been single all his life and proud of it. Recently he met Teresa D., who sets his "heart aflame." The problem, said the rugged Texan, "is that the fire's out before we get cooking."

When Earl's doctor asked him a series of questions, he discovered that Earl was consuming three or more drinks before each sexual encounter to loosen up. The end result was that he physically shut down. On his doctor's advice, Earl limited his alcohol consumption to one drink for the evening. The result? "Sparks flew!"

Most people don't realize that alcohol is a drug. In addition, our tolerance for alcohol diminishes with age, so that we feel its effects from smaller and smaller amounts. As in Earl's case, a few drinks can affect sexual performance. A depressant, alcohol dulls impulses of the central nervous system, including those that stimulate the penis. In men, erections may be less firm and ejaculation more difficult. Women may have problems reaching orgasm.

It's best not to drink alcohol for several hours before a sexual encounter, or at least to limit yourself to one drink. People who drink regularly should limit themselves to a maximum of 1½ ounces of hard liquor, one 6-ounce glass of wine, or two 8-ounce glasses of beer per day. Anyone taking prescription or over-the-counter drugs should avoid alcohol until talking with a physician about the potential side-effects of combining the medications with alcohol.

Tobacco. For more than forty years, George A. has been a heavy smoker. While he knew this put him at increased risk of cancer and heart disease, he didn't realize that smoking could affect his potency, too.

Nicotine constricts blood vessels—sometimes including the vessels in the penis that enable a man to have an erection. Even smoking a few cigarettes can cause erectile problems. Potency can usually be restored by kicking the habit, unless atherosclerosis (hardening of the arteries) has been accelerated by nicotine and has led to obstruction of blood flow to the penis. This was what happened to George, who had his potency restored by having a penile implant (discussed later in this chapter).

Drugs. When Ted S., a 63-year-old psychology professor, developed high blood pressure, his doctor prescribed an antihypertensive medication that lowered his blood pressure. However, this treatment also made him impotent and left him feeling depressed. Ted switched to a different drug that somewhat improved his sexual capacity, but at times he is still unable to maintain an erection.

Ted is angry at the pharmaceutical manufacturers whom he thinks should be able to develop effective drugs that don't have severe side-effects. People who are unhappy with the side-effects of their prescription medications need a physician who will take the time to work with them to find the best combination and dosage of medication for their health problems and their lifestyle.

Many prescription and over-the-counter drugs can cause other sexual problems as well as impotence. Most of these problems dis-

Table 8-2 Common Prescription Drugs That Can Cause Impotence

Generic Name	*Brand Name*
Blood Pressure Medications	
Methyldopa	Aldomet, Aldoclor, Aldoril
Clonidine hydrochloride	Catapres, Combipres
Guanethidine sulfate	Ismelin
Prazosin	Minipress
Propranolol	Inderal[1]
Atenolol	Tenormin[1]
Nadolol	Congard[1]
Antidepressant Medications	
Amitriptyline hydrochloride	Elavil, Amitril
Phenelzine sulfate	Nardil
Isocarboxazid	Marplan
Weight Reduction Aids	
Chlorphentermine	Pre-State
Fenfluramine	Pondimin
Ulcer Medications	
Cimetidine	Tagamet
Methantheline bromide	Banthine
Antihistamines for Allergy and Motion Sickness	
Dimenhydrinate	Dramamine
Diphenhydramine	Benadryl
Medication for Bladder and Bowel Spasms	
Propantheline	Pro-Banthine
Atropine[2]	

Source: Adapted from AUA Update Series, American Urological Association Office of Education, Houston, Texas.

[1]A beta blocker.

[2]Often combined with other drugs.

appear when the dosage is lowered or an alternative drug or other treatment is substituted. Never take any of these steps without first consulting your physician.

Psychological Causes of Impotence

It's normal for a man to be unable to have an erection occasionally. But dwelling on an isolated episode may lead to a self-fulfilling prophecy. Giving too much attention to loss of erection, or believing that it means loss of manhood, can build psychological roadblocks to future functioning. Other psychological roadblocks include anger, jealousy, depression, job stress, and financial worries. Most cases of psychological impotence can be helped.

After he had been widowed for five years, 62-year-old Ernie J. remarried. Anxious to impress his new bride (who was twelve years younger) with a sexual "master performance," to his consternation Ernie found that he couldn't raise the curtain with her at all. Counseling with a sex therapist helped him and his wife learn to relax and gradually progress to a state of sexual arousal resulting in intercourse.

Impotence cannot be cured by willpower or by force, but it may disappear when the emotional problem is treated. If the impotence remains, a comprehensive medical evaluation is advisable.

Treatment for Impotence

A number of treatment options can help men who are experiencing chronic impotence, although it has been estimated that only 5 percent of the 10 million men in this country who are affected seek treatment. Some men accept impotence as an inevitable part of illness or aging. Others are unaware that some intervention might help them, so they don't ask. A survey of older men conducted by the Impotence Information Center (run by a maker

Figure 8-2 What treatment options for impotence, if any, do you know of?

MEN RESPONDED:

NONE 69%

PENILE IMPLANTS 14%

PSYCHOLOGICAL OR SEX THERAPY 12%

VASCULAR SURGERY 9%

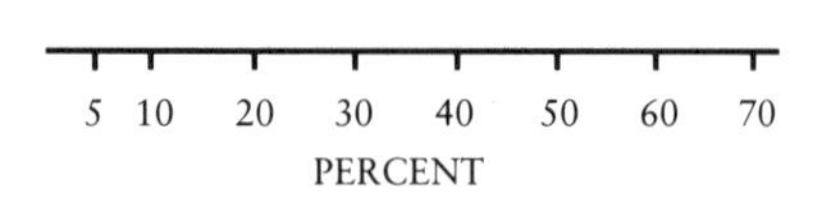

Courtesy of American Medical Systems, Inc., Minnetonka, Minnesota.

of penile prostheses) revealed that 69 percent of the respondents knew of no treatment options for the disorder (see figure 8.2).

The choice of appropriate treatment depends on the cause of the problem. Even if impotence has a physical cause, psychological and sex therapy along with medical treatment can be beneficial. Both partners should be involved in the therapy, because understanding and support are important in overcoming impotence. The five types of treatment available are drugs, vacuum or suction devices, penile implants, surgery, and psychosexual therapy (sex therapy).

Drugs. Drugs used in treating impotence may be taken orally or by injection. Three kinds of drug treatment are currently available.

Hormone therapy usually involves injections to increase the level of testosterone or decrease estrogen, or pills to decrease the production of prolactin.

Papaverine, an experimental drug, is available from some physicians. The drug is injected directly into the penis each time a man wants an erection. Papaverine increases blood flow to the penis and keeps it firm for a few hours. The treatment is used for impotence caused by disorders that impair nerves such as diabetes, multiple sclerosis, spinal-cord injury—essentially any condition other than complete blockage of the main artery to the penis. Papaverine should not be used more than three times a week, and usage of the drug requires close monitoring for side-effects. The most serious complication involves an erection that lasts more than four hours, which could result in serious damage.

Yohimbine, another experimental drug that increases blood flow to the penis, is a traditional African aphrodisiac. Side-effects from the drug may include nausea, anxiety, and headaches.

Vacuum or suction devices. This type of treatment involves placing a mechanical device around the penis. As air is drawn out

FROM THE OTHER SIDE OF THE BED: A PARTNER'S PERSPECTIVE

When most people think about impotence, their primary concern is the man's distress. But what about his partner? Woman's Day *reports that experts believe a partner suffers as much—and sometimes more.*

What feelings do partners experience? Often frustration, rejection, guilt, loneliness, and anger. If your partner is impotent, some of the following scenarios may be familiar to you:

- *Your partner may withhold all expressions of affection for fear he'll eventually be expected to perform.*
- *He may blame you for his impotence.*
- *Your self-esteem may hit bottom. You may blame yourself or worry that your partner is having an affair.*
- *Your partner may drink too much, gamble compulsively, work long hours, or make passes at other women to cope with his anxiety and prove that he's still attractive.*
- *If your partner refuses to discuss the situation, your frustration may be turning to anger that is driving the two of you further apart.*
- *You may find the issue too private to discuss even with close friends or relatives.*
- *You may have migraines, backaches, colitis, or other stress-related illnesses.*

of the chamber of the instrument, it creates a vacuum that draws blood into the penis, causing an erection. Some devices maintain the erection by placing a band around the base of the penis. Some devices stay on the penis during intercourse.

Many physicians are very encouraged by preliminary reports on the use of vacuum devices. However, if not used properly, they may cut off circulation to the penis and cause permanent injury.

Penile implants. Penile implants are surgically placed within the body to allow a man to stiffen his penis mechanically. Implants are most suitable for impotence caused by chronic organic problems such as diabetes, heart disease, rectal or prostate surgery, pelvic-nerve injury, or spinal-cord injury. Occasionally, if psychotherapy has been ineffective, implants are used to treat psychological impotence. Most men who have penile implants are able to ejaculate because ejaculation is a separate function from erection.

Implants vary in complexity, cost, and ability to mimic a natural erection. According to the Impotence Information Center, three types are available:

- Rod prostheses, in which two silicone cylinders are placed in the penis, creating a permanent erection. Most rods can be manipulated so the erect penis is not noticeable during daily activities.
- Inflatable prostheses, in which two balloon-like cylinders are placed in the penis. The man controls inflation and deflation by pressing a pump in the scrotum. Erections are more natural-looking than with other prostheses.
- Self-contained prostheses, in which two balloon cylinders are placed in the penis, each with a self-contained pump, allowing the man to control the erection. The erection is not as full or firm as with the inflatable device.

COPING WITH IMPOTENCE: STRATEGIES FOR THE PARTNER

If you are involved with a man who is impotent, discuss the situation openly with him. Don't avoid the issue to spare your partner's feelings. He may assume you don't care, causing hostility to build and jeopardize your relationship. Try the following suggestions to help you both cope with the situation:

- *Avoid placing blame. Instead, try to find out what's causing the problem and how it can be treated. Your partner's physician can refer him to a urologist, if necessary, possibly in combination with an endocrinologist and a sex therapist.*
- *Seek professional help, preferably with your partner; if not, then on your own. Individual counseling and support groups can help you carry on with your life.*
- *Engage your partner in other forms of physical intimacy such as manual stimulation, oral sex, and cuddling.*

The cost of a penile implant ranges from $3,000 for a rod device, to $8,000 to $10,000 for a self-contained prosthesis, to $12,000 for an inflatable device. When impotence has a physical cause that has been documented by your doctor, Medicare and most insurance policies reimburse about 80 percent of the cost for the prosthesis, doctor's services, and hospital stay. It is important to check beforehand, though, and clearly establish that the surgery is classified as rehabilitative, not cosmetic. The best way to ensure that you will be reimbursed is to obtain written approval for the procedure from your insurance provider before surgery.

Sexual activity can usually be resumed within four to six weeks after the prosthesis has been implanted. While the physical operation is successful in more than 90 percent of cases, the emotional attitudes of both the man and his partner are also very important to the outcome.

Vascular surgery. Vascular surgery can sometimes repair damaged blood vessels and restore blood circulation to the penis, allowing a man to have an erection.

Short-term psychosexual therapy. This type of treatment is usually effective for men whose impotence has a psychological cause. The earlier treatment is sought, the more effective treatment can be. Sex therapy by a licensed, specially trained psychotherapist can also help to solve other problems with one's sexual relationships.

One popular technique used by sex therapists is Masters and Johnson's three-stage method called sensate focus. Partners are taught to progress from nongenital pleasuring to genital touching and caressing to sexual intercourse. The focus is always on pleasure rather than performance.

Support groups allow people to share their feelings about impotence with others who are experiencing the same problems.

INFORMATION AND COUNSELING ABOUT IMPOTENCE

Now that people are admitting the problem exists, and public discussion is no longer a taboo or a poor joke, sources of information and counseling about impotence have multiplied. They include:

- *American Association of Sex Educators, Counselors, and Therapists, 435 N. Michigan Avenue, Suite 1717, Chicago, IL 60611. Telephone: (312) 644-0828. This association will provide a registry of members by city and state upon request and a copy of the Code of Ethics for Sex Therapists.*
- *American Urological Association, 1120 N. Charles Street, Baltimore, MD 21201. Telephone: (301) 727-1100.*
- *Impotence Foundation, P.O. Box 60260, Santa Barbara, CA 93160. Telephone: (800) 221-5517. This is a national information service run by a maker of penile prostheses.*
- *Impotence Information Center, Department USA, P.O. Box 9, Minneapolis, MN 55440. Telephone: (800) 843-4315. This center is also run by a maker of penile prostheses.*
- *Impotents Anonymous, Bruce and Eileen MacKenzie, 119 S. Ruth Street, Maryville, TN 37801. Telephone: (615) 983-6064. This is a national self-help network for impotent men and their partners, with about 100 chapters. For information, send a stamped, self-addressed envelope.*
- *Many medical schools, Veterans Administration hospitals, and large medical centers also offer information and treatment.*

These meetings provide education for couples about the medical and emotional aspects of impotence, including treatment alternatives. At meetings people can ask questions and voice their concerns about impotence.

Many untrained persons label themselves sex therapists (the practice is not licensed or regulated in most states), and many of these people cause more grief and damage than they cure. To be certain you are working with a well-trained person, ask your physician for a referral, and then ask the therapist whether he or she is certified by the American Association of Sex Educators, Counselors and Therapists (AASECT). This association will send you a list of certified professionals in your area.

Quick cures—buyer beware. Understandably frustrated and unhappy about having erectile difficulties, some men are willing to try anything to solve the problem quickly. And there are plenty of "youth doctors" and entrepreneurs ready to take advantage of this plight, despite the Food and Drug Administration's attempts since 1985 to ban the sale of nonprescription aphrodisiacs.

So what's the bottom line for consumers? Beware of any device, medication, or treatment that claims to cure sexual problems. The Impotence Foundation warns that these so-called miracle cures are a waste of time and money and sometimes a danger to health. Complications from self-doctoring can lead to the emergency room and surgery. For example, Spanish fly (catharides) is derived from a common European beetle, ground into a powder, and taken orally for improved sexual arousal and performance. However, Spanish fly can be dangerous and even fatal. Large doses produce inflammation of the stomach and intestines and can seriously damage the urinary tract.

Looking Good and Feeling Great

In addition to dealing with normal physical changes and common illnesses that occur with age, you're probably facing some lifestyle changes as well. If you've been married many years, you may be looking for ways to spice up the romance in your life. If your spouse is ill, you may need alternative ways of making love. Many people who are single—whether widowed, divorced, or never married—are coping with dating and with concerns about remarriage and living together. And then we must deal with our adult children about the choices we have made. Probably the single most important factor that affects our relationships with others is how we feel about ourselves.

In an effort to feel good about themselves, many older people have gone in search of the fountain of youth. But that's changing today. Now, more older adults are feeling that it's okay to look their age—as long as they look their best.

People who are sexually attractive have high self-esteem. They feel good about themselves, and it shows. Alex Comfort commented, "Sexual attractiveness has little to do with age, and the appearance of a partner is a poor index of sexual skills. . . . Most continued attractiveness is the outward and visible sign of inward and spiritual self-esteem."

A woman's self-esteem may be shaken by the prospect of a hysterectomy or mastectomy. If performed correctly, hysterectomy (removal of the uterus) does not harm sexual functioning. If you believe that you've been damaged by a hysterectomy, however, or that your partner considers you less feminine after surgery, seek counseling. Mastectomy (removal of the breast) can also reduce a woman's self-esteem. Peer support from groups like Reach to Recovery, sponsored by the American Cancer Society, help women to adjust. The American Cancer Society also offers referrals for professional help with selecting a prosthesis (a carefully fitted artificial breast). Some women choose to have reconstructive surgery after a mastectomy. Medical insurance carriers are required to pay for reconstructive surgery for a woman who has had a breast removed.

Cosmetic Procedures and Products

Plastic surgery. Some people have plastic surgery to correct a physical problem (such as very large breasts that get sore), while others choose plastic surgery to restore a more youthful image. If you're in good health and believe you can benefit from plastic surgery, there's no reason not to proceed. Most people are pleased with the results.

Ask your doctor for a referral, then make an appointment to interview the plastic surgeon. Ask about the surgeon's experience, where the surgery will be done, what the procedure is, and how long the recovery period is. Ask to see photos of other patients who have had similar surgery. Ask for referrals to satisfied patients with whom you can talk. Inform yourself about the risks and costs. Many insurance policies do not cover cosmetic surgery, and the price tag is high—up to $3,000 for nose reconstruction and $5,000 or more for a face-lift. One last caution: Although plastic surgery changes your appearance, it may not improve your feelings about yourself. If your feelings of low self-esteem stem from psychological problems, you might achieve better results with short-term psychotherapy, which can be very helpful in adjusting your self-image.

Products with beautiful promises. Often we long for some magic potion to restore our youthful hairline, smooth skin, or muscle tone. Some products, such as Rogaine (a prescription anti-baldness drug containing minoxidil) and Retin-A (an acne medication now popularly prescribed as a wrinkle remover), have been shown to be somewhat effective. At $50 to $60 for a month's supply of Rogaine, consumers pay heavily for any new hair growth; Retin-A is cheaper, about $45 for a three-month supply. Both products must be used on an ongoing basis to maintain the desired results.

One of the newest developments in the beauty business is facial toning, which involves mild electrical stimulation of face muscles. Advocated as a painless, effortless workout for facial muscles, proponents claim that ten to twelve treatments—at $45 to $150 each—can make a person's face look as much as fifteen years younger.

According to the Food and Drug Administration (FDA), electric muscle stimulators (EMSs), if used for cosmetic purposes, are misbranded and fraudulent even if a physician or a licensed practitioner is using the device. The *Wall Street Journal* reports that even though the FDA hasn't investigated facial toning specifically, EMSs of any sort are cleared only for relieving muscle spasms, preventing blood clots, retarding muscle atrophy, and increasing blood circulation.

Don't be exploited by quacks who capitalize on emotional insecurities. One person recently questioned a "doctor's" claim for a formula to eliminate arterial plaque and prevent strokes and heart attacks. This concerned consumer was only one of many. The Subcommittee on Health and Long Term Care of the House Select Committee on Aging has reviewed hundreds of such anti-aging cures. None proved beneficial except for the marginal value of some cosmetic products that were generally less effective than other products available at lower prices. Some of the phony cures reviewed were dangerous in that they caused people to postpone a more effective therapy for chronic disease. If you suspect someone of offering a bogus product or procedure, contact your state attorney general or consumer-affairs agency.

'Til Death Do Us Part

Self-esteem is a vital part of a good sexual relationship, even one established for many years. At this point in their lives, people in long-term marriages may be experiencing either a peak in sexual interest or a lack of sexual desire. In fact, our private image of a normal sex life may have more to do with our fantasies and what we've seen in movies than with reality. We may judge ourselves harshly against unrealistic standards. Most sex therapists and counselors advise clients that if both partners are happy with the level and frequency of sexual activity, they are normal.

Some couples rediscover each other after the kids leave home. Relaxed roles, more leisure time together, less stress, and fewer financial pressures can lead to renewed love, intimacy, and sexual vitality. Generally, partners have also become better at commu-

nicating and being more understanding and tolerant of each other. The result? A relationship that combines the romance of newlyweds with the comforts of longtime friends.

Many couples find that the completion of menopause and freedom from the fear of becoming pregnant enhances their sexuality. Says 63-year-old Ted S.: "When my wife finished menopause, it was like a second honeymoon—better than the first—because we were more relaxed and could communicate better."

Retirement

Retiring from the workplace may also enhance sexual activity in a long-term relationship. Researchers Starr and Weiner found that 60 percent of retired respondents in their study said that sex has always been good and continues that way. Some 24 percent said that retirement allowed for more relaxed lovemaking and heightened enjoyment. Only 17 percent reported a decrease in sexual activity after retirement.

People's identities are often closely associated with their work, so retirement can have a major impact on feelings of well-being and self-esteem. Before you retire, think carefully about how you'll spend your time. If you're happy with your retirement choices, you're more likely to feel good about yourself—and your sexuality.

Sometimes partners feel they are spending too much time together after retirement; each person feels emotionally crowded. In addition to pursuing mutual interests, it is important to maintain friendships outside the marriage. Pursuing some activities separately will also allow needed breathing space.

Keeping Life in the Old Relationship

When couples have been married for many years, one or both partners may lose interest in sex. Causes include depression, lack of foreplay or romance, pain, inability to achieve orgasm, medications, and hormonal changes. Boredom is a killer in long-term relationships.

So how do you go about rejuvenating an old-shoe love life? In *Dr. Ruth's Guide to Good Sex,* Dr. Ruth Westheimer, creator of radio's *Sexually Speaking* and television's *What's Up, Dr. Ruth?,* offers the following suggestions:

- Vary the time of intercourse.
- Vary the place. Have sex in the kitchen sometimes, or in the living room, in front of the fireplace, under the stars, at a motel (It doesn't have to be expensive!).
- Try some wine.
- Fantasize.
- Experiment with different positions.
- Read *The Joy of Sex,* by Alex Comfort.

Use your imagination to expand on Dr. Ruth's list. Try taking a bath or shower together. Change your home environment to create a sensual mood. Buy flowers and go out for a quiet dinner; when you get home, leave the television off and play soft music. If you do drink alcohol, limit yourself to small amounts. To avoid having your bedroom look like an infirmary (and for safety's sake), put all medications out of sight and at walking distance from the bed. (If you have to get up at night to get your medication, you'll probably be alert enough by then to take the correct drug and dosage.) Exceptions would be drugs for emergencies, such as nitroglycerin.

Some couples face the problem of one partner being a day person and the other a night person. Ted's schedule is early to bed, early to rise, while his wife, Eunice, enjoys working into the wee hours of the morning on their computer. Ted and Eunice have found that one solution, at least on nonworking days, is to engage in some "afternoon delight."

Oral sex. Oral sex can be an enjoyable form of sexual expression as a regular part of intercourse, an occasional variation from the old routine, or an alternative form of sexual pleasure for people with physical disabilities. As with any other expression of intimacy, it's important that both you and your partner feel comfortable with the activity and that you communicate what gives you pleasure.

Even someone who has always been slightly reluctant may learn to enjoy this form of mutual pleasuring. For example, Dr. Ruth recommends that a woman new to oral sex put only the tip of the man's penis in her mouth and lick along the ridge near the tip. If a man feels that a woman's vagina is unclean, he can ask her to shower or bathe beforehand. But there's no point in forcing something that either of you is uncomfortable doing. Just focus on other sexual activities that you and your partner enjoy.

Changing with the times. Perhaps we can all learn to keep the flame burning from the experiences of Yvonne and Alphonse L., whose progressive ideas mark them as a couple ahead of their time. Born in 1908 and 1900, respectively, they had one son. Yvonne worked in a large-city school district for forty-two years as a teacher and administrator, and her husband was employed in the men's clothing industry. Although it was rare in those days for women to juggle the triple roles of career woman, wife, and mother, it came naturally to Yvonne, and her husband was very supportive.

Yvonne's desire to learn and to teach others extends to all areas of her life and continues to be an important mission. These days, she is known for her talks to various groups on the topic of sexuality.

A vibrant, distinguished-looking woman, Yvonne speaks of her own exposure to sexuality. "In the 1920s, the prevailing attitude was that sex was only to please the man. Sex education was hit-and-miss, and likely to be gotten from friends." Married in

1931, Yvonne was a "good girl" who waited until the wedding night to engage in sexual intercourse. She describes her husband as a macho man who taught her a lot about sex but was nonetheless ignorant himself.

Later, in the 1960s, "the sexual revolution was a great boon to me," says Yvonne. When David R. Reuben's 1969 bestseller, *Everything You Always Wanted to Know about Sex, But Were Afraid to Ask,* was published, Yvonne purchased a copy that the couple read together. By educating themselves, Yvonne and Alphonse were better able to understand the needs of both partners and enhance their sex life.

Intimate details of the couple's love life "never went beyond the bedroom door," says Yvonne. "I began giving talks on sexuality because, as an educator, I felt the need to share my experiences with my peers. The emphasis is on opportunities for educating oneself correctly."

When age or disability creates changes in sexual functioning, "you adapt," says Yvonne. Alphonse has suffered several strokes and now lives in a nursing home. "For most people, sexuality is related to the sex act," says Yvonne. "For us, it now means talking, kissing, and hugging. When Alphonse says to me, 'You make me feel so good,' it's the most sensuous thing in the world."

Nursing-home privacy. Unlike Yvonne and Alphonse, some couples have found their intimate relationship cut off when one or both partners entered a nursing home. The American Civil Liberties Union Handbook, *The Rights of Older Persons,* states that in a nursing home, "You may visit privately with your doctor, your friends and relatives, your minister, your social worker, your lawyer, and others. . . . If you are married, you are entitled to private visits with your spouse, and if both of you live in the home, you are entitled to share a room."

Federal regulations provide some guidelines on your right to privacy, but most privacy rights are limited to married couples and to nursing homes that participate in Medicare and Medicaid (more than two-thirds don't). You probably have privacy rights under your state's laws. If a nursing home fails to observe your right to privacy, speak with the administrator of the facility. If you don't get the response you want, contact your state nursing-home ombudsman or regulatory office (see chapter 6).

The Single Life

In *A Good Age,* Alex Comfort wrote, "Probably the best defense is to enter age as a couple and hope that both of you die in the same accident." This will not be the experience of most couples, however. Whether widowed, divorced, or never married, most of us will spend part of our adult life as a single person. If you are accustomed to functioning as one-half of a comfortable partnership, being on your own may require major adjustments.

Widowhood

The Bureau of the Census reports that in 1987, half of all women aged 65 and over were widows. Cecile P. was widowed after forty-seven years of marriage. Following her husband's death, she felt so numb she didn't cry. Several weeks later, she cooked his favorite meal and set her table for two, although she lives alone. But Cecile wasn't going crazy. What Cecile experienced is part of normal grief.

For both men and women, the initial reaction to loss of a spouse is often a shocked numbness. This dreamlike state can help one cope with funeral arrangements, visitors, and the impact of the loss. Commonly, this numbness is followed by denial. Although Cecile knows what has happened intellectually, on a deeper level her habits and memories are denying death. Hence the table for two. These episodes will fade as she has less need for this mechanism.

Widows and widowers often feel angry. This anger can be directed at God for letting such a tragedy happen, the medical staff for not saving the loved one, or even the deceased person for leaving. When anger is directed inward, the survivor feels guilt. Guilt and regret almost always well up at some time during the grieving process.

Depression commonly follows these initial reactions, manifested by lethargy, sleeplessness, loss of appetite, withdrawal from other people, and other symptoms. It will be important for Cecile to pay attention to her physical health during this time because she will be most vulnerable to illness.

With time and support, most people gradually recover, although grief reactions tend to last longer in older people. One excellent source of support is the Widowed Persons Service, which is sponsored by the American Association of Retired Persons (AARP). Now available in more than 200 communities, this program trains widowed volunteers to work one-on-one with newly widowed persons. A variety of other services are also offered at no charge. Single copies of AARP's guide for widowed persons, *On Being Alone,* are available free (see Recommended Reading).

According to AARP, the average age of widowhood in the United States is 56, but widowhood at any age can present special difficulties for people who find themselves single in a couple-oriented society. Often the widowed person must cope with changes in housing, family relationships, and social life, as well as with unfamiliar financial and legal matters. At the same time, the person must deal with the emotional reactions of guilt, loneliness, fear, anger, or resentment, along with loss of identity and self-esteem.

Furthermore, losing a spouse means losing a sexual partner. It's normal to have feelings ranging from a strong interest in sex to a lack of sexual desire. But what many widowed persons miss most is the closeness that comes with marriage. Before you leap into a new sexual relationship, consider what you really want from it—sex? intimacy? cuddling? companionship? admiration? Conflicts may arise between societal taboos and your personal needs, so do what feels comfortable for you.

Divorce

Rose C. is 51 and her former husband is 57. After twenty-eight years of what she thought was a good marriage, her husband left her for another woman. Rose is shocked and feels alone; she wonders what happened.

The number of separations after twenty or more years of marriage has been rapidly increasing in recent years. Life changes—such as midlife crisis, menopause, loss of adult children, and career dissatisfaction—are often the culprits. Panic reactions to unmet goals, unfulfilled dreams, and fear of old age can cause one partner to break away abruptly, leaving a spouse in shock.

A marriage may break up for many reasons: People aren't ready for the demands of marriage; they grow and change at different rates; their lives take them in different directions; or they are dissatisfied and think they deserve better. Another lover is often involved in a marital breakup, but this person usually represents a symptom, not the problem itself. In fact, the Canadian Mental Health Association reports that most new loves break up within a few months of the marital split.

If you're having problems in your marriage, you need to consider events in your life that may have contributed to your partner's dissatisfaction. Have you been unhappy or depressed for an extended period of time? Have you lost interest in sex? Are you struggling with your roles as spouse, parent, homemaker, or working professional?

Often people react to trouble in the primary relationship by looking for a new partner. This approach saves them from having to recognize how much of the problem is within themselves. Talk with your spouse about marriage counseling. If your spouse is unwilling to go with you, make an appointment for yourself with a mental health professional. (One source of help is your local community mental health center.) You can't change your spouse's behavior, but you can learn to make adjustments in your own life.

If separation occurs, low self-esteem and depression are common feelings, especially in the partner who feels left behind. A divorced older woman in particular may have to cope with a variety of problems, including fewer eligible men for companionship or remarriage, a jeopardized financial situation, and limited or no job experience (see chapter 9 for ideas about joining the work force). AARP's helpful booklet, *Divorce after 50: Challenges and Choices,* examines issues related to late-life divorce, discusses the necessary financial and legal tasks, and touches on the range of emotions that may occur during and after the divorce (see Recommended Reading).

Both men and women will probably find after so many years that dating is a foreign experience and that it is difficult to trust again. Although we all need affection, companionship, and sex, jumping blindly into a new relationship may only add to our insecurities. A good way to reestablish a social life is on the basis of strong personal interests. Special relationships of all kinds can grow naturally from these associations. Many single-parent groups such as Parents Without Partners also offer social programs (see Resources).

Same-Sex Relationships

Some people's lifelong sexual preference is homosexual or lesbian, while for others sexual involvement with a same-sex partner follows the death of a heterosexual one. In *Gay and Gray,* Raymond Berger points out that about 10 percent of Americans are homosexual. Many of them have long-term relationships and face the same interpersonal problems that heterosexuals face. In many communities, homosexuals have established centers that provide counseling and other services sensitive to homosexual concerns. For example, Senior Action in a Gay Environment (SAGE) in New York City and Gay and Lesbian Outreach to Elders (GLOE) in San Francisco offer a network of social services for older lesbians and gay men (see Resources).

Unfortunately, rights that are unquestionable for a heterosexual couple may not be freely granted to a homosexual one. Hospitals and other institutions may not recognize a homosexual relationship in terms of visitation privileges and consultation with medical personnel, and legal rights are often unclear and unprotected. A major concern for male homosexuals is the AIDS epidemic, discussed later in this chapter.

Some people prefer same-sex relationships for companionship in the later years. Such relationships help fill the need for close communication and at the same time allow the person to retire sexually if they wish. Although same-sex friendships are important throughout life, they are particularly important for older single women, who outnumber their male counterparts by three to one.

The Dating Game

Whether you are widowed, divorced, or never married, the time will come when you're ready to establish a new love relationship. To do this, you may decide to draw upon some skills you haven't practiced in many years—the art of dating.

Where to go. If you're a single woman, you probably know that you're entering the dating game at a disadvantage because older women significantly outnumber older men. This disparity makes finding eligible men more difficult but not impossible.

Jenny S. says: "I can only believe that finding dates must be much easier for a man. Other older women and I need some guidelines on how to find dates." Here are a few suggestions: To meet new singles, get out and get involved. Do volunteer work, attend church socials, enroll in adult-education classes, or take tennis or dance lessons. Choose activities you enjoy, with an eye toward those that attract both sexes. Also, let friends know you'd like to meet someone. Introductions are one of the most common ways dating partners find one another. Chance encounters can develop into close relationships; be open to meeting new friends in public places such as restaurants or museums.

Some older adults find dates through singles clubs, personal ads, or dating services and video match-ups, which increasingly are being targeted to the 50-plus crowd. If you're interested in exploring these activities, check the personals column of your local newspaper or look in the yellow pages under dating or clubs.

Finally, if you're a woman, consider breaking with tradition: Next time you meet someone you like, take the initiative and ask him out.

Who's dating whom. Some adults are looking at options other than dating an unmarried person of approximately the same age and the opposite sex. In a Consumer's Union survey of 4,246 women and men aged 50 to 93, 69 percent of unmarried male respondents and 29 percent of unmarried female respondents in ongoing heterosexual relationships reported that their partner was at least five years their junior. Forty percent of unmarried women with sexual partners had taken a married man as a lover. Others had older or same-sex partners.

At least initially, think of a potential date as someone you're going to spend a little time with—not as a candidate for remarriage. Focus on making a friend, whatever the long-term outcome might be. When you go out together, have fun and get to know the other person. Enjoy!

Date or mate? If you are dating, it may or may not be with an eye toward marriage. There are pros and cons with either choice. Single and married people share similar satisfactions, disappointments, pleasures, and problems. When people feel frustrated, it's usually because they aren't living the way they would like.

If you are reentering the dating game in hopes of finding a lifetime mate, don't assume that your new friends share similar expectations. When the Consumer's Union survey asked unmarried respondents with sexual partners why they didn't get married, almost half indicated that they preferred to remain single. The biggest difference between the women and the men was that 43 percent of the women—but only 16 percent of the men—said they couldn't get married because their partner was already married to someone else.

Today's social climate is generally more permissive than it was in your younger years. You need to think about your views on marriage, living together, and the circumstances under which sexual activity is acceptable to you. What's important is that you make choices *you* feel comfortable with. You may prefer to keep a relationship open-ended because remarriage would mean giving up new-found independence. You may not want to be responsible for your partner's finances or health. You may not wish to put your economic benefits in jeopardy or give up your own home. Says 75-

year-old Wil B., a widower for six years: "I have women friends who'd like to get close, but I like my life the way it is. If I could find a woman who wanted sex but no companionship, I'd take her."

If you're looking for marriage, then someone who is committed to another person or uninterested in a long-term relationship is not for you. Howard Halpern, author of the column "On Your Own," recommends keeping your perspective about time running out, and cautions against building expectations for a new relationship that are based on little more than wishful thinking. Compatibility goes far beyond deciding which house to live in and establishing a pleasurable sexual relationship.

Anita B. says: "I am afraid I found that the same principles apply to my thinking today as in 1940 when I first started dating. After all, these are the basic thoughts and feelings that make long-term relationships possible. If you don't agree with each other's moral standards (which are much more than just the sexual behavior), then there is very little to hold on to. I was married for twenty-two years to a wonderful man who gave me all the important things in life, and I would feel that I would compromise all that we had together if I lowered my standards now. If God wills it, maybe there will be another great guy out there to fill the terrible emptiness. But it will have to be the RIGHT one, with the right standards."

Single and Sexual

Living without a partner does not preclude sexuality. Whether or not you're dating, masturbation can be a satisfying alternative to sex with a partner. In fact, you may feel safer pleasuring yourself than having a relationship with someone you don't know well.

Masturbation. You may not have an available partner. Or if you've lost a partner with whom you enjoyed lovemaking, you may not be ready to start with someone new. Many people release sexual tension by masturbating. Masturbation can also be incorporated into lovemaking with a partner to enhance pleasure and reduce pressure on both partners to satisfy the other.

If your beliefs allow masturbation but your adult life hasn't included the experience, it may take time to adjust to the idea and to find the way that gives you the most pleasure. Give yourself time and privacy; enjoy whatever feels good to you. For older women, the covering of the clitoris may become easily irritated, so it may help to use a lubricating jelly.

AIDS and other sexually transmitted diseases. A major concern about beginning a sexual relationship with someone new is the possibility of contracting a sexually transmitted disease. If you're going to engage in sexual activity, talk with your potential partner about your concerns and his or her sexual history. If you can't trust him or her to tell you the truth about a history of herpes or possible exposure to AIDS, you shouldn't consider having a sexual relationship with that person.

The incidence of transmission of AIDS through heterosexual

intercourse is increasing. Says Wil B., the 75-year-old widower: "I've had sex with prostitutes in the past, but now with AIDS I don't take chances. Mostly I masturbate." Aside from abstinence, condoms appear to be the most effective prevention against sexually transmitted diseases.

If you believe that you or your partner may be infected with the AIDS virus, or if you are not sure, avoid any sexual activity that involves contact with body fluids—blood, semen, urine, feces, and possibly vaginal secretions. Both you and your partner should consider getting an AIDS antibody test as well as professional counseling before and after the test. For more information about AIDS, call the National AIDS Hotline toll-free at (800) 342-AIDS (Spanish language, (800) 344-SIDA; hearing impaired, (800) AIDS-TTY).

Remarriage: Practical Considerations

If you're planning to remarry, congratulations! Take time to plan and celebrate the joyous occasion. Take time, too, to consider the practical aspects of the relationship:

- Are you and your spouse making a prenuptial agreement?
- If you or your spouse own a house, will the owner continue to keep it in his or her name? Will a trust be established to ensure that the surviving spouse has a place to live?
- Will your spouse make you a beneficiary of his or her life-insurance policy? health-care policy? disability policy?
- Do you have enough income or savings between you to take care of you both?
- Will both partners contribute to family expenses?
- Who will pay the rent or mortgage?
- What are the terms of both wills or living trusts?

- Have you considered establishing two irrevocable trusts before marriage to preserve both your nest eggs in case one of you needs Medicaid coverage for nursing-home care?
- Have you each executed a financial durable power of attorney and a durable power of attorney for health care in the event that one or both of you becomes incapacitated? (See chapter 5.)

Financial and inheritance matters can be handled through marriage contracts and other arrangements. Look out for gold diggers, whether you are a man or a woman.

You have a right to live your own life, choose your friends, and manage your financial affairs. However, if you and your new partner decide to marry or live together, your children may object (see chapter 7). If your children have trouble accepting your new partner—and that person is decent, kind, and loving to you—then you may need to encourage them to seek psychological counseling or other help to accept this change in their parent's life.

In your later years, you may maintain a relationship with a long-term partner, start over with someone new, or go solo. Exploring new forms of sexual expression may be in store, or you may stick with old standbys that feel comfortable. Perhaps sexuality will take on a new meaning, or you may retire sexually. Whatever the outcome, remember that while changes with age may call for modifying your sexual activity, chances are you can have an active sex life if you choose.

Resources

Look in your telephone book for local chapters of these national organizations:

American Diabetes Association, 1660 Duke Street, Alexandria, VA 22314. Telephone: (800) ADA-DISC.

American Heart Association, 7320 Greenville Avenue, Dallas, TX 75231. Telephone: (214) 373-6300.

Arthritis Foundation, P.O. Box 19000, Atlanta, GA 30326. Telephone: (800) 283-7800.

Parents Without Partners, 8807 Colesville Road, Silver Spring, MD 20910. Telephone: (301) 588-9354.

Reach to Recovery, American Cancer Society, 1599 Clifton Road, NE, Atlanta, GA 30329. Telephone: (800) ACS-2345.

Widowed Persons Service, American Association of Retired Persons, 601 E Street, NW, Washington, DC 20049. Telephone: (202) 434-2277.

Contact these organizations for information:

Gay and Lesbian Outreach to Elders (GLOE), 1853 Market Street, San Francisco, CA 94103. Telephone: (415) 626-7000 (V/TTY).

National AIDS Hotline. Telephone: (800) 342-AIDS, (800) 344-SIDA (Spanish language), (800) AIDS-TTY (hearing impaired).

Senior Action in a Gay Environment (SAGE), 208 W. 13th Street, New York, NY 10011. Telephone: (212) 741-2247.

Recommended Reading

American Association of Retired Persons. *Divorce after 50: Challenges and Choices*. Single copies available free from AARP Fulfillment, 601 E Street, NW, Washington, DC 20049.

Also recommended is *On Being Alone,* available from the same address.

American Heart Association. *Sex and Heart Disease*. Single copies available free from your local chapter of the AHA, or write to 7320 Greenville Avenue, Dallas, TX 75231.

Arthritis Foundation. *Living and Loving: Information about Sex*. Single copies available free from your local chapter, or write to the Arthritis Foundation, P.O. Box 19000, Atlanta, GA 30326.

Berger, Raymond M. *Gay and Gray*. Boston: Alyson Publications, 1982.

Brecher, Edward M., and the Editors of Consumer Reports Books. *Love, Sex, and Aging*. Boston: Little, Brown and Company, 1984.

Brown, Robert N., and Legal Counsel for the Elderly. *The Rights of Older Persons*. 2nd ed. (American Civil Liberties Union Handbook). Carbondale: Southern Illinois University Press, 1989.

Butler, Robert N., and Myrna I. Lewis. *Love and Sex after 60*. New York: Harper and Row, 1988.

Comfort, Alex. *The Joy of Sex*. New York: Simon and Schuster, 1987.

Doress, Paula Brown, Diana Laskin Siegal, and the Midlife and Older Women Book Project. *Ourselves, Growing Older*. New York: Simon and Schuster, 1987.

Starr, Bernard D., and Marcella Bakur Weiner. *The Starr-Weiner Report on Sex and Sexuality in the Mature Years*. New York: McGraw-Hill, 1981.

Westheimer, Ruth. *Dr. Ruth's Guide to Good Sex*. New York: Warner Books, 1983.

Whitehead, E. Douglas. "Impotence." Reprints of this article are available from your local chapter or state affiliate of the American Diabetes Association. (There may be a nominal fee.) To locate your state affiliate, call the American Diabetes Association on their toll-free line (800) ADA-DISC.

CHAPTER NINE

In and Out of the Workplace

It is only well with me when I have a chisel in my hand.

—Michelangelo

WANTED: *A productive, conscientious worker who brings experience and mature judgment to the job. Demonstrated decisionmaking and leadership skills a must. Ability to learn new skills required. Prefer applicants who work well with others and are willing to make a commitment to the company.*

Does that description fit someone you know? How about yourself? Most older men and women have these strong qualifications and would be desirable job candidates. Studies of older workers have repeatedly shown that, contrary to stereotype, age is an asset in the workplace. Consider the facts:

- Older workers are just as productive as younger workers in most jobs. Moreover, older employees stay on the job longer than younger employees, averaging about fifteen years with the same company.
- Older workers possess interpersonal skills comparable to those of younger workers. In addition, older workers have highly developed decisionmaking capabilities, bolstered by the knowledge they've accumulated over the years.
- Older workers are rarely absent or tardy; their attendance record equals or surpasses that of other age groups. Furthermore, older employees have fewer accidents on the job.
- Older workers are as capable of learning and acquiring new skills as younger employees. The slight decline in memory generally does not impede job performance.

As this country moves into the twenty-first century, there will be fewer and fewer people aged 18 to 25. U.S. businesses will learn to compete more vigorously for these younger workers, but they will also learn to discard negative stereotypes of seasoned workers. As Natalie Gold, a Los Angeles project manager with the National Council on the Aging, Inc., points out, businesses will need older, experienced workers to fill out their workforce. In the last decade, the number of organizations offering employment programs and benefits designed to retain, recruit, and accommodate the needs and preferences of mature workers has surged. Yet, despite evidence that older employees are in growing demand, many mature workers will have to commit themselves to educating the business world about the valuable contribution they can make.

Misperceptions about the abilities of older workers abound, and so to compete in the workplace, you'll need the spirit and confidence of someone like North Dakota Senator Quentin Burdick, who at 79 defiantly declared: "If you hear from anyone that my age is an impediment, name the gym, name the opponent, and I'll be there." And you'll need the courage and motivation of people like Charles B. After retiring from the banking business at age 63, Charles shattered stereotypes and hushed nay-sayers when he turned a desire to help others into a nursing degree, and eventually, a pediatrics position tending ailing infants.

Today's older workers have an important job to do. Often praised as role models for the young, they act as role models for their peers as well by changing the way mature employees are perceived. They are trendsetters, pioneering exciting opportunities for renewal through their continued contributions to the workplace in later life.

Whether you work to make ends meet or to enjoy the psychological benefits that work provides, whether you want to prolong your career or start a new one, this chapter will help you choose work that enhances other aspects of your life. We provide tips for defending yourself against age discrimination in the workplace; we consider ways to balance the demands of career with the needs of a dependent older relative; we evaluate the pros and cons of various employment options designed to extend your working years or help you phase into retirement; and we review a step-by-step plan for finding the job that's right for you.

Defending Yourself against Age Discrimination

The federal Age Discrimination in Employment Act (ADEA) prohibits discrimination in employment against most persons 40 years old and over. Because age discrimination in the workplace is illegal, can we assume it never occurs? Not on your life. It happens all the time. We know that, you know that, the men and women who filed over 17,000 charges of age discrimination in fiscal 1986 know that, and George G. knows that, because it happened to him.

A veteran sales manager for a clothing manufacturer, George and seventeen other executives lost their jobs in a company reorganization. As a result of the terminations, the average age of the sales staff was substantially lowered. Indeed, most of the remaining managers were about the same age as the newly hired 32-year-old company president. A coincidence? George didn't think so. He filed an age discrimination charge against his former employer.

The case ultimately was resolved in his favor partly because George thoroughly understood the age discrimination law and the rules of the Equal Employment Opportunity Commission (EEOC), which enforces the law. He had written the equal-opportunity manual for his sales division. If you want to protect your rights, you must understand these rules, too.

Under the ADEA, it is unlawful for employers with twenty or more employees to discriminate against workers aged 40 and

MANDATORY RETIREMENT: SOMETIMES IT'S LEGAL

Although the Age Discrimination in Employment Act (ADEA) generally prohibits mandatory retirement at any age, there are exceptions. Under the ADEA, it is legal to mandate retirement for the following employees.

- *Executives or policymaking employees who reach age 65 if they (1) are entitled to an annual retirement benefit of $44,000 provided solely by that employer, and (2) have served in an executive or high policymaking position for at least two years immediately before the proposed retirement date.*
- *Tenured college professors who reach age 70, effective January 1, 1987, through December 31, 1993.*
- *Law-enforcement officers and firefighters who reach the age of retirement set by state or local laws, effective January 1, 1987, through December 31, 1993.*

older in hiring, discharge, pay, promotions, and most other aspects of employment. (Exceptions apply for employee benefits. In a 1989 landmark decision, the U.S. Supreme Court ruled that employee benefits are exempt from coverage under the ADEA. The National Senior Citizens Law Center states that employers can now legally deny, terminate, or reduce fringe benefits for workers age 40 and older. As of this writing, legislation to reverse the Supreme Court decision is pending.) It is also illegal under the ADEA to discriminate within the protected group (for example, by hiring a 41-year-old rather than a 50-year-old on the basis of age alone) and to require retirement at a specific age in most occupations.

Although one purpose of the ADEA is to promote the employment of persons on the basis of ability rather than age, many observers believe that the law has merely encouraged employers to disguise their age-based decisions. Often an older worker suspects, rather than knows for certain, that he or she has been a victim of age discrimination. Consider these examples:

- An older secretary asks to enroll in a word-processing class that younger secretaries have attended. Her manager denies her request, explaining that the company no longer grants time off for such training.
- A retired school teacher calls a summer youth camp to inquire about a counselor position the camp has advertised. He's invited to complete an application, but when he gets to the camp, the program director tells him the job has been filled.
- A senior magazine writer attends a staff meeting to discuss strategies for capturing a larger segment of the baby-boom market. Over the next few months, he notices that he's being assigned more and more to write fill-in copy rather than feature articles.

HELP FROM STATE AND LOCAL FAIR EMPLOYMENT PRACTICE AGENCIES

Most states and many local governments have their own laws against age discrimination. These laws take precedence over the ADEA only when they provide greater protection.

Under the ADEA, the Equal Employment Opportunity Commission (EEOC) is authorized to refer discrimination charges to state and local agencies that meet the commission's criteria. Thus, age-discrimination cases may be handled by either the EEOC or the state or local agency. A person who files with the EEOC or with the state or local agency automatically files with both.

For the addresses and telephone numbers of EEOC field offices and state and local agencies dealing with age discrimination, check the government section of your telephone book under headings such as "Equal Employment Opportunity," "Fair Employment Practices," and "Human Relations."

If you've had a similar work experience, you might have wondered how you could prove that your boss or prospective employer had run afoul of the law. If so, you exaggerated your responsibility under the ADEA. To pursue an age-discrimination case, you need only establish an apparent violation of the law. According to Martin Levine, gerontologist and professor of law at the University of Southern California, you are only responsible for showing that you are in the protected age group (40 years or older), that you were adversely affected by a personnel action, and that you met the basic qualifications for an opening or were performing satisfactorily in your job.

Let's suppose, for example, that you've applied for a promotion in your organization. You're 56. You've read the job requirements, and you know that you're as qualified as the only other applicant, a younger worker in her thirties. Nevertheless, your competitor gets the job. If you want to press charges, you have an age-discrimination case. Once you've proved your points, the burden shifts to your employer, who must defend his or her actions.

When charged, few employers will admit to having discriminated against a worker because of age. In most cases, employers try to defend their actions by proving that their policies and practices are legal. They may do this by showing that the use of age as an employment criterion is necessary to the normal operation of a particular business (as it would be in hiring a child actor for a toy commercial, for example); that their actions were based on reasonable factors other than age; that they terminated or disciplined a worker for good cause; or that they observed the terms of a bona fide seniority system or employee-benefits plan. Now you know half of what George explained in his division's equal-opportunity manual. What you may not know is the second half: how to file an age-discrimination charge.

If you've been discriminated against, you can file a charge either in person or by mail with the EEOC. You must do this within 180 days of the discriminatory act (in states with age-discrimination laws, you have 300 days). The charge must be in writing and include your name, the name of the person who discriminated (the respondent), and a description of the alleged discriminatory act.

To pursue the case, you must agree to let your name be revealed to the respondent (let's assume it's your employer). The EEOC will notify your employer of the charge. If you are still on the job when your employer is notified, expect some fallout. Although it's illegal under the ADEA to retaliate against a worker who has filed a charge, it's likely that your employer will be displeased with the situation and, without crossing the law, can make you uncomfortable at work. Also, once all your cards are on the table, it may be difficult to obtain information substantiating your case. So before filing the charge, it's wise to gather documents, personnel policies, minutes or notes from meetings, and other data that can support your claim.

If you wish to remain anonymous, you should file a complaint, a confidential statement that your employer has violated the ADEA. However, complaints usually wind up at the bottom of a tall stack of charges, and you may have to file a charge in any case if you decide to pursue a private lawsuit.

Assuming you want to press charges, what happens next? In most cases, the EEOC invites you, your employer, and pertinent witnesses to an informal fact-finding conference. Here, an EEOC representative will try to resolve your charge with a settlement satisfactory to both you and your employer. If a settlement can't be reached, the EEOC may decide to close the case, investigate it further, or file a suit against your employer.

These procedures take time. You may wait a year or more after

HOW TO BE AN ADVOCATE FOR YOUR CASE

In 1988 the Equal Employment Opportunity Commission failed to investigate more than 200 age-discrimination claims within the two-year statute of limitations. What's an older worker to do? Take heart. Victims of age discrimination can help ensure they don't become victims of the bureaucracy as well, according to Christine Masters, a Los Angeles attorney who specializes in age-bias cases. Here's the action she suggests:

- *Investigate your state as well as federal rights. Most states prohibit age discrimination, and state law may provide for speedier investigations and broader remedies for successful litigants. To take full advantage of such provisions, consider filing charges with your state's Fair Employment Practice Agency.*
- *Start a discriminatory action as soon as possible. You must file a charge with the EEOC within 180 days of the discriminatory act (in states with age-bias laws, you have 300 days). If you wish to file a private lawsuit, you must do so within two years of the discriminatory action.*
- *File a charge, not an anonymous complaint—the practical equivalent of doing nothing. If you're worried your employer will retaliate, consult an attorney. It is illegal under the ADEA to retaliate against a person for complaining about age discrimination.*
- *File your charge in person; don't rely on the mail.*
- *Advocate your case in a persistent, businesslike manner. Call the EEOC or state agency periodically—Masters suggests monthly—to check on the status of your claim. Then send a letter to the person you spoke with, confirming the conversation and any follow-up plans.*
- *Consider seeking legal advice. Attorneys who specialize in labor or fair-employment practices can assess your claim and tell you whether other legal options apply to you.*

you've filed your charge before an EEOC investigator is assigned to your case.

If you want faster action, consider filing a private lawsuit. You can do this sixty days after filing with the EEOC, and generally you must do it within two years of the discriminatory action. (You have three years if the violation was in reckless disregard of the ADEA; however, this condition is extremely difficult to prove.) What you save in time you may spend in cash. Age-discrimination suits can be complicated, and most lawyers want to be paid up front. (See chapter 5 for tips on finding a good lawyer.)

By now you may be wondering whether an age-discrimination charge is worth the aggravation. Probably not, if the situation can be resolved informally or by using established grievance procedures. For example, Mary J., a 55-year-old salesperson for a

large department store, believed she was being harassed by her manager, a younger man who often made snide remarks about Mary's age. Unwilling to tolerate her boss's behavior, Mary applied for and received a transfer to a more hospitable division of the store.

Engineering manager Jim R., 59, was outraged after his employer, an aerospace corporation, refused to help finance his master's degree in business, despite the fact that the company typically subsidized education related to the job. Strongly suspecting that the review committee had based its decision on his age and not on his qualifications, Jim lodged a complaint with the personnel department, requesting that the committee reconsider his application. It did so, and this time it approved Jim's college grant.

If such remedies are unavailable, appealing to the EEOC may be your best recourse. An older worker who has been fired, laid off, or forced to retire because of age has little to lose by filing a charge, and potentially, he or she has much to gain, including back pay and reinstatement.

Protecting your rights against age discrimination in the workplace takes courage. Few older employees will receive medals for filing age-discrimination charges, but many should. When Pan American pilots who had reached age 60 challenged and eventually overturned a company rule barring them from becoming flight engineers because of their age, they not only shattered stereotypes about older workers, but also won rights for future flight engineers.

Many other older men and women are changing the way mature employees are perceived. In response, a growing number of employers are beginning to accommodate the needs of their more experienced workers. One way employers are changing is by offering greater flexibility to mature employees who are responsible for the care of elderly family members.

In and Out of the Workplace

Balancing Elder Care and Your Career

Ellen K., 55, works a double shift. An executive secretary, she spends her eight-hour workdays typing, filing, scheduling appointments, and making travel arrangements for her boss. At 5:00 P.M., she reports to her next job—at home. There she cooks, cleans, entertains, and supervises her 86-year-old mother, who has Alzheimer's disease.

Juggling her home and work responsibilities isn't easy. Although an attendant cares for Mom during the day, Ellen sometimes has to leave work early, take long lunch hours, or use sick leave to handle emergencies at home. She also spends about an hour each week on the office phone taking care of business for her mother. Her boss notices these interruptions, but he hasn't said anything—yet. She dreads the day he does.

It would be a relief if Ellen's boss called her into his office and said, "Ellen, I've noticed lately that you're having trouble concentrating on your work. I suspect it has a lot to do with your mother's illness. You're an excellent secretary, and I'd hate to let you go. But I've got a business to run. I need to be able to count on your performance. How can I help you balance your responsibilities here with those you have at home?"

Does Ellen's situation sound far-fetched? It's not. With one-quarter to one-third of workers 40 years and older sandwiched between demands at work and care for a frail elderly relative, a growing number of employers are asking what they can do to lighten the burden of these hard-working men and women. Although formal elder-care programs (note that this name is deceptive because services are usually provided to caregivers, not directly to aging relatives) are presently offered by only a small percentage of businesses, these programs are expected to spread rapidly.

In a recent survey of benefits directors at 100 large industrial companies, 77 percent of respondents predicted that elder-care benefits would see "major growth" by 1995. Only 66 percent said that employer-sponsored child care would be more prevalent. What's fueling the growth of these services?

First, the influx of women into the workforce has spurred demand for corporate elder care. Today, more than half of all women aged 40 to 60 work outside their homes—and this percentage is growing. Middle-aged women have traditionally assumed primary responsibility for the care of frail older relatives, but their increased participation in the labor force and their consequent need to share elder care will draw more men into the pool of caregivers. The result? Growing numbers of working women *and* men have been clamoring for elder-care benefits. With the burgeoning of the aged population, this trend will continue.

Second, more employers are recognizing that providing assistance to employed caregivers is often the cheapest and most efficient way to retain valuable workers, many at the peak of their productivity, while alleviating some of the caregiving stresses that interfere with job performance. Finally, executive decisionmakers are likely to support these programs because many are shouldering caregiving responsibilities themselves.

Apart from specially designed programs for caregivers, employers are finding that they can boost productivity and morale among workers of all ages by letting them select from a flexible menu of benefits and work options. Benefits directors predict that flexible medical plans, long-term-care insurance, and flexible work schedules—all of which can make life more manageable and secure for working caregivers—will soon be common in employee-benefits packages.

Programs and benefits for working caregivers vary from company to company, but they generally address caregivers' needs for flexible work schedules, financial assistance, emotional support, and information about community services available to frail older persons and their families (see Employee Programs and Benefits for Caregivers, this chapter). These services are usually administered by the organization's personnel or employee-assistance department.

Suppose that you contact the personnel department to find out whether your company offers special services and benefits for caregivers. You're told it doesn't. Does this mean that, like Ellen, you'll wind up walking on eggshells at the office because no matter what you do, there will be times when your caregiving responsibilities interfere with work? Not necessarily. You can do several things to reduce conflict between competing demands. Not all of these strategies will help every employed caregiver, because circumstances vary depending on the particular job, employer, and elder-care responsibilities. But many of these strategies are helpful. Consider the following guidelines.

Plan ahead. If you suspect your older relative is neglecting social, physical, financial, or other needs, express your concerns before the problem becomes a crisis. Early involvement offers several advantages. It gives you, your older relative, and other family members an opportunity to discuss the situation thoroughly and plan for the future. You'll have time to explore and mobilize family and community resources. Consequently, having a family conference to encourage family members to become involved before the crisis develops can promote the sharing of responsibilities among several caregivers. Finally, timely intervention may enhance your older relative's ability to live independently longer.

Recognize your limits and give yourself permission to seek help with elder care. Contrary to popular assumption, studies show that family members provide 80 percent of the care given to frail older relatives. Employed caregivers frequently pass up promotions, forego business trips, trim work hours, and even quit their jobs to tend to the needs of older relatives. Despite these and other personal sacrifices, many people feel guilty about not doing enough for their dependent relative.

Rather than ask what you should be doing for your relative, ask what commitments you feel comfortable making. Being at ease with your role can help prolong both your professional and caregiving careers.

Remember that your time is limited, so spend it wisely. In many cases, "wisely" means delegating some elder-care duties. In every community you're likely to find an array of services for frail older persons. These services may include transportation, in-home meals, help with finances, and assistance with home chores. Although caregivers may be aware of such services, many use them inefficiently. Research has shown that families typically seek help from formal service providers only as a last resort, after they've reached the end of their rope. Yet, most of us would agree that it's better to prevent burnout by obtaining timely assistance. So why the resistance?

Many people mistakenly assume that support services constitute charity and are available only to low-income elderly. In fact, eligibility for many services, such as Meals on Wheels, depends not on income but on the recipient's physical or social need for assistance. And services at senior centers, for example, are offered to all persons over a certain age.

Family caregivers may also overextend themselves because, in their minds, doing less means shirking family obligations. But service providers don't replace you; rather, they should support and complement your caregiving efforts. Their help with meal preparation, house cleaning, and other chores permits you greater flexibility in managing tasks you can't entrust to others. You can be freer to provide the companionship Mom or Dad might prefer instead of spending your time doing routine chores.

Sometimes the older person, fearing loss of independence, resists accepting outside help. If this happens, you and other family members need to talk with your relative in an open, caring manner. Listen to his or her feelings and concerns and offer support, remembering that older people should have the opportunity to make their own lifestyle decisions to as great a degree as possible. If solutions can't be found, consider asking the family doctor, close friends, or other trusted individuals to talk with your relative.

Be prepared to address your employer's concerns. The dual demands of career and care for a frail relative can affect productivity at work. Studies of employed caregivers have found that they miss work, arrive late, take sick leave, and use the office telephone for personal calls more often than other employees. Consequently, many managers worry that they can't afford to employ family caregivers. To alleviate their concerns, there are several things you can do:

- Your best strategies for reducing conflicts between work and elder care are, again, to plan ahead and enlist support from other family members, friends, and community service providers. If, despite these efforts, you need time off or find yourself running late for work, inform your supervisor as soon as possible so that he or she can plan accordingly. Offer to make up the time or charge it to your vacation period. Most employers will appreciate that you've considered their needs, and they may therefore grant you time off more freely.

• Limit the amount of time you spend on the office telephone researching services for your older relative by first contacting senior organizations that offer information and referral programs (see Resources). These organizations can help identify the services your relative needs and refer you to agencies that provide them. Once you know which organizations to call, make a list of questions to ask before you place the call.

• If you must make elder-care calls from work, do so before or after your shift, or during your break or lunch period. Any calls made during work hours should be as brief as possible. Make them when you're least busy, and if your boss or colleagues need you, tell the person you'll call back. If the other party must return your call, ask him or her to do it during nonworking periods. Consider charging calls to your home or using a pay phone.

• Take care of yourself. Although caring for an aging relative can be rewarding, it frequently is also physically and emotionally draining. The caregiver's health may suffer. Besides eating properly and exercising regularly (see chapter 1), working caregivers need to address their often-neglected social and emotional needs. Though elder-care responsibilities may preclude your long-overdue vacation, at a minimum you should take a daily block of time —even 30 minutes will help—exclusively for yourself. Use this time to relax or do something you enjoy. If you can't unwind, it may help to discuss your concerns with family members, close friends, clergy, professional counselors, or members of a caregiver support group. As one working caregiver noted, "When you have somebody no further away than the telephone to help, it's comforting."

• Many senior organizations can refer you to support programs for family caregivers. Ask them about such services when exploring resources for your older relative.

Pioneer new elder-care benefits within your organization. It's not necessary for your employer to offer flexible benefits and formal caregiver services if you can negotiate with your supervisor for the support you need. Bookkeeper Geri G., 57, arranged a short-term elder-care benefit that few (if any) companies report offering.

After her 78-year-old mother was treated for depression, Geri enrolled her in an adult day-care program. However, there was a three-day lag between her mother's discharge from the hospital and admission to the day-care center. Unable to leave her mother home alone, Geri asked her boss if the older woman could come to the office. "Certainly," said her supervisor. A mother who occasionally brought her child to work when the sitter cancelled unexpectedly, the supervisor empathized with Geri's dilemma.

As this example illustrates, special arrangements and company support for employed caregivers may be available on request. It's probably safe to assume that most supervisors will try to accommodate their employees' needs, if only because they recognize how costly and difficult it is to replace workers. Keep in mind, however, that you need to help your employer help you. For example, Geri took responsibility for ensuring that her mother's office visits did not disrupt anyone's work. Before discussing arrangements, assess the situation from your employer's point of view to determine what you can reasonably expect. Also, consider how your position in the organization might be affected if your request is denied.

Consider advocating for corporate elder care on a broader scale. You might do this by asking members of Congress to support legislation favoring elder care, raising the issue with your union, or slipping a note into the company suggestion box.

Finally, read on. In recent years, a growing number of organizations have created work and retirement options that can help employed caregivers as well as other mature workers.

Employee Programs and Benefits for Caregivers

What elder-care services should you look for at your current job? Or if you are looking for a job, what services should you inquire about? The most widely available employee programs and benefits for working caregivers include the following:

• *Information and referral services.* Trying to find the right services for an aging relative can be a time-consuming, frustrating task. To save the time that individual employees have to spend researching available services, a number of employers offer to do it for you.

• *Caregiver support groups.* Held at the office, these are convenient to attend, easy to fit into work schedules, and immensely reassuring to employed caregivers, who often feel isolated and alone.

• *Lunch-time seminars.* These programs typically feature a guest speaker, often a community professional, who discusses some aspect of aging or caregiving. Because they may be attended by hundreds of employees, brown-bag seminars can be particularly important to caregivers who prefer to get help anonymously.

• *Individual counseling.* Working caregivers can maintain their anonymity in confidential individual counseling. If you're looking for short-term help with managing your job and caregiving responsibilities, an employee-assistance counselor familiar with aging issues can assist you.

• *Care-assistance plans for dependents.* Salary deductions, in amounts specified by the worker, may be used to defray certain medical, in-home, and day-care expenses incurred for elderly dependents. These deductions are *not* taxable income.

• *Long-term-care insurance.* More employers are offering workers, their dependents, and company retirees the chance to buy long-term-care insurance, which covers certain nursing-home and home health-care expenses. Frequently, the insured individual pays the full premium. Because long-term-care insurance is relatively new, its reliability and comprehensiveness have been questioned. Caregivers should examine policies carefully before purchase (see chapter 4 for guidelines to consider).

• *Extended leaves of absence.* Some employers offer extended leaves to workers caring for seriously ill family members. These leaves can range from a few weeks to three or more months. Although most such leaves are unpaid, employers may continue to contribute their share of the cost of medical insurance and other benefits during the time the employee is on leave.

• *Flextime.* A favorite among employed caregivers, who often have time constraints at home because of caregiving arrangements, this program allows employees to vary the beginning and end of their workdays within certain hours. For example, at one corporation, employees may start work any time between 7:00 and 9:00 A.M. and leave after their full shift.

Evaluating Your Work and Retirement Options

Since graduating from college, Sam T. had been working toward it. In his mid-thirties he began saving for it. After his fifty-fifth birthday he began planning for it. And at age 62 he took it: retirement. In many respects, Sam's retirement was typical, down to the office farewell party and the inscribed watch.

Like Sam, Kevin A. planned to retire sometime in his mid-sixties. But three months after he turned 55, his employer of thirty years made him an offer he couldn't refuse. In return for an early retirement, he'd receive a full pension, half his salary until he qualified for social security, and comprehensive medical coverage for life. With these benefits, he and his wife could maintain their present lifestyle without having to work. Five months later, Kevin was a full-time retiree.

Ruth K.'s employer also offered her an opportunity she hadn't counted on. As a high-school teacher, Ruth couldn't imagine a more rewarding job. What could be better than watching young faces light up with new knowledge? But keeping pace with her ninth graders required immense energy, and after thirty-four years in the classroom, Ruth felt her spark diminishing. Somewhat reluctantly, she decided to retire. Informed of this decision, her boss, eager to retain such an experienced instructor, arranged for Ruth to share her job with a recently hired teacher. Ruth was thrilled. Her half-day schedule gave her enough classroom time to feel stimulated but not drained.

As these examples demonstrate, the concept of retirement is rapidly changing. A few decades ago, when most Americans retired at age 65, Sam would have been the exception to the rule. Today, with the average worker clocking out at age 62, he exemplifies it. But Sam, Kevin, and Ruth may not represent the future. With demographic shifts expected to rock the economy over the next decade, many observers predict that the current trend toward early retirement will either accelerate or, conversely, begin moving in the opposite direction. Let's look at some of the big changes that are causing people to reassess when they leave work.

Over the last three decades, there has been a dramatic shift toward early retirement. Between 1950 and 1984, the proportion of men over 65 years who were still in the workforce plummeted

from 50 percent to 16 percent, according to the U.S. Special Committee on Aging. Despite the influx of women into the labor force, the percentage of older working women also dropped during that period, from 10 percent to 7.5 percent.

The decline in workforce participation extends to people younger than age 65 as well. Labor Department statistics show that 21 percent of men aged 55 to 59 had left the workforce in 1986—up from about 8 percent in 1960. According to the General Accounting Office, the number of persons aged 55 to 61 who were receiving pension benefits doubled during the last ten years.

Experts attribute the rush toward early retirement to the combined effect of several social, demographic, and economic forces:

- The availability of social security benefits, better and more widely offered pension benefits, and the increased number of two-career families mean that more men and women can afford to retire early.
- Americans are enjoying longer, healthier lives. For some people good health is a reason to prolong a successful career. For others, good health and longevity are incentives to trade their jobs for earlier opportunities to pursue personal interests with more vigor and intensity.
- Expectations about retirement are changing. Today the average man spends about 19 percent of his lifetime in retirement—up from 3 percent at the turn of the century. With new opportunities for leisure, many Americans feel entitled to quit work early.
- To survive in competitive regional and international markets, many companies are trimming the payroll to make room for younger, less expensive workers by offering older employees attractive early-retirement packages.

NEGOTIATING WORK OPTIONS

Depending on your circumstances, you may want to negotiate with your employer for job sharing, phased retirement, or another work option not presently offered. Keeping in mind that the most effective employment practices typically benefit both employee and employer, you should first find out the answers to these questions:

- *What are the advantages and disadvantages of the work option in terms of your time, pay, responsibilities, fringe benefits, pension benefits, and so on? How do these compare with your present job or other work options that interest you?*
- *If the option involves reducing your hours, does your job lend itself to the new schedule? If the option entails new responsibilities, are you qualified to assume them?*
- *How will the organization benefit if you alter your job? For example, will you be able to work more productively? Prolong your career? Will co-workers benefit or gain new opportunities?*
- *What obstacles might your employer face in implementing the option? For instance, would the company incur extra expenses? Will a co-worker or temporary replacement have to assume some of your responsibilities?*
- *What actions can you take or suggestions can you offer to help your supervisor overcome any obstacles?*
- *Will your position in the organization be compromised in any way if your employer denies your request?*

While early retirement remains alluring, reasons to buck this trend are mounting:

- Older workers are growing in demand as employers look to fill labor shortages caused by a steadily diminishing supply of younger workers.
- Recognizing what many of us know from personal experience—that older adults are valuable workers—employers are creating a variety of job options designed to accommodate the preferences of mature employees. For example, a survey of 400 randomly selected companies showed that about one-quarter of these organizations offered job-sharing progams while another one-fourth had phased retirement plans.
- Recent government actions have eliminated deterrents to work for many older adults and created incentives that will promote a longer work life. The 1986 amendments to the ADEA

outlaw mandatory retirement at any age for most occupations. Another recent ADEA amendment requires employer pension contributions to accrue for workers who stay on the job past age 65. The social security credit earned for each year a person delays collecting benefits past the normal retirement age will gradually increase from 3 percent in 1989 to 8 percent in 2008. Finally, after the turn of the century, the eligibility age of 65 for full social security benefits will begin rising, until it reaches age 67 in 2022.

Although signals to older workers are mixed, the message is clear: The range of work and retirement options is expanding, making room for people to exercise individual preferences.

With the business world becoming more receptive to flexible work options, planning for later life should include a look at innovative employment practices. To help you begin thinking creatively about how these can contribute to a more satisfying lifestyle, let's consider the pros and cons of the most prevalent work and retirement options.

Early-Retirement Incentive Programs

If you could maintain your present standard of living without working, would you retire? "Probably yes," says a former AT&T employee whose decision to accept his company's early retirement plan boiled down to "simple economics." "Why work," asked this person, "when I could have more net income as a retiree?" This powerful argument, considered in light of leisure and second-career opportunities available to early retirees, helps explain why 1.5 million workers accepted the "golden handshake" in the 1980s. However, incentive programs sometimes lure into early retirement employees who are financially and psychologically unprepared to leave work. Furthermore, some employees feel compelled to accept early retirement to avoid being "put out to pasture" at a later date (see the discussion earlier in this chapter regarding your rights under the ADEA).

Retirement Transitions

Until recently, older workers could find out if they were adequately prepared for retirement only by diving into it full time. With the deed done, it was a case of sink or swim. But in the last decade, a sizable number of companies have created transition programs that allow would-be retirees to get their feet wet before taking the plunge.

Phased retirement programs. These programs allow employees to reduce their work hours gradually during the year or two before retirement. For example, quality-control manager Mike N. recently trimmed his work week from forty to thirty hours. Next year he'll work twenty hours a week, before taking full-time retirement. With the extra time, he's attending a fiction-writing class, committing literary mayhem in his spy novel. Meanwhile, at the office, a junior colleague is training to assume some of Mike's responsibilities.

Depending on company policy, employees in a phased-retirement program can reduce their hours per day, days per week, or weeks per month. Although participants continue to receive full benefits, they may receive lower pension benefits at retirement because of salary reductions during the transition period.

Sabbaticals. A sabbatical of a few months to a year offers older workers a chance to explore personal interests in preparation for retirement. In addition, older workers may use the time to upgrade job skills, prepare for a second career, or rekindle interest in work through a refreshing change of pace. A sabbatical's major drawback is loss of pay during the leave.

Part-time work schedules. Doris L., a 63-year-old nurse, feels she's finally leading a balanced life. Before retiring, Doris discussed with her employer the possibility of working on call. Today, she turns down as many assignments as she accepts. "I'm free to set my own schedule. One week I work full time, the next I'm visiting Hawaii. I have the best of both worlds," she says.

Doris is one of a growing number of retirees who have been rehired part time by their former employers. Members of this contingency workforce may return to their old stomping grounds to help with special projects, train new employees, or substitute for vacationing or ill employees. Some work part time for extended periods; others work full time for a few weeks or months. They may be hired directly or through job banks and employment agencies.

Banks, insurance companies, aerospace corporations, and many other organizations have actively recruited retirees for various reasons. Besides offering dependability, maturity, and good interpersonal skills, retirees bring an irreplaceable institutional memory to the job. In addition, they are often more efficient than outside temporary replacements because they have experience with company policies and practices.

Job sharing. While not every job lends itself to part-time work, some full-time positions can be filled by part-time employees. Sometimes two part-time workers can divide the tasks of one full-time job. To be successful, the partners must carefully plan the allocation of tasks and maintain good communication. Workers interested in job sharing sometimes discuss the possibility with their employer after finding their own partners and devising a feasible workplan.

While part-time work offers several advantages, including more time for leisure and special interests, there's a flip side to consider. Part-timers typically receive lower wages and fewer benefits than their full-time counterparts. They may be passed over for advancement opportunities and terminated from a job with little notice. Also, pension rules may hamper the rehiring of retirees; in some cases, benefits cease with reemployment.

Job Modifications

Have you ever had something like this happen to you? You're sitting in the office reading a report. A colleague drops by to ask about a project you're working on. Later, as she's walking out, she stops in the doorway. "How about some light?" she says and flips on the switch. Wow! What a difference. Now why didn't you think of that?

Many of us are so accustomed to adapting to our work environment that we find ourselves in the dark when it comes to reversing the relationship and modifying the surroundings to suit our needs. Yet job accommodation or job redesign, which also includes restructuring work tasks, can reduce stress, bolster productivity and morale, and enable some older workers to prolong their careers. Job redesign can take many forms:

- Because of her arthritis, a machine operator had trouble reaching up and across the machine to perform certain tasks. An adjustable stool with back support and a platform for her feet corrected the problem.
- When her hearing loss began to hamper communication with patients, a nurse discussed the situation with her boss. With help from the hospital's rehabilitation personnel, the nurse's job was restructured around administrative tasks.
- A plant supervisor with multiple sclerosis was unable to move around the plant's tool room. After the company bought him

a motorized three-wheeled cart, his co-workers had trouble keeping up with him.

Many employers view job redesign as too difficult and expensive to implement. But as the Job Accommodation Network points out, "Modifications need not be costly, complex, or technical to be successful. Often, the simpler modifications are more effective." In addition, job-accommodation programs can save money by extending the work life of valued employees who otherwise might take disability leave or retirement.

Another type of modification, job transfer, involves assigning a worker to a different job or a special project without actually changing the person's permanent position. Such options can offer new challenges and help retain older employees who are burned out with their jobs or whose careers have stalled because of clogged promotion channels. Job transfer can also benefit mature employees who want fewer responsibilities or reduced physical demands. Although lateral moves to jobs with comparable responsibilities do not usually trigger a reduction in salary, downward transfers often do.

Retraining

Technical knowledge is expanding so rapidly that if workers of all ages don't continually upgrade their skills, they are soon left in the dust of technological change. The retraining of older, experienced workers usually involves updating their skills to keep pace with developments in their field. However, many older workers resist or are denied such training because of myths about the learning abilities of older adults. Yet, several studies have shown that older workers can and do learn effectively. Although they may be more deliberate decisionmakers, where time pressure is not a fac-

NEED HELP WITH YOUR JOB SEARCH?

Looking for a job can be lonely, frightening, and depressing. But the going's easier with someone to lend a hand. These organizations offer you job-search assistance, career counseling, and vocational testing.

Forty Plus. *Designed for older professionals, these membership organizations have a self-help focus. Their primary function is to help members help themselves get jobs. There are 16 independent Forty Plus organizations located in metropolitan areas across the United States.*

Members generally pay an initial membership fee and monthly dues. Usually members do volunteer work to take the place of paid staff. Telephones, desks, word processors, support groups, job-search seminars, want ads, and other publications are available. To find a Forty Plus near you, check the white pages of your telephone book, or inquire at your local senior center.

Regional Coordinating Councils (RCCs). *Nationwide, eight older-worker RCCs (in Arkansas, Michigan, Vermont, southeastern Nebraska, Los Angeles County, Boston, Chicago, and New York City) offer free or low-cost job-search assistance and other services to older job seekers. Contact a local senior center or check the yellow pages under "employment" for the address of an RCC in your area.*

Job Training Partnership Act (JTPA). *This federal program provides funds to local "service-delivery areas" for job training and placement services. Most JTPA programs have both on-the-job and classroom training opportunities.*

To be eligible, a single person must have an average income lower than $523 per month for the last 6 months (in 1991); for a family of two, the income limit is $701 per month. These limits may change each year. To find out about JTPA programs in your area, contact your State Unit on Aging (see appendix B) or the Job Training Coordinating Council in your state capitol.

Senior community service employment programs. *These organizations help place workers over 55 years in part-time positions with nonprofit organizations. No previous training is required; the purpose is to provide on-the-job training, and the federal government pays the wages.*

To qualify, your annual income cannot exceed 125 percent of the poverty standard ($8,275 for a single person in 1991; the limits are $10,363 and $9,513 respectively for residents of Alaska and Hawaii). For more information and the address of a senior community service employment program in your area, contact a senior center or your State Unit on Aging (see appendix B).

Displaced Homemakers Network. *This national organization provides counseling, workshops, training, and job placement assistance to displaced homemakers (women who have lost their source of income because of events such as divorce or the death of a spouse). More than 1,000 programs are offered through YWCAs, women centers, community colleges, and the like. For information about programs in your area, contact the national office at 1411 K Street, NW, Suite 930, Washington, DC 20005. Telephone: (202) 628-6767.*

tor, their performance equals that of younger workers.

Mature workers need to keep these facts in mind and take responsibility for puncturing negative stereotypes that may obstruct their access to training. Also, many employers need to be apprised of the cost benefit of training older workers, who typically stay with a company longer than their younger counterparts. An investment in their future frequently yields a high return. (See chapter 10 for information about educational opportunities available to older adults.)

Even if you've set your retirement date or have already retired, it's a good idea to keep these job options in mind. Someday you may want to return to work. At that point you may need to refresh your job-search skills.

Finding the Job That's Right for You

When Mary, a 64-year-old retired secretary, decided to look for a job, she did what millions of Americans do: She scoured the classified ads, clipping and answering those that interested her. Three weeks, thirty-six applications, and two disappointing interviews later, Mary signed up with an employment agency. The woman who interviewed her was encouraging and promised to call "real soon." Two weeks passed and still Mary hadn't heard from her.

What's wrong? she wondered. She had eight years of experience working for a manager who had scared off two previous secretaries in six months. Mary lasted because she knew how to get along with others and was good at her job. Since retiring two years ago, she had traveled, volunteered at church, and kept busy in other ways before deciding she missed the challenges and benefits of a job. She hadn't anticipated much difficulty finding one.

Now, tired of waiting for the employment agency to call, she contacted a senior center, hoping that someone there might help. She was pleasantly surprised when a woman suggested she report to a certain address by 10 A.M. the next day. She went expecting to be interviewed for a job.

Instead, she found herself in a small group at a placement agency for older workers. The woman in charge was explaining that the agency didn't find jobs for participants; rather, it offered an approach that enabled them to find jobs. Mary wasn't interested until she learned that the names posted on two walls belonged to older workers who had found jobs using methods the woman was now describing.

If it worked for them, it might work for me, she thought. It did. Mary eventually accepted a secretarial job that not only suited her skills, interests, and talents, but paid the salary she wanted.

What's the secret to her and many others' success? No secret—just a widely recommended job-search plan in which the job seeker takes control by following certain steps. Whether you're reentering the workforce, looking for a new job, or seeking paid employment for the first time, this plan can help you land the job you've been dreaming about.

Take Stock of Yourself

Assessing yourself is a critical first step because it lays the groundwork for your job-search plan. It entails describing—in writing!—your skills, interests, work values, personal attributes, preferred work environment, and salary needs. So grab pen and paper and make a list of the following attributes.

Your skills. Don't be modest; list everything you're good at. Consider skills you've acquired not only through work and school, but also through hobbies, volunteer positions, recrea-

tional activities, family responsibilities, reading, and the like. Your skills will fall into three categories: skills in working with (1) people, (2) information, or (3) objects such as tools, materials, and machines. A thorough analysis of your skills can help you begin thinking creatively about a number of job opportunities.

Your special interests. Your interests are often acquired during your leisure time. A possible list might include reading, gardening, traveling, and sports. Think of all the things you enjoy doing, and jot them down. Special interests are activities to which you're drawn naturally, so they may better represent the type of job you should seek than your education or previous training. A special interest may be more marketable if you develop it formally through volunteer work or educational classes.

Your work values. What do you want most from a job? Why do you want to work? People work for all kinds of reasons: to earn money, be of service, meet new people, gain prestige, and so on. A job that fits well will reflect your work values.

Your personal attributes. What type of person are you? What personal qualities do you bring to a job? One person may be patient, detail-oriented, able to follow instructions to the letter. Another may be energetic, self-directed, always ready for a new challenge.

Your preferred work environment. Where and with whom do you want to work? Consider the organization's size, location, administration, and physical facilities. Also, consider the types of people—supervisors, co-workers, and clients—with whom you prefer to work.

Your salary needs. It helps to determine your financial needs early in your job search so that you can rule out positions that don't meet your requirements for earnings and fringe benefits. Remember that in a job you may incur additional expenses for transportation, clothing, lunches, and so on. Also, if you continue to work once you've started receiving social security payments, your earnings may affect your benefit amount (see chapter 5).

Set Employment Goals

Using your personal inventory as a guide, jot down several job possibilities consistent with your skills, interests, values, and preferences. You might list specific job titles, such as teacher, banker, or sales manager, but add some broader goals, too. For example, perhaps you would like to break into the movie industry or find a job working with other older adults. These broader definitions include a range of jobs you might work toward.

Research the Job Market

Your task now is to identify potential employers. You can use the traditional approach—scanning newspaper ads and contacting employment agencies and personnel departments. However, you should also tap into the hidden job market, which many experts believe is a richer source of job leads.

Start by visiting the library. Ask the reference librarian to recommend books, catalogs, directories, and other materials that can help direct your job search. Also, check trade journals, business sections of newspapers, and the yellow pages for organizations that interest you. Scan local job boards in schools, churches, senior centers, and other public gathering places. Contact college placement offices and professional organizations for more information and ideas.

Build Your Network

Another important source of job information is the people you know and the people they know, as well. Networking means informing your relatives, friends, and acquaintances that you are looking for work so that they can refer you to others who might employ you. By networking you may discover existing openings or some that have not yet been advertised. You may also find opportunities to create a position that matches your skills.

"The majority of professional, managerial, and technical jobs are filled through networking," writes personnel consultant Fred Merrill in *Job Search Manual for Mature Workers*. Many mature job seekers, he adds, "have a networking advantage because they know people further along in their careers and have higher levels of contacts."

To start networking, get in touch and stay in touch with the people you know. Your network will expand as your original contacts link you with new people and organizations. Start with

- relatives, friends, and casual and business acquaintances (your sister-in-law, banker, barber, neighbors, and so on)
- former employers, supervisors, and co-workers
- members of alumni, professional, social, and religious organizations

When talking with these people, stress that you are not asking for a job, but would appreciate any information, suggestions, and referrals they might offer. When referred to someone you do not know, send a letter requesting a brief (fifteen to twenty minute) interview, and then follow up with a phone call. After each interview, send a thank-you note. Although many job seekers feel that networking is an imposition on friends and strangers, remember that most people enjoy helping others and feel flattered when asked for advice.

Sell Yourself

Through your research and networks, you will discover interesting job openings. Your ability to parlay an application into an offer will depend partly on how well you market yourself. You need to convey to potential employers that you are a top-notch worker with the qualities, skills, and experience they need. How will you do this? By communicating—verbally, nonverbally, and in writing.

Resumes, cover letters that accompany them, applications, and thank-you letters—all should be carefully prepared. They represent you and reflect the quality of your work. Alone, they won't win you the job. But if their message is precise, brief, and upbeat, they can net you an interview, your goal at this stage. Guidelines for preparing these marketing tools and using them to your advantage are available in the books listed at the end of this chapter.

The interview gives you an opportunity to relate your skills, experiences, and personal qualities to the employer's needs. More than resumes and cover letters, the interview allows you to convey what you're like as a person, how you get along with others, and your desire to work. There are several things you can do to shine during an interview.

Prepare. At the library and through your networks, find out all you can about the employer and the job. For example, what are the duties to be performed and skills required for the position you want? What does it typically pay?

What's happening in the employer's field and how is the organization doing? Be prepared to explain how your skills and accomplishments match the needs of the position and employer.

Rehearse. Ask a family member or friend to help you prepare for the interview by asking you typical interview questions such as, "Why did you choose this organization?" "What are your strengths and weaknesses?" "What can you tell me about yourself?" Your answers should be crisp, articulate, and focused on the subject at hand.

Although federal legislation (ADEA) prohibits employers from asking your age, some employers are unaware that this question is illegal. If asked about your age, use discretion. Some experts suggest emphasizing your job qualifications and focusing on positive attributes, such as maturity and dependability, often associated with age. Others caution that ducking the age issue may result in a lower rating or leave the interviewer with the impression that you are older than you are. Whatever you do, don't apologize for your age. Take pride in those years of experience!

Pay attention to appearance and level of enthusiasm. Making a positive first impression is critical because many interviewers decide on an applicant during the first few minutes of the interview. Wear clothing appropriate to the position, be well groomed, offer a firm handshake and a ready smile, take pride in past performance, and show a genuine interest in the employer's operation to impress the interviewer favorably.

Make sure your nonverbal cues are sending positive messages. Maintain eye contact, nod agreement when appropriate, and keep an energetic posture.

Ask relevant questions. Questions about the job and the organization not only indicate your interest in the position, but allow you to weigh responses against your work preferences.

Negotiate Salary

Your research should have informed you about the typical salary range for this position. Consider this range in light of fringe benefits and advancement opportunities offered to determine what you can reasonably request.

Until you have a firm job offer, your response to interview or application questions about salary should be that it's negotiable. If pressed to state a salary, mention a salary range. As a contingency measure, be prepared to accept a wage near the low end of the

range. However, you can and should negotiate for a salary at the high end.

How about Starting Your Own Business?

Bored stiff after a year of retirement, Janice N. was eager to return to work, not as an employee but as her own boss.

"I was a highly successful tax accountant for a large firm for more than fifteen years," says the vibrant 63-year-old. "My former employer would probably rehire me, but why sell myself short? With my experience and professional contacts, I think I can establish my own accounting business."

Perhaps a similar idea has occurred to you. Maybe you're bored with your current job, and the idea of working for another company is just as boring. Maybe there is something you always dreamed of trying. Or maybe, like Janice, you want a new challenge in retirement. Whatever the reason, you want to start your own business. What are the ingredients for success? Your skills and professional networks count, but you'll also need a good idea, then money and plenty of hard work.

Typically, a good idea translates into a product or service that appeals to buyers and matches your skills and interests. If you decide to enter a field where you lack experience, consider developing new skills through temporary employment or volunteer activities. Also, be aware that a good idea often needs a good location in order to flourish.

A written business plan will help you determine how much money you'll need. In addition to a description of the business, its purpose, and its market, the plan should include sales projections for the first few years, a detailed strategy for achieving those sales, and cash-flow projections of expected income and expenses.

If you decide to apply for a loan, a practical and well-thought-out business plan will improve your chances. If your application is turned down, consider asking your banker for a Small Business Administration (SBA) loan guarantee. For loans of less than $750,000, the SBA may guarantee up to 90 percent of the balance to the bank.

Hard work in small business parlance means more than toiling for long hours each day. It also includes taking risks, managing crises, tending to details both large and small, making quick and firm decisions, and assuming responsibility for failures as well as successes. Are you up to the challenge? If you think so, you can obtain more information and a free business start-up kit from the Small Business Administration, toll-free (800) 368-5855.

Have You Considered Consulting?

Darren T., 67, liked the idea of being his own boss, but not the thought of assuming responsibility for a full-time business. When a friend suggested that Darren offer his services as a consultant, the retired engineer was intrigued.

"Consulting would be the ideal solution," Darren muses. "I could get paid well for doing what I like to do when I want to do it."

But before Darren prints new business cards, he should take time to evaluate himself. So should you if you're considering consulting. Consultants need to be entrepreneurial risk takers who are self-starters and self-motivated. Although you may have had an office full of support previously, as a novice consultant you may find yourself doing everything from typing to paying taxes.

Next, consider not only your product—your professional advice—but how to market it. While many consultants capitalize on skills they've honed over the years, others pioneer new fields. Either way, you'll have to market your expertise. Many consultants fail because they don't market their services. Instead of expensive ads and bulk mailings, you might join professional groups, write articles, speak at conferences, and prime your network.

Finally, do some financial reality testing. Even if you plan just to supplement your retirement income, calculate your overhead costs and any additional taxes you may have to pay. Yes, it's true that consultants charge handsome fees: in 1990, the average daily billing rate was around $1,050. Despite this, only one in three consultants makes a living at it. Why? Because most do not have full-time practices. It's important to assess realistically the time and energy you want to invest in "doing your own thing" and trying to make money at it.

Mark Twain once said: "Work and play are words to describe the same thing under differing conditions." Many older folks agree. According to a survey by the American Association of Retired Persons, most employees age 63 and older work because they enjoy it. For some, like Fred W., working is a favorite pastime. "Every New Year's, I make a resolution to only work Monday, Wednesday, and Friday, and every January 2, I violate the resolution," the 90-year-old housing developer says. He reports to his office every day because he views his job as fun.

Opportunities for older people to have fun at work are increasing as employers develop flexible work programs to accommodate the needs and preferences of an aging labor force. Still, for many mature adults, work will continue to be just one of the many ways they choose to express themselves, stay active, and be of service. After all, employment options aren't the only ones that are expanding for older men and women. Today, seniors can select from such a wide variety of leisure and recreational activities that the porch rocking chair may never see action again.

Resources

Write to these organizations for information about services available to older persons and their families. Many of these groups have local or regional chapters that can provide information about programs in your community.

Alzheimer's Association, 70 E. Lake Street, Suite 600, Chicago, IL 60601. Telephone: (800) 621-0379; in Illinois, (800) 572-6037.

American Association of Retired Persons, 601 E Street, NW, Washington, DC 20049. Telephone: (202) 434-2277.

American Health Care Association, 1201 L Street, NW, Washington, DC 20005. Telephone: (202) 842-4444.

Children of Aging Parents, 2761 Trenton Road, Levittown, PA 19056. Telephone: (215) 945-6900.

National Association of Area Agencies on Aging, 600 Maryland Avenue, SW, Suite 208, West Wing, Washington, DC 20024. Telephone: (202) 484-7520.

National Association of State Units on Aging, 2033 K Street, NW, Suite 304, Washington, DC 20006. Telephone: (202) 785-0707.

National Council on the Aging, Inc., 600 Maryland Avenue, SW, Suite 100, West Wing, Washington, DC 20024. Telephone: (202) 479-1200.

National Council of Senior Citizens, 925 15th Street, NW, Washington, DC 20005. Telephone: (202) 347-8800.

National Senior Citizens Law Center, 2025 M Street, NW, Suite 400, Washington, DC 20036. Telephone: (202) 887-5280.

Older Women's League, 730 11th Street, NW, Suite 300, Washington, DC 20001-4512. Telephone: (202) 783-6686.

Recommended Reading

Books about all aspects of finding a job—networking, resume writing, interviewing, negotiating, and so on—are widely available in bookstores and libraries. Here are some of the most popular:

Azrin, Nathan H., and Victoria Besalel. *Finding a Job.* Berkeley, CA: Ten Speed Press, 1983.

Bolles, Richard N. *What Color Is Your Parachute?* Berkeley, CA: Ten Speed Press, 1989.

Cohen, Herb. *You Can Negotiate Anything.* Secaucus, NJ: Citadel Press, 1983.

Jackson, Tom. *The Perfect Resume.* New York: Doubleday, 1981.

Lathrop, Richard. *Who's Hiring Who?* Berkeley, CA: Ten Speed Press, 1989.

Merrill, Fred L. *Job Search Manual for Mature Workers.* Los Angeles: Los Angeles Council on Careers for Older Americans, 1987. Order from the publisher: Los Angeles Council on Careers for Older Americans, 5225 Wilshire Boulevard, Suite 204, Los Angeles, CA 90036. Cost: $15; California residents, add 8¼ percent sales tax.

Parker, Yana. *The Damn Good Resume Guide.* Berkeley, CA: Ten Speed Press, 1989.

Pettus, Theodore. *One on One: Win the Interview, Win the Job.* New York: Random House, 1981. To order, call toll-free: (800) 726-0600.

CHAPTER TEN Life in the Leisure Lane

A purposeless leisure breeds nothing good.

—Sophocles

With early retirement and longer life expectancy, many of us will spend one-quarter to one-third of our lives—between nineteen and twenty-five years—in retirement. What will we do with those extra eight hours a day? Pretty much the same things we do now during nonworking hours, say people who have studied retirees.

Think about that for a minute. What do you do now with your free time? Watch television? Read? Volunteer? Travel? Visit with relatives and friends?

How satisfied are you with these activities? Are they stimulating or boring? Relaxing or stressful? Varied or monotonous? Do they offer opportunities for companionship? Intellectual growth? Physical challenge? Self-expression? Do they foster a sense of achievement? Usefulness? Wellness?

Do you want to continue with these activities or find some new ones? Chances are that unless you devote time and effort to developing a range of rewarding pursuits, you'll find yourself in retirement agreeing with Bernard Shaw's observation that "a perpetual holiday is a working definition of hell." And even if you plan never to retire, it's important to take stock of your leisure life. As researchers John Verduin and Douglas McEwen so aptly note, "Just as learning of math is fundamental to engineering, so is learning about art, sport, and music fundamental to individual fulfillment." So discard any notions you might have that leisure is the time left over when all the important stuff is done. Consider it instead a prime ingredient in a satisfying, healthful, well-balanced life.

Planning and Managing for Satisfying Leisure

To make the most of your free time, leisure counselors recommend that you use the same planning and management skills that you apply to work and other aspects of your life. Let's look at how to do this.

Analyze Your Leisure Time

Leisure counseling pioneer Patsy G. Edwards, owner of Constructive Leisure in Los Angeles, recommends making a time study: Jot down your daily activities for one or two weeks, and then cross off those related to work and personal maintenance (for example, shopping, laundry, and housecleaning). What's left is your leisure time. If you're not pleased with the results, consider ways to improve them. For example, can you eliminate some activities you don't like to allow more time to do those you enjoy? Will accomplishing a series of maintenance tasks in one day give you more discretionary time during another?

Assess Your Leisure Preferences

"Tell me what you do when you are free to do as you wish, and I will tell you what kind of person you are," said educator Charles Brightbill. More than work and other obligatory activities, freely chosen leisure pursuits reflect our basic values and priorities. Although critics may argue that this is too heady an interpretation, they are likely to agree that rewarding leisure requires self-discovery.

"All of us like some things more than others," notes Edwards. But how many of us organize our leisure to be driven by what we *think* we should be doing or what others *say* we should enjoy? Thus, the introvert winds up in group activities because she's

heard those are the norm. And the recent retiree runs from one pursuit to another so he can report his day is full.

It's better to ask, say researchers, not what should you be doing, but how much will you enjoy it. Would you rather collect Indian sand paintings or join a search-and-rescue team? Study the stars or design a stage set? Sing with a church choir or jog around the park?

Take time, recommends Edwards, to list leisure activities that you currently enjoy as well as ones that you tried and liked in the past. Also, record pastimes you hope to pursue in the future. Now examine the list. Can you spot a pattern to your preferences? For example, do physical activities outnumber intellectual pursuits? Do you prefer doing things alone or with other people? How many activities entail travel? Creating something new? Volunteering? Or simply relaxing? The picture that emerges is your leisure profile. Use it to guide your future actions.

Identify Alternatives

Now that you've listed more activities than anyone could reasonably carry out, you need to narrow your selection. Concentrate on pursuits for which you have sufficient time, money, and energy; don't stretch yourself too thin. However, accurately assessing the time and money an activity requires often entails research. For example, are you aware that some colleges and universities offer free or reduced tuition for older learners? And that some volunteer positions require only minimal time commitments? This chapter describes a wide range of popular leisure-time pursuits for a variety of budgets, schedules, and interests. Use the information to help decide whether you have the time and resources to pursue a favorite activity.

Also, select some activities that you can enjoy alone and others that you can share with family and friends. Many people find that a balanced agenda that taps a range of interests, abilities, and skills is most rewarding. A varied schedule also helps preserve continuity in the event something must be dropped. Finally, make sure that some of your activities are challenging enough to provide opportunities for continual striving and development.

Take Action

Now that you've identified practical leisure activities that appeal to you, develop a plan for pursuing them. Gather more information about your special interests. In this chapter, you'll find out where to go and whom to contact for further information about educational pursuits, travel opportunities, volunteer activities, and other pastimes. Augment these leads by exercising imagination, initiative, and commitment. You'll quickly discover that even if one activity doesn't work out, a comparable one will suit you just fine. In the process, don't be surprised if your outlook on life improves and your curiosity and zest for living start to blossom.

Leisure at its best has that effect on people.

A Back-to-School Guide

Marge retired from a teaching career that spanned twenty-seven years. Now she's back in school again—studying.

"I was listening to Mozart one evening when it dawned on me that I loved music but didn't know a thing about it," recalls the lively 72-year-old. "I had always wanted to play in an orchestra for the fun of it, so I signed up for a wind instrument class at the community college. The instructor told me that the concert band was short a bassoonist, so I signed up for that too. Soon afterward I enrolled in a music history class and then a music theory course at a private university. Altogether, I'm carrying 12 units this quarter. That's a full load," she adds proudly.

Marge is one of the record number of older Americans who are enjoying the good old golden-rule days of school. According to a survey by the National Center for Education Statistics, participation in adult education by people over age 55 jumped from 9 percent in 1975 to 12 percent in 1984, or from 1.6 to 2.7 million.

One reason for the surge in older students is demographic. The traditional applicant pool of 18- to 25-year-olds is shrinking, and to fill classes and raise revenues, schools are actively courting members of the senior set, whose numbers in the general population continue to climb. Consider, for example, the college Marge attends. It has a special center for mature students who are returning to school after a break in their education. Besides academic, personal, and career counseling, the Center for New Options offers workshops, films, and a variety of special-interest programs. "It's also a nice place to relax between classes," adds Marge.

The college extension program is also popular among older students. It features noncredit courses in subjects with practical significance to mature participants. A typical class schedule includes offerings such as "Personal Growth and Communication," "The Pleasures of Traveling Alone," "Physical Fitness for Older Adults," and "Financial Planning—Getting Started."

The chance to audit a class free of charge is another back-to-school incentive for seniors. "I'm on a fixed income. I can't afford the tuition at a private university, certainly not the one I attend now," says Marge. "If I had to pay for my music theory class, it'd cost me $1,200. But if you're over 60, the university lets you listen in on one class free each quarter. This way I'm also exempt from doing the homework." (A good student, she does it anyway.)

Other enticements for lifelong learning include evening and

BARGAIN TUITION

Tuition for a three-credit course at Delaware State College is $67.50. But for students over 62, it's free (although they still have to pay a registration fee and purchase books). Savings are even higher at Western New England College, where students age 65 and older pay $20 for a three-unit course worth $588.

Many other colleges and universities offer older learners similar bargains. In fact, thirty-five states have enacted legislation or adopted policies mandating that state-supported schools offer free or reduced tuition to older adults.

Contact the admissions office of the school you plan to attend to find out if it offers special tuition for older learners. Also, AARP's Institute of Lifetime Learning publishes two helpful booklets:

- Tuition Policies in Higher Education for Older Adults *lists more than 500 colleges and universities that offer tuition waivers or reductions.*
- State Legislative and Administrative Policies Affecting Older Adults in Higher Education *outlines older-student tuition policies in 35 states.*

To request free copies, write to the Institute of Lifetime Learning, AARP, 601 E Street, NW, Washington, DC 20049.

weekend classes held at convenient off-campus locations such as senior centers, churches, high schools, and community centers; reduced or free tuition for older residents at some state-supported and private colleges; and opportunities to enroll in specially designed centers for older learners and to earn credit for life experience (more information about these programs is given later in this chapter).

These inducements, while appealing, pale in comparison to some of the other rewards of lifelong learning. Says Marge, "I advise all my friends to go back to school. I tell them life gets more exciting when you associate with people who are learning and are interested in new challenges. Look at me. I'm busier now than I was when I was teaching. I've met a lot of people I wouldn't have met otherwise, many of them much younger than I am. If I feel closer to their age, it's probably because I've realized that age differences are largely irrelevant when you're discussing something of interest with fellow students.

"All this," she adds, "is to say nothing of the money I've saved." How so? "I'm too busy to shop," she explains.

Marge's enthusiasm is characteristic of the older student's gusto. Reports the American Association of Retired Persons (AARP): "As important as exercise is for the body, mental stimulation and creative pursuits generate a sense of accomplishment and contribute to health and well-being." Moreover, studies show that people who exercise their learning skills throughout life maintain intellectual vigor well into their later years.

Many older men and women doubt this last point. One of the most common reasons older adults give for not enrolling in educational programs is that they think they're too old to learn. Those who return to school despite such fears are often pleasantly surprised.

Recalls Marge, "Going into the first music-theory exam, I had my reservations. The other students were majoring in music. I knew they were brighter, more accomplished than I was. I was nervous, but maybe that helped. I got an A." Only six of the other forty students matched her achievement.

Research shows that older learners do as well as and often better in the classroom than younger students. In fact, one study found that the most frequent problems encountered by older learners are not academic but related to parking and registration. What's the secret of their scholastic success? Motivation. According to a Louis Harris poll, personal interest is by the far the main reason given by older adults for participation in educational activities.

"I don't have to go to school," says Marge, who never misses a class. "I go because I truly love music." Says another student, "If I live to be 110, I'll never be able to take all the courses that interest me."

Your reasons for returning to school may differ. Perhaps you want to upgrade your job skills, acquire new ones, or earn a degree you've always wanted. Whatever the reason, pairing it with a keen desire for lifelong learning will enrich your educational experience. Once you've identified an objective for your studies, explore your options for achieving it. Today's mature student can choose from a variety of programs and places of learning. Here are some of the most popular.

High-School Diplomas

Fifty-one percent of Americans over age 65 never graduated from high school. For many, school days were interrupted by more pressing needs to earn a wage or to help at home. Often, these men and women moved on to successful careers. "We have

many students who hold responsible positions," observes one adult-school supervisor. "No one knows they never finished high school. Still, they want the diploma. It's a matter of self-esteem."

Older persons can earn high-school diplomas by taking the General Educational Development (GED) tests sponsored by the American Council on Education (ACE) and state departments of education. The GED is a series of five tests designed to measure broad concepts and general knowledge (writing skills, social studies, science, interpreting literature and the arts, and mathematics). Few questions require knowledge of details or definitions, according to ACE.

Available in large print, Braille, and audiocassette editions, GED tests are administered frequently at more than 3,500 testing centers in the United States and Canada. Successful candidates receive high-school equivalency credentials authorized by local school districts or state departments of education. These documents are widely recognized by employers, colleges, and universities.

Classwork is not required to take the GED. However, those who want assistance can enroll in preparation classes offered at adult high schools, community colleges, and other institutions. GED study guides, with review sections for the different exam areas and sample tests, are available in bookstores and libraries for people who wish to study on their own.

For more information about taking the GED, contact your school district (typically listed in the city or county government section of the telephone book), nearby community college, or the GED Testing Service (see Resources).

Adult Education

If you live in a school district with an adult school, chances are you've received its schedule of classes. The catalog, addressed to "resident," may have been a slick glossy publication, or it may have been a couple of newsprint pages stapled together. Inside were listed an array of courses in business, homemaking, arts and crafts, self-improvement, family living, health and recreation, academics, and more. Almost all classes were offered at night for non-credit. Some lasted a few hours on one evening only. Others met once a week for a couple of months. Many instructors lived in the community and practiced the subjects they taught. Fees were reasonable and, in some cases, discounted for seniors.

Remember that catalog? If not, don't worry. You can probably get one like it by calling your school district or nearby public and private schools. Or call your local library to find out if they have copies available. Increasingly, these institutions are offering adult-education programs like the one described above. Such programs provide an excellent opportunity to sharpen old skills, learn new ones, or study for personal pleasure.

Two-Year Colleges

Community and junior colleges offer two-year programs equivalent to the first two years of a four-year college; vocational and technical schools offer a more specialized curriculum. Depending on the courses taken, graduates receive associate degrees or career certificates.

Two-year colleges are designed for adult learners. On many campuses, 50 percent or more of the students are 25 years or older. These institutions have also taken the lead in attracting seniors by offering a wide variety of courses with special appeal for older learners, such as classes in the humanities and sciences as well as crafts, nutrition, travel, homemaking, and carpentry.

Fees and admissions policies at two-year colleges also attract mature students. In general, these predominantly public institutions charge lower fees and tuition than most four-year colleges. For example, the community college Marge attended charged only $5 per unit per semester, up to a maximum of $50 per semester. Also, as in most two-year colleges, the school had an open admissions policy, whereby virtually all applicants are accepted. Marge didn't have to fuss with entrance exams, transcripts, or letters of reference. She simply completed a two-page application.

Most two-year colleges maintain continuing-education or extension programs, which offer noncredit courses. These courses are often held at night, and sometimes they are held at off-campus locations which may be more convenient.

Check your local library or bookstore for catalogs of two-year colleges in your area as well as national directories of these institutions. For more detailed information about enrollment, degree programs, and continuing-education classes, contact the college's admissions office.

Four-Year Colleges and Universities

A four-year college offers credit courses for bachelor's and, sometimes, graduate degrees. In some cases, students can audit courses, that is, attend a class without the requirement to turn in homework or take exams.

Admissions policies vary. Although many colleges have open admissions, others require applicants to meet certain minimum requirements. For example, new students may need three years of high-school math or science, or else a minimum score on standardized admissions tests. Don't let admissions criteria discourage you. Most of these institutions rate their entrance requirements "noncompetitive" or only "minimally" to "moderately" difficult. The key to success may be your persistence in assembling the necessary application materials.

Like two-year colleges, most four-year institutions offer continuing-education or extension courses without credit. For more information about local and national four-year degree programs, check your local library or bookstore for relevant catalogs and directories. Once you've narrowed your selection, telephone the admissions office at each institution and ask that a school catalog and enrollment packet be mailed to your home.

College Centers for Older Learners

At last count, ninety-three colleges in twenty-eight states and the District of Columbia offered continuing-education programs specially designed for older adults. According to AARP's Institute of Lifetime Learning, these college centers for older learners (CCOLs) "offer the mental stimulation, educational resources, and social opportunities usually associated with college life without the aspects of regular college programs that sometimes make them unappealing to retirement-aged people."

At Harvard's Institute for Learning in Retirement, for example, the students (average age of 70) create the curriculum, help schedule the classes, and lead the study groups. Participants are neither tested nor graded; they are just expected to join in lively discussions. A flat fee (in 1989, $155 per semester) covers tuition for all program courses.

In the Southwest, the Phoenix College Senior Adult Program offers sixty or so noncredit classes each semester to its middle-aged and older student body. Participation includes use of the campus library, career center, and other college facilities. Although some lectures are free, course fees usually average $2 per hour of instruction.

Want to learn more about CCOLs? Consult AARP's free booklet, *College Centers for Older Learners,* which lists CCOLs nationwide (see Recommended Reading).

College Level Examination Program

You don't have a college degree, but over the years, you've learned a thing or two. Can you earn credit for this life experience? Yes, at the more than 1,900 colleges and universities that recognize the College Level Examination Program, better known as CLEP. CLEP tests in thirty-five topics are offered monthly at some 1,100 test centers nationwide for a modest fee (in 1991, $38 per exam). Participating schools translate the test scores into credits that count toward a bachelor's degree. One older learner in pursuit of a nursing degree took nineteen separate CLEP tests to satisfy general requirements at a local college. By the time she matriculated, she had sophomore status and had saved herself considerable time and money.

"If you're self-motivated and bright, you can generally do pretty well," said Jean Paine of the Educational Testing Center, which develops and administers CLEP exams. But it often pays to prepare, particularly if it's been some time since you last took an exam. Paine recommends the *College Board Guide to the CLEP,* which describes each test and includes sample questions (see Recommended Reading). To find out whether the college you plan to attend accepts CLEP credit, contact the school's admissions office. For a free list of CLEP colleges and a test registration form, contact CLEP (see Resources).

External Degree Programs

Offered by some colleges and universities, external degree programs also give credit for life experience. In addition, students can satisfy graduation requirements through nontraditional learning experiences such as independent study, assessment of previous education, internships, and credit by examination (including CLEP tests). These programs are perfect for persons who want to pursue a bachelor's or master's degree, but find it difficult to attend regularly scheduled classes.

For more information about external degree programs, contact the college you plan to attend or consult the directory, *Who Offers Part-Time Degree Programs*. This directory lists external degree, daytime, evening, weekend, and summer programs at more than 2,500 institutions nationwide (see Recommended Reading).

Correspondence Courses

Correspondence courses are convenient, self-paced, and individualized. They range from a few lessons that require only weeks to complete to a hundred or more assignments that entail extensive study over years. Colleges, universities, and private institutions offer courses on a wide variety of subjects—from accident prevention to zoology. Students prepare written assignments, and then mail them to qualified instructors. Corrected papers with comments are quickly returned.

Because no campus work is required, these courses are ideal for those who want to earn while they learn or pursue a special interest without leaving home. The credits earned can usually be applied toward a degree program, although it's best to check with the college to determine whether the courses are acceptable. For more information, consult *The Independent Study Catalog* or the *Directory of Accredited Home Study Schools,* both of which list correspondence schools around the country (see Recommended Reading).

Learning Vacations

Grandchildren call it wacky, but these days, more and more older adults are taking vacations not from school but to it. Witness the enormous popularity of Elderhostel, a nonprofit organization that combines travel and learning for older Americans. It attracts more than 160,000 participants each year to several hundred participating colleges and universities nationwide and abroad.

Elderhostelers, aged 60 and older, together with their spouses or companions aged 50 and older, spend a week studying, sightseeing, and socializing. A wide range of liberal arts and science courses exploring all aspects of human experience are offered. In keeping with the college spirit, students sleep in dormitories and eat together in dining rooms. Such accommodations also keep costs down. In 1991, the charge for a six-night program in the United States ranged from $260 to $300. (Institutions in Hawaii and Alaska may charge somewhat more.) Fees cover room and board, three daily classes, and a variety of extracurricular activities.

Information about other short-term educational holidays lasting three days to a week can be found in *Learning Vacations*, a directory of more than 500 such programs for a variety of budgets and interests (see Recommended Reading). Many colleges also offer summer learning institutes for alumni and their friends. Contact your college for more information.

Other Educational Options

A lecture on picking the right pet. A beginner's class in quilt making. A discussion of the current administration's domestic policies. A workshop for writers. Classes in gem identification, real estate licensing, massage, or hypnosis. These are just a sampling of the learning opportunities you may find listed in the calendar section of your local newspaper; in the yellow pages under "schools"; or on bulletin boards at libraries, museums, churches, senior centers, and other community gathering places. These avenues for intellectual stimulation are ideal for those who prefer self-directed study. Of course, they're not the only ones. Traveling provides another excellent learning opportunity for those who enjoy charting their own path.

Travel

Having been around the block a few times, many older Americans now feel a wanderlust. Their bags are packed, they're ready to go. Someday (as in "Someday I'll visit . . . ") has arrived.

Today, mature travelers are cruising in style aboard luxury liners and roughing it in river rafts. They're shaping up on walking tours and sweating it out on mountain treks. They're visiting national parks and zoos and exploring African wildlife sanctuaries. They're taking the water in Biarritz and lounging beside it in Hawaii. With time and good health on their side, they're discovering that travel restrictions are often just nuisances that the airlines impose. Apparently, even these aren't too great an imposition. Consider that Americans over 50 years old

- travel more often and buy more expensive travel products than any other age group
- buy more hotel and motel room nights than the under-50 population
- purchase 80 percent of all luxury travel

The travel industry has greeted this news by wooing even more older customers with attractive discounts on transportation, accommodations, tours, and much more. Although it's tempting to respond to such come-ons by packing your knapsack and hitting the road, lack of planning can spoil a getaway: You wind up worrying about survival when you should be enjoying your new surroundings. To ensure that you have a wonderful time, let's review some important travel considerations.

Choosing a Destination

Sit back, relax, and picture yourself . . . where? doing what? People select a particular destination for many reasons. Some choose a country, state, region, or city to explore. Others head for the hills or make for the beach. Some people use a travel experience to relax and unwind. Others view it as an opportunity to pursue favorite activities. You may want to check out retirement communities, learn about foreign cultures, meet new people, trace your roots, or . . . .

Take a minute to get in touch with your travel preferences. Remember, just because the Smiths had a great time wind-surfing in Florida doesn't mean you will. Let your imagination, past travel experiences, and personal predilections whisk you away to your special destination. Then get up and go. Not to your paradise, but to a library or travel agency for help with planning your trip.

Doing research. Think of a remote place. Chances are someone's not only been there before, but written about it for other travelers. Find out about a particular destination—how to get there; where to stay; what to see, do, expect, and beware of—by reading books and articles. Start by browsing through travel articles in your local newspaper. Also, check the travel section of bookstores and libraries. Use the library's *Readers' Guide to Periodical Literature* to locate magazine articles about appealing vacation spots.

Consult a travel agent. Their services and advice are usually free to the traveler, and they can save you time, money, and frustration. To select a good one, ask friends for recommendations. When you visit the agency, are you treated in a professional manner? Does the staff appear to work well as a team? Does the office have a computer hookup? Also, check for logos such as ASTA (American Society of Travel Agents), IATAN (International Airlines Travel Agent Network), and ARC (Airlines Reporting Corporation). These affiliations mean the agency complies with certain industry standards.

A good travel agent will listen attentively to your ideas, clarify what you want, and make suggestions you may not have considcrcd. Hc or shc should also givc you thc pros and cons of each option, including possible discounts for seniors and any applicable restrictions.

Other good sources of information are free brochures, guides, and other publications produced by the tourist and travel industry. Ask your travel agent for these materials, or contact appropriate vacation spots and tourist offices in the cities you plan to visit. Most foreign countries maintain national tourist offices that will send you beautiful, informative tourist literature. Just write to the nearest consulate. Many hotels, resorts, cruise lines, travel agencies, and tour operators are just a toll-free phone call away (for directory assistance, call 1 (800) 555-1212).

Finally, talk with family and friends who have visited the destination you're considering. Ask them to show you slides or pictures from the trip. These may help them recall specific details, which you can use in planning your excursion.

Getting There

Getting there can be half the fun, provided you select a mode of transportation that matches your travel needs and preferences. Let's review the options.

Flying. In a hurry? Take a plane. A trip that takes three days on wheels takes about three hours in flight. On board, you can read, take a nap, enjoy a meal, and take comfort in knowing that flying is one of the safest modes of travel.

Discounted airfares are often available if you book reservations in advance, usually fourteen days or more. In addition, most major airlines sponsor senior programs that offer discounts on selected fares for travelers over a certain age, often age 62. For information about airline specials or a particular airline's senior program, call the airline or your travel agent. Restrictions may apply, so ask about them.

To minimize pre-travel stress, arrive at the airport in good time. Secure boarding passes in advance from travel agents and check baggage with a porter outside the terminal so that you can proceed directly to the gate. Once aloft, after the seatbelt sign goes off, take regular strolls down the aisle to reduce flight fatigue and increase circulation.

You'll experience jet lag after a long-distance flight, so don't overbook at first. Allow about one day for each time zone change to adjust to a new wake-sleep cycle.

Cars and recreational vehicles. Ah, the freedom of the road, the sense of control, the thrill of adventure, the lure of wide vistas! Today, about 80 percent of vacationers travel by car. Thousands more, particularly midlife and older travelers, are enjoying the comforts of home on the road in a recreational vehicle, or RV.

In addition to room-and-board expense, the American Automobile Association recommends vacationers budget $8 per 100 miles for gas, oil, and auto maintenance. RVs cost more to operate, but you'll save on overnight accommodations and on meals, if you eat in. Before investing in an RV (fully equipped, they cost upwards of $30,000), rent one for the first few trips. RV rental agencies usually are listed in the yellow pages under "recreational vehicles."

For a safe, comfortable trip, start in the morning when you're fresh, and try not to drive more than five hours per day. Eat a light lunch and plan to have your main meal in the early evening after reaching your stopping point. It's best not to arrive after dark

GETTING MORE BANG FOR YOUR BUCK

Before calculating the cost of a trip, determine how much you can afford to spend. You can always trim expenses by economizing:

- *Travel during off-season, when airlines, hotels, cruise lines, and car-rental agencies clip prices to attract customers.*
- *Stay over weekends to save on airfare and hotel stays.*
- *Book travel reservations in advance to qualify for Supersaver or other promotional fares. (Purchase tickets soon afterward to lock in savings. If the price drops, you can request a refund.) Discount tickets may be subject to stiff penalties for changes or cancellations, so ask about restrictions.*
- *Join a club. Membership in the American Automobile Association, American Association of Retired Persons, National Council of Senior Citizens, and other large consumer-oriented associations can get you bargains on airfare, hotel rooms, car rentals, cruises, and tourist attractions. Keep membership numbers handy to receive benefits.*
- *Ask about discounts and special deals for seniors, whether you're making travel reservations, securing overnight accommodations, or entering an amusement park, campground, or other tourist attraction. Be aware that some senior discounts are not valid with other promotional offers. To qualify for senior discounts, be prepared to show proof of age.*
- *Go with a group. Sign up for packaged tours to take advantage of group rates on airfare, hotel rooms, meals, tourist outings, and more.*
- *Enroll in airline frequent-flier programs and hotel frequent-stay plans. Often, you can earn points toward free flights and overnight accommodations just by signing up. Call the airlines and hotels you typically patronize for applications.*

when road signs are more difficult to see in unfamiliar territory. A brisk walk after supper is good for digestion, stretching leg muscles, and exploring.

Buses and trains. You'd rather leave the driving to someone else? Consider hopping a bus or train. You'll enjoy excellent views of the countryside and probably meet friendly tourists. You can also keep travel costs down.

Greyhound Lines discounts its fares by 10 percent for customers over age 65. Depending on your destination, you may get a better deal by booking seats two weeks or, preferably, thirty days in advance. In 1991, any one-way ticket purchased three weeks in advance costs $68.

Amtrak, which runs the U.S. passenger railroads, knocks 25 percent off round-trip coach fares for travelers age 65 or older.

While this sounds good, it pays to ask about excursion prices because these may be lower than the specials for seniors.

Overseas travelers can purchase train and bus passes that allow unlimited travel for a specified period. These include Eurailpass, BritRail Pass, and Japan Rail Pass, all of which must be purchased before departure in the United States or Canada (see Resources).

Finding Accommodations

Where you stay can profoundly affect your travel experience. For example, imagine that you've checked into a luxury hotel. Here you'll be pampered by doormen, bell boys, maids, and tour directors. You'll enjoy twenty-four-hour room service, spa privileges, nightly entertainment, and easy access to shops and tourist attractions. Over cocktails at poolside, you and other guests will swap tourist stories and perhaps arrange to meet later at a popular restaurant. Ah, you say, this is the life.

Now, suppose you're a guest at a bed-and-breakfast. You have to carry your own luggage and share a bathroom. But the atmosphere's homey and the company's great. The owners, a retired couple, rent three of their home's five bedrooms to supplement their income. At breakfast, the three of you discuss family, work, and retirement. Afterward, they direct you to local stores with super sales and tell you which restaurants serve the best lunch specials. If your evening's free, they add, they'd be delighted if you'd join them for dinner.

To make the most of your trip, consider all your housing options. These include commercial hotels and motels; bed-and-breakfasts, guest homes, and country inns; private houses and apartments that you rent or swap; and no-frills lodgings at public campgrounds. Prices depend on location and services and amenities offered. For example, you'd expect accommodations at the luxury hotel to cost more than those at the bed-and-breakfast.

For more information about housing options, consult your travel agent. Also, many foreign and domestic cities have tourist bureaus that can help you find comfortable, affordable accommodations. Most countries have tourist offices in major U.S. cities such as New York and Los Angeles.

Hassle-free Tours and Cruises

If assembling all parts of a trip seems like work to you, look into tours and cruises.

Cruises. For many, cruises are synonymous with travel comfort. Just unpack your bags and go with the flow. You'll visit exotic ports of call, enjoy dazzling nightly entertainment, feast on sumptuous cuisine, and be pampered by the ship's crew. On board these floating communities, you can post letters, fill prescriptions, have your hair styled, call home, cash checks, and browse through the library. You can also participate in a variety of daily events, from bridge games to money-management seminars to dance and aerobics classes.

Cruises are prepaid and rarely cheap. Consider, however, that prices include lodging, meals, and transportation between ports of call. You can cut costs by booking in advance (six months isn't too soon), traveling off-season, and reserving a minimum, or least expensive, stateroom. Remember to budget for extras such as port taxes, shore excursions, tips, alcoholic beverages, shopping, and, possibly, travel to the embarkation point.

Your travel agent can help find a cruise for you. Ask for free pamphlets and brochures on specific ships or ports of call. You can also call or write to the appropriate cruise line for information.

Tours. Packaged tours would probably be even more popular if

TOURS FOR OLDER TRAVELERS

In recent years, a number of organizations have designed tours especially for older travelers:

- *American Association for Retired Persons (AARP) Travel Services, 5855 Green Valley Circle, Culver City, CA 90230. Telephone: (800) 227-7737. Arranges domestic and foreign escorted tours for AARP members.*
- *Seniors Abroad, 12533 Pacato Circle North, San Diego, CA 92128. Telephone: (619) 485-1696. Arranges three-week homestays for people over age 50 in Australia, Denmark, Japan, New Zealand, Norway, and Sweden.*
- *Grandtravel, 6900 Wisconsin Avenue, Suite 706, Chevy Chase, MD 20815. Telephone: (800) 247-7651; in Maryland: (301) 986-0790. Organizes domestic and foreign escorted tours for grandparents and their grandchildren.*
- *Grand Circle, 347 Congress Street, Boston, MA 02210. Telephone: (800) 221-2610. Primarily arranges international tours for mature travelers (no age restrictions).*

travelers thought of them in the same way they do flowers. We know that flowers come in a variety of shapes, sizes, and colors—hardly any two are alike. Similarly, tours, though sometimes dismissed as all alike, vary one from another.

Tours are prepaid excursions that usually include transportation, lodging, and sightseeing. Tours may visit one destination or several. They may be open to persons of all ages or be specially designed for older travelers. On some, an escort accompanies the travelers. On others, a host is a phone call away.

Tours are typically assembled by tour operators, who sell the excursions directly or through travel agents. A travel agent can help identify tours that match your travel preferences. For best results, be precise. If you've got your heart set on seeing the Louvre, the Eiffel Tower, and the Leaning Tower of Pisa with a group no larger than twenty people, all aged 50 or older, tell your travel agent just that. Also, let him or her know what types of accommodations you prefer, how structured you'd like the trip, and how much you can afford.

For a Healthy Trip

To make sure your travel plans don't unravel because of illness on the road, experts recommend you think prevention, but go prepared. Here are some fitness tips for travelers.

- Consult your physician before a trip, especially if you have heart trouble, high blood pressure, diabetes, or another chronic condition. He or she can alert you to special precautions, if needed, and write prescriptions for any necessary medications.
- Find out whether your medical insurance carrier provides adequate coverage if you're traveling abroad. Medicare

generally does not pay for health services provided outside the United States. However, some Medicare supplemental policies offer limited coverage abroad. Consult your health-insurance agent. He or she can tell you what coverage you have and explain procedures for seeking and paying for medical treatment abroad. If you need extra coverage, consider buying a policy designed specifically for travelers. Ask your travel agent or health-insurance carrier for referrals.

- Before traveling abroad, find out whether you need immunizations to enter the countries you plan to visit. The state or local health department (listed in the government section of the telephone book) can tell you which shots, if any, are required and where to get them. Also, consider joining the International Association for Medical Assistance to Travelers, which provides listings of English-speaking physicians in foreign countries (see Resources).
- Pack a small medical kit. Include aspirin, antacid tablets, a mild laxative, Band-Aids, sunblock lotion, vaseline, antiseptic cream or lotion, a nasal decongestant, insect repellent, a thermometer, and a medical information sheet prepared with your doctor's assistance. Ask your doctor about other items, including diarrhea medications and allergy treatments. If you are allergic to insect bites, travel with an emergency kit and be sure you know how to use it.
- Carry personal prescriptions with you on planes. Don't pack them in your luggage because you and your bags may be separated.
- Eat properly and limit your consumption of alcohol. If you're on a special diet, notify the airline, cruise ship, or

tour operator in advance so that the staff can accommodate your needs.
- Exercise regularly and get adequate rest.

While more and more older Americans are broadening their horizons through travel, many others are experiencing new adventures close to home. Some of these new adventures include volunteer activities.

Help Yourself: Volunteer

In November they gave him notice; in January he was out of a job. Starting over at age 56 wasn't easy. Later, after life had settled down, he would write about the challenges confronting him and his wife that winter: "An involuntary end of a career and an uncertain future; the realization that 'retirement' age is approaching; the return to a home without the children we had raised there; new family relationships, for which there had been no preparation."

Under such circumstances, what's a man to do? Volunteer. That's one thing former President Jimmy Carter did. Several months after leaving the White House and returning home to Plains, Georgia, Jimmy Carter and his wife, Rosalynn, offered their services to Habitat for Humanity. This nonprofit organization, based in Americus, Georgia, builds housing for those who need it. "Of all the activities we have undertaken since leaving the White House, [working with Habitat] was certainly one of the most inspiring," write the former president and his wife in their book, *Everything to Gain: Making the Most of the Rest of Your Life.**

*Reprinted with permission, Random House.

Jimmy Carter may be more famous than Milton T., but their midlife stories share similarities. At age 60, Milton, then a mid-level sales manager, was laid off. Unable to find a job that matched his skills and interests and unwilling to sit idly watching television, he sought out volunteer opportunities. He finally accepted one at the Andrus Gerontology Center at the University of Southern California. One thing led to another.

Today, about the only time you'll find Milton at home is before 7:00 A.M. or after 5:00 P.M. Otherwise, he's active at the Andrus Center and on more than ten community task forces, action committees, and boards of directors, most of which address senior concerns.

"I'm a full-time volunteer," says Milton, now 75, who never had time to donate while he was working. "And I get much more back than I put in. Volunteer service keeps me active and involved and presents challenges I enjoy meeting."

Ask older volunteers why they do it, and you'll hear similar praises: "I like helping others," one older volunteer told us. "It gives me a chance to meet new people," said another. "It gets me involved and that keeps me young," said an 84-year-old who "feels 60."

Volunteering is also an option if you want to learn new skills to help you obtain a paid position later. Moreover, it can improve your outlook on life. Research has shown that volunteering can boost self-esteem, foster a sense of competence and accomplishment, and counteract stress and depression.

Given these benefits, why don't even more older Americans volunteer? Time constraints, health problems, and competing family responsibilities are often the reasons. But another frequently cited reason for not volunteering is that they've never been asked. If that's your problem, then consider this chapter your invitation!

Today, many nonprofit agencies are struggling to meet growing demands with shrinking resources. Increasingly, they are recruiting help from older volunteers, known for their dependability, motivation, and experience. You can lend a hand by following these steps.

Establish a Goal

Take a tip from Milton T.: "Set a goal, just as you would if you were looking for a job." Making a concerted effort to match your interests, abilities, and needs to a particular volunteer activity will probably reinforce your commitment to the cause you select. A self-inventory will help point you in the right direction. To start, consider the following.

With whom do you want to work? Some older volunteers enjoy being with members of the younger generation. Others prefer working with adults. One volunteer may be suited to assisting the disabled; another may be skilled at helping the homeless. An introvert may be happiest in small group activities, while an extrovert may revel in larger events. Some volunteers like helping clients. Others favor assisting staff. Some prefer to work with people; others prefer to work with materials or machines. Whatever your preferences, there's bound to be a volunteer activity to match them.

What do you want to do? You can choose a volunteer activity that taps skills and talents you've honed over the years. Conversely, you might select an opportunity that allows you to develop new interests. Consider also whether you want a physically demanding position or one that's more sedentary.

Where do you want to volunteer? Think, for the moment, of location, not specific organizations. Determine how far you are willing to travel, calculating any costs in both time and money.

Once you reach the volunteer site, do you prefer to stay put or are you willing to travel to other places as needed?

How much time can you devote? Be realistic. Don't overextend yourself. Volunteer activities should blend with your lifestyle, not create competing demands on your time. There is likely to be an organization that can accommodate your schedule, whether you're available several days a week or a few hours on Saturday every other month.

What interests you most? Above all, select a cause to which you feel a strong commitment, perhaps from your personal experience. Irma, 56, volunteers at a halfway house for alcoholic women because "this is where I got sober five years ago. Now I want to give back some of the love and support I received." Other volunteers are largely directed by strong feelings and deep beliefs. "You have to care about people just as people," said Joan, 67, a volunteer who works with developmentally disabled children. Before researching volunteer opportunities, do some soul-searching to discover where you want to make a difference.

Explore the Possibilities

After pinpointing your preferences, seek out volunteer programs whose needs and interests match your own. Friends may be good sources of referrals, but you should look outside your network, too.

Start by contacting a volunteer placement program (see Resources) or a local volunteer bureau (listed in the white pages of your phone book under "volunteer"). These agencies match men and women with local voluntary organizations. You can also contact organizations whose work you already know—such as the Red Cross and United Way, or local civic organizations and religious institutions. Check the yellow pages under "social services," "volunteer services," and "senior citizens' service organizations." The calendar or community section of your local newspaper may also provide leads. Through your research, you will identify several promising organizations. For more information about the volunteer activities each offers, contact the agency's volunteer director or supervisor. Often, these professionals "are of one breed: we're social animals who love to chat, particularly about our programs," said Norma Jacobs, volunteer director at Olive View Medical Center in Sylmar, California.

Ask about the agency's needs, but be specific about what you want to do as well. Application procedures vary, so ask about them. For some higher level positions, you may have to submit a resume, provide references, run for election, or win committee approval. More often, volunteer candidates complete applications, and then they are interviewed by the volunteer director or invited to a group orientation or training session. Participation in these events will help you determine whether both you and the agency will benefit from your involvement.

Know Your Rights

"Volunteer rights?" you ask. "I don't expect anything from the agency," said an older volunteer, "just the satisfaction I get from knowing I'm helping others." That's an admirable sentiment, not uncommon among volunteers. Yet charitable providers do have rights. When these are respected, we often take them for granted, but once violated, they may become painfully obvious.

For one thing, these rights are nothing new to many volunteer directors, particularly the good ones. Said Jacobs, "Volunteers should have someone to report to, someone who really listens to them. They deserve respect from staff members and recognition for their contributions."

Added volunteer director Wendy Free of the Andrus Gerontology Center, "Volunteers are entitled to a job description that outlines their responsibilities and adequate training and supervision. They have a right to information about the agency's purpose and the policies governing [volunteer] conduct, transfers, terminations—all the things you'd want to know about if you were a paid employee."

In addition, they need to know about any expenses they may incur. For example, does the agency provide free parking? If a uniform is required, who pays for it? What happens in case of an accident? Does the organization's liability insurance cover volunteers?

Discuss your rights with the volunteer director. If you don't want to describe them as such, you can cover the same ground by requesting a job description and asking about training, supervision, how you and paid staff will relate to each other, and so on.

Recognize Your Responsibilities

To hear their supervisors tell it, *responsible* is the middle name of most older volunteers. Still, for those new to the world of volunteerism, it helps to know what's expected. In a word, consideration. That means being punctual, keeping to your schedule, and notifying your supervisor in advance if you're running late or need time off. If your supervisor asks you to submit a time card, sign in, or complete other required paperwork, do it religiously. Many nonprofit agencies must document volunteer participation in order to maintain funding.

When you volunteer, you become an important contributor to the agency's operations, and as such, you'll be expected to complete your assigned duties in a timely manner. Don't modify tasks without first discussing changes with your supervisor. If you anticipate having difficulty meeting a deadline, let someone know, the sooner the better, so that extra help can be recruited.

If you counsel clients or are involved with them in any way, make sure you protect their confidentiality. Do not reveal their identities and histories to people outside the agency or anyone else without legal authorization or a written release from the client. Finally, if you must relinquish your position, give your supervisor adequate notice.

Responsible, reliable performance is fast becoming the trademark of older volunteers. Strive to make it yours.

Join the Crowd

Thirty-nine percent of Americans over age 45 participate in volunteer programs during the year, according to a 1988 survey commissioned by AARP. That's more than 29 million men and women. How and where do they spend their volunteer time?

Well, at least two serve as "cuddlers" for very sick newborns at a county hospital near Los Angeles. Within the same medical center, more than forty other older volunteers visit patients of all ages, help with office work, staff the gift shop, translate for Spanish-speaking patients, and raise funds for the auxiliary.

Halfway across the country, 150 men and women over age 60 are learning about the legislative process in Missouri while developing bills on issues that concern seniors. These "representatives" and "senators" were elected by their peers to the state's Silver Haired Legislature, one of twenty-six across the country.

Speaking of civics, that's one of the many subjects older volunteers help teach to public-school students. According to the National School Volunteer Program, more than 4.3 million adults participate in some 3,000 school volunteer programs. And about a quarter of all public-school volunteers are senior citizens, according to the School Management Study Group.

Teaching is also a familiar activity among older Peace Corps volunteers, who numbered 462 in 1987, up from 82 in 1962.

Among those who have donated their services is a 60-year-old school teacher from New England, who taught math and science to young villagers in Nepal. Other volunteers do two-year stints in parts of Africa, Latin America, the Caribbean, and the Pacific.

Some older volunteers assist overseas countries without leaving home. Members of VITA (Volunteers in Technical Assistance) respond by mail to requests for technical assistance from individuals, organizations, and businesses in developing countries. One volunteer may offer suggestions for building a water-treatment system in Brazil; another, ideas for controlling poultry diseases in Nigeria.

VITA should not be confused with VISTA (Volunteers in Service to America), whose members work full time for one year to alleviate poverty through locally sponsored projects nationwide.

VISTA, a program of ACTION, the federal government's domestic volunteer agency, is open to adults of all ages. Other ACTION programs are geared especially toward older volunteers like Helen W. Under the Foster Grandparent Program, Helen, 73, works with and listens to troubled youngsters confined to a detention center. Joan, 67, helps people at the other end of the age spectrum. A volunteer for the Senior Companion Program, she visits the homebound elderly, letting them know that someone cares. George, 81, is fond of saying he's done it all—through RSVP, the Retired Senior Volunteer Program. Thanks to RSVP's placement services, he has enjoyed volunteer experiences at a hospital, elementary school, senior center, and family counseling clinic. Nationwide, these three federal programs involve 438,500 older volunteers who devote 110 million hours of service each year to their local communities. Impressed? We were.

Equally impressive are the 13,000 volunteers for SCORE/ACE (Service Corps of Retired Executives/Active Corps of Executives) who use their skills and experience to help people start their own businesses or improve existing ones. Sponsored by the U.S. Small Business Administration, SCORE has 750 locations across the country.

While we're on the subject of government volunteer programs, consider those sponsored by the National Park Service and U.S. Forest Service. For the privilege of communing with nature, many older wilderness buffs spend the summer conducting natural history walks, maintaining trails, improving wildlife habitat, and performing other conservation services in national parks and forests. These volunteer programs are perfect for those who want to vacation with a purpose and are willing to pay for their food and lodging.

Another popular "volunteer vacation" is available through Earthwatch, a nonprofit organization in Massachusetts that matches amateur volunteers with scientific expeditions around the world. Outings may involve unearthing Egyptian temples, tracking turtles during egg-laying season, and hiking into volcanoes. Earthwatch volunteers pay for travel to and from the site and contribute between $450 to $2,500 to the cost of the expedition.

We've accounted for only a fraction of the older men and women who participate in volunteer programs. Others donate their services to

- youth groups
- family-service organizations
- men's and women's clubs
- senior centers
- adult day-care programs
- nursing homes
- halfway houses

- alcohol and drug rehab centers
- shelters for the homeless
- community kitchens
- food co-ops
- churches, temples, and synagogues
- museums
- music centers
- theater groups
- arts councils
- libraries
- civic clubs
- neighborhood watch councils
- police and fire departments
- courts
- legal aid bureaus
- zoos
- animal shelters

. . . the list goes on. There's something for everyone. What's more, everyone has something to give.

In addition to volunteering, another excellent way to express yourself and showcase your talents is through hobbies and recreational activities.

Hobbies and Recreational Activities

Joe was released from a Japanese-American relocation camp in 1943 to serve as an interpreter during World War II. That year he started snapping photos to include with the letters he sent to his parents, who were still in the camp. Looking back, Joe, now 68, describes the pictures as his diary. They document a particularly trying stage of his life.

The war ended, but Joe's interest in photography did not. A modest man, he gently concedes that his camera work has gotten better with time. In the past year or so, at the request of friends and acquaintances, he's artfully wielded his camera and video recorder at high-school reunions, weddings, church functions, and other affairs. For a friend's 99th birthday, he turned photos of the man's life from boyhood into a slide presentation to be shown during the party. Another time, he created a slide show of pre-war Japanese-Americans, using pictures from high-school annuals from 1926 to 1944 that he found in libraries.

"When I do projects like these," he notes, "I familiarize myself with a lot of interesting people and events. History unfolds before my eyes."

Barbara picked a rock out of a bin in the stone quarry where her brother-in-law works. "It's beautiful," she said, admiring its rosy glint against the Wyoming setting sun. A native of Los Angeles, the 62-year-old retired nurse never paid much attention to rocks before. "It's yours," said her brother-in-law.

At home, she placed the stone among her potted house plants and there it sat until a friend told her about a local rock and mineral club. A call to the city's parks and recreation department led her to the club's president, who invited her to the monthly meetings.

Today the rock is in two polished pieces, each with one flat surface that hugs the books in her living room. Now adept at using the club's polishing and cutting equipment, Barbara is fashioning earrings, pendants, and rings from ordinary and semiprecious stones she collects in the hills around Los Angeles.

Lois, 72, is a family therapist with a deep, dark secret. "I want to be a writer," she confesses. Members of a local writers' group she attends remind her that she already is one. She just hasn't been published—yet.

With their support, she's been writing and rewriting a series of short stories for and about disabled children. Tales of pain and joy, frustration and triumph, loss and renewal. "Frankly, I don't know why I started writing them," she says with a gesture toward her heart. "I enjoy reading mysteries myself," she adds ironically.

Perhaps that's why she's begun writing everything but the ending for each story. Once a month she reads the unfinished narrative to young students at a school for the disabled. "They provide the ending," says Lois, "and my inspiration."

Joe calls photography his hobby. Barbara describes her stone work as "just something I like to do." And Lois labels her writing "a special interest." However you characterize them, these pleasant pastimes are some of many that older men and women engage in for personal satisfaction, relaxation, intellectual development, and involvement. Such activities may be solitary or social, sedentary or physical, cerebral or creative. In the following sections, we discuss a sample of popular leisure time pursuits. For additional ideas and suggestions, investigate hobby books, adult-education schools, and college extension programs, as well as city departments of human services or parks and recreation (listed in the government section of your phone book). Friends and acquaintances who are active and involved are also good sources of referrals.

Sports

Par for 70-year-old Helen S. is about forty-five rounds of golf each summer—a round of nine holes every three days. "After umpteen years of playing, you'd think I'd tire of the game. Not so. In fact, I doubt I'll ever retire my clubs," she says.

Helen is one of nearly 10 percent of Americans over age 60 (about 3.2 million people) who enjoy golf, according to the National Golf Foundation. The game has been described as the "quintessential retirement recreation," but in fact it's only one of the many sports and fitness activities in which older Americans engage.

In recent years, organized recreational activities designed especially for older athletes of all skill levels have expanded in a variety of sports. For instance, skiers over age 50 qualify for the Over the Hill Gang, an international club with 1,500 members in sixteen "gangs" nationwide and many more chapters in the works (see Resources).

For those who like to combine sports with travel, the nonprofit National Senior Sports Association organizes once-a-month trips to senior tennis, golf, and bowling tournaments in some of the country's most famous resorts. The association uses its group purchasing power and off-season scheduling to obtain good rates (see Resources).

Other older competitors are challenging one another in events such as tennis, cycling, badminton, and horseshoes during local, state, and national Senior Olympic games. A variety of sponsors, including government departments of aging and parks and recreation, host more than 100 such competitions in thirty-five states (see chapter 1).

Pets

"Sammy keeps tabs on me, and I keep tabs on him. We're quite a team, aren't we, pooch?" said Ed, 81, to the golden-haired pup nestled on his lap. Sammy, a cross between a cocker spaniel and God-knows-what, thumped his tail, all the while seeming to smile at Ed with his angelic copper eyes.

Owning a pet—a dog, cat, rabbit, bird, or snake—can enhance your health, say some researchers, who have found that pet companionship can lower blood pressure and increase the chances of survival for heart-attack patients. Whether or not they provide health benefits, animals offer amusement, unconditional love, encouragement for daily exercise, and a sense of purpose and commitment.

If you'd like to adopt a pet, one source to consider is a local animal shelter or humane society. The Purina Pets for People Program funds adoption of dogs and cats to qualifying persons 60 years or older. The program pays the initial cost for adoption fees, spaying or neutering, first veterinary visits, inoculations, pet supplies, and a starter kit of pet food (see Resources). The program is administered by humane societies in many cities across the country and funded by the Ralston Purina Company.

Gardening

William, a busy corporate executive, discovered gardening on his sixty-fifth birthday when a friend gave him the necessary tools, enough seeds to see him through the year, and a how-to book to get him started. Last year, for his sixty-seventh birthday, his wife gave him a sports cap emblazoned "The Happy Horticulturist." He wears it proudly on his regular escapes from the rat race to his backyard flower and vegetable beds.

Obviously, there's great diversity among the estimated 24 million amateur gardeners over 55 years old. But whether they're pruning petunias in a windowsill planter or cultivating corn on an acre lot, chances are they all thrill at the sight of the season's first seedlings.

If you've got a green thumb, consider contributing your skills to Operation Green Plant, a program of the America the Beautiful Fund, which distributes free vegetable, flower, and herb seeds to volunteers who grow them for community distribution or to beautify neglected neighborhoods (see Resources).

Genealogy and Life Reviews

Throughout her life, Elaine had heard fascinating stories about relatives on both sides of her family. Since retirement, she's become the family sleuth, sorting through old diaries, letters, and other records of the past and tracking down distant relatives to record their stories on tape. The family tree, or pedigree chart, she started two years ago now encompasses several generations. "But it's far from complete," she says, not wearily, but with verve and anticipation.

The time and detective work spent tracing your family tree can be immensely rewarding. Besides creating a record of vital family statistics, you'll learn about the people and historical events that helped shape you. Your journey into the past may produce surprises as well: You may discover a famous—or infamous—relative or family secret.

Recording or writing your own life story can be equally satisfying. As James Birren and Donna Deutchman note in their book, *The Fabric of Life: Guiding Autobiography Groups for Older Adults,* "Writing an autobiography puts the contradictions, paradoxes, and ambivalence of life into perspective. It restores our sense of self-sufficiency and personal identity that has been shaped by the crosscurrents and tides of life." If you want help getting started, contact senior centers and adult- or continuing-education programs for information about autobiography or life-story workshops.

Reading

When the youngest of his five children graduated from college, signaling the end of steep tuition fees, Gene R. vowed to buy—in hardcover—any and all books he desired. Few visitors to his home would call him deprived. The living room, dining room, and den are lined with crammed bookshelves. "I've read them all," Gene, 62, explains, "I'm looking for new adventures now."

When researchers ask people how they spend their leisure, reading is among the top-ranked activities. If it's not something you usually do, turn off the television and try it. Choose a book, magazine, or newspaper that interests you. If the reading material at home is unappealing, visit the library. In addition to a treasure trove of books, you'll find magazines and newspapers, records, audiocassettes, and compact discs as well as instructional and popular videotapes. A variety of special events such as book discussions, writers' workshops, and computer classes may also be offered.

For visually impaired readers or those tired of straining over small print, many libraries maintain collections of books on audiocassette and large-print reading materials. Some also offer home-delivery services to patrons who can't visit the library. Call your local branch for more information.

Creative and Performing Arts

Doug and Linda met and fell in love backstage during a high-school production of *Hamlet*. Now married, they're performing together again after forty-eight years in *Annie, Get Your Gun,* an amateur production featuring a stellar cast all age 50 and older. Notwithstanding an occasional missed cue, the community troupe plays to appreciative audiences in nursing homes and retirement centers.

Inspired by contemporary artists and performers such as Ruth Gordon, who starred in films and plays until her death at age 88, and Georgia O'Keeffe, who continued painting past age 90, older men and women increasingly are finding creative outlets for self-expression. Many people simply dream of pursuing such activities, but lack confidence or fear failure. What they don't realize is that the best way to overcome these obstacles is to persist despite them.

Books for beginning writers, photographers, and painters are widely available in libraries and bookstores. Many colleges and adult-education schools offer courses for novices in these and other subjects, including dancing, singing, and acting. To find out about local groups for creative and performing artists, contact community centers, libraries, and city departments of human services or recreation.

Handicrafts

Elsa, 63, enjoys landscaping—of a sort. Before starting, she visualizes the finished scene, imagining how the rich colors of the rose bushes will blend with the greenery of the shrubs and how the rough textures of the trees will highlight the velvet smoothness of the lawn. Then she threads her needle and starts embroidering. Despite failing vision, she "can still zero in on small details." This focus makes her work remarkable and draws interested buyers to her door.

In an era in which almost everything seems machine-made, items fashioned by hand take on special appeal. "It's a labor of love," say older craftspeople of their work with wood, stone, beads, thread, or clay. Finished products may be used for personal pleasure, given as gifts to friends, or sold for extra income. Craft and hobby books available in libraries and bookstores can get you started. Or enroll in craft courses offered by adult-education schools and college extension programs.

Collecting

Personal satisfaction and a keen interest in history motivate Vincent M. to collect. The "over 50" president of the Society of Inkwell Collectors owns some 600 inkwells, valued between 25¢ and $2,500. The hobby "grows on you," he says. "There's not a movie I go to that I don't watch for inkwells." He also spends a lot of time studying historical pictures that include inkwells because that's how collectors date these coveted items.

Although popular among all age groups, collecting holds special appeal for older men and women who want to stay active and involved. Those who do it say collecting is difficult to plan. "It's something you fall into. It's a lot like love," explains Vincent. Once started, many collectors join groups that promote their hobby through meetings and newsletters. These groups also facilitate the exchange of collectibles. Debates within the various groups about whether collecting is primarily a hobby or an investment are common. Novices, however, should approach collecting as a hobby, spending only discretionary funds, at least until they learn more about their specialty. For more information, check your local library or bookstore for books on collecting. Or consult the *Encyclopedia of Associations,* which lists national organizations for collectors of everything from stamps to thermometers. Copies are usually available in the reference section of your local library.

The leisure activities we've described in this chapter give you some idea of the pleasant pastimes in which older people engage. Although leisure—the time free from work and duties—is something people enjoy at any age, late life offers a special opportunity to relish it as a time for self-expression and self-realization.

Resources

Here's more information about the organizations mentioned in this chapter as well as a few others you might find helpful.

Education

Elderhostel, 80 Boylston Street, Suite 400, Boston, MA 02116. Telephone: (617) 426-8056.

GED Testing Services, American Council on Education, One Dupont Circle, NW, Washington, DC 20036. Telephone: (202) 939-9490.

Institute of Lifetime Learning, American Association of Retired Persons, 601 E Street, NW, Washington, DC 20049. Telephone: (202) 434-2277. Publishes educational resource materials for older persons and offers free study materials in print, audio, and video formats for individual or group use.

Travel

BritRail Pass, c/o BritRail Travel International, Inc., 630 Third Avenue, New York, NY 10017. Telephone: (212) 599-5400.

Eurailpass, c/o French National Railroad, 610 Fifth Avenue, New York, NY 10020. Telephone: (212) 582-2110.

International Association for Medical Assistance to Travelers, 417 Center Street, Lewiston, NY 14092. Telephone: (716) 754-4883. Membership is free, but donations are appreciated.

Japan Rail Pass, c/o East Japan Railway Company, 45 Rockefeller Plaza, New York, NY 10111. Telephone: (212) 757-9070.

Volunteering

AARP Volunteer Talent Bank, American Association of Retired Persons, 601 E Street, NW, Washington, DC 20049. Telephone: (202) 434-2277. Matches volunteers with AARP programs and programs of other national voluntary organizations.

Earthwatch, 680 Mt. Auburn Street, Box 403, Watertown, MA 02272. Telephone: (617) 926-8200. Matches volunteers with scientific expeditions around the world.

Foster Grandparent Program, c/o ACTION, 1100 Vermont Avenue, NW, 11th Floor, Washington, DC 20525. Telephone: (202) 634-9108. Matches volunteers over age 60 with disabled or troubled children in need of companionship and guidance. Some stipends are available.

Habitat for Humanity, Habitat and Church Streets, Americus, GA 31709. Telephone: (912) 924-6935. Builds homes with help from low-income residents in the United States, Canada, and South Africa.

National Park Service, Volunteer Office, U.S. Department of the Interior, P.O. Box 37127, Washington, DC 20013-7127. Telephone: (202) 523-5270. Contact the park you're interested in or write for a brochure on volunteering in national parks.

National School Volunteer Program, 601 Wythe Street, Suite 200, Alexandria, VA 22314. Telephone: (703) 836-4880. Ask how to start or join a school volunteer program.

Peace Corps, 1990 K Street, NW, Washington, DC 20526. Telephone: (800) 424-8580. Volunteers help people of developing countries meet basic needs.

RSVP, c/o ACTION, 1100 Vermont Avenue, NW, 11th Floor, Washington, DC 20525. Telephone: (202) 634-9108. Write for a free brochure or check your yellow pages under listings such as "volunteer services," "social services," and "senior citizen service organizations." RSVP matches adults over age 60 with community volunteer programs. Participants may be reimbursed for transportation expenses and a portion of meal costs. Liability insurance is provided for volunteers while on assignment.

SCORE/ACE (Service Corps of Retired Executives/Active Corps of Executives), 1441 L Street, NW, Washington, DC 20416. Telephone: (800) 368-5855. Volunteers offer help for new or struggling businesses.

Senior Companions, c/o ACTION, 1100 Vermont Avenue, NW, 11th Floor, Washington, DC 20525. Telephone: (202) 634-9108. Matches volunteers over age 60 with other adults, primarily the frail elderly, who need care and assistance. Some stipends are available.

Silver Haired Legislatures. Convened annually in 26 states, these nonpartisan, mock legislatures are supported by a variety of state departments, including aging, social services, and health. Contact these departments, local "members of congress," or the State Unit on Aging (see appendix B) to find out whether your state sponsors a senior legislature.

U.S. Department of Agriculture, Forest Service, Human Resource Programs, P.O. Box 37483, Washington, DC 20013. Telephone: (202) 535-0920. Write for a brochure on volunteering in national forests.

VISTA (Volunteers in Service to America), c/o ACTION, 1100 Vermont Avenue, NW, 11th Floor, Washington, DC 20525. Telephone: (202) 634-9108. Helps low-income persons improve the conditions of their own lives. Volunteers receive subsistence allowances.

Volunteers in Technical Assistance (VITA), 1815 N. Lynn Street, Suite 200, P.O. Box 12438, Arlington, VA 22209-8438. Telephone: (703) 243-1865. Volunteers share their knowledge, skills, and experience with people in developing countries.

Hobbies and Recreation

National Genealogical Society, 4527 North 17th Street, Arlington, VA 22207-2399. Telephone: (703) 525-0050. Write for a free pamphlet, *Suggestions for Beginners in Genealogy.* Enclose a self-addressed, stamped envelope.

National Library Service for the Blind and Physically Handicapped, Reference Section, Library of Congress, 1291 Taylor Street, NW, Washington, DC. Telephone: (202) 707-5100. Write for information about books and other reading materials for blind and physically handicapped persons.

National Senior Sports Association, 10560 Main Street, Suite 205, Fairfax, VA 22030. Telephone: (703) 385-7540. Arranges senior tennis, golf, and bowling tournaments at domestic and foreign resorts.

Operation Green Plant, America the Beautiful Fund, 219 Shoreham Building, Washington, DC 20005. Telephone: (800) 522-3557. Distributes free vegetable, flower, and herb seeds to volunteers for community distribution and neighborhood revitalization.

Over the Hill Gang International, 13791 E. Rice Place, Aurora, CO 80015. Write for information on membership or organizing a "gang" for skiers over age 50.

Purina Pets for People Program, Ralston Purina Co., Checkerboard Square, OCA, St. Louis, MO 63164. Telephone: (314) 982-1000. Offers adoption of dogs and cats to qualifying persons age 60 and over.

U.S. National Senior Olympics, 14323 S. Outer Forty Road, Suite N-300, Chesterfield, MO 63107. Telephone: (314) 878-4900. Ask for information about regional, state, and national Senior Olympic games for older athletes.

Recommended Reading

College Board Guide to the CLEP. New York: Macmillan Publishing Company, Inc., 1989. Widely available in bookstores.

College Centers for Older Learners. Information about CCOL programs around the country is available free from the American Association of Retired Persons, P.O. Box 2400, Long Beach, CA 90801.

Directory of Accredited Home Study Schools. A listing of more than 100 accredited home-study schools across the country is available free from the National Home Study Council, 1601 18th Street, NW, Washington, DC 20009.

Eisenberg, Gerson G. *Learning Vacations.* Princeton, NJ: Peterson's, 1990. Widely available in bookstores.

Kennedy, Joyce Lain. *The Independent Study Guide.* Princeton, NJ: Peterson's, 1990. Widely available in bookstores.

Who Offers Part-time Degree Programs? Princeton, NJ: Peterson's, 1990. Widely available in bookstores.

APPENDIX A

Being Your Own Advocate

From time to time, we all face situations that we need help to resolve. You've moved to Florida, but your mail is still being delivered in New York. Your health insurer denies a claim for a service that you understood was covered. You have a pressing tax question, but whenever you call the IRS you get an irritating recorded message. At times like these, it helps to know that people can be very effective in advocating their own cases.

Take the case of Elizabeth S. Her driver's license was to expire on her sixtieth birthday while she was abroad on a three-month holiday, so she submitted the license-renewal form before her departure. On returning home, she discovered that she had not received her new license. She tried calling the Department of Motor Vehicles for two days, but always got a busy signal. Frustrated and wary of driving without a valid license, Elizabeth complained to her state assemblyman's office. The next day, the assemblyman's staff informed her that a new license was being issued. Two days later, Elizabeth received her license. She was delighted, and the assemblyman had her vote for life.

If you have a problem you can't resolve despite your best efforts, ask an elected official for help. These public servants have assigned staff to handle constituents' problems. As one official said: "Constituency services are our bread and butter. We are happy to help."

Often, the key to success is knowing whom to approach for assistance. Here's a guide:

- U.S. Senators and Representatives can help resolve problems arising within federal programs such as Social Security, Medicare, and Veterans programs.
- State governors, senators, and members of the assembly provide help managing problems involving state departments, such as the Department of Motor Vehicles,

and state-regulated businesses and institutions, such as nursing homes.

- Local elected officials offer assistance untangling community problems such as those involving traffic, garbage collection, rent control, and health and safety issues.

After you decide whom to approach, review the facts of your situation. Can the problem be handled by telephone or is a letter preferable? When calling, be sure to get the name of the person with whom you are speaking. At the end of the conversation determine what course of action and follow-up steps are needed. If you send a letter, write it in your own words. Focus on the facts and be as specific as possible. Also, briefly explain what action you've taken and the results of your efforts. If you have relevant correspondence from the agency involved, send copies with your letter.

If you're interested in advocating either for or against particular legislation, it often helps to join forces with people or groups that have similar interests. You and other proponents might also find it useful to meet with your legislator(s) to discuss the proposed legislation. Develop a fact sheet and flyer summarizing the benefits of the bill, or conversely, its pitfalls. Be willing to testify at public hearings or identify someone who can.

If your elected official supports your cause, helps resolve a problem, or clarifies a situation for you, write a letter thanking him or her. You never know when you may need help again.

APPENDIX B

What Are State Units on Aging?

Throughout this book we have referred to State Units on Aging, or SUAs. This is a generic term, which in some states may refer to a bureau, office, department, or commission.

The SUA is part of the state government. The agency is headed by a director appointed by the governor and charged with addressing issues and concerns that affect older residents and acting as an advocate on behalf of older adults. The SUA is responsible for funding and evaluating regional and local programs for older adults. Although SUAs typically do not provide services for seniors, they have a wealth of information about programs that do. SUAs can direct you to your local Area Agency on Aging (AAA), a nonprofit or public agency that administers local or regional programs for adults age 60 and older.

A primary goal of both SUAs and AAAs is to develop a community-based service-delivery system that includes the following:

- access services such as transportation, outreach, information, and referral
- community services including group meals, continuing education, legal services, and counseling and assistance
- in-home services such as home health, homemaker, home-delivered meals, and home chore and maintenance

SUAs and AAAs work to improve existing and establish new partnerships between government agencies and private organizations that offer services and opportunities to older persons.

SUAs and AAAs are good places to begin your search for support services. For the address and telephone number of your SUA, check the directory below. The SUA and local AAA may also be listed in the government section of your telephone directory or in the yellow pages under "senior citizen service organizations" or "social services."

Alabama Commission on Aging, 136 Catoma Street, 2nd Floor, Montgomery, AL 36130. Telephone: (205) 261-5743.

Older Alaskans Committee, P.O. Box C, Mail Stop 0209, Juneau, AK 99811. Telephone: (907) 465-3250.

Territorial Administration on Aging, Government of American Samoa, Pago Pago, American Samoa 96799. Telephone: (684) 633-1252.

Aging and Adult Administration, Department of Economic Security, 1400 W. Washington Street, Phoenix, AZ 85007. Telephone: (602) 255-4446.

Division of Aging and Adult Services, Arkansas Department of Human Services, Main & 7th Streets, Donaghey Building, Suite 1428, Little Rock, AR 72201. Telephone: (501) 682-2441.

California Department of Aging, 1600 K Street, Sacramento, CA 95814. Telephone: (916) 322-3887.

Aging and Adult Services, Department of Social Services, 1575 Sherman Street, 10th Floor, Denver, CO 80203-1714. Telephone: (303) 866-3851.

Department of Community and Cultural Affairs, Civic Center, Commonwealth of the Northern Mariana Islands, Saipan, Mariana Islands 96950.

Connecticut Department of Aging, 175 Main Street, Hartford, CT 06106. Telephone: (203) 566-3238.

Delaware Division on Aging, Department of Health and Social Services, 1901 North Dupont Highway, 2nd Floor, New Castle, DE 19720. Telephone: (302) 421-6791.

District of Columbia Office on Aging, Executive Office of the Mayor, 1424 K Street, NW, 2nd Floor, Washington, DC 20005. Telephone: (202) 724-5626.

Program Office of Aging and Adult Services, Department of Health and Rehabilitative Services, Building 2, Room 328, 1323 Winewood Boulevard, Tallahassee, FL 32399-0700. Telephone: (904) 488-8922.

Office of Aging, Department of Human Resources, 6th Floor, 878 Peachtree Street, NE, Atlanta, GA 30309. Telephone: (404) 894-5333.

Division of Senior Citizens, Department of Public Health and Social Services, P.O. Box 2816, Government of Guam, Agana, Guam 96910. Telephone: 0-11-671-734-7399.

Hawaii Executive Office on Aging, 335 Merchant Street, Room 241, Honolulu, HI 96813. Telephone: (808) 548-2593.

Idaho Office on Aging, Statehouse, Room 108, Boise, ID 83720. Telephone: (208) 334-3833.

Illinois Department on Aging, 421 E. Capitol Avenue, Springfield, IL 62701. Telephone: (217) 785-2870.

Indiana Department of Human Services, P.O. Box 7083, 251 North Illinois, Indianapolis, IN 46207-7083. Telephone: (317) 232-7006.

Department of Elder Affairs, Jewett Building, Suite 236, 914 Grand Avenue, Des Moines, IA 50319. Telephone: (515) 281-5187.

Kansas Department on Aging, Docking State Office Building, 122-S, 915 S.W. Harrison, Topeka, KS 66612-1500. Telephone: (913) 296-4986.

Division for Aging Services, Cabinet for Human Resources, Department for Social Services, 275 E. Main Street, Frankfort, KY 40621. Telephone: (502) 564-6930.

Governor's Office of Elderly Affairs, P.O. Box 80374, 4550 North Boulevard, 2nd Floor, Baton Rouge, LA 70898-0374. Telephone: (504) 925-1700.

Bureau of Maine's Elderly, Department of Human Services, State House, Station 11, Augusta, ME 04333. Telephone: (207) 289-2561.

State Agency on Aging, Department of Social Services, Republic of the Marshall Islands, Marjuro, Marshall Islands 96960. Telephone: 0-11-692-9-3384.

Maryland Office on Aging, 301 W. Preston Street, Baltimore, MD 21201. Telephone: (301) 225-1100.

Massachusetts Executive Office of Elder Affairs, 38 Chauncy Street, Boston, MA 02111. Telephone: (617) 727-7750.

Office of Services to the Aging, P.O. Box 30026, Lansing, MI 48909. Telephone: (517) 373-8230.

Minnesota Board on Aging, 444 Lafayette Road, 4th Floor, c/o DHS Building, St. Paul, MN 55155-3843. Telephone: (612) 297-2544.

Mississippi Council on Aging, 421 W. Pascagoula Street, Jackson, MS 39203-3092. Telephone: (601) 949-2070.

Division of Aging, Department of Social Services, P.O. Box 1337, 2701 W. Main Street, Jefferson City, MO 65102. Telephone: (314) 751-3082.

Department of Family Services, P.O. Box 8005, Helena, MT 59604. Telephone: (406) 444-5900.

Department on Aging, P.O. Box 95044, 301 Centennial Mall South, Lincoln, NE 68509. Telephone: (402) 471-2306.

Nevada Division for Aging Services, Department of Human Resources, 505 E. King Street, Room 101, Carson City, NV 89710. Telephone: (702) 885-4210.

Division of Elderly and Adult Services, New Hampshire Department of Health and Human Services, 6 Hazen Drive, Concord, NH 03301. Telephone: (603) 271-4394.

New Jersey Division on Aging, Department of Community Affairs, 101 S. Broad Street, CN 807, Trenton, NJ 08625-0807. Telephone: (609) 292-4833.

New Mexico State Agency on Aging, La Villa Rivera Building, 4th Floor, 224 E. Palace Avenue, Santa Fe, NM 87501. Telephone: (505) 827-7640.

New York State Office for the Aging, Agency Building 2, Empire State Plaza, Albany, NY 12223-0001. Telephone: (518) 474-4425.

North Carolina Division of Aging, Department of Human Resources, 693 Palmer Drive, Raleigh, NC 27603. Telephone: (919) 733-3983.

Aging Services Division, North Dakota Department of Human Services, State Capitol Building, Bismarck, ND 58505. Telephone: (701) 224-2577.

Ohio Department of Aging, 50 W. Broad Street, 9th Floor, Columbus, OH 43215. Telephone: (614) 466-5500.

Aging Services Division, Department of Human Services, P.O. Box 25352, Oklahoma City, OK 73125. Telephone: (405) 521-2281.

Senior and Disabled Services Division, Department of Human Resources, 313 Public Service Building, Salem, OR 97310. Telephone: (503) 378-4728.

State Agency on Aging, Department of Social Services, Republic of Palau, Koror, Palau 96940.

Pennsylvania Department of Aging, 231 State Street, 6th Floor, Barto Building, Harrisburg, PA 17101. Telephone: (717) 783-1550.

Puerto Rico Office of Elderly Affairs, P.O. Box 11398, Santurce, Puerto Rico 00910. Telephone: (809) 721-4010.

Department of Elderly Affairs, 79 Washington Street, Providence, RI 02903. Telephone: (401) 277-2858.

South Carolina Commission on Aging, 400 Arbor Lake Drive, Suite B-500, Columbia, SC 29223. Telephone: (803) 735-0210.

Office of Adult Services and Aging, Richard F. Kneip Building, 700 Governor's Drive, Pierre, SD 57501-2291. Telephone: (605) 773-3656.

Tennessee Commission on Aging, 706 Church Street, Suite 201, Nashville, TN 37219-5573. Telephone: (615) 741-2056.

Texas Department on Aging, P.O. Box 12786, Capitol Station, Austin, TX 78711. Telephone: (512) 444-2727.

Utah Division of Aging and Adult Services, P.O. Box 45500, 120 North 200 West, Room 4A, Salt Lake City, UT 84103. Telephone: (801) 538-3910.

Vermont Office on Aging, Waterbury Complex, 103 S. Main Street, Waterbury, VT 05676. Telephone: (802) 241-2400.

Virgin Islands Department of Human Services, Barbel Plaza South, Charlotte Amalie, St. Thomas, Virgin Islands 00802. Telephone: (809) 774-5884.

Virginia Department for the Aging, 700 E. Franklin Street, 10th Floor, Richmond, VA 23219-2327. Telephone: (804) 225-2271.

Aging and Adult Services Administration, Department of Social and Health Services, Mail Stop OB-44-A, Olympia, WA 98504. Telephone: (206) 586-3768.

West Virginia Commission on Aging, State Capitol Complex, Holly Grove, 1710 Kanawha Boulevard, Charleston, WV 25305. Telephone: (304) 348-3317.

Department of Health and Social Services, P.O. Box 7851, 1 W. Wilson, Room 480, Madison, WI 53707. Telephone: (608) 266-2536.

Commission on Aging, Hathaway Building, 1st Floor, Cheyenne, WY 82002. Telephone: (307) 777-7986.

APPENDIX C Nursing-Home Ombudsmen

Alabama
Commission on Aging, 136 Catoma Street, 2nd Floor, Montgomery, AL 36130. Telephone: (205) 261-5743.

Alaska
Office of the Long Term Care Ombudsman, 3601 C Street, Suite 260, Anchorage, AK 99503. Telephone: (907) 279-2232 (Accepts collect calls).

Arizona
Aging and Adult Administration, P.O. Box 6123-950A, 1400 W. Washington Street, Phoenix, AZ 85007. Telephone: (602) 542-4446.

Arkansas
Division of Aging and Adult Services, Arkansas Department of Human Services, 1417 Donaghey Plaza South, P.O. Box 1437, 7th & Main Streets, Little Rock, AR 72203-1437. Telephone: (501) 682-2441.

California
California Department of Aging, 1600 K Street, Sacramento, CA 95814. Telephone: (916) 323-6681 or (800) 231-4024.

Colorado
The Legal Center, 455 Sherman Street, Suite 130, Denver, CO 80203. Telephone: (303) 722-0300 or (800) 332-6356.

Connecticut
Connecticut Department on Aging, 175 Main Street, Hartford, CT 06106. Telephone: (203) 5667770.

Delaware
Division on Aging, 11-13 Church Street, Milford, DE 19663. Telephone: (302) 422-1386, (800) 223-9074 (New Castle County), or (800) 292-1515 (Kent and Sussex County).

District of Columbia
Legal Counsel for the Elderly, 1909 K Street, NW, Washington, DC 20049. Telephone: (202) 662-4933.

Florida
State LTC Ombudsman Council, Executive Office of the Governor, Holland Building, Suite 94, 600 S. Calhoun Street, Tallahassee, FL 32399-0001. Telephone: (904) 488-6190.

Georgia
Office of Aging, Department of Human Resources, 878 Peachtree Street, NE, Room 642, Atlanta, GA 30309. Telephone: (404) 894-5336.

Hawaii
Hawaii Executive Office on Aging, 335 Merchant Street, Suite 241, Honolulu, HI 96813. Telephone: (808) 545-2593 or (800) 468-4644.

Idaho
Idaho Office on Aging, State House, Room 108, Boise, ID 83720. Telephone: (208) 334-3833.

Indiana
Indiana Department of Human Services, Division of Aging, P.O. Box 7083, 251 N. Illinois Avenue, Indianapolis, IN 46207-7083. Telephone: (317) 232-7020 or (800) 545-7763.

Iowa
Department of Elder Affairs, Jewett Building, Suite 236, 914 Grand Avenue, Des Moines, IA 50319. Telephone: (515) 281-5187 or (800) 532-3213.

Illinois
Department on Aging, 421 E. Capitol Avenue, Springfield, IL 62701. Telephone: (217) 785-3140 or (800) 252-8966.

Kansas
Department on Aging, Docking State Office Building, 122-S, 915 SW Harrison, Topeka, KS 66612-1500. Telephone: (913) 296-4986 or (800) 432-3535.

Kentucky
Division for Aging Services, Cabinet for Human Resources, CHR Building, 6th Floor, West, 275 E. Main Street, Frankfort, KY 40621. Telephone: (502) 564-6930 or (800) 372-2991.

Louisiana
Governor's Office of Elderly Affairs, P.O. Box 80374, 4550 North Boulevard, Baton Rouge, LA 70898-0374. Telephone: (504) 925-1700.

Maine
Maine Committee on Aging, State House, Station 127, Augusta, ME 04333. Telephone: (207) 289-3658 or (800) 452-1912.

Maryland
Maryland Office on Aging, 301 West Preston Street, Room 1004, Baltimore, MD 21201. Telephone: (301) 225-1083 or (800) 243-3425.

Massachusetts
Massachusetts Executive Office of Elder Affairs, 38 Chauncy Street, Boston, MA 02111. Telephone: (617) 727-7273 or (800) 882-2003.

Michigan
Citizens for Better Care, 1627 E. Kalamazoo, Lansing, MI 48912. Telephone: (517) 482-1297 or (800) 292-7852.

Minnesota
Minnesota Board on Aging, Office of Ombudsman for Older Minnesotans, 444 Lafayette Road, St. Paul, MN 55155-3843. Telephone: (612) 296-7465 or (800) 652-9747.

Mississippi
Mississippi Council on Aging, 21 W. Pascagoula Street, Jackson, MS 39203. Telephone: (601) 949-2070 or (800) 222-7622.

Missouri
Division of Aging, Department of Social Services, P.O. Box 1337, 2701 W. Main Street, Jefferson City, MO 65102. Telephone: (314) 751-3082.

Montana
Governor's Office on Aging, P.O. Box 232, Capitol Station, Helena, MT 59620. Telephone: (406) 444-4676 or (800) 332-2272.

Nebraska
Department on Aging, P.O. Box 95044, 301 Centennial Mall South, Lincoln, NE 68509. Telephone: (402) 471-2307.

Nevada
Division of Aging Services, Department of Human Resources, Kinkead Building, Room 101, 505 E. King Street, Carson City, NV 89710. Telephone: (702) 885-4210 or (800) 222-0400 (Las Vegas only).

New Hampshire
New Hampshire LTC Ombudsman Program, Division of Elderly and Adult Services, 6 Hazen Drive, Concord, NH 03301-6508. Telephone: (603) 271-4375 or (800) 442-5640.

New Jersey
Office of the Ombudsman for the Institutionalized Elderly, 28 W. State Street, Room 305, CN808, Trenton, NJ 08625-0808. Telephone: (609) 292-8016 or (800) 624-4262.

New Mexico
State Agency on Aging, LaVilla Rivera Building, 4th Floor, 224 E. Palace Avenue, Santa Fe, NM 87501. Telephone: (505) 827-7640 or (800) 432-2082.

New York
Office for the Aging, Agency Building 2, Empire State Plaza, Albany, NY 12223. Telephone: (518) 474-7329 or (800) 342-9871.

North Carolina
North Carolina Department of Human Resources, Division of Aging, Taylor Hall, 693 Palmer Drive, Raleigh, NC 27603. Telephone: (919) 733-3983.

North Dakota
Aging Services Division, Department of Human Services, State Capitol Building, 600 East Boulevard Avenue, Bismarck, ND 58505. Telephone: (701) 224-2577 or (800) 472-2622.

Ohio
Ohio Department on Aging, 50 W. Broad Street, 9th Floor, Columbus, OH 43266-0501. Telephone: (614) 466-9927 or (800) 282-1206.

Oklahoma
Division of Aging Service, Department of Human Services, P.O. Box 25352, Oklahoma City, OK 73125. Telephone: (405) 521-2281.

Oregon
Office of LTC Ombudsman, 2475 Lancaster Drive, Building B, 9, Salem, OR 97310. Telephone: (503) 378-6533 or (800) 522-2602.

Pennsylvania
Department of Aging, Barto Building, 231 State Street, Harrisburg, PA 17101. Telephone: (717) 783-7247.

Puerto Rico
Gericulture Commission, Department of Social Services, G.P.O. 11398, Santurce, Puerto Rico 00910. Telephone: (809) 721-0734 or (809) 722-2429.

Rhode Island
Rhode Island Department of Elderly Affairs, 160 Pine Street, Providence, RI 02903. Telephone: (401) 277-6883.

South Carolina
Long Term Care Ombudsman, Office of the Governor, Division of Ombudsman and Citizens' Services, 1205 Pendleton Street, Columbia, SC 29201. Telephone: (803) 734-0457.

South Dakota
Office of Adult Services and Aging, Department of Social Services, Richard F. Kneip Building, 700 Governor's Drive, Pierre, SD 57501-2291. Telephone: (605) 773-3656.

Tennessee
Commission on Aging, 706 Church Street, Suite 201, Nashville, TN 37219-5573. Telephone: (615) 741-2056.

Texas
Department on Aging, P.O. Box 12786, Capitol Station, 1949 IH 35, South, Austin, TX 78471-3702. Telephone: (512) 444-2727 or (800) 252-9240.

Utah
Division of Aging and Adult Services, Department of Social Services, P.O. Box 45500, 120 North, 200 West, Salt Lake City, UT 84103. Telephone: (801) 538-3910.

Vermont
Department of Rehabilitation and Aging, 103 S. Main Street, Waterbury, VT 05676. Telephone: (802) 241-2400 or (800) 642-5119.

Virginia
Virginia Department for the Aging, 700 E. Franklin Street, 10th Floor, Richmond, VA 23219-2327. Telephone: (804) 225-2271.

Washington
South King Co. Multi-Service Center, Department of Community Development, 1200 S. 336, Federal Way, WA 98003. Telephone: (206) 838-6801 or (800) 562-6028.

West Virginia
Commission on Aging, State Capitol Complex, Charleston, WV 25305. Telephone: (304) 348-3317 or (800) 252-9240.

Wisconsin
Board on Aging and Long Term Care, 819 N. 6th Street, Suite 619, Milwaukee, WI 53203-1664. Telephone: (414) 227-4386.

Wyoming
Wyoming Long Term Care Ombudsman, Wyoming State Bar Association, P.O. Box 94, 953 Waters Street, Wheatland, WY 82201. Telephone: (307) 322-5553.

References

Chapter 1. Keeping Fit

Bailey, Covert. *Fit or Fat?* Boston: Houghton Mifflin, 1978.

Brody, Jane E. "Intriguing Studies Link Nutrition to Immunity." *New York Times,* March 21, 1989.

"Can Exercise Alter the Aging Process?" *New York Times,* Nov. 28, 1988.

Doheny, Kathleen. "An Overweight Partner Can Sabotage the Best Diet Plan." *Los Angeles Times,* Aug. 22, 1989.

Doress, Paula Brown, Diana Laskin Siegal, and the Midlife and Older Women Book Project. *Ourselves, Growing Older.* New York: Simon and Schuster, 1987.

"Exercise Reduces Pain and Improves Mobility." *Gerontology News,* Sept. 1989, 7.

Fiatarone, Maria A., et al. "The Effect of Exercise on Natural Killer Cell Activity in Young and Old Subjects." *Journal of Gerontology: Medical Sciences* 44, no. 2 (March 1989):M37–45.

"Growing Old, Feeling Young." *Newsweek,* Nov. 1, 1982, 56–65.

Harris, Raymond. "Fitness and Exercise: A Day in the Life of Dr. H." *Generations,* Spring 1983, 23–25.

Harris, T. George. "Heart Disease in Retreat." *Psychology Today,* Jan./Feb. 1989, 46–51.

Larsen, David. "Fit for a Lifetime." *Los Angeles Times,* April 11, 1989.

Levine, Art, Stacy Wells, and Curtis Kopf. "New Rules of Exercise." *U.S. News and World Report,* Aug. 11, 1986, 52–56.

National Heart, Lung, and Blood Institute, National Institutes of Health. "Facts About . . . Exercise: How to Get Started." Nov. 1987. Washington, DC: U. S. Department of Health and Human Services, Public Health Service.

National Institute on Aging, National Institutes of Health. "Don't Take It Easy—Exercise!" *Age Pages,* Jan. 1984, 14–15. Washington, DC: U.S. Government Printing Office.

Neal, Iris. "Athletes Prepare for Senior Olympics: Nationals Slated in St. Louis in June." *Senior World/San Diego,* May 1989, 6.

Pardini, Alan, and Connie Mahoney. *A Resource Guide for Fitness Programs for Older Persons*. Washington, DC: U.S. Department of Health and Human Services, Administration on Aging, 1987.

Pennington, Jean A. T. *Bowes & Church's Food Values of Portions Commonly Used,* 15th ed. Philadelphia: Lippincott, 1989.

Pressley, Sue Anne. "Stretching into the Golden Years of Life: After 3 Decades, Montgomery Fitness Teacher Is Still Kicking." *Washington Post,* May 23, 1989.

Rowe, John W., and Robert L. Kahn. "Human Aging: Usual and Successful." *Science* 237 (July 10, 1987):143–49.

Stockton, William. "Each Idle Day Requires 2 Days of Exercising." *Los Angeles Times,* April 10, 1989.

Stones, M. J., Brenda Dornan, and Albert Kozma. "The Prediction of Mortality in Elderly Institution Residents." *Journal of Gerontology: Psychological Sciences* 44, no. 3 (May 1989):P72–79.

Toufexis, Anastasia. "Older—But Coming on Strong." *Time,* Feb. 22, 1988, 76–79.

Verity, Larry S. "Testing and Modifying for Individual Needs." In *Aerobic Dance-Exercise Instructor Manual,* edited by Naneene Van Gelder, 169–204. San Diego, CA: International Dance-Exercise Association (IDEA) Foundation, 1987.

Whitten, Phillip, and Elizabeth J. Whiteside. "Can Exercise Make You Sexier?" *Psychology Today,* April 1989, 42–44.

Chapter 2. To Your Good Health

1988 Joint National Committee. "The 1988 Report of the Joint National Committee on Detection, Evaluation, and Treatment of High Blood Pressure." *Archives of Internal Medicine* 148 (1988):1023–38.

Arnst, Dennis J. "Presbycusis." In *Handbook of Clinical Audiology,* edited by J. Katz. Baltimore: Williams and Wilkins, 1985, 707–20.

Beck, John C., et al., eds. *Geriatrics Review Syllabus: A Core Curriculum in Geriatric Medicine.* New York: American Geriatrics Society, 1989.

References

Campion, Edward W., et al. "Hip Fracture: A Prospective Study of Hospital Course, Complications, and Costs." *Journal of General Internal Medicine* 2 (1987):78–82.

Capino, Diosdado G., and Howard M. Leibowitz. "Age-Related Macular Degeneration." *Hospital Practice* 23, no. 3A (1988):23–42.

Consensus Conference. "Urinary Incontinence in Adults." *Journal of the American Medical Association* 261, no. 18 (May 12, 1989):2685–90.

Cox, E. B. "Breast Cancer in the Elderly." *Clinical Geriatric Medicine* 3 (1987):695–713.

Cummings, Jeffrey L., and Douglas F. Benson. "Dementia: Definition, Prevalence, Classification, and Approach to Diagnosis." In *Dementia: A Clinical Approach,* edited by Jeffrey L. Cummings, and Douglas F. Benson. Boston: Butterworths, 1984.

Cummings, Steven R., et al. "Epidemiology of Osteoporosis and Osteoporotic Fractures." *Epidemiology Review* 7 (1985):178–208.

Gersh, Bernard J., Richard A. Kronmal, and Hartzell V. Schaff. "Comparison of Coronary Bypass Surgery and Medical Therapy in Patients 65 Years of Age or Older: A Non-Randomized Study from the Coronary Artery Surgery Study (CASS) Registry." *New England Journal of Medicine* 313 (1985):217–24.

Grotta, James C. "Current Medical and Surgical Therapy for Cerebrovascular Disease." *New England Journal of Medicine* 317 (1987): 1505–16.

Keating, Herbert J. "Preoperative Considerations in the Geriatric Patient." *Medical Clinics of North America* 71, no. 3 (May 1987):569–83.

Larson, Eric, et al. "Dementia in Elderly Outpatients: A Prospective Study." *Annals of Internal Medicine* 100 (1984):417–23.

Lipowski, Zbigniew J. "Delirium in the Elderly Patient." *New England Journal of Medicine* 320 (1989):578–82.

Lipson, Loren G. "Diabetes in the Elderly: Diagnosis, Pathogenesis, and Therapy." *American Journal of Medicine* 80, Suppl5A (1986):10–21.

Lyss, Alan P. "Systemic Treatment for Prostate Cancer." *American Journal of Medicine* 83 (1987):1120–28.

Mader, Scott. "Hearing Impairment in Elderly Persons." *Journal of the American Geriatrics Society* 32 (1984):548–53.

Moskowitz, R. W. "Primary Osteoarthritis: Epidemiology, Clinical Aspects, and General Management." *American Journal of Medicine* 83 (1987):5–10.

Oboloer, Sylvia K., and F. Mark LaForce. "The Periodic Physical Examination in Asymptomatic Adults." *Annals of Internal Medicine* 110 (1989):214–26.

"Osteoporosis." National Institutes of Health Consensus Development Conference Statement 5 (1984).

Ouslander, Joseph G., ed. "Urinary Incontinence." *Clinical Geriatric Medicine* 2 (1986).

Reuben, David B. "Taking Drugs Wisely—Concerns for Seniors." In *Medical and Health Annual of the Encyclopaedia Britannica* (1990): 463–66.

Rowland-Morin, Pamela A., and David B. Reuben. "Getting the Most from Your Visit to the Doctor: Make Your Office Visit Work for You." *Diabetes Forecast* (October 1987):27–28.

Schoenberger, J. A. "Epidemiology of Systolic and Diastolic Systemic Blood Pressure Elevation in the Elderly." *Journal of American Cardiology* 57 (1986):45C–51C.

Straatsma, Bradley R., et al. "Aging-Related Cataract: Laboratory Investigation and Clinical Management." *Annals of Internal Medicine* 102 (1985):82–92.

Tinetti, Mary E., Mark Speechley, and Sandra F. Ginter. "Risk Factors for Falls among Elderly Persons Living in the Community." *New England Journal of Medicine* 319 (1988):1701–7.

Tipton, Toni. "What's Their Secret?" *Los Angeles Times,* May 17, 1990.

U.S. Preventive Services Task Force. "Guide to Clinical Preventive Services." Report presented to the Department of Health and Human Services, May 2, 1989, xxxi–lii.

Weinbech, M., and J. Erchenbrecht. "Motor Function of the Large Intestine. Constipation and Diarrhea." In *Gastrointestinal Tract Disorders in the Elderly,* edited by J. Helleman and G. Vantrappen. Edinburgh: Churchill-Livingstone, 1984.

Wheat, Mary E. "Exercise in the Elderly." *Western Journal of Medicine* 147 (1987):477–80.

Winslow, Constance M., et al. "The Appropriateness of Performing Coronary Artery Bypass Surgery." *Journal of the American Medical Association* 260 (1988):505–9.

Chapter 3. Keeping Your Emotional Balance

Berkman, Lisa F., and Leonard S. Syme. "Social Networks, Host Resistance and Mortality: A Nine-Year Follow-up Study of Alameda County Residents." *American Journal of Epidemiology* 109, no. 2 (Feb. 1979):186–204.

Blazer, Dan G. "Depressive Illness in Late Life." In *America's Aging: Health in an Older Society,* Committee on an Aging Society, Institute of Medicine and National Research Council. Washington, DC: National Academy Press, 1985.

Blazer, Dan G. "Social Support and Mortality in an Elderly Community Population." *American Journal of Epidemiology* 115, no. 5 (May 1982): 684–94.

Busse, Ewald W., and Dan G. Blazer, eds. *Geriatric Psychiatry.* Washington, DC: American Psychiatric Press, 1989.

Butler, Robert N., and Myrna I. Lewis. *Aging and Mental Health.* 3d ed. Columbus, OH: Charles E. Merrill, 1982.

Davis, Jim. "Mental Well-being of Elders: Seeking Positive Solutions." *Generations* 67 (Spring 1983):30–33.

Kinney, Jean, and Gwen Leaton. *Loosening the Grip: A Handbook of Alcohol Information.* St. Louis: Mosby, 1983.

Mercer, Susan O. *Elder Suicide: A National Survey of Prevention and Intervention Programs.* Washington, DC: American Association of Retired Persons, 1989.

Milam, James R., and Katherine Ketcham. *Under the Influence: A Guide to the Myths and Realities of Alcoholism.* Toronto: Bantam, 1981.

National Center for Health Statistics. *Monthly Vital Statistics Report* 36, no. 6 (Sept. 30, 1988):25.

National Center for Health Statistics, and M. G. Kovar. "Aging in the Eighties, Age 65 Years and Over and Living Alone, Contacts with Family, Friends, and Neighbors." *Advance Data from Vital and Health Statistics,* No. 116, DHHS Pub. No. (PHS) 96–1250. Hyattsville, MD: Public Health Service, May 9, 1986.

Njeri, Itabari. "Coming to America." *Los Angeles Times,* July 2, 1989.

Roark, Anne C. "Most Older Persons Say They're Happy With Lives." *Los Angeles Times,* May 4, 1989, Part I.

Rowe, John W., and Robert L. Kahn. "Human Aging: Usual and Successful." *Science* 237 (July 10, 1987):143–49.

Shneidman, Edwin S., Norman L. Farberow, and Robert E. Litman. *The Psychology of Suicide.* New York: Jason Aronson, 1983.

Toufexis, Anastasia. "Older but Coming on Strong." *Time,* Feb. 22, 1988, 76–79.

Wayne, G. J. "Electroconvulsive Treatment in the Elderly." *Journal of the National Association of Private Psychiatric Hospitals* 11 (1980): 25–27.

Chapter 4. The Health-Insurance Puzzle

Bacon, Kenneth H. "Plan to Overhaul Payment of Doctors Under Medicare Is Agreed to by Conferees." *Wall Street Journal,* November 21, 1989.

Boston University, Health Policy Institute. *More Health for Your Dollar, An Older Person's Guide to HMOs.* Washington, DC: American Association of Retired Persons, 1983.

Budish, Armond D. *Avoiding the Medicaid Trap: How to Beat the Catastrophic Costs of Nursing-Home Care.* New York: Henry Holt, 1989.

California Department of Insurance. *Consumer's Guide to Group Health Insurance.* Sacramento, CA: California Department of Insurance, 1988.

"Company Earnings Face a Big Hit from Accounting for Health Benefits." *Wall Street Journal,* May 6, 1989.

Dobris, Joel C. "Medicaid Asset Planning by the Elderly: A Policy View of Expectations, Entitlement, and Inheritance." *Real Property, Probate and Trust Journal* 24, no. 1 (Spring 1989):1–32.

Gillam, Jerry. "Assembly Panel OKs Brown's Worker Health Insurance Bill." *Los Angeles Times,* June 8, 1989.

"Good Health-Care News." *Los Angeles Times,* May 30, 1989.

Hamilton, Frederick & Schneiders. *Health Care in America: Views and Experiences of Mature Adults.* Washington, DC: American Association of Retired Persons, 1987.

Hankin, Marc B. "Medicaid and Medi-Cal, After the Medicare Catastrophic Coverage Act of 1989 ("MCCA"): Is There Salvation in MECCA?" *Fulbright & Jaworski's ElderLaw Newsletter* 1, no. 2 (Fall 1989):1–3.

Health Insurance Association of America. *What You Should Know about Health Insurance.* Washington, DC: Health Insurance Association of America, 1987.

Iacocca, Lee. "The Competitive Pull to National Health Care." *Los Angeles Times,* April 16, 1989.

Jones, Lannie. "National Physicians' Group Urges Broad Federal Health Plan." *Los Angeles Times,* Jan. 12, 1989.

National Association of Insurance Commissioners. *Guide to Health Insurance for People with Medicare.* Washington, DC: U.S. Department of Health and Human Services, Health Care Financing Administration, 1989.

———. *Model Regulation to Implement the NAIC Medicare Supplement Insurance Minimum Standards Model Act.* Kansas City, MO: National Association of Insurance Commissioners, 1988.

"Paying for a Nursing Home." *Consumer Reports,* Oct. 1989, 664–67.

Reinhardt, Uwe E. "Toward a Fail-Safe Health Insurance System." *Wall Street Journal,* January 11, 1989.

Roark, Anne C. "Health Care: A Confusion of Choices." *Los Angeles Times,* April 23, 1989.

Rosenblatt, Robert A. "Bill Would Cap Total Medicare Fees for Doctors." *Los Angeles Times,* June 14, 1989.

Scott, Diana J., and Wayne S. Upton. "Postretirement Benefits Other

Than Pensions." *Highlights of Financial Reporting Issues*. Norwalk, CT: Financial Accounting Standards Board, February 1989.

Steinbrook, Robert. "Fundamental Challenges Face U.S. Health System." *Los Angeles Times,* April 25, 1989.

Tilly, Jane. *Public Policy Institute Fact Sheet: Long-Term Care*. Washington, DC: American Association of Retired Persons, 1989.

———. *Public Policy Institute Fact Sheet: Medicaid and Long-Term Care for Older Americans*. Washington, DC: American Association of Retired Persons, 1989.

U.S. Congress. House. Select Committee on Aging. *Catastrophic Health Insurance: The Medigap Crisis*. 99th Congress, 2d sess., 1986.

———. *Long Term Care and Personal Impoverishment: Seven in Ten Elderly Living Alone Are at Risk*. 100th Congress, 1st sess., 1987.

U.S. Congress. Senate. Special Committee on Aging. *Aging America: Trends and Projections*. Washington, DC: U.S. Government Printing Office, 1987.

U.S. Department of Health and Human Services, Health Care Financing Administration. *The Medicare Handbook*. Washington, DC: U.S. Department of Health and Human Services, 1989.

"Who Can Afford a Nursing Home?" *Consumer Reports,* May 1988, 300–311.

Chapter 5. Planning Your Financial Future

Agran, Libbie. *Your Personal Financial Statement and Supporting Schedules*. Los Angeles, CA: Libbie Agran Financial Services and Seminars, 1983.

American Association of Retired Persons. *A Guide to Planning Your Retirement Finances*. Washington, DC: U.S. Government Printing Office, 1982.

———. *Your Money Matters*. Washington, DC: American Association of Retired Persons, 1986.

American Financial Services Association. *Consumer Budget Planner.* Washington, DC: American Financial Services Association.

References

Barker, John F. *Investment Fraud, Current Problems in Regulation and Enforcement.* Washington, DC: American Association of Retired Persons, 1989.

Better Business Bureau. *Tips on Financial Planners.* Arlington, VA: Council of Better Business Bureaus, 1986.

Bezaire Law Offices. *The Benefits of the Revocable Living Trust.* San Marino, CA: Bezaire Law Offices, 1988.

Blankinship and Associates. *Thoughts for Improved Financial Health.* Del Mar, CA: Blankinship and Associates, 1989.

Blankinship, John T., Jr. "Breaking the Psychological Barrier." *Life Association News,* July 1986.

California Department of Insurance. *Buyer's Guide to Life Insurance.* Sacramento, CA: State of California, Department of Insurance, 1987.

Consumer Reports. "How Much Life Insurance Do You Need?" *Consumer Reports,* Dec. 1987, 120–24.

Foundation for Financial Planning. *Consumer Guide to Financial Independence.* Atlanta, GA: Foundation for Financial Planning.

Green, Wayne E. "Taking Your Own Counsel." *Wall Street Journal,* May 8, 1989.

Institute of Certified Financial Planners. *How to Select a Financial Planner.* Denver, CO: Institute of Certified Financial Planners, 1989.

Jacobs, Sanford L. "Investment City, Brokers, Bankers and Planners Swarm to Leisure World's Affluent Retirees." *Wall Street Journal,* Dec. 2, 1988.

Moschis, George P. *Consumer Behavior of Older Adults: A National View.* Atlanta, GA: Center for Mature Consumer Studies, 1988.

National Pension Assistance Project, Pension Rights Center. *A Guide to Understanding Your Pension Plan.* Washington, DC: American Association of Retired Persons, 1989.

Pension Benefit Guaranty Corporation. *Your Pension, Things You Should Know about Your Pension Plan.* Washington, DC: U.S. Government Printing Office, 1989.

Porter, Sylvia. *Your Financial Security: Effective Financial Strategies for Every Stage of Life.* New York: Morrow, 1987.

Regan, John J. *Your Legal Rights in Later Life*. Washington, DC: American Association of Retired Persons, 1989.

"Secure Retirement Is Top Goal for Most People. But Is It Beyond Reach?" *Wall Street Journal,* July 11, 1989.

Senior Life. "Looking at Durable Powers of Attorney." *Senior Life,* Dec. 1988, 3.

Slater, Karen. "Stockbrokers Dress Up Life Insurance for New Pitch." *Wall Street Journal,* Feb. 2, 1989.

Society for the Right to Die. *What You Should Know about Durable Powers of Attorney*. New York: Society for the Right to Die, 1989.

———. *You and Your Living Will.* New York: Society for the Right to Die, 1989.

Steinbrook, Robert, and Bernard Lo. "Decision Making for Incompetent Patients by Designated Proxy." *New England Journal of Medicine,* 310, no. 24 (June 14, 1984):1598–99.

U.S. Congress. Senate. Special Committee on Aging. *Aging America: Trends and Projections*. Washington, DC: U.S. Government Printing Office, 1988.

U.S. Department of Health and Human Services, Social Security Administration. *Retirement.* Washington, DC: U.S. Government Printing Office, 1989.

———. *SSI*. Washington, DC: U.S. Government Printing Office, 1989.

———. *SSI in California*. Washington, DC: U.S. Government Printing Office, 1989.

———. *Survivors*. Washington, DC: U.S. Government Printing Office, 1989.

White, James A. "The 401(k) Grows Popular as Nest for Retirement Eggs." *Wall Street Journal,* June 21, 1989.

Chapter 6. A Place Called Home

Alternative Living for the Aging. *Alternative Living for the Aging*. West Hollywood, CA: Alternative Living for the Aging, 1986.

American Association of Retired Persons. *Establishing a Nursing Home*

References

Council. Washington, DC: American Association of Retired Persons, 1988.

———. *Understanding Senior Housing*. Washington, DC: American Association of Retired Persons, 1986.

American Health Care Association. *Thinking about a Nursing Home: A Consumer's Guide to Long Term Care*. Washington, DC: American Health Care Association.

Blank, Thomas O. *Older Persons and Their Housing Today and Tomorrow*. Springfield, IL: Charles C. Thomas, 1988.

Boyer, Richard, and David Savageau. *Retirement Places Rated*. Chicago: Rand McNally, 1987.

Cohen, Marc A., et al. "Attitudes Toward Joining Continuing Care Retirement Communities." *The Gerontologist* 28, no. 5 (1988):637.

Cohen, Marc A., Eileen J. Tell, and Stanley S. Wallack. "The Lifetime Risks and Costs of Nursing Home Use Among the Elderly." *Medical Care* 24, no. 12. (Dec. 1986).

deCourcy Hinds, Michael. "Communal Living for Elderly People." *New York Times,* Jan. 31, 1985.

Dickinson, Peter A. *Travel and Retirement Edens Abroad*. Glenview, IL: Scott Foresman, 1989.

FitzGerald, Frances. *Cities on a Hill: A Journey through Contemporary American Cultures*. New York: Simon & Schuster, 1986.

Gordon, Paul A. *Developing Retirement Facilities*. New York: Wiley, 1989.

Hancock, Judith. *Housing the Elderly*. New Brunswick, NJ: Rutgers University Press, 1987.

Hare, P., and L. Hollis. *ECHO Housing: A Review of Zoning Issues and Other Considerations*. Washington, DC: American Association of Retired Persons, 1987.

Haske, Margaret. *A Home Away from Home*. Washington, DC: American Association of Retired Persons, 1986.

Hing, Esther. "Use of Nursing Homes by the Elderly: Preliminary Data from the 1985 National Nursing Home Survey." *Advance Data*. Washington, DC: National Center for Health Statistics, 1987.

References

Hubbard, Linda, *Housing Options for Older Americans.* Washington, DC: American Association of Retired Persons, 1984.

Jacobs, Paul. "Landlady Charged with Eight More Murders." *Los Angeles Times,* April 1, 1989.

Kasper, Judith D. "Aging Alone Profiles and Projections." In *The Commonwealth Fund Commission on Elderly People Living Alone.* Baltimore, MD: The Commonwealth Fund, 1988.

Kleyman, Paul. "Nursing Home Reform: Chaos or Progress?" In *The Aging Connection.* San Francisco, CA: American Society on Aging, Aug./Sept. 1989.

Langdon, Philip. "Housing an Aging Nation." *The Atlantic Monthly,* April 1988.

Laughlin, James L., and S. Kelley Moseley. *Retirement Housing: A Step by Step Approach.* New York: Wiley, 1989.

Lebow, Joan. "Customized Condos Marketed to the Elderly." *Wall Street Journal,* September 26, 1989.

Liang, Jersey, and Edward Jow-Ching Tu. "Estimating Lifetime Risk of Nursing Home Residency: A Further Note." *The Gerontologist* 26, no. 5. (Oct. 1986).

McConnell, Stephen R., and Carolyn E. Asher. *Intergenerational Housesharing: A Research Report and Resources Manual.* Los Angeles: University of Southern California, 1980.

Morgan, Dala. "The Sun Also Sets." *Arizona Trends,* June 1988.

Newcomer, Robert, Powell M. Lawton, and Thomas Byerts. *Housing an Aging Society: Issues, Alternatives and Policy.* New York: Van Nostrand Reinhold, 1986.

Otten, Allen. "The Young Old Often Stay Put." *Wall Street Journal,* July 21, 1988.

Pynoos, Jon. "Continuum of Care Retirement Communities: Option for Mid-Upper Income Elders." *Generations* (Spring 1985):31–33.

———. "Public Policy and Aging in Place: Identifying the Problems and Potential Solutions." In *Aging in Place: Supporting the Frail Elderly in Residential Environments,* edited by D. Tilson. Chicago: Scott Foresman, 1990.

Quinn, Jane Bryant. "On Reverse Mortgages." *Newsweek,* March 30, 1981, 75.

Quirk, Dan, Diane Justice, and Terry Nixon. *State Tax Policy Options for the Elderly: A Guide for Aging Advocates.* Washington, DC: National Association of State Units on Aging, May 1985.

Regnier, Victor, and Jon Pynoos. *Housing the Aged: Design Directives and Policy Considerations.* New York: Elsevier, 1987.

Richards, Bill. "Tired and Scared of Living Alone—More Elderly Try Sharing Homes." *Wall Street Journal,* September 22, 1986.

Silverman, Abner. *Users' Needs and Social Services.* Washington, DC: House Committee on Banking and Currency, 1971.

Spitz, Laura A., and Shelah Leader. *A Consumer Guide to Life-Care Communities.* Washington, DC: National Consumers League, 1986.

Tiren, M., and B. Ryther. *State Initiatives in Elderly Housing: What's New, What's Tried and True.* Washington, DC: Council of State Housing Agencies, December 1986.

United Press International. "Landlady in Boardinghouse Death Pleads Innocent to One Murder Count." *Los Angeles Times,* January 14, 1989.

U.S. Congress. Senate. Special Committee on Aging. *Aging America: Trends and Projections.* 1987–88 ed.

U.S. Congress. Senate. Special Committee on Aging. *Turning Home Equity into Income for Older Homeowners.* 1982.

U.S. Department of Health and Human Services. *How to Select a Nursing Home.* Washington, DC: U.S. Department of Health and Human Services, December 1980.

U.S. Department of Housing and Urban Development. "Home Equity Conversion Mortgage Insurance." *Federal Register,* Part III, June 9, 1989.

Welch, P., V. Parker, and J. Zeisel. *Independence through Interdependence: Congregate Living for Older People.* Boston: Department of Elder Affairs, 1984.

Welfeld, Irving. *Where We Live: A Social History of American Housing.* New York: Simon & Schuster, 1988.

References

Chapter 7. Changing Family Roles

Brazelton, T. Berry. *Families: Crisis and Caring.* Reading, MA: Addison-Wesley, 1989.

Brody, Elaine M. "Women's Changing Roles and Care of the Aging Family." In *Aging: Agenda for the Eighties, A National Journal Issues Book.* Washington, DC: Government Research Corporation, 1979.

Butler, Robert N., and Myrna I. Lewis. *Aging and Mental Health.* 3d ed. Columbus, OH: Charles E. Merrill, 1982.

Cherlin, Andrew J., and Frank R. Furstenberg, Jr. *The New American Grandparent: A Place in the Family, a Life Apart.* New York: Basic Books, 1986.

DeAngelis, Tori. "Alzheimer's Research Promising, Panel Says." *APA Monitor* 9 (August 1989).

Doka, Kenneth J., and Mary Ellen Mertz. "The Meaning and Significance of Great-Grandparenthood." *The Gerontologist* 28, no. 2 (April 1988):192–97.

Jarvik, Lissy, and Gary Small. *Parentcare: A Commonsense Guide for Adults and Children.* New York: Crown, 1988.

Johnson, Colleen Leahy. *Ex Familia: Grandparents, Parents, and Children Adjust to Divorce.* New Brunswick, NJ: Rutgers University Press, 1988.

McKain, W. C. *Retirement Marriage.* Storrs: University of Connecticut, 1969.

Norris, Jane, ed. *Daughters of the Elderly: Building Partnerships in Caregiving.* Bloomington: Indiana University Press, 1988.

Palmer, Verne. "They're Back: Dubbed 'the Boomerang Kids,' Adults Return Home in Trendsetting Numbers." *The Los Angeles Daily Breeze,* June 25, 1989.

Parker, Marcie, and Cynthia L. Polich. *What Is a Case Manager and How Do You Know if You Need One? How to Be a Wise Consumer and Find the Health and Social Services You Need for Long-Term Care.* Excelsior, MN: InterStudy, March 1989.

Rosenthal, C. J. "Kinkeeping in the Familial Division of Labor." *Journal of Marriage and the Family* 47 (1985).

Silverstone, Barbara. "Informal Social Support Systems for the Frail Elderly." In *America's Aging: Health in an Older Society*. Committee on an Aging Society, Institute of Medicine and National Research Council. Washington, DC: National Academy Press, 1985.

Troll, Lillian E. "New Thoughts on Old Families." *The Gerontologist* 28 (5):586–91.

Van Buren, Abigail. *The Best of Dear Abby*. Kansas City, MO: Universal Press, Andrews and McMeel, 1989. "A Divorce after 44 Years Is No Disgrace for Family." *Los Angeles Times*, August 21, 1989.

Weishaus, S. S. "Determinants of Affect of Middle-Aged Women toward Their Aging Mothers." Unpublished doctoral dissertation. Los Angeles: University of Southern California, 1978.

Chapter 8. Intimacy

American Association of Retired Persons. "On Being Alone." Washington, DC: American Association of Retired Persons, 1988.

American Heart Association. *Sex and Heart Disease*. Dallas: American Heart Association, 1983.

American Medical Systems. "Impotence Answers: Where to Go, What to Ask." Minneapolis, MN: Impotence Information Center, 1989.

———. "Impotence—Help in the USA." Minneapolis, MN: Impotence Information Center, 1986.

———. "Insurance and Your Implant." Minneapolis, MN: Impotence Information Center, 1984.

Boggs, Jo Ann. *Living and Loving: Information about Sex*. Atlanta: Arthritis Foundation, 1982.

Brecher, Edward M., and the editors of Consumer Reports Books. *Love, Sex, and Aging*. Boston: Little, Brown and Company, 1984.

Brody, Jane E. "Personal Health: Impotence Is More Common but Increased Understanding of the Causes Offers Men Hope." *New York Times*, August 11, 1988.

———. "Personal Health: Treatments of Impotence Range from Sex Therapy to Drugs and Surgical Implants." *New York Times*, August 18, 1988.

References

Browder, Sue. "A Husband's Impotence: A Wife's Dilemma." *Woman's Day,* May 6, 1986, 44–48.

Brown, Robert N., and Legal Counsel for the Elderly. *The Rights of Older Persons,* 2d ed. American Civil Liberties Union Handbook. Carbondale, IL: Southern Illinois University Press, 1989.

Butler, Robert N., and Myrna I. Lewis. *Love and Sex after 60.* New York: Harper and Row, 1988.

Calistro, Paddy. "Ageless Grace." *Los Angeles Times Magazine,* September 17, 1989.

Canadian Mental Health Association. *Coping with Separation and Divorce.* 1985. Distributed by National Mental Health Association, Alexandria, VA.

Comfort, Alex. *A Good Age.* New York: Simon and Schuster, 1976.

———. *The Joy of Sex.* New York: Simon and Schuster, 1987.

Doress, Paula Brown, Diana Laskin Siegal, and the Midlife and Older Women Book Project. *Ourselves, Growing Older.* New York: Simon and Schuster, 1987.

Fowles, Donald G., American Association of Retired Persons, Program Resources Department, and U.S. Department of Health and Human Services, Administration on Aging. *A Profile of Older Americans: 1988.* Washington, DC: American Association of Retired Persons, 1988.

Guyon, Janet. "New Wrinkle in Search for Youth." *Wall Street Journal,* March 22, 1989.

Halpern, Howard. "On Your Own: For Singles Who Want to Be Married." *Los Angeles Times,* November 7, 1988.

Hodge, Marie, and Jeff Blyskal. "Report to Singles—Part II: Flying Solo." *50 Plus,* May 1988, 60–65.

Kiester, Edwin, Jr. "Science Takes the Wrinkles Out of Aging." *50 Plus,* February 1988, 23–26.

Levitt, Shelley. "The New Intimacy." *New Choices,* September 1989, 38–43.

Masters, William H., and Virginia E. Johnson. *Human Sexual Response.* Boston: Little, Brown and Company, 1966.

Mentor Corp. *Overcoming Impotence.* Santa Barbara, CA: Impotence Foundation, 1986.

———. *Sexual Fraud: Purported Cures for Impotence Found Ineffective and Dangerous.* Santa Barbara, CA: Impotence Foundation, 1989.

Shelley, Florence D. *When Your Parents Grow Old.* 2d ed. New York: Harper and Row, 1988.

Shulman, Bernard H., and Raeann Berman. *How to Survive Your Aging Parents.* Chicago: Surrey Books, 1988.

Solomon, Neil. "Heart Patients' General Guidelines for Safe Sex." *Los Angeles Times,* February 12, 1988.

Starr, Bernard D., and Marcella Bakur Weiner. *The Starr-Weiner Report on Sex and Sexuality in the Mature Years.* New York: McGraw-Hill, 1981.

Stipp, David. "Better Prognosis: Research on Impotence Upsets Idea That It Is Usually Psychological." *Wall Street Journal,* April 14, 1987.

U.S. Congress. House. Select Committee on Aging, Subcommittee on Health and Long-Term Care. *Quackery: A $10 Billion Scandal.* Washington, DC: U.S. Government Printing Office, 1984.

U.S. Department of Health and Human Services, Public Health Service, National Institutes of Health, National Institute on Aging. "Age Page: Sexuality in Later Life." Washington, DC: U.S. Government Printing Office, 1981.

Walz, Thomas H., and Nancee S. Blum. *Sexual Health in Later Life.* Lexington, MA: D.C. Heath and Company, 1987.

Weg, Ruth B. "Sexuality in Aging." In *Principles and Practice of Geriatric Medicine,* edited by M. S. J. Pathy. New York: Wiley, 1985.

Weg, Ruth B., ed. *Sexuality in the Later Years: Roles and Behavior.* New York: Academic Press, 1983.

Westheimer, Ruth. *Dr. Ruth's Guide to Good Sex.* New York: Warner Books, 1983.

Chapter 9. In and Out of the Workplace

American Association of Retired Persons. *The Age Discrimination in Employment Act Guarantees You Certain Rights. Here's How.* Washington, DC: American Association of Retired Persons, 1987.

———. *Work and Retirement: Employees Over 40 and Their Views.* Washington, DC: American Association of Retired Persons, 1986.

———. *Working Options, How to Plan: Your Job Search, Your Work Life.* Washington, DC: American Association of Retired Persons, 1985.

Anderson-Ellis, Eugenia. "Elder Care Needn't Keep Employees Out of the Office." *Wall Street Journal,* August 8, 1988.

Barber, Mary. "Banker Among Babes." *Los Angeles Times,* March 3, 1988.

Brody, Robert. "Getting Off Your Workaday Treadmill." *50 Plus,* Sept. 1988, 23–28.

Dessler, Gary. *Personnel Management.* 4th ed. Englewood Cliffs, NJ: Prentice-Hall, 1988.

Farney, Dennis. "No One Ever Called Sen. Burdick, 80, a Retiring Fellow." *Wall Street Journal,* Nov. 4, 1988.

Fleischer, Dorothy. "Alternative Work Options." In *Retirement Preparation,* edited by Helen Dennis. Lexington, MA: Lexington Books, 1984, 53–60.

Hager, Philip. "Pan Am to Pay Former Pilots $17.2 Million in Age Bias Case." *Los Angeles Times,* Feb. 4, 1988.

Job Accommodation Network. *Employers Are Asking . . . About Accommodating Workers with Disabilities.* Washington, DC: President's Committee on Employment of the Handicapped, 1989.

Larsen, David. "Golden Choices: Work-Some, Play-Some Life Style Appealing to More Older Workers." *Los Angeles Times,* Oct. 9, 1989.

Levine, Martin Lyon. "Age Discrimination: The Law and Its Underlying Policy." In *Fourteen Steps in Managing an Aging Work Force,* edited by Helen Dennis. Lexington, MA: Lexington Books, 1988, 25–35.

May, Lee. "No-Frills Jobs: More Work for Less." *Los Angeles Times,* June 15, 1988.

Merrill, Fred. *Job Search Manual for Mature Workers.* Edited by Vicki J. Plowman and Ann H. Ransford. Los Angeles, CA: Los Angeles Council on Careers for Older Americans, 1987.

Morrison, Malcolm H. "The Aging of the U.S. Population: Human Resource Implications." *Monthly Labor Review,* May 1983, 13–19.

Paul, Carolyn E. "Implementing Alternative Work Arrangements for Older Workers." In *Fourteen Steps in Managing an Aging Work Force,* edited by Helen Dennis. Lexington, MA: Lexington Books, 1988, 113–19.

Root, Lawrence S. "Corporate Programs for Older Workers." *Aging* 351 (1985):12–16.

Ryon, Ruth. "Developer Is Still Going Strong at 90." *Los Angeles Times,* Jan. 22, 1989.

Solomon, Jolie. "The Future Look of Employee Benefits." *Wall Street Journal,* Sept. 7, 1988.

U.S. Department of Health and Human Services, Office of Human Development Services, Administration on Aging. *Older Workers: Myths and Realities.* Washington, DC: U.S. Department of Health and Human Services, 1984.

U.S. Equal Employment Opportunity Commission. *Filing a Charge, About Filing a Charge . . . Job Discrimination.* Washington, DC: Government Printing Office, 1983.

Work/Family Elder Directions, Inc. *Elder Care Handbook.* Watertown, MA: Work/Family Elder Directions, Inc., 1988.

Chapter 10. Life in the Leisure Lane

ACTION, the Federal Domestic Volunteer Agency. "Fact Sheet—Older American Volunteer Programs." Washington, DC: ACTION, Jan. 1988.

Birren, James. "Age, Competence, Creativity, and Wisdom." In *Productive Aging: Enhancing Vitality in Later Life,* edited by Robert N. Butler and Herbert P. Gleason. New York: Springer, 1985.

Carter, Jimmy, and Rosalynn Carter. *Everything to Gain.* New York: Random House, 1987.

References

Center for Adult Learning and Educational Credentials, American Council on Education. *General Educational Development Testing Service.* Washington, DC: American Council on Education, 1989.

College Level Examination Program, College Board. *Moving Ahead with CLEP.* Princeton, NJ: College Board, 1989.

Edwards, Patsy B. *Leisure Counseling Techniques: Individual and Group Counseling Step-by-Step.* Los Angeles: Constructive Leisure, 1980.

Growald, Eileen Rockefeller, and Allan Luks. "Beyond Self." *American Health,* March 1988, 51–53.

Hamilton, Frederick & Schneiders. *Attitudes of Americans over 45 Years of Age on Volunteerism.* Washington, DC: American Association of Retired Persons, 1988.

Hegener, Karen C. *National College Databank: The College Book of Lists.* Princeton, NJ: Peterson's Guides, 1984.

Institute for Lifetime Learning, American Association of Retired Persons. *College Centers for Older Learners.* Washington, DC: American Association of Retired Persons, 1986.

———. *Learning Opportunities for Older Persons.* Washington, DC: American Association of Retired Persons, 1987.

Kunkel, Suzanne. "An Extra Eight Hours a Day." *Generations,* Spring 1989, 57–60.

Levitt, Shelley. "Pet Two Poodles and Call Me in the Morning." *50 Plus,* July 1988, 56–61.

Long, Huey B. "Academic Performance, Attitudes, and Social Relations in Intergenerational College Classes." *Educational Gerontology* 9 (1983):471–81.

Merenda, Daniel W. *School Volunteers: Partners in Education.* Alexandria, VA: National Association of Partners in Education.

Nichols, Wade. "An Age of Advancing Travelers: The Mature Traveler." *Travel Weekly,* Aug. 31, 1988, 6.

Russell, Ruth V. "The Importance of Recreation Satisfaction and Activity Participation to the Life Satisfaction of Age-Segregated Retirees." *Journal of Leisure Research* 19, no. 4 (1987):273–83.

U.S. Congress. Senate. Special Committee on Aging. *Aging America:*

Trends and Projections. Washington, DC: U.S. Government Printing Office, 1987.

Verduin, John R., and Douglas N. McEwen. *Adults and Their Leisure: The Need for Lifelong Learning*. Springfield, IL: Charles C. Thomas, 1984.

Versen, Gregory R. "Senior Adults in the Undergraduate Classroom." *Educational Gerontology* 12(1986):417–28.

Index

Index

Index

Index

Index

Index

Index

Index

Index

Index